Asia-Pacific Environment Monograph 3

Customary Land Tenure and Registration in Australia and Papua New Guinea: Anthropological Perspectives

Asia-Pacific Environment Monograph 3

Customary Land Tenure and Registration in Australia and Papua New Guinea: Anthropological Perspectives

Edited by James F. Weiner
and Katie Glaskin

ANU
THE AUSTRALIAN NATIONAL UNIVERSITY
E PRESS

ANU
E PRESS

Published by ANU E Press
The Australian National University
Canberra ACT 0200, Australia
Email: anuepress@anu.edu.au
This title is also available online at: http://epress.anu.edu.au/customary_citation.html

National Library of Australia
Cataloguing-in-Publication entry

Customary land tenure and registration in Australia and
Papua New Guinea : anthropological perspectives.

Bibliography.
ISBN 9781921313264 (pbk.)
ISBN 9781921313271 (online)

1. Aboriginal Australians - Land tenure - Social aspects -
Australia. 2. Papuans - Land tenure - Social aspects -
Papua New Guinea. 3. Land titles - Registration and
transfer - Australia. 4. Land titles - Registration and
transfer - Papua New Guinea. 5. Land use - History -
Australia. 6. Land use - History - Papua New Guinea. I.
Weiner, James F. II. Glaskin, Katie. (Series : APEM
Monographs Series).

306.32

Cover design by Duncan Beard.
Cover photograph: Landowner of Goare Village, Goaribari Island, Gulf Province,
Papua New Guinea (photo by James F. Weiner).

Table of Contents

List of Figures

List of Tables

Foreword

Anthropologists 50 years ago would probably have regarded a collaborative presentation of essays on indigenous land tenure in Australia and Papua New Guinea (PNG) as a dubious undertaking, if not a category error. Aboriginal and Melanesian systems were functionally distinct, one adapted to the needs of a hunting and gathering economy, the other to sedentary horticulture. Going back another 50 years, such a conjunction would have been intelligible only if its purpose was to exhibit lower and higher stages in cultural evolution. As the authors of the present volume are not motivated by a desire either to overturn functionalism or advance evolutionism, what brings them together in common cause?

An important clue is to be found in the curious fact that the *Native Title Act* of 1993, passed by the Federal Government on behalf of the indigenous people of Australia, grew directly out of a High Court action by three Torres Strait Islanders whose ancestors probably came from PNG and whose people traditionally lived as subsistence cultivators. In the course of documenting the denigration of Aborigines in colonial legal history, Justice Brennan made it clear he would have no sympathy with any attempt to represent the plaintiffs as belonging to a higher level of native society than any that existed on the mainland (Bartlett 1993: 27). His colleague Justice Toohey acknowledged significant cultural differences between the two peoples but insisted that the principles relevant to a determination of interests in land were the same (ibid: 140).

Although the Mabo decision was the first positive determination by the judiciary of the rights of native Australians to land at common law, it was heralded by political and legislative forerunners in PNG as well as Australia. In the early 1970s, government inquiries were carried out independently to consider the issue of land rights in two Commonwealth territories — the Commission of Inquiry into Land Matters (1973) in PNG, and the Aboriginal Land Rights Commission (1973) in the Northern Territory. Two Acts of Parliament ensued shortly afterwards: the PNG *Land Groups Incorporation Act 1974* and the Australian *Aboriginal Land Rights (Northern Territory) Act 1976*.

It need hardly be said that the consequences of this legislation for the intended beneficiaries were profound. Less conspicuous, though no less profound, were the side-effects on the practice of anthropology. Whereas in the first three quarters of the twentieth century investigations of traditional land tenure in Australia and PNG were pursued at a leisurely pace, in response to the needs of an academic discipline, in the last quarter they were more often carried out under contract and under pressure in the context of indigenous land claims or externally-financed resource exploitation. While I am a relic of the old order, all the other contributors in this book belong to the new.

My interest in customary land corporations began while I was an undergraduate at Sydney University. In 1952, two years before I enrolled in anthropology, A.R. Radcliffe-Brown published his collected essays and addresses under the title of *Structure and Function in Primitive Society*, which enshrined unilineal descent as a key principle in the occupation, ownership, and use of land in pre-industrial social formations. In his first article on Aboriginal social organisation, *Three Tribes of Western Australia* (1913), he identified the primary territorial group in the Port Hedland region as a patrilineal clan. In his seminal treatise, *The Social Organization of Australian Tribes* (1931), he argued that the patrilineal clan formed the basis of landowning corporations throughout the continent.[1]

Radcliffe-Brown was professor of anthropology at Sydney University from 1926 to 1931. Scholars attracted by his theoretical approach after he returned to England, particularly E.E. Evans-Pritchard and Meyer Fortes, emerged as leading exponents of descent theory in the analysis of African societies. In Aboriginal and Melanesian ethnography his abiding influence dominated the research agenda throughout the 1950s, particularly following the establishment of anthropology at The Australian National University. Most of my contemporaries regarded themselves in some sense as 'British structuralists'. One of the most thoroughgoing applications of the school's doctrines was carried out by my teacher M.J. Meggitt, who first consolidated descent theory in the Australian desert and then planted its flag in the New Guinea Highlands (Meggitt 1962, 1965).

While post-war anthropology was thus preoccupied with the documentation of indigenous corporate culture, post-war native policy under the direction of Paul Hasluck (Minister for Territories) viewed communal ideologies as barriers to the assimilation of individuals into the workforce and lifestyle of Western civilisation. As time passed, the pragmatic and philosophical assumptions underpinning this approach came to be regarded as repressive by indigenous activists as well as members of the Australian intelligentsia, and by the end of the 1960s the policy had effectively given way to demands for autonomy and self-determination. Of particular significance was a mounting support for land rights. The rejection of communal title by Judge Blackburn in the Gove case of 1971, followed by the election of a Labour federal government in 1972 and the approach of Independence in PNG, all helped to mobilise administrative and legislative machinery in the desired direction. As we have seen, two progressive Acts were passed in the mid-1970s, one by the Somare government in PNG and the other by the Fraser government in Australia. The principle architects were C.J. Lynch and A.E. Woodward respectively — both lawyers of liberal inclination.

---

[1] Neither of these two publications was included in *Structure and Function in Primitive Society*.

While the essays in the present volume take for granted that the land legislation in question was intended for the protection and benefit of the indigenous peoples, the authors situate themselves as observers of troubled waters downriver from the confluence of the two streams I have traced in the preceding paragraphs. Anthropology, in its classical Radcliffe-Brownian form, provided the administration with a single-criterion, unambiguous model of the customary land corporation, admirably suited for registration and incorporation into the modern world of commerce and capitalism. Unfortunately, it is now apparent that in many parts of Australia and PNG patriliny is unlikely ever to have been a sole exclusive principle of recruitment to land groups, and that in some places it was barely acknowledged.

Scepticism began in PNG somewhat earlier than in Australia. In 1962, John Barnes, an Africanist trained in the best traditions of British structuralism before migrating to Australia, drew attention to recurring reports from the New Guinea Highlands of non-agnates comfortably embedded in patrilineal descent groups (Barnes 1962).[2] Fieldwork over the next 25 years continued to undermine classical descent theory by demonstrating a range of strategic and opportunistic considerations, besides patriliny, that contributed to the composition of groups in the contexts of production, exchange, marriage arrangements, and warfare (Wagner 1967; Strathern 1968; Kelly 1977; Modjeska 1982). Reviewing this material in 1987, Daryl Feil concluded that 'social structures in the Highlands contain many interrelated elements, the relative emphasis of a single feature, say patrilineal descent, being only one and not necessarily the dominant one' (Feil 1987: 125).

In Australia, anomalies began to appear during the 1970s, particularly in the findings of Fred Myers (1976) in Central Australia and John von Sturmer (1978) in North Queensland. Among the Pintupi of the Western Desert, admission to landowning groups depends mainly on conception at a particular site, or close cognatic links to individuals of previous generations conceived there. Cognatic kinship is likewise important among the Kugu-Nganychara of Cape York, but the basis of site ownership is not conception but male dominance through which an individual comes to be acknowledged as the 'boss' for a particular camping location. In both cases incipient patrilineal tendencies may appear but are regularly submerged by other considerations. In the Northern Territory a variety of departures from the classical patrilineal model emerged in the course of land claim research subsequent to the proclamation of the *Land Rights Act*, most conspicuously the recognition of matrifiliation as a ground for ownership status. In a review of evidence of this kind from widely separated parts of Australia

[2] During his first visit to PNG in 1960, John Barnes met a Land Commissioner in Rabaul 'who had been taught by Radcliffe-Brown that land was owned by patrilineal descent groups and was finding such groups all over the Gazelle Peninsula' (personal communication).

(Hiatt 1984), I concluded that 'patrifiliation has been accorded an undue pre-eminence in the definition of landownership, at the expense of other cognatic links (especially matrifiliation) and of criteria such as putative conception-place, birth-place, father's burial place, grandfather's burial place, mythological links, long-term residence, and so on' (Lakau 1995: 98).[3]

Given that anthropological orthodoxy was not seriously challenged in Australia until after the *Northern Territory Act* had been passed, it is noteworthy (not to say surprising) that the term 'patrilineal' does not appear in the wording. The landowning group is described merely as a 'local descent group'. In the early hearings the Land Commissioner was persuaded that patrilineality was implied in the definition; subsequently, faced with continuing pressure from claimants to include matrifiliates in the list of registered owners, he felt free to interpret the wording literally (and therefore more flexibly).

Patrilineality is likewise not specified by PNG's *Land Groups Incorporation Act*, whose preamble states that the purpose of the law is 'to recognise the corporate nature of customary groups and to allow them to hold, manage and deal with land in their customary names'. A recurrent criticism in the present essays is that, despite the broad ambit of the legislation, the government and its agents have represented patrilineal descent groups ('clans') as the appropriate bodies through which indigenous people should protect and pursue their interests in relation to modern commercial enterprises. In areas where criteria other than patriliny have been traditionally recognised as valid alternative grounds for land group affiliation, non-agnates may be excluded from membership through lack of officially required patrilineal credentials. In some places where patriclans did not exist traditionally, the people have 'invented' them on the understanding that the government and the developers require them for the purpose of distributing royalties.

The guiding principle of the Commission of Inquiry into Land Matters was that land policy 'should be an evolution from a customary base'. In that case it is obviously important to get the customary base right, and the present volume makes a timely and valuable contribution in that direction. There can no longer be any excuse for imposing a rigid anthropological dogma on people for whom it was never valid; or worse, tempting them to invent fictions in order to conform to it. But the issues discussed in the book raise a more radical question: to what extent will the current preoccupation with cementing customary institutions into the foundations of political economy in PNG and Aboriginal Australia in fact impede further 'evolution' or even bring it to a halt? Any society that treats

---

[3] Writing generally of PNG a decade later, Andrew Lakau noted that, although inheritance is through patrilineal or matrilineal descent, individuals in competition for scarce resources in land and survival resorted to various other recognised credentials, such as 'affinity, adoption, birthplace, conception place, father's or mother's birthplace, mythological links and so on' (ibid).

its traditions as sacrosanct and not subject to inquiry, criticism, revision, or rejection must sooner or later confront the consequences of stasis.

Several essays raise the question whether capitalist development is compatible with the perpetuation of communal landownership. The issue is currently the subject of public argument in both PNG and Australia; and, while no one seriously expects a consensus to emerge on the basis of either economic facts or moral values, it seems necessary in the interests of clarity to distinguish among the kinds of benefits ownership might confer. Where legal title confers rights to royalties in respect of natural resources (minerals, petroleum, forests), justice would seem to require equal distribution within the incorporated customary landowning group. It might even be argued that the appropriate landowning group in such cases is one of maximal proportions (such as a tribe rather than a constituent clan). But where legal title confers the right to transmit the products and improvements of human labour by inheritance (for example, to descendants), pragmatism probably dictates a system of individual ownership. There is no need to assume that the two forms are mutually incompatible: the principle of leasehold with payment of rent makes it possible for communal and individual ownership to coexist within the same community.

I commend the essays in this volume to all concerned with the social and economic future of the Indigenous peoples of Australia and PNG. Combining professionalism with humanism, they seek to protect the land reforms of the late-twentieth century against over-zealous traditionalism as well as against a dissipation of cultural and natural resources in the name of modernism.

Lester R. Hiatt
April 2007

References

Barnes, J.A., 1962. 'African Models in the New Guinea Highlands.' *Man* 62: 5–9.

Bartlett, R.H., 1993. *The Mabo Decision*. Perth: Butterworths.

Feil, D.K., 1987. *The Evolution of Highland Papua New Guinea Societies.* Cambridge: Cambridge University Press.

Hiatt, L.R., 1984. 'Traditional Land Tenure and Contemporary Land Claims.' In L.R. Hiatt (ed.), *Aboriginal Landowners*. Sydney: University of Sydney (Oceania Monograph 27).

Kelly, R., 1977. *Etoro Social Structure*. Michigan: University of Michigan Press.

Lakau, A., 1995. 'Options for the Pacific's Most Complex Nation.' In R. Crocombe (ed.), *Customary Land Tenure and Sustainable Development*. New Caledonia: South Pacific Commission.

Meggitt, M.J., 1962. *Desert People*. Sydney: Angus and Robertson.

————, 1965. *The Lineage System of the Mae Enga of New Guinea*. New York: Barnes and Noble.

Modjeska, N., 1982. 'Production and Inequality: Perspectives from Central New Guinea.' In A.J. Strathern (ed.), *Inequality in New Guinea Highland Societies*. Cambridge: Cambridge University Press.

Myers, F., 1976. To Have and to Hold: A Study of Persistence and Change in Pintupi Life. Michigan: University of Michigan (PhD thesis). Published (1986) as *Pintupi Country, Pintupi Self*. Canberra: Australian Institute of Aboriginal Studies.

Radcliffe-Brown, A.R., 1913. 'Three Tribes of Western Australia.' *Journal of Royal Anthropological Institute of Great Britain and Ireland* 43: 54–82.

————, 1931. *The Social Organization of Australian Tribes*. Sydney: University of Sydney (Oceania Monograph 1).

————, 1952. *Structure and Function in Primitive Society: Essays and Addresses*. London: Routledge and Kegan Paul.

Strathern, A.J., 1968. 'Descent and Alliance in the New Guinea Highlands: Some Problems of Comparison.' *Proceedings of the Royal Anthropological Institute of Great Britain and Ireland:* 37–52.

Von Sturmer, J., 1978. The Wik Region: Economy, Territoriality, and Totemism in Western Cape York Peninsula, North Queensland. Brisbane: University of Queensland (PhD thesis).

Wagner, R., 1967. *The Curse of Souw*. Chicago: University of Chicago Press.

Abbreviations

AAPA	Aboriginal Areas Protection Authority
ACAA	*Aboriginal Councils and Associations Act 1976*
ALA	*Aboriginal Land Act 1991*
ALRA	*Aboriginal Land Rights (Northern Territory) Act 1976*
ALT	Aboriginal Land Trust
ASSA	*Aboriginal Sacred Sites Act 1978*
ASSPA	Aboriginal Sacred Sites Protection Authority
ATSIC	Aboriginal and Torres Strait Islander Commission
BHP	Broken Hill Proprietary Ltd
BP	British Petroleum
CDEP	Community Development Employment Projects
CILM	Commission of Inquiry into Land Matters
CLC	Central Land Council
CLRA	Customary Land Registration Area
CNGL	Chevron Niugini Limited
ENB	East New Britain
DOGIT	Deed of Grant in Trust Lands
DPE	Department of Petroleum and Energy
ILG	Incorporated Land Group
ILUA	Indigenous Land Use Agreement
LGIA	*Land Groups Incorporation Act 1974*
NFM	North Flinders Mines
NLC	Northern Land Council
NTA	*Native Title Act 1993*
PBC	Prescribed Body Corporate
PDL	Petroleum Development Licence
PNG	Papua New Guinea
RAC	Resource Assessment Commission
ROT	Registrar of Titles

Contributors

Peter Blackwood is a consultant anthropologist specialising in native title, Aboriginal cultural heritage and land claim work. His work with Aboriginal groups spans more than two decades, including positions as senior anthropologist with the Cape York Land Council and Aboriginal Areas Protection Authority in the Northern Territory. He is currently researching native title and statutory land claims in central and north Queensland, Cape York and the Gulf region.

John Burton is a Fellow in the Resource Management in Asia-Pacific Program with current research interests in Papua New Guinea, Torres Strait and North Queensland. He specialises in social mapping, landowner identification and land ownership in Melanesia, the social impacts of mining on traditional owners, and native title research.

Derek Elias is a UNESCO Programme Specialist currently working in Bangkok in Education for Sustainable Development and Technical and Vocational Education and Training. He received his PhD in anthropology from The Australian National University and has worked in central Australia with Aboriginal people for nearly 10 years. His work there focused on the preparation of Aboriginal land claims, sacred site protection and the negotiation of mining agreements with Aboriginal landowners throughout the Northern Territory as well as the rest of Australia. He has consulted for a wide range of stakeholders including Aboriginal organisations, universities and the private sector.

Colin Filer holds a PhD in social anthropology from the University of Cambridge. He has taught at the Universities of Glasgow and Papua New Guinea, and was Projects Manager for the University of Papua New Guinea's consulting company from 1991 to 1994, when he left the University to join the PNG National Research Institute as Head of the Social and Environmental Studies Division. Since 2001, he has been the Convenor of the Resource Management in Asia-Pacific Program at The Australian National University's Research School of Pacific and Asian Studies.

Jim Fingleton is a lawyer-anthropologist with more than 30 years' experience advising governments in two dozen countries in the Pacific Islands, Asia, Africa and the Caribbean. During the 1970s and 1980s he conducted fieldwork on the reform of customary land tenures in a number of provinces of PNG, and he has returned many times since to work on projects for the development of customary land. From 1993–95 he was head of the Native Title Research Unit, Australian Institute of Aboriginal and Torres Strait Islander Studies. He is a Fellow of the Australian Anthropological Society.

Katie Glaskin has undertaken applied and academic research with Aboriginal people of the Kimberley region of Western Australia since 1994. Her research interests include legal anthropology, applied anthropology, property relations, tradition and innovation, cosmology, ontology and dreams. She is currently a Senior Lecturer at the University of Western Australia.

Laurence Goldman was an Associate Professor of Anthropology at the University of Queensland from 1984–2004. He joined Oil Search Ltd as a community affairs consultant in 2005. He has authored and co-edited various books and articles principally dealing with the Huli people of Papua New Guinea. His research interests include dispute resolution, child play, and sociolinguistics.

Alex Golub is an Assistant Professor in the Department of Anthropology at the University of Hawai'i at Manoa in the United States. His past research involves kinship, identity, and land tenure in Papua New Guinea and his current research focuses on policy elites in Port Moresby, the capital of Papua New Guinea.

Dan Jorgensen began his fieldwork among the Telefolmin in 1974–75, and he has returned for five subsequent visits, most recently in 2004. During that time his research has increasingly focused on two of the most profound influences on Telefol life: large-scale mining and evangelical Christianity. He is currently chair of the Department of Anthropology at the University of Western Ontario in London, Canada.

Robert Levitus is an anthropologist practising as a private consultant on issues of Australian indigenous land relations and native title. His main area of field research has been the Kakadu National Park region, and he has published papers on social history, human ecology and contemporary issues in indigenous policy.

Scott McDougall is a lawyer and Director of the Caxton Legal Centre Inc. in Brisbane. Scott has worked extensively on legal issues with indigenous organisations and communities in Queensland.

Keir Martin completed his PhD in social anthropology at the University of Manchester in 2006. He is currently employed as a lecturer in anthropology at the same university, where he is involved in the coordination of an ongoing project examining moral reasoning and social change in the Asia-Pacific region.

Paul Memmott is the Director of the Aboriginal Environments Research Centre, based in the School of Geography Planning and Architecture at the University of Queensland. He is an anthropologist and an architect who operates a research consultancy practice on Aboriginal projects, specialising in the cross-cultural study of people-environment relations among indigenous peoples. His research interests encompass Aboriginal housing and settlement design, Aboriginal access to institutional architecture.

James Weiner received his PhD in anthropology from The Australian National University in 1984 and has taught anthropology at the ANU, the University of Manchester and the University of Adelaide. Since 1979, he has conducted over three years of fieldwork among the Foi of Papua New Guinea and has worked extensively as a consultant in the petroleum project area in Papua New Guinea since 1999. He has also conducted native title research throughout Australia since 1998. He is the co-editor, with Alan Rumsey, of the volume, *Mining and Indigenous Life Worlds in Australia and Papua New Guinea.*

Chapter One

Customary Land Tenure and Registration in Papua New Guinea and Australia: Anthropological Perspectives

James F. Weiner and Katie Glaskin

In 2005, the mechanism of indigenous customary land tenure was again under assault in both Australia and Papua New Guinea (PNG).[1] It was claimed that communal customary land tenure was impeding economic development; that it was inconsistent with the exercise of individual autonomy and freedom in a liberal society, and that it was an archaic base upon which to build and develop a national economy in the modern world. Steven Gosarevksi, Helen Hughes and Susan Windybank (2004: 137) thus asserted: 'communal ownership has not permitted any country to develop. In PNG, where 90 per cent of people live on the land, it is the principal cause of poverty.' Since 2004, comments by such persons as member of the National Indigenous Council Warren Mundine, Prime Minister John Howard, and Senator Amanda Vanstone[2] have all advocated that communal landownership was acting as a brake on wealth creation in Australian Aboriginal communities.[3]

The notion that communal customary landownership is an impediment to economic development is not a recent one. As Lund (2004) demonstrates with respect to customary land tenure in Ghana, colonial authorities there actively promoted the development of private property rights in land, seeing an 'evolution' from customary communal land tenure to individual property as being necessary and desirable. In the African context generally, Besteman (1994: 484) says that government interventions in customary land tenure regimes have stemmed from arguments linking customary tenure arrangements with low agricultural productivity. To this end, many African countries have pursued the path of 'individualisation in the form of title registration programmes, either freehold or individual leasehold on state-owned land' (ibid). Yet in the case of

---

[1] For example, Brown and Ploeg (1997: 513) record Hasluck's (1960) policy position as being one that advocated individual as opposed to communal land titles.
[2] See Bradfield (2005) for citations and summaries of these comments reported in the Australian national media.
[3] The intellectual *fons et origo* for these comments are located in de Soto's (2000) book *The Mystery of Capital*.

Somalia, contrary to the link made between economic development and private ownership, Besteman shows that individual land registration has led to a 'concentration of ownership, speculation, and decreased agricultural productivity' (ibid: 503). Drawing on Channock's work, Lund (2004) notes a paradox — that while colonial authorities in Africa began their rule convinced of the superiority of their understandings of property in individual terms, individual property rights were not looked on favourably by the end of the colonial period.

The recent debates concerning private property ownership in PNG and Australia have also drawn responses providing evidence contrary to the notion that the individualisation of property rights amongst their indigenous peoples would constitute an economic panacea to current problems. In relation to PNG, Jim Fingleton, one of the contributors to this volume, edited a collection of papers demonstrating the health and vigour of entrepreneurship in PNG based on customary communal landownership (Fingleton 2005). In Australia, an Oxfam commissioned report found no evidence to support the idea that individual landownership is a necessary pre-condition to economic development on Aboriginal land in the Northern Territory, and drew on the Aotearoa/New Zealand context to demonstrate that 'individualising title can actually compromise sustainable economic development on indigenous land' (Altman et al. 2005: 5).

As the African studies referred to particularly indicate, recent concerted efforts to overturn remaining customary land tenure regimes must be placed within the broader historical development of world capitalism, and indeed colonialism. However, our goal in this volume is not in the first instance to make a case for the protection of customary land tenure *per se,* but to understand the mechanics of the translation process in which non-Western cultural and social forms are incorporated and regulated by Western legal and statutory bodies. While the chapters in this volume[4] all apparently describe episodes within an ever-expanding 'culture clash' between indigenous peoples and Western governments or capital, our conclusions will be provocative — that in a fundamental cultural sense, 'the customary' is a *product* of the expansion of state and capital formations, rather than foreign or external to it (Weiner 2006; Weiner and Glaskin 2006).

As neighbouring countries linked by a colonial past as well as by more recent political and economic developments, Australia and PNG share commonalities and differences with respect to customary land registration. Lakau (1997: 537) and Fingleton (this volume) remind us that the primary instrument of customary land registration in PNG, the *Land Groups Incorporation Act 1974 (LGIA),* arose

---

[4] This collection had its genesis in a conference held in Brisbane in 2000, entitled 'Problems and Perspectives on Customary Land Tenure and Registration in Australia and Papua New Guinea', organised by Laurence Goldman and John Bradley of the University of Queensland.

from one of the recommendations of the 1973 Commission of Inquiry into Land Matters that was established during the period of PNG self-government preceding independence.

> It is for the most part only since independence (1975), and to an increasing degree in the past few years, that the people of Papua New Guinea have developed claims to land expropriated by missions, previous administrators, private individuals, and development groups … Local people now seek to reclaim their land and resources or demand new compensation for land and resources formerly granted to administration, mission, or companies (Brown and Ploeg 1997: 512–3).

Even though indigenous claims against land alienations go back to the early 1900s in PNG, and local Papua New Guineans acquired the opportunity to seriously contest land alienation in the 1960s through the Public Solicitor's Office, as the papers in this volume attest, much landowner registration in that country has been specifically elicited in response to mineral exploration and other recent development projects. In his chapter, Fingleton discusses the East Sepik land legislation of 1987, which was prompted by 'a new "reality" — modern demands being put on people's customary land'. As he says, such laws are 'an attempt to channel the response to that new reality'.

In Australia, the Commonwealth *Aboriginal Land Rights (Northern Territory) Act 1976* granted communal inalienable freehold title to Aboriginal groups in the Northern Territory who could demonstrate traditional ownership according to the criteria set down in that Act. While most other Australian states also had some form of land rights legislation, the first and only nation-wide land rights legislation, the Commonwealth *Native Title Act (NTA)*, only came into existence in 1993. This legislation followed the High Court's Mabo decision[5] that Aboriginal or native title existed and could be recognised within the common law of Australia (an issue which presumably was never in doubt in PNG). Yet in Australia, similarly to the PNG situation, many Aboriginal groups have been required to lodge claims in response to mining or other development on their country (following the issue of Section 29 notices). Nor is there any real doubt that the legal mechanism of native title is at least as concerned with identifying and codifying Aboriginal land interests in order that development may proceed, as it is with recognising pre-existing Aboriginal rights.

The main theme of the volume is thus to show that legal mechanisms, such as the *LGIA* in PNG and the *NTA* in Australia, do not, as they purport, serve merely to identify and register already-existing customary indigenous landowning groups in these countries. Because the legislation is an integral part of the way in which indigenous people are defined and managed in relation to

---

[5] *Mabo & Ors v Queensland (No 2)* (1992) 175 CLR 1.

the State, it serves to elicit particular responses in landowner organisation and self-identification on the part of indigenous people. These pieces of legislation actively contour the indigenous social, territorial and political organisation at all levels in these nation-states — or at least in the way that indigenous people present them to the wider society (Weiner 2000, 2003, 2007).

One of the significant features of the current Australian government's strategy with Aboriginal Native Title and Land Rights is to assert that this process will have an end — at some point, all indigenous interests will be mapped, accounted for and ultimately compensated for in some way that will historically draw a line under the era of indigenous struggle for recognition of customary ownership. But if local regimes of property are brought into being by enduring relations of structural asymmetry between the State and 'indigenous interests', then the struggle for land rights will always be poised against such state agencies. It is a defining condition of the State, rather than a finite episode in its evolution.

Those anthropologists who have been working in settled Australia, where dispossession and removal to Reserves and Missions were common experiences of Aboriginal people throughout the nineteenth and twentieth centuries, have confronted the crucial role that Norman Tindale's (1974) tribal map plays in the formation and recognition of native title claim groups. Tindale's map and his collection of genealogies now serve as the resource with which most native title claim groups in settled Australia begin the process of identifying their ancestors and their traditional country. For many families who have experienced severe impairments to the transmission of cultural knowledge across generations, Tindale's identifications of people, tribes and territories become highly authoritative. Because the entire continent is wholly divided into parcels of discrete tribal territories, there is an attractive and compelling completeness and lack of 'fuzziness' in Tindale's scheme. Notwithstanding the authority which Tindale's map is typically given by various parties involved in native title in Australia, its authority has been brought into serious question by many anthropologists working on this subject.[6]

Recent advances in mapping wrought by satellite and computer technology will have a profound effect on the future of customary land registration. The difficulties in mapping sacred sites that the Central Land Council has encountered in the past, as described by Elias in his chapter, will be greatly ameliorated. National Native Title Tribunal president Graeme Neate observes that in the United States, the Intertribal Geographic Information System Council was recently set up to promote 'tribal self-determination by improving management of

---

[6] For example, in a recent native title decision the judge noted that 'Professor Sutton devoted considerable effort to reanalysing Tindale's surviving fieldwork data from his 1933 expedition to the Mann and Musgrave Ranges in order to refute the latter's hypothesis' (*Jango v Northern Territory of Australia* [2006] FCA 318, at paragraph 223).

geographic information and building intertribal communications networks' (1998: 2). The Global Positioning System will serve to calibrate to a single Cartesian system for *all* territorial information, Western and non-Western, and will provide the empirical basis for what Burton (1991) has called the 'cadastral landscape'. Drawing on the established legal sense of this term, Burton intends it to mean 'the end result of dealings in land; it is the cumulative record of legal decisions — arising from customary or state law — in the formation of the cultural landscape' (ibid: 197).

Mapping indigenous ownership of land is part and parcel of a more general attempt by Western governments to define and 'manage' their own internal indigenous relations to land. In his chapter, Jorgensen draws on Scott's (1998) discussion of legibility: the State's implementation of its plans requires legibility, and for those affected by such plans, recognition is reciprocal to the requirement for legibility. Recognition of customary landownership creates such legibility, identifying the groups that have to be considered at any given time in relation to land, and mapping their interests onto the landscape (Weiner 2004). In Australia at least, a significant part of this exercise under the *NTA* includes clarifying the areas where indigenous landowners do not have to be dealt with, either because their native title has been extinguished, or because they have been unable to demonstrate that it continues according to the criteria of recognition in the *NTA*, and its interpretation by the judiciary in litigated cases.

At the time of writing (2006), Western Australia is considered to be in the midst of a resource boom that is significantly fuelling Australia's current economic growth and prosperity. Resource extraction and development on such a large scale is inevitably contingent on accessing land, much of which is currently under native title claim. The issue of customary land registration in PNG and Australia, then, is inexorably slanted towards the requirements of the resource industry to deliver the financial benefits of extractive projects. With the exception of Martin's chapter on the Tolai and Glaskin's chapter on Bardi and Jawi, all case studies in this collection proceed under the shadow of some large-scale resource project in which the landowners are involved. And as Fingleton and Weiner point out in their chapters, the registration of landowning groups in PNG is not so much oriented towards the management of *land* but to the management of *resource rents and incomes* to indigenous landowners. The local landowners of the petroleum project area in PNG have, from the inception of the land group registration process, never really construed the Incorporated Land Group as having anything to do with ownership or management of customary activities on land. In this respect, landowner registration has very little to do with empowering customary control and management of land, but a great deal to do with eliciting 'the validation of *landowner consent*', as Filer says in his chapter.

The idea of the 'corporation' is a pervasive theme in this collection (see also Sullivan 1997). The corporation is the form that modern indigenous customary groups (if one can call them that) must take according to the legislation; it is also a technical term both legally and anthropologically (for example, Radcliffe-Brown 1965); and it embodies some of the most central tenets of democratic and managerial culture that comprises the modern Western polity (Weiner 2003). In PNG and Australia, registration of indigenous customary land is only partly about securing 'land rights' for indigenous people — it is also about creating a managerial and legal capacity for them through various processes of *incorporation*. Identifying in some anthropological sense customary landowning groups is thus only half of the problem. Both the *NTA* and *LGIA* are as much oriented towards specifying the obligations, functions and conduct of such groups for the purposes for which they have been formally and legally registered. But as Weiner says in his chapter on the incorporation of Foi land groups in PNG, it is often 'wrongly assumed that the *internal* affairs and composition of landowning social units are both practically and ontologically prior to their external relations'. These groups are, after all, brought into being in order to make decisions concerning actions that take place on customary land. Customary landowners are usually less interested in acquiring legal certification of their landholdings than in entering into what Filer (this volume) identifies as 'social relations of compensation' with government and developers (see also Filer 1997).

There is a significant difference in the ability of PNG and Australia respectively to fund, manage and administer the effects of procedures for registering and supporting indigenous corporations. With respect to native title claim groups in Australia, Mantziaris and Martin (2000: 186) have noted that the paperwork, accounting and administrative responsibilities demanded of a native title group far exceed the capacity of communities characterised by 'high levels of residential mobility, poor literacy, and poor understanding of formal legal and administrative processes'.[7] Edmunds (1995) makes the important observation that increasing governmental and administrative support for indigenous people within Western states has served to increase the degree to which indigenous persons can act autonomously, and attenuate the strength of 'customary' obligations that kinsmen have to each other in indigenous societies. Applicants are therefore less dependent upon the support of indigenous kinsmen or other political bodies within the indigenous community. In Australia, this is one factor that has led to an increasing tendency for larger quasi-'tribal' native title claim groups to fragment into constituent extended families. In short, the availability of state support for the maintenance and functioning of indigenous landowner groups has often had the opposite effect.

---

[7] These same conditions have created the conditions for widespread abuse and manipulation of the royalty delivery system, also based on the incorporation of local landholding groups, in the petroleum project area in PNG.

If 'customary law' and 'customary social groups' are elicited as responses from indigenous people to pressures placed on them by the state and developers, then we should be aware that different conditions and stimuli will call forth different versions of 'customary' and hence different versions of 'customary groups'. In her chapter, Glaskin discusses the outstation movement among Bardi and Jawi of the Dampierland Peninsula, Western Australia, which encourages the formation of small and separate residential incorporated groups, while the requirements of the *NTA*, in which the same people are also involved, requires them to make claim to land and sea on behalf of a much larger category of rights holders. Both require a specific form of corporate group to manage rights in property. Applications for outstations in this area have largely, though not entirely, been lodged by single, patrifilially composed estate groups. In contrast to these lower-level landed groupings, recent court decisions in Aboriginal Australia have focused on more encompassing groups said to constitute the 'society' of native title holders, this being understood as that society from which the laws and customs giving rise to rights and interests in land flow, and which is held to have continuity with the normative society that existed at the time of colonisation. In some cases, this has meant that courts have recognised regional configurations of more than one socio-linguistic grouping or 'tribe', based on similar realisations of shared custom, social interaction, and shared occupation of a larger territorial domain.[8] Such strategies, foreshadowed in the Miriuwung Gajerrong (Ward) Full Federal Court decision, have been used to characterise the recent Wanjina (Neowarra) and Alyawarr native title claims.[9]

In their chapter, Memmott, Blackwood and McDougall describe the active design of the *prescribed body corporate,* the legally prescribed body that holds, manages, preserves and transmits native title. The *NTA* allows that such bodies corporate can be based on either customary or non-customary laws of governance and composition. In Australia and PNG, we witness what Filer (1996: 69) has called 'the incorporation of the local community through the adoption or imposition of bureaucratic management methods'. The legal mechanism of incorporation is not a neutral organisational and administrative template: like the mythologies that indigenous people bring to bear in the face of their own explanatory challenges, it is a systematisation of core components of personhood, autonomy, consensus and will in Western culture. As such, the language of incorporation, so widely adopted by indigenous communities in their

---

[8] However, in *Sampi v Western Australia* [2005] FCA 777, the determination of the Bardi and Jawi peoples' claim (to which Glaskin refers in her chapter), the judge held a converse view: that Bardi and Jawi people had not constituted a single 'society' at the time of colonisation, but instead were two 'societies' at that time. Given the implications of this decision for Jawi people in particular, this determination is currently being appealed in the Full Federal Court of Australia.

[9] *Western Australia v Ward* [2002] HCA 28; *Neowarra v State of Western Australia* [2004] FCA 1092; *Alyawarr, Kaytetye, Warumungu, Wakay Native Title Claim Group v Northern Territory of Australia* [2004] FCA 472.

confrontation with governments and companies over control of resources and land, has been the most effective agent of their own sociopolitical transformation. Whether a truly indigenous form of the corporation — something anthropologists took for granted in Radcliffe-Brown's hey-day but which seems far more perilous a proposition now — can emerge from this conjunctural arena is only one of a number of questions that an anthropology of indigenous communities in Australia and PNG will have to closely attend to now.

By the same token, different statutory bodies charged with protecting and promoting differently-situated 'traditional' interests in land can often be at odds with each other, as Levitus makes evident in his absorbing account of negotiations over the early Coronation Hill gold mining site in the Northern Territory and the contested positions taken by the Northern Land Council and the former Aboriginal Sacred Sites Protection Authority. While anthropologists have conventionally been involved in describing the holistic nature of social life in small-scale societies, the complex legal framework in which indigenous people have to register different kinds of rights fragments and compartmentalises their various interests in land.

Neither the *NTA* nor the *LGIA* stipulates a specific form that a customary landowning group must take; the two pieces of legislation are notable for their lack of specificity in regards to the nature of indigenous sociality. Both demonstrate a lack of awareness that the units of social affiliation or membership and the units of property ownership might be different things in both PNG and Australia (and by implication generally in indigenous 'communal' society worldwide). It is not just 'groups' that are brought into being in this intercultural process, but the very notion of 'custom' itself. While Western law can recognise varying degrees of non-Western customary law, it draws a line at what it considers 'repugnant' to the common law. In a Land Titles Commission hearing of 1998, the Chief Commissioner Josepha Kanawi and her co-commissioners (both men) found that the asserted practice of allowing a woman to pass on rights in land in a situation where there remained no other adult men in the clan, was consistent with the avowed constitutional promise of PNG to promote equity and equality among all its citizens — including women (Kanawi et al. 1998). Therefore, even though it was not a traditional custom, the Land Titles Commission went 'against' tradition in order to promote 'change'. The very opposite has occurred in Australia, where the courts have not legitimated any marked degree of socio-cultural transformation in Aboriginal society and have employed a static and over-literal sense of the 'traditional' (Glaskin 2003a). This is the case both in terms of the basis on which claims to native title are evaluated, and in terms of the kinds of native title rights and interests that may be recognised. The latter have tended to be confined to so-called 'traditional' rights to hunt and gather, to conduct ceremonies and protect places of significance, and so on. They have to date explicitly excluded commercial rights to resources, even over land where 'full exclusive possession' determinations of native title have been made (Glaskin 2003b). This significantly curtails Indigenous Australians' capacity to generate their own wealth from land that has been 'recognised' as traditionally theirs, but this is not generally articulated in those discussions in Australia suggesting that communal customary landownership is an impediment to Aboriginal economic development.

Most of the contributors to this volume have had experience both as academic and consulting anthropologists and have taken seriously the relation between these two areas of anthropological practice. The consultant anthropologist must not only manage the translation between Indigenous and Western lifeworlds, he or she must also negotiate the divergent expectations of developer, government and indigenous community, as well as the often structurally conflictual relationship between Law and Anthropology. In his chapter, Laurence Goldman, long-time ethnographer of the Huli people of the Southern Highlands Province and currently Manager of Community Affairs for the PNG Gas Project, makes a strong case that the role of the anthropologist is not just to passively annotate the traditional structures of indigenous project landowners, but to actively design and configure special-purpose units and groups that will best serve their own interests and those of governments and developers. He found that Huli social organisation, which is not based on a unilineal descent rule, does not lend itself to the registration of discrete, non-overlapping units of property holders. Instead, he devised a system of spatial 'zones' within the Hides gas project licence area which preserved the historically and socially regnant configuration of most enduring social and political alliances, 'conceived as loosely drawn territorial areas in which an aggregated set of clans and clan sections resided which sustained long-term relationships based on intermarriage and exchange'. The Ipili of the Porgera Valley, as described by Golub in his chapter, evince similar characteristics — 'the focus … was on regional embeddedness and connections with — rather than divisions between — different areas of settlement' The Ipili do not even have a word for 'clan'. Rather, like the word *ruru* for the Kewa of the Southern Highlands Province, the Ipili term *yame* refers to any group of people, at any level of organisation, who coalesce for any reason, and thus can refer, among other things, to a cognatic grouping at any level of inclusiveness.

Golub and Jorgensen both make the point in their chapters that in the absence of identifiable 'clans', the system will inevitably manufacture them. Because of the theoretically unambiguous manner in which it can allocate people to discrete social groups, unilineal descent as a social recruitment mechanism has been in effect endorsed as a 'most favoured indigenous institution' by the legal establishment in both countries. Anthropologists have in both countries had to argue strenuously against the applicability of unilineal descent in certain cases, not always successfully.[10] Needless to say, unilineal descent lends itself more readily to the conditions of legibility required by the state than other mechanisms of group recruitment and attachment to land, such as those of the Australian Western Desert (Sutton 2003: 140–4).

Introducing his chapter, Burton draws attention to what this has produced in both cases — a serious disjunct between the necessity to identify the property owning unit on the one hand, and to officially endorse some unit of indigenous governance and self-management on the other. Thus, as Filer suggests in his chapter, the question can be raised 'whether land boundaries are more or less substantial, flexible, or porous than group boundaries'. Martin, in his chapter on contemporary Tolai land tenure in East New Britain, and Elias, in his chapter on Warlpiri relations to land and heritage protection in the Tanami Desert, also confront this major anthropological discrepancy that has emerged in legislation designed to recognise customary entitlements to land: a failure to distinguish between laws and customs pertaining to territorial group membership and those pertaining to the exercise of property rights. In Australia, Sutton (2003: 111–34) has described a 'dual structure of traditional land tenure' in which there is a distinction between underlying and proximate title to land — that although individuals and local descent groups assert immediate control of any given territory, the wider group recognising shared custom is the source of customary entitlements that are recognised by the 'jural' Aboriginal public. This means, among other things, that where local organisation is that of estates or clan groups, the higher level grouping has mechanisms for succession to deceased estates, so that the underlying title to those estates is not lost when they no longer have living members. The courts of Australia, since the Yorta Yorta High Court decision,[11] have more or less taken on this distinction, concluding that native title claims in Australia must be located at the level of underlying title — the wider 'society' within which members of lower-level groupings, such as clans, recognise they belong. In PNG, however, where perhaps a similar distinction could be drawn — although ethnographically it has received scant attention — no landowner would ever agree to relinquish control of clan land to such a putative entity. Such entities never had political functions in traditional PNG society (at least not in the interior).

An examination of the Torres Strait also provides an important contribution to the consideration of these issues. The islands lie between the Australian mainland and PNG, are considered part of Australian territory, and gave rise to the Mabo decision that established the existence of native title in Australia. In his chapter, Burton discusses the ways in which proximate titles have been handled in Australia and PNG, with his discussion of native title focusing on

---

[10] For example, see *Jango v Northern Territory of Australia* [2006] FCA 318.
[11] Members of the *Yorta Yorta Aboriginal Community v State of Victoria* [2002] HCA 58.

the islands of the Torres Strait. The tendency in Australia has been for the courts to resist recognising the discrete property rights of smaller units or individuals as constitutive of native title, instead keeping native title tied to the level of encompassing linguistic, territorial and cultural unity. Burton argues, however, that for the Meriam people of the island of Mer in the Torres Strait, the Mabo determination has given the Meriam 'something that they did not want in the form of the *forced collectivisation* of traditional land'. Many Australian anthropologists have pointed out that the concept of the 'tribe' has been a mainstay to theorising about the nature of the Aboriginal polity for anthropology's entire history.[12] Merlan (1998: 149) has pointed out that 'in recent times, the "tribal" level and other forms of organisation have been elicited from Aborigines, and given greater concreteness and fixity than they previously had, as part of a wider project of management of Aboriginal affairs'.

Not only are non-Western social groups over-simplified in legislation; so is the range of different indigenous relations to places themselves. Aboriginal people in general did not see 'places' in isolation. Sites were always linked to other sites, because when the landscape was originally created by ancestral beings, it was the result of a purposeful *movement* over terrain and through the landscape. Sites that are linked as points along the journey of a single creator being thus have a mythological connection and coherence rather than a purely spatial or geographical one. Present-day communities whose territories are linked in this way are 'related' in the sense that they have important and recognised social obligations to each other, particularly in religious terms. But when economic development takes place on indigenous land, developers inevitably focus on sites of development as discrete and unconnected. They wish to negotiate over rights to particular sites in isolation from the range of other sites to which they are connected in traditional and mythological ways. As Elias describes in his chapter, developers therefore have difficulty in understanding the spatial and genealogical distribution of interests in particular sites, and also the range of different connections that often include people located at some distance from any particular site.

As the preceding discussion demonstrates, the registration of customary land tenure has a number of complexities. Not least of these is the kind of groupings for which the recognition of landownership takes place, the relationship between the landowning groups thus recognised, and the exercise of proprietary rights and interests in land or waters by individuals and groups that may not fall within these statutory definitions or be a consequence of their application. Thus Filer's chapter, which examines the 'interaction of law, policy and ideology in the social construction of "land groups", "land boundaries", and "group boundaries"' in relation to resource development in PNG, has as one of its conclusions that the

---

[12] For example, see Sutton (2003: 42–3, 46, 92–3) for an overview.

'ideology of landownership also conceals a real variety of "local customs in relation to land"'.

In his chapter, Fingleton opens his discussion by referring to the 'protests, riots and police killings in Port Moresby which accompanied the World Bank's attempt to promote customary land registration in 2001'. Customary landownership is of considerable significance to indigenous people, and responses to government proposals for 'recognition', and indeed to indigenous demands for recognition, will vary significantly according to the terms upon which such recognition is offered or sought. In Australia, Aboriginal people talk about fighting for their country, for the recognition of their pre-existing ownership of the land, and the right to control what happens on their country. As the contributions to this volume demonstrate though, the recognition of customary landownership is located within complex matrices of colonial history, government policy and legislation, ideology, indigenous property rights and relations to land, indigenous responses to requirements for customary land tenure registration or 'land reform', and economic development or large-scale mineral extraction on which the wealth of nations may considerably depend. The Indigenous and the 'Western' are thus defined against each other, and the articulation of each includes the other in its foundation. The struggle for recognition of customary land tenure is as much a moment in the development of Western social economy as it is an historical trope for indigenous peoples of the world. In bringing this collection together, we hope to make a contribution to the understanding and analysis of this conjunctural field.

References

Altman, J.C., C. Linkhorn and J. Clarke, 2005. 'Land Rights and Development Reform in Remote Australia.' Fitzroy: Oxfam Australia.

Besteman, C., 1994. 'Individualisation and the Assault on Customary Tenure in Africa: Title Registration Programmes and the Case of Somalia.' *Africa* 64(4): 484–515.

Bradfield, S., 2005. 'White Picket Fence or Trojan horse? The Debate Over Communal Ownership of Indigenous Land and Individual Wealth Creation.' Canberra: Australian Institute of Aboriginal and Torres Strait Islander Studies, Native Title Research Unit (*Land, Rights, Laws: Issues of Native Title* — Issues Paper 3-3).

Brown, P. and A. Ploeg, 1997. 'Introduction.' In P. Brown and A. Ploeg (eds), op. cit.

——— (eds), 1997. *Change and Conflict in Papua New Guinea Land and Resource Rights.* Special Issue 7(4) of *Anthropological Forum.*

Burton, J., 1991. 'Social Mapping.' In P. Larmour (ed.), *Customary Land Tenure: Registration and Decentralisation in Papua New Guinea*. Port Moresby: Australian National University, New Guinea Research Unit (Bulletin 40).

De Soto, H., 2000. *The Mystery of Capital: Why Capitalism Triumphs in the West and Fails Everywhere Else*. New York: Basic Books.

Edmunds, M., 1995. 'Conflict in Native Title Claims.' Canberra: Australian Institute of Aboriginal and Torres Strait Islander Studies, Native Title Research Unit (*Land, Rights, Laws: Issues of Native Title* — Issues Paper 1-7).

Filer, C., 1996. 'The Policy and Methodology of Social Impact Mitigation in the Mining Industry.' In D. Gladman, D. Mowbray and J. Duguman (eds), From Rio to Rai: Environment and Development in Papua New Guinea up to 2000 and Beyond — Volume 4: Warning Bells. Waigani: University of Papua New Guinea Press.

———, 1997. 'Compensation, Rent and Power in Papua New Guinea.' In S. Toft (ed.), *Compensation for Resource Development in Papua New Guinea*. Boroko: Law Reform Commission (Monograph 6). Canberra: Australian National University, National Centre for Development Studies (Pacific Policy Paper 25).

Fingleton, J. (ed.), 2005. 'Privatising Land in the Pacific: A Defence of Customary Tenures.' Canberra: Australia Institute (Discussion Paper 80).

Glaskin, K., 2003a. 'Representations of "Tradition": Native Title and the Recognition of Indigenous Land Rights in Australia.' *Anthropology News*, December 2003.

———, 2003b. 'Native Title and the "Bundle of Rights" Model: Implications for the Recognition of Aboriginal Relations to Country.' *Anthropological Forum* 13(1): 67–88.

Gosarevski, S., H. Hughes and S. Windybank, 2004. 'Is Papua New Guinea Viable *with* Customary Land Ownership?' *Pacific Economic Bulletin* 19(3): 133–136.

Kanawi, J., B. Noki and C. Malaisa, 1998. 'Gobe South East Gobe Customary Landownership Dispute Appeal: Reasons for Judgement.' Port Moresby: Land Titles Commission.

Lakau, A.L., 1997. 'Customary Land Tenure, Customary Landowners and the Proposals for Customary Land Reform in Papua New Guinea.' In P. Brown and A. Ploeg (eds), op. cit.

Lund, C., 2004. 'The Situation is Incongruous in the Extreme. The History of Land Policies in the Upper Regions of Ghana.' Sahel-Sudan Environmental Research Initiative (Working Paper 46).

Mantziaris, C. and D. Martin, 2000. *Native Title Corporations: A Legal and Anthropological Analysis.* Sydney: Federation Press.

Merlan, F., 1998. *Caging the Rainbow: Places, Politics and Aborigines in a North Australian Town.* Honolulu: University of Hawai'i Press.

Neate, G., 1998. 'Native Title: The Spatial Information Sponge'. Address to the National Conference of the Mapping Sciences Institute, Fremantle, 24–28 May.

Radcliffe-Brown, A.R., 1965 (1952). *Structure and Function in Primitive Society.* New York: The Free Press.

Sullivan, P., 1997. 'A Sacred Land, a Sovereign People, an Aboriginal Corporation: Prescribed Bodies and the Native Title Act.' Casuarina: Australian National University, North Australia Research Unit (Report 3).

Sutton, P., 2003. *Native Title in Australia: An Ethnographic Perspective.* Cambridge: Cambridge University Press.

Tindale, N., 1974. *Aboriginal Tribes of Australia: Their Terrain, Environmental Controls, Distribution, Limits and Proper Names.* Berkeley: University of California Press.

Weiner, J., 2000. 'The Anthropology of and for Native Title.' *The Asia Pacific Journal of Anthropology* 1(2): 124–132.

———, 2003. 'The Law of the Land: A Review Article.' *The Australian Journal of Anthropology* 14(1): 97–110.

———, 2004. 'Introduction: Depositings.' In A. Rumsey and J. Weiner (eds), *Mining and Indigenous Lifeworlds in Australia and Papua New Guinea.* Wantage (UK): Sean Kingston Publishing.

———, 2006. 'Eliciting Customary Law.' In J. Weiner and K. Glaskin (eds), op. cit.

———, 2007. 'Anthropology vs. Ethnography in Native Title: A Review Article in the Context of Peter Sutton's *Native Title in Australia.*' *The Asia Pacific Journal of Anthropology* 8(2): 151–168.

——— and K. Glaskin, 2006. 'Introduction: The (Re)-Invention of Indigenous Laws and Customs.' In J. Weiner and K. Glaskin (eds), op. cit.

——— and K. Glaskin (eds), 2006. *Custom: Indigenous Tradition and Law in the 21st Century.* Special Issue 17(1) of *The Asia Pacific Journal of Anthropology.*

Chapter Two

A Legal Regime for Issuing Group Titles to Customary Land: Lessons from the East Sepik[1]

Jim Fingleton

Recently, there has been renewed interest in the subject of customary land reform in Papua New Guinea (PNG). Although it was never really off the agenda, the protests, riots and police killings in Port Moresby which accompanied the World Bank's attempt to promote customary land registration in 2001 meant that land tenure reform moved to the margins of the political debate. But the subject is too important for it to remain marginal for long, and customary land registration was placed on the agenda for a high-level 'land summit' held in PNG in August 2005. In preparation for that meeting, I wrote four articles on customary land registration that were published in the *PNG Post-Courier* during March 2005,[2] leading to lively debate there over the desirability of land tenure reform.

Meanwhile, another debate was running in Australia, over the direction of aid policy in PNG and the Pacific Islands generally, and on the use of development aid to promote land tenure reform. On one side, the economist Helen Hughes from the libertarian Sydney-based Centre for Independent Studies called for aid to be tied to the privatisation of customary tenures (Hughes 2004), while others with extensive practical experience in PNG and elsewhere defended customary land tenures as a viable basis for development (Fingleton 2004, 2005). Again, the question was raised whether customary land tenures are an impassable barrier to growth and sustainable development. For those who take the view that they are not, the challenge is to show how development strategies based on customary land tenures would work in practice. In responding to that challenge, attention must be given to the role of customary groups in the ownership and management of their customary land.

As other contributors to this volume have pointed out, attempts to identify indigenous groups and give them legal recognition are part of a two-way process,

---

[1] The author is grateful to Tony Power, James Weiner and Martha Macintyre for their comments on an earlier draft of this chapter.
[2] The articles appeared in the *Post-Courier* on 9, 15, 22 and 29 March 2005.

whereby 'laws, practices and customs of both the Western nation state and indigenous people embedded in it, are developing and evolving out of each other' (Sahlins 1976). In this chapter I present information on a 'scheme of legislation'[3] for customary land registration introduced almost two decades ago in the East Sepik, one of the provinces of PNG. The main components of that scheme of legislation were: the *East Sepik Land Act* of 1987, which set out the law applying generally to land in the province, and the regulation of dealings in land; the *East Sepik Customary Land Registration Act* of 1987, which set out a process for the selective registration of group titles in customary land in the province and provided for the legal effects of such registrations; and PNG's *Land Groups Incorporation Act (LGIA)* of 1974,[4] which is a national law providing for the legal recognition of customary landowning groups and their operations with regard to land.

A study of that scheme of legislation — its origins, aims, processes and results — can provide useful information on what is involved in issuing titles to customary groups in their customary land, and where the problems lie. I lived in PNG and worked as a government lawyer specialising in land matters from 1970 to 1978, and returned in 1987 to draft the East Sepik land legislation, so I can comment personally on the origins, aims and processes of the legislation being studied here. As for their results, while I have some personal experience I must rely mainly on the accounts of others.

In what follows, each law will be outlined first, before examination of their results. My personal involvement in the preparation of the above laws means that, while I cannot claim complete impartiality, at the same time I do have an insight into the legislation and can document what the laws were attempting, and how they were intended to operate.[5] This is not well understood today, and that detracts from the important lessons which can be learnt from the experience under that scheme of legislation.

The three Acts mentioned above were designed to work together as a 'scheme', interacting with each other. I will first examine the East Sepik land legislation of 1987, and then the national law for the legal recognition of customary landowning groups. That law came into operation in 1974, and was invoked by the East Sepik legislation to provide for the bodies that would be issued with land titles and authorised to carry out dealings in registered customary land.

---

[3] The term 'scheme of legislation' is used by lawyers to denote a number of separate Acts intended to operate together in a co-ordinated way, as part of a 'scheme' to implement a policy goal.

[4] Enacted in 1974 as the *Land Groups Act* No 64 of 1974, the law was re-named after Independence in 1975.

[5] My own involvement should not be overstated. Many individuals have an impact on the final form of legislation including: policy-makers and planners (Tony Power, in the case of the East Sepik laws); members of drafting committees (Nick O'Neill, Rudi James and Abdul Paliwala in the case of the national land legislation); legislative draftsmen (Joe Lynch, in the case of the land groups legislation), in addition to members of the legislatures themselves.

The period under consideration for present purposes mainly relates to PNG's post-Independence period after 1975, but a brief account of previous developments in land legislation and customary group recognition will be given as necessary background to what followed.

East Sepik Land Legislation of 1987

The East Sepik land legislation was an exceptional body of law, but it was not unprecedented. When writing about the legislation in 1991, I said:

> Those Acts, with their supporting Regulations, represent the most significant breakthrough in the field of customary land tenure reform, not only in PNG but in the South West Pacific generally, since the current period of independent nationhood began (Fingleton 1991: 147).

The inability of governments in the Pacific to pass legislative reforms affecting land tenure means that my comment still holds true today, over a decade later. Most Pacific Island nations are still operating under land legislation from their colonial period. In PNG, this means that the land registration laws comprise remnants of a scheme of legislation introduced by the Australian Administration in the mid-1960s.

One of those laws was the *Land Registration (Communally Owned Land) Ordinance 1962*.[6] This law, based on Fijian precedents,[7] provided for the registration of customary land in declared areas as either individually owned or communally owned.[8] A Register of Communally Owned Land was established, in which those persons or groups found to be the owners of land would be registered. Land entered in the Register remained subject to custom, but an entry in the Register was conclusive evidence of the stated ownership, as at the date of the finding. The law made no provision, however, for dealings in the registered land, or for the legal recognition and operation of the landowning groups.

The other main land law introduced by the Australian Administration in the mid-1960s was the *Land (Tenure Conversion) Ordinance* of 1963. In contrast to the previous law, this legislation expressly provided that the individual freehold titles in customary land registered under its provisions would thereafter be free from custom, and all customary interests in the land and controls over it would be extinguished. Both this law and the previous one were administered by a special body, the Land Titles Commission, made up mainly of experienced senior field officers from the Administration.

---

[6] The operation of the 1962 law was suspended in 1970, and the law was subsequently repealed.
[7] The 1962 law replaced the *Native Land Registration Ordinance 1952*, which drew directly from the *Fijian Native Lands Ordinance 1905*.
[8] For a criticism of the term 'communal' with respect to customary land tenures, see Fingleton (2005: 3–4).

In the early 1970s the Australian Administration proposed another major scheme of land legislation, but introduction of such reforms on the eve of Independence was controversial, and in the face of strong opposition the proposed laws were withdrawn. After the 1972 national election, the coalition government led by Michael Somare set up a Commission of Inquiry to make recommendations for reform of land policies, laws and administration in preparation for Independence. The Commission of Inquiry into Land Matters (CILM) made comprehensive recommendations for reform in its 1973 report, its guiding principle being that land policy 'should be an evolution from a customary base not a sweeping agrarian revolution; collective and individualistic extremes should be avoided' (GoPNG 1973: 15). The CILM based this principle on the Government's 'Eight Point Programme', the forerunner of the National Goals and Directive Principles of the PNG Constitution, one of which (Section 5) calls for development to be achieved 'primarily through the use of Papua New Guinean forms of social, political and economic organisation'.

Recommendations were made by the CILM for a new system of land dispute settlement, for dealing with problems over alienated lands (such as plantations), for land resettlement and other land matters. With respect to customary land, the CILM's main views were that:

- the previous emphasis on individualisation of titles was not appropriate;
- new legislation for customary land registration should be introduced, but that it should be used sparingly, and only where there was a clear demand from the landowners concerned and a real need to replace customary tenures;
- the 'basic pattern' should be to register group titles, and provide for the group to grant registrable occupation rights (to group members) or leases (to non-members);
- the landowning groups should be incorporated, with a constitution defining their membership, powers and decision-making processes;
- the system of using 'representatives' to make decisions on a group's behalf should be abandoned;
- the main controls on dealings in registered land should be through restrictions on the titles themselves — titles would not be fully negotiable, and limits would apply to grants of occupation rights and leases, while mortgages would only be available to secure loans from approved lending bodies (GoPNG 1973: 17–44).

The CILM Report became the basis for land policy making and legislative reform during the 1970s, including notably for present purposes passage of the *Land Groups Act* (later renamed the *Land Groups Incorporation Act*) of 1974, and the *Land Disputes Settlement Act* of 1975. By the end of the 1970s, however, the Somare-led coalition government was experiencing political instability. In 1978 the National Executive Council approved policy submissions that would have implemented reform in the main outstanding areas of the CILM report, including for the registration of group titles in customary land. But bureaucratic delays during 1979 and a change of government following a no-confidence vote in 1980 meant that no laws to implement the National Executive Council decisions were ever drafted. There has been no important change in PNG's land legislation at the national level since then.

Meanwhile, a number of provincial governments were becoming frustrated by the failure at the national level to provide new legislation for customary land registration. The existing legislation, providing for conversion of customary land tenures to individual freehold titles, had been discredited by the CILM report, and the Land Titles Commission was in the process of being replaced by the new land dispute settlement machinery. The East Sepik leadership was firmly committed to basing economic development on customary tenures and Melanesian forms of organisation as called for by the PNG Constitution. When a World Bank consultant's criticism of Port Moresby's latest proposals for land law reform led to their being shelved, the East Sepik Provincial Government decided to invoke its legislative powers under the *Organic Law on Provincial Government* and proceed with its own land legislation.[9] In 1987, this resulted in passage by the East Sepik Provincial Assembly of the *East Sepik Land Act* and *Customary Land Registration Act*. The two laws were prepared on the basis of the CILM's recommendations.[10]

East Sepik Land Act 1987

The *East Sepik Land Act* sets out the general principles of land tenure in the province, providing in particular, that all land is either held under the State (alienated from customary ownership) or owned by customary groups under customary tenure.[11] Custom applies to all land in the province, except to the extent that it has been removed or modified by legislation. Land can only be removed from customary tenure by government acquisition. The Act also made provision for three kinds of dealing with customary land — sales, leases and charges.[12]

With respect to sales, the Act provides that customary land could only be sold to the National or Provincial Government, or to another customary group. Leases of customary land could be granted to a wide list of persons and bodies,

---

[9] I have written previously on the lead-up to this ground-breaking initiative (Fingleton 1991: 147–53).

[10] I drafted both these Acts, and their supporting Regulations, as a consultant engaged by the Australian International Development Assistance Bureau (AIDAB — the predecessor of AusAID) to work with the national and provincial authorities in drafting the necessary provincial legislation.

[11] Much of the *East Sepik Land Act* was concerned with the administration of leases over State-owned land in the province, which does not concern us here.

[12] The East Sepik Provincial Government decided to subsume occupation rights — recommended by the CILM for members of the landowning group — under leases. 'Charge' is the generic term for such things as mortgages.

including incorporated land groups and business groups, local and registered foreign enterprises, citizens and non-citizens resident in the province. Both sales of customary land to customary groups and leases of customary land are 'controlled dealings', requiring approval from either the Provincial Land Management Committee (for all sales and some leases) or the Local Land Management Committee for the area concerned, depending on the nature of the parties. Charges over customary land could only be made to secure a debt to prescribed lending bodies, and restrictions were imposed on the lender's ability to foreclose and exercise a power of sale.

East Sepik Customary Land Registration Act 1987

The *East Sepik Customary Land Registration Act* provides for registration of customary land at two levels: registration of full ownership, and registration of interests which are less than full ownership.

The other basic dichotomy drawn by the Act is between registration in declared Customary Land Registration Areas (CLRAs), and registration outside such areas. CLRAs were those parts of the East Sepik Province officially identified as having a priority for registration — based on criteria of local need and demand, and the availability of administrative resources necessary to carry out and maintain the registration of land titles. In CLRAs, the group ownership of land would be systematically investigated and registered. In addition, subordinate rights (for leases and so forth) granted by landowning groups to individual members or others could — subject to the requirements of the *East Sepik Land Act* outlined above — also be registered upon application. Within CLRAs, a registration was conclusive evidence of title.

Outside CLRAs, people could also apply for registration of their rights in customary land, either in full group ownership or as subordinate right holders. Because they would *not* be preceded by systematic investigations, the effect of these registrations was to confer only *prima facie* evidence of title. In effect, this was not much more than an official recording service, providing documentation of interests in land but no statutory protection for them.

The legislation specified that customary land registered under its provisions would remain subject to custom, although a claim based on custom could not defeat a registered title in a CLRA. Landowning groups were required to incorporate under the *Land Groups Incorporation Act* before they could be issued with a certificate of title and start entering into dealings with their land.

Key features of the East Sepik land legislation are:

1. All land in the province is either owned by the State, or is owned by customary groups under customary tenure (that is, customary land cannot be held in absolute individual ownership).

2.   Custom applies to all land in the province, except to the extent that its application has been excluded or modified by legislation.

3.   Subject to specified controls, three kinds of dealings could be entered into over customary land — sales, leases and charges (for mortgages and such).

4.   Registration of titles in customary land would be introduced selectively, in CLRAs identified by reference to the criteria of: general support from the local landowners; genuine need for registration of titles; and availability of administrative resources.

5.   In CLRAs, the group ownership of all land would be systematically investigated and registered.

6.   Group titles issued in CLRAs would be indefeasible — that is, given statutory protection from competing claims.

7.   Groups could enter into dealings with their titles, but first they had to incorporate under the *LGIA*.

8.   Outside CLRAs, a service was available for recording interests in customary land, but such interests would be given no statutory protection.

9.   Transfers (to other customary groups), leases and mortgages entered into by incorporated land groups (ILGs) could also be registered, and in CLRAs the titles so gained would also be indefeasible.

10. Registered customary land would remain subject to custom, but a claim based on custom could not defeat a registered title in a CLRA.

The East Sepik land legislation was an attempt to balance the economic need for greater certainty of interests in land with the desire, for social and cultural reasons, to retain customary tenures. The East Sepik Provincial Government of the day was committed to village-based development and the retention of traditional communities, and the legislation was designed to cause minimal interference with customary tenures. Registration would only be introduced selectively, where customary tenures were unable by themselves to adapt to changing circumstances. Even in such cases, the application of custom would only be removed to the extent necessary to meet the changing circumstances. Customary groups would remain the key actors under the province's land reform, holding ownership of the registered land and having the power to enter into dealings with the land. The legislation was a statement of belief in the continued viability of customary groups.

Results of the East Sepik Land Legislation

What was the result of this vote of confidence in customary groups? As with so many of PNG's attempts at land tenure reform, the tangible results were negligible. The East Sepik Provincial Assembly passed the two Acts by early March 1987, and they were brought into force on 19 May 1987. Later in that year I returned to East Sepik Province to draft the implementing regulations — the *Land Regulation* and *Customary Land Registration Regulation*, both of which were approved by the Provincial Executive Council in November 1988.[13] They prescribed the forms and procedures to be used in application of the two Acts. I also prepared a detailed Manual of Laws and Procedures, to assist officials in performing their land administration duties under the land legislation. Many anthropologists, linguists, geographers and other social scientists have conducted fieldwork in the East Sepik Province, and I prepared a Background Paper explaining the new legislation and a Land Tenure Questionnaire, which was sent to them seeking data for use in applying the new laws. Information Papers on the new regime were prepared for banks, financial bodies and others.

Meanwhile, at the national level, the World Bank was becoming increasingly involved in land affairs. In 1986 a World Bank Project Identification Mission visited PNG, following which the PNG Government approved preparation of the Land Evaluation and Demarcation (LEAD) Project. The Australian Government agreed to fund a feasibility study for the proposed project, the main objective of which was to create more favourable conditions for the implementation of agricultural and forest development projects (GoPNG 1988: 8). The Project Preparation Report proposed a project with a number of components, one of which was for a two-year trial of East Sepik's *Customary Land Registration Act*. Based on this trial, consideration would be given to national legislation for customary land registration.

But this was too tardy progress for some provinces whose governments, encouraged by East Sepik's example, also decided to go ahead with their own provincial land legislation. My assistance was sought, but the national authorities, worried about losing the initiative, arranged in 1988 for the World Bank to fund me to prepare Drafting Instructions for national 'framework' legislation for customary land registration. This approach would have allowed provinces to have their own legislation like that of the East Sepik, but within the 'framework' of a national law which would lay down the basic requirements to be met by provincial laws. In this way, it was hoped to ensure consistency and coordination across the country on this important subject.

In 1989, a World Bank loan to PNG was approved for the Land Mobilisation Project (LMP), based on the LEAD Project feasibility study. Under the LMP there was some support given to the East Sepik legislation, but not enough to produce any registrations. A land titles consultant was engaged in 1989 to review the legislation. His report (Levy 1989) supported its general thrust,[14] and made recommendations on the form and contents of the Customary Land Register under the new law. Despite this endorsement, the Department of Lands and Physical Planning delayed putting in train the necessary legislative,

[13] My follow-up work on the activities mentioned in this paragraph was also conducted in my capacity as an ADAB consultant.
[14] Levy did suggest some minor refinements.

administrative and financial arrangements to allow the East Sepik legislation to come into operation. In 1995, when the provincial government system was substantially re-organised, the legislative powers of provincial governments were greatly reduced. The East Sepik land legislation never came into effective operation, and as it was not 're-enacted' under the new provincial government arrangements it has now lost its legal status.[15]

One of the requirements of the East Sepik legislation was that, before a customary group could be issued with a registered title in its land, it had to be incorporated under the *LGIA*. The rationale for this requirement was the need for customary groups to be set up for effective decision making before being issued with a title and entering into dealings. The requirement provided protection both for the landowning group and persons dealing with the group. As it was a major component of the East Sepik's scheme of legislation, that law will now be examined.

National Legislation for Land Group Incorporation

The *Land Groups Incorporation Act*, passed by PNG's House of Assembly in 1974,[16] was another exceptional law, like the East Sepik land legislation which followed it over a decade later. In 1998, in a review of laws for the recognition of indigenous groups published by the United Nations Food and Agriculture Organization (FAO), I described the Act as 'one of the most innovative laws on the general subject of group recognition' (Fingleton 1998: 11). As previously mentioned, the Commission of Inquiry into Land Matters in PNG recommended in 1973 that, for purposes of the registration of titles in customary land, landowning groups should be incorporated, with a constitution defining their membership, powers and decision-making processes. The person who drafted the legislation to give effect to these proposals was C.J. (Joe) Lynch, then PNG's Chief Legislative Draftsman.

As it happened, Lynch had already been considering the general subject of legal recognition of customary institutions for some years. It was clearly a subject which interested him, both intellectually and professionally. From the mid-1960s until his death in the late 1980s he wrote prodigiously on subjects ranging from the recognition and enforcement of custom (including deliberations by 'grass-roots' courts) to the question of how legal provision could be made for traditional leadership — sometimes writing about a particular country and sometimes comparing the approaches taken to these matters across the Pacific Islands. Not only did he prepare the legislation passed by the law-making bodies of Pacific countries, he frequently produced papers debating the issues or

---

[15] Under the new arrangements, the Governor of East Sepik, Sir Michael Somare, failed to move for the re-enactment of the land legislation by the Provincial Assembly within the 60 days provided (personal communication, Tony Power, 2005).

[16] The House of Assembly became the National Parliament upon Independence in 1975.

commenting on the outcomes. He drafted PNG's Constitution in the mid-1970s, and was engaged in the early 1980s as Legislative Counsel in both Marshall Islands and Kiribati, shortly after their Independence.

Lynch's (1969) paper on 'Legal Aspects of Economic Organization in the Customary Context in Papua and New Guinea and Related Matters' dealt with four interrelated subjects, one of which was 'Community Landholding'.[17] The paper starts with an introductory part where Lynch outlines the purpose and scope of his endeavours:

> The theme of the whole paper is simply that for too long we have all acted on the theory that indigenous forms of organization are not apt for 'Westernized' economic development and that the latter must wait on a long period of 'Westernizing' economic education. In my view, it is high time that we asked 'Why not?' and tried to find remedies for specific deficiencies in the indigenous system. It is hoped that this paper may furnish a starting-point at least in the field of statutory requirements (Lynch 1969: 3).

In arguing for the adaptation of indigenous forms, Lynch's approach was radical for the time — especially for a lawyer. PNG was only just emerging from what has recently been termed the 'replacement paradigm', where development was seen as requiring replacement of customary institutions with their Western counterparts.[18] Paul Hasluck's influential reign as Australia's Minister for Territories (1951–63) was not long over, and his views on land reform saw no future for customary tenures (Hasluck 1976: 126). The Derham Report of 1960 advising on the administration of justice in PNG also saw no place for a village-based system of courts applying custom (Oram 1979: 61–4). Even the then Public Solicitor, W.A. (Peter) Lalor, a champion of indigenous rights and often a thorn in the Administration's side, was a legal conservative when it came to embracing customary institutions.

Among the sources for his own paper, Lynch mentions publications by the New Guinea Research Unit of The Australian National University dealing with indigenous business enterprises (Lynch 1969: 4). He also set out the 'propositions' on which he based his approach,[19] including the 'undesirability of unnecessarily interfering with custom by forcing it into an artificial legal framework', and the 'need for simplicity and flexibility and for leaving alternatives open' (ibid: 2).

---

[17] The other three topics were group businesses, the use of customary land as security for loans and taxing customary land.
[18] Movement away from the 'replacement paradigm' towards the 'adaptation paradigm' in land tenure reform is discussed in FAO (2002: 223).
[19] Some of the quotes which follow are from the part of Lynch's paper dealing with group businesses, but he made it clear that his views also applied to land groups (Lynch 1969: 8).

In discussing the particular requirements of a land groups' law, Lynch notes that the need for a legal form for landholding by customary groups arises from 'external factors'.

> The needs of people dealing with the land-holding group ... the general (though not necessarily individual) need for overall land registration in some form, the need to have some recognized authority who can be made legally responsible in legal matters affecting the land, and so on ... [the need to] interfere with the internal structure and working [of land groups] to the minimum, even allowing for the fact that the observer does influence the observed and the mere description of a custom may affect it either immediately or in relation to its development ... [the need for] the utmost flexibility in our requirements as to the constitution and powers of our corporate body ... [and the need to recognise] that we are not dealing with social organizations which have been worked out ad hoc, but with highly developed organizations with existing implications for many fundamental aspects of community life (Lynch 1969: 9–10).

His conclusion was that 'we should not *impose* a structure, but should concentrate on *describing* one' (ibid: 9, emphasis in the original), and he proposed a simple method to recognise and give corporate legal status to existing customary groups (ibid: 8), and then to regulate their external dealings — 'and even in this to interfere as little as possible' (ibid: 6).

Lynch recognised that what was being undertaken was 'attempting to fit a non-English institution into the framework of English law' (Lynch 1969: 12),[20] and he acknowledged that he was approaching the task as a lawyer, recommending that the views of anthropologists should be sought on his proposals.[21] He attached to his paper a preliminary draft bill for a 'Group Land Ordinance', which included the procedure for recognition of land groups and the requirements for a land group's constitution (ibid: 58–70).[22] Apart from enabling customary groups to own and deal with land in their own right, Lynch saw that his proposed legislation would also do away with the existing provision for the use of agents in land dealings (ibid: 15), and — in what, with hindsight, might now be seen as an inopportune prediction — he saw it as providing a method for making payments under mining and forestry legislation 'in safety' (ibid: 15–16).

---

[20] Here he was referring to the concept of land ownership, but his comment applies also to group recognition.

[21] In fact, it seems from a copy of Lynch's paper in my possession that he received comments from the lawyer-anthropologist A.L. (Bill) Epstein on his completed paper.

[22] Proposed laws are called 'bills' before they are passed by the legislature. Before self-government (1973), the principal legislation in PNG were Ordinances. They became Acts after self-government.

Notable features of the above views are Lynch's regard for customary institutions, his belief that they could be adapted to meet modern needs, and his perceptions that the law's task was to recognise the corporate nature of groups already existing under custom rather than create corporate bodies *de novo*. Legal recognition was mainly for the benefit of outsiders; groups did not require much internal regulation and the goal was minimum interference by the legislation in the group's internal affairs. At the same time, he clearly understood that even such minimal interference would affect the groups, and 'mere description of a custom may affect it either immediately or in relation to its development' (Lynch 1969: 9).

In 1974, the task began of bringing forward recommendations of the CILM for government consideration.[23] Most pressing were the problems of claims to alienated lands, mainly foreign-owned plantations which in some areas were contributing to pressures on land and racial conflict. The Plantation Redistribution Scheme, adopted in 1974, was underpinned by a scheme of four laws, one of which was the *LGIA*.[24] The CILM had called for such a law to enable the vesting of land titles in customary groups, but the Act was brought in initially to allow the vesting of registered titles in redistributed plantations.

As PNG's Chief Legislative Draftsman, Joe Lynch drafted the Act, but it was more than just a dusting-off of his 1969 preliminary draft of the Group Land Ordinance.[25] Two of the CILM's small support staff of advisers were the anthropologist Professor Ron Crocombe, then Professor of Pacific Studies at the University of the South Pacific in Fiji, and Dr Alan Ward, then a Senior Lecturer in History at La Trobe University in Melbourne and an authority on Maori land affairs. They lent their authority to the CILM's recommendation that landowning groups should be incorporated with a constitution defining their membership, powers and decision-making processes. Furthermore, a drafting committee of government officials and lawyers from the University of Papua New Guinea participated in the drafting of the new Act during 1974.[26] But the approach taken in the *LGIA* of 1974 followed the main views and proposals formulated by Joe Lynch in his 1969 paper, and he is, therefore, entitled to be regarded as the true 'architect' of that innovative piece of legislation.

---

[23] From 1974 to 1978 I was employed in the PNG Department of Lands (under its different names), with responsibility for advising the PNG Government on land policy and legislation.

[24] The other laws were the *Land Acquisition Act*, *Land Redistribution Act* and *Land Trespass Act*.

[25] In the scheme of land reform legislation prepared in 1971, provision was made for customary groups to be registered as the owners of land, but the legislative machinery provided for the 'incorporation of landowning groups' was rudimentary and fell back on the use of 'group representatives' — a practice not favoured by the CILM (GoPNG 1973: 30).

[26] I chaired the drafting committee in my capacity as a government lawyer seconded to the Department of Lands to assist in implementing the CILM report.

Land Groups Incorporation Act 1974

The preamble to the *LGIA* states that it is a law 'to recognize the corporate nature of customary groups and to allow them to hold, manage and deal with land in their customary names'. The following treatment will first spell out the main provisions of the Act, then list its key features.

The Act provides a simple process for the incorporation of land groups, which begins with preparation of the group's constitution. This document must set out:

- the name of the group;
- the qualifications for (and any disqualifications from) membership of the group;
- the title, composition and manner of appointment of the committee or other controlling body of the group;
- the way in which the group acts, and its acts are evidenced;
- the name of the custom under which the group acts;
- details of the group's dispute-settlement authority;
- any limitations or conditions on the exercise of powers conferred on the group under the Act; and
- any rules applicable to the conduct of the group's affairs.

A group applies to the Registrar of Incorporated Land Groups for incorporation, sending in its constitution. The application is given publicity in the area concerned, and checks are carried out on the group's suitability for incorporation. After considering comments received and any objections, the Registrar can issue a certificate of recognition, whereupon the group becomes legally incorporated, gaining legal status as a corporation with perpetual succession and the capacity to sue and be sued, and do other things a corporation can do.

Upon incorporation, the rights and liabilities of the customary group become rights and liabilities of the ILG. The powers of the ILG relate only to land, its use and management, and they must be exercised in accordance with the group's constitution and the relevant custom as nominated in the ILG's constitution. Subject to these requirements, an ILG may acquire, hold and dispose of customary land, enter into agreements for its use and management, and distribute any product or profits from the land. Evidentiary provisions protect persons who enter into transactions with ILGs which are in formal compliance with the provisions of its constitution.

Each ILG must have a dispute-settlement authority, for dealing with disputes between group members or between the ILG and a member, including disputes over entitlement to membership. The dispute-settlement authority may be a person or persons specified by name or position, or determined in the manner specified in the ILG's constitution. Dispute-settlement authorities are required to do 'substantial justice' between all interested persons, in accordance with the Act, the ILG's constitution and any relevant custom.

Provision is made for the dissolution of an ILG, in cases where it has ceased to function as such, or its affairs are being conducted in an oppressive or unfair manner, or for some other reason 'it is just and equitable that the affairs be wound up'. In general, customary land belonging to an ILG which has been dissolved reverts to the persons who would be its customary owners if the ILG had never been recognised.

Key features of the *Land Groups Incorporation Act* are:

1. It is a process for the recognition of existing groups — that is, bodies which already have a corporate identity under custom.
2. Groups have considerable freedom in preparing their constitutions. The Act prescribes certain matters upon which rules must be made (on membership, the way the ILG acts and its acts are evidenced), but it does not dictate the content of those rules.
3. ILGs remain subject to custom. They are required to identify in their constitution the custom under which they operate, but this may be done by simply naming it. There is no requirement for the custom to be written down.
4. The powers of ILGs are confined to their land — its ownership, use and management, and the distribution of its product and profits. An ILG may place limits or conditions on the exercise of those powers in its constitution.
5. Upon incorporation, the assets and liabilities of a customary group are transferred to the ILG. Upon dissolution, the ILG's customary land is vested back in its customary owners.
6. Protection is given to outsiders dealing with an ILG. They are entitled to rely on its constitution, and if the ILG has entered into a dealing — other than a transaction disposing of its land[27] — in accordance with the formal requirements set out in its constitution, that is generally conclusive as to its power to enter into the dealing.
7. Special machinery is provided for settlement of internal disputes within ILGs.

Results of the National Legislation for Land Group Incorporation

The *LGIA* was passed in 1974, but for many years there was virtually no action taken to use its provisions. This was partly because the Act was initially introduced as a component of the Plantation Redistribution Scheme, and when

---

[27] An ILG's power to dispose of its land would have to be proved under the normal rules of evidence.

that measure started to experience delays (Fingleton 1981), the immediate need for the Act declined. A second reason was the division of responsibility for land group incorporations between the Registrar-General (responsible for incorporations) under the Ministry of Justice, and the Ministry of Lands (responsible for land administration). A capacity for carrying out the special responsibilities involved in supervising the incorporation of customary land groups was never developed.

The third and main reason, as explained above, was that the national legislation for registration of titles in customary lands did not eventuate. The main purpose of the *LGIA* was to enable customary groups to hold, manage and deal with their customary land in their own names. The most important legal device to facilitate the management of land — affording security of tenure for its owners and for those entering into dealings with its owners — is a registered title. It was anticipated that, once the customary land registration law was in place, ILGs would be the bodies in which the group titles would be vested.[28] That was the clear intention of the CILM.

In 1988 I was engaged as a consultant, under the UNDP-funded Urban Settlement Planning Project in PNG, to design the land tenure arrangements for provision of low- and medium-cost housing to persons occupying customary lands at two sites — Buko settlement (40 ha) near Butibam village on the edge of Lae, and Kreer settlement (131 ha) within the Wewak town boundary. The arrangements were approved after extensive consultations with the customary owners of both sites and the people already occupying much of the land (so-called 'squatters' — nearly 500 households at Buko and over 400 at Kreer). A meeting was also held with the main commercial banks operating in PNG, whose managers agreed in principle that the proposed land tenure arrangements would provide acceptable collateral for lending to the settlers for their house construction and improvement. One aspect of the arrangements was for the customary groups which owned the land in question (six clans for the Buko site and two clans for the Kreer site) to be incorporated under the *LGIA*.

This was my first 'hands-on' experience of the Act I had been involved in drafting in 1974. My inquiries showed that only a handful of incorporations had been carried out by 1988 — 14 years after the Act was passed. During the period 1988–90, I visited the two sites on a number of occasions, holding village meetings and collecting data for the preparation of clan genealogies. Based on that information I drafted constitutions for the proposed ILGs, setting out their membership rules, decision-making processes, dispute-settlement authorities and so on, as required by the Act. Applications for incorporation were prepared

---

[28] Although Section 13(3) of the Act provides that the grant of an interest in land to a group member could not be registered under existing registration laws, this was only a temporary provision until the appropriate arrangements for customary land registration were in place.

and sent to the Registrar of Incorporated Land Groups and, after lengthy delays,[29] the ILGs were incorporated. The next step was for the ILGs to re-incorporate as companies under the *Companies Act* — one company made up of the six ILGs for Buko and another company made up of the two ILGs for Kreer. The companies would then be authorised to manage the settlement sites on behalf of the ILGs under management agreements, which included the granting of leases to the individual settlers.

Although by 1991 all the legal arrangements were in place, and house block surveys and the provisions for power, water and sewerage infrastructure had reached an advanced stage at the two sites, the project became a victim of PNG's financial crisis following the Bougainville rebellion. Negotiations were held with the World Bank, but the project was not included for funding under the Structural Adjustment Program or the Special Interventions Project, possibly partly because of the Bank's aversion at the time to working with customary land groups. Funding dried up, and the land tenure arrangements were never completed by the grant of leases to the settlers.

In 1992, I had my only other 'hands-on' experience of land group incorporation. That year I was engaged by Chevron Niugini Limited (CNGL), together with an anthropologist Dr Tom Ernst, to advise on the incorporation of customary groups within the Kutubu oilfields of the Southern Highlands Province. Tony Power, who had been the moving force behind the East Sepik land legislation in the 1980s, was now working for CNGL as their Business and Community Development Manager, and he drew on the East Sepik experience in conceptualising how ILGs could be used to improve participation by customary landowners in the benefits of the project. After a field trip with Ernst and Power to the area and some brief village meetings, I prepared the 'Manual of Laws and Procedures for Incorporation of Customary Landowning Groups', drawing on my previous experience in incorporating the eight ILGs for the Urban Settlement Planning Project. This manual was then used by CNGL staff to incorporate ILGs in the project area for the purposes of royalty distribution and participation in 'spin-off' business opportunities.

Mention must now be made of two developments which were to have major significance for administration of the *LGIA*. In 1992, the new *Forestry Act* of 1991 came into operation. One goal of the Act was to improve the arrangements for gaining access to PNG's forest resource, almost all of which stood on customary land. For this purpose, the Act provided that, as a general rule, the timber rights in customary land could only be acquired if the title to the land

---

[29] I had to chase up the Registrar more than once to carry out his registration functions — a sign that there was no routine in place for ILG incorporation.

was vested in land groups incorporated under the *LGIA*.[30] This requirement threw open the gates for a stream of ILG applications. In anticipation, the PNG Forest Authority adopted my CNGL manual prepared for the petroleum project at Kutubu as the model for its Manual on Land Group Incorporation (GoPNG 1995). Then, in 1998, a new *Oil and Gas Act* was passed. By one of its provisions (Section 169), payments of landowner entitlements had to be made to ILGs. What had begun as the brainchild of Tony Power, to facilitate involvement of customary landowners in the Kutubu petroleum project, had now become a statutory requirement for all forestry and petroleum projects across the country.[31] And the same basic manual, which I prepared privately for CNGL, was now being used for the purposes of all forestry and petroleum projects in PNG.

The result was that, after almost two decades of negligible activity under the *LGIA*, the last decade had seen a flood of ILG incorporations. In March 2004 I interviewed the Titles Officer (ILGs) in the Department of Lands and Physical Planning in Port Moresby, who informed me that a total of over 10,000 ILGs had been incorporated by then, and that between 10 and 15 applications for new incorporations were being processed daily. All the duties of checking the suitability of new incorporations, as well as the oversight of existing ILGs, had fallen on the shoulders of this one officer. He had no special training, and was manifestly unable to carry out the statutory responsibilities in anything other than a perfunctory fashion. Most of the applications for incorporation related to forestry and petroleum projects,[32] and it is apparent that the manuals were being slavishly followed without regard to local variations in custom. It was a situation where breakdown in the operation of ILGs was inevitable.

When to this was added the fact that the great majority of ILGs were being incorporated *not* for the main purpose for which they were designed — holding and managing land — but for the subsidiary purpose of receiving and distributing royalties from their land, then problems were even more to be expected. Management of a group's money was fertile ground for disputes everywhere: the greatest problems with ILGs in PNG arose from royalty distribution.

Issues Raised by the Legal Recognition of Customary Groups and Their Land Titles

I have been considering legislation which had two main aims — the legal recognition of customary landowning groups, and the registration of land titles in the names of such customary groups. Two main findings from the above

---

[30] Section 57 of the *Forestry Act* was originally headed 'Verification of tenure of customary owners'. This was later changed to 'Obtaining consent of customary owners to Forest Management Agreement'.
[31] But not, apparently, for mining projects. The *Mining Act* of 1992 has no similar requirement for ILGs.
[32] A newspaper advertisement early in 2004 referred to 599 ILGs in one Forest Management Area in the Gulf Province.

account are that a great many customary groups were recognised as ILGs, but no land titles were ever issued to them.[33]

In these circumstances, most of the critical comment has been on the problems of group recognition and organisation, but some critics have also attacked the attempt to vest registered titles in customary groups. I have not carried out a systematic review of the literature, but sufficient, I think, to give a representative account of the main problems being encountered by ILGs. These can be divided into two main kinds — problems with the way the legislation is implemented, and problems with the legislation itself. A clear-cut division is not possible, but for purposes of analysis — in particular, for identifying the lessons to be learnt in the final part of this paper — I will consider the problems raised in the literature under those two headings, and then give a brief response to the criticisms.

Problems in Implementing the Legislation

As mentioned above, only the *LGIA* was implemented, so only the problems in implementing that legislation can be considered. It is worth repeating that the great majority of ILGs were incorporated for the purposes of forestry and petroleum projects, not for the vesting of land titles. Indeed, the anthropologist Colin Filer, who was much involved in developing the methodology for improving landowner participation in resource projects, describes how the *LGIA* was captured by the 'heavy' industries — oil and gas, mining, timber and palm oil — for their purposes (Filer, this volume). Another much-involved anthropologist, James Weiner, makes a similar point about CNGL's 'managerial approach' to the landholding groups in the Kutubu oil project area (Weiner, this volume).

A very good account is given by Samuel Koyama, an officer of the PNG Department of Petroleum and Energy, of problems which have arisen in the petroleum sector, in using ILGs as a mechanism for the distribution of royalties and other benefits. He discusses the main problems under the following headings:

- leadership struggles;
- unlawful and unfair sharing of benefits;
- complaints about leaders misusing ILG funds;
- lack of representation and responsibility of ILG leaders;
- lack of accountability and transparency;
- inability of ILGs to solve their problems internally;
- political alliances as a means of facilitating rent-seeking;

---

[33] To be quite accurate, I should say 'no land ownership titles' were ever issued to ILGs. Under the 'lease-lease back' system used mainly for oil palm development, landowners leased customary land to the State, which then leased the land back to ILGs made up of the customary landowners, who then subleased the land to an oil palm company.

- bribery and corruption within ILGs;
- failed landowner business enterprises (Koyama 2004: 23–8).

Koyama concludes that these are 'mostly principal-agent problems arising from the poor design and lack of oversight of the ILGs — effectively, a failure of the government after it approved of these new institutions through legislation' (ibid: 20).[34] Taylor and Whimp made a similar finding in their report on land issues for PNG's Department of Mining and Petroleum. Although they had their reservations about aspects of the *LGIA*, they noted that 'there are almost no government facilities for the proper management of ILG incorporation processes, and little support for ongoing maintenance outside that offered by developers' (Taylor and Whimp 1997: 12).

The academic David Lea, in his recent study of the forest industry and the role of incorporated entities, concludes that 'ILGs have been less than successful in resolving problems besetting the forestry industry' (2005: 169). Having mentioned the requirement under the new *Forestry Act* for landowners to form ILGs for logging projects, he continues:

> In most cases, however, it seems that, when landowners proceed to associate with the logging company, they persist in setting up so called landowner companies in particular to receive financial benefits which accrue to the landowners under the terms and conditions of the Timber Permit (2003/2004 Review Team 2004: 29). This is generally promoted by the PNG Forest Authority and the logging companies because it is easier to deal with a single entity than a large number of individual incorporated land groups (ILGs) (ibid).

Although Lea does make some important criticisms of the ILG concept, the problems he refers to are mainly caused by inadequate administration of the legislation — indeed, in this case, not just the *LGIA* but also the *Companies Act*.

Problems with the Legislation Itself

The criticism of the scheme of legislation in PNG for recognition of customary groups and registration of titles in their customary land generally takes the approach that what was being attempted was misconceived.. Some critics take the view that ILGs are inappropriate entities to be involved in benefit sharing, while others challenge the legitimacy of attempts by 'Western' legislation to reconcile 'traditional' custom with development. Anthropologists in particular are concerned by what they see as attempts to 'reify' or 'entify' custom (Ernst 1999)[35] and perpetuate an 'ideology' of landownership (Filer 1997).

---

[34] I take Koyama to be referring here to the Government's 'approval' for the incorporation of the particular ILGs, not approval of the ILG concept.
[35] 'Entify' is defined as meaning to make an entity, or to attribute objective existence to something.

For David Lea, ILGs have been unsuccessful actors in forestry operations because they are based on social relationships rather than on trust, and because they are essentially 'wealth-distributing' rather than 'wealth-creating' bodies (Lea 2005: 171–3). For him, the solution lies in abandoning ILGs and installing in their place companies created on a voluntary basis (ibid: 173).

James Weiner (this volume) asserts that the whole purpose of the *LGIA* is misconceived.

> [It] is based on a quite erroneous assumption of the communal nature of landholding and transmission within the Melanesian 'clan', and of its essentially 'collective' interest ...

> There is thus a fundamental conflict at the heart of the ILG mechanism, which crops up constantly. This conflict can be stated as follows: the *Land Groups Incorporation Act* of 1974 was purportedly designed to enshrine the *traditional landowning group as a legal landowning corporation*. The purpose of this was to give *legislative protection* to the traditional landowning units in any given area of PNG ...

> The conclusion we must face is that *traditional custom cannot be protected by an Act of legislation* [my emphasis]. The legislation is composed and empowered by a cultural and legal system very much at odds with the way local 'traditional custom' arises and is implemented.

Weiner seems to be making two different points here — the *LGIA* has wrongly understood the nature of Melanesian customary tenures, and in any case, legislation cannot be used to protect custom — but his fundamental criticism is that Western-style legislation cannot faithfully capture customary institutions, values and processes. Colin Filer (this volume) represents this as an argument that there is 'no way of reconciling custom with development, either in theory or in practice'. His own argument is that 'Melanesian custom does not really *exist* in a form which would allow us to ask how it could or should be recognised in modern national law, because it was actually born out of the armpit of Australian colonial law'.

A Response

There is no doubt that the scheme of legislation for land group recognition and the registration of group titles has been dogged by problems of implementation. In many cases it is clear that the breakdown in ILG operations can be attributed to failure to follow the Act's requirements in setting up ILGs and supervising their operations, not to the Act itself. In commenting elsewhere on Koyama's list of problems above, I have made the further point that it 'is no coincidence that these are precisely the problems facing the PNG State, in its grappling with the new responsibilities of nationhood' (Fingleton 2004: 101). One can hardly blame the ILG concept for 'leadership struggles' and lack of leadership responsibility, misuse of funds, political alliances being formed to maximise benefits, bribery and corruption, and the failure of 'spin-off' business enterprises.

To the extent that malfunctions are due to poor administration, the way forward lies in putting in place a suitable administrative structure, with adequate staff, trained to carry out their functions and provided with the funds and facilities to do so. Without the necessary capacity for a law to be properly implemented, it cannot be given a fair trial. Only when a law has been properly implemented can a true impression be gained of how well the law is suited to achieve its purposes. As with any new legislation, it is important to keep its operations under review, and be prepared to make amendments and other adjustments where the need arises. Acts usually require implementing regulations, to carry them more fully and effectively into operation. There is a basic *Land Groups Incorporation Regulation* providing the forms and procedures for incorporation, but no provision has been made for distribution of benefits, for example — an obvious area for better regulation when the Act was being mainly used for that purpose.

As for the arguments that the legislation is fundamentally misconceived, I would first of all point out that the views of some commentators seem to be based on some basic misunderstandings. It is not the purpose of the legislation to codify custom. The *LGIA* is a measure which is based on custom and which applies custom, but it does not seek to set out custom. Nor, as some people seem to think, was the Act intended to record land boundaries and the ownership of land. That is the function of a customary land registration system — the missing element in implementing the reforms based on the CILM report of 1973. Unfortunately, many commentators seem to base their views of the legislation on how it has been applied — or, too often, misapplied. One main purpose of this paper is to provide a better information base, so that the legislation can be more constructively analysed.

The biggest concern is the view that to legislate for the legal recognition of customary landowning groups was attempting the impossible. Taken to its full extent, this would mean that the legislatures of countries which have adopted constitutional democracies and the rule of law can never bring that law to the aid of their traditional systems of social, political and economic organisation. Such a result approaches the prescriptions of critics like Helen Hughes (see Weiner and Glaskin, this volume), who see no ongoing role for customary tenures, but only their replacement by Western-style freeholds. The same sort of dismissal of custom lay behind the objections of the colonial judges and legal officers, which delayed the introduction of Village Courts in PNG for three decades (Oram 1979: 58–64). Such was emphatically not the view of the framers of PNG's National Constitution, which makes custom part of the nation's underlying law, which lays down as a National Goal that development should be achieved 'primarily through the use of Papua New Guinean forms of social, political and economic organisation' (Section 5), and which requires all governmental bodies (including the National Parliament) to apply and give effect to such National Goals (Section 25(2)).

Conclusion

The underlying purpose of the East Sepik land legislation was to give effect to the National Goals of PNG's Constitution as they relate to customary land in the province, in particular for development to take place primarily through the use of Papua New Guinean forms of organisation, and for traditional communities to remain as viable units of society. What prompted the laws was a new 'reality' — modern demands being put on people's customary land[36] — and the laws are an attempt to channel the response to that new reality. As observed by Nigel Oram, the aim of such laws is 'to bring about a synthesis of the modern with the traditional systems' and 'attempt to close the gap between Western and indigenous systems, which are products of different cultural milieux' (Oram 1979: 71).

Are the critics saying that these attempts by elected legislatures in PNG to adapt to new realities and further the National Goals are never valid? If so, then they invite the response which the pioneer Pacific anthropologist Bronislaw Malinowski gave in 1930 to the dismissive views of the British authorities on African systems of land and property law. Weiner himself quotes Malinowski's response:

> It is absurd to say that such a system 'cannot be reconciled with the institutions or the legal ideas of civilised society'. To reconcile the two is precisely the task of Colonial statesmanship (cited in Weiner 2000: 124).

The aim of the legislative recognition of custom, customary tenures and customary groups is to provide a legal process which maintains their basic character and dynamism, and enables them to adapt to new demands. ILGs in PNG are not meant to be the actual clans or other indigenous groups, but their legal representation.[37] Weiner calls the results 'legal transformations' (ibid: 3), but then judges them according to their sameness. The important question is not 'Are they the same?', for they are not meant to be, but 'How will they work?' In other words, the attention should be on *how* to recognise custom, not on

---

[36] Weiner (this volume) acknowledges the new 'reality' among the customary landowners in the Kutubu project area, that the land was now valuable 'in a way that traditional land was not'.

[37] It should be noted that, upon the dissolution of an ILG, ownership of its customary land reverts to the customary owners. The implication is that the indigenous group continues to exist, and is not replaced by the ILG.

whether to recognise it. As the accounts of abuses by the leaders of ILGs show, this is a challenging task, but it should not be regarded as impossible.

References

Ernst, T.M., 1999. 'Land, Stories and Resources: Discourse and Entification in Onabasulu Modernity.' *American Anthropologist* 101(1): 88–97.

FAO (Food and Agriculture Organization of the United Nations), 2002. 'Law and Sustainable Development Since Rio: Legal Trends in Agriculture and Natural Resource Management.' Rome: FAO Legal Office (Legislative Study 73).

Filer, C., 1997. 'Compensation, Rent and Power in Papua New Guinea.' In S. Toft (ed.), *Compensation for Resource Development in Papua New Guinea*. Boroko: Law Reform Commission (Monograph 6). Canberra: Australian National University, National Centre for Development Studies (Pacific Policy Paper 25).

Fingleton, J.S., 1981. 'Comments on Report by the Committee of Review into the Plantation Redistribution Scheme, August-September 1979.' In M.A.H.B. Walter (ed.), *What Do We Do About Plantations?* Boroko: Institute of Applied Social and Economic Research (Monograph 15).

———, 1991. 'The East Sepik Land Legislation.' In P. Larmour (ed.), *Customary Land Tenure: Registration and Decentralisation in Papua New Guinea*. Boroko: National Research Institute (Monograph 29).

———, 1998. 'Legal Recognition of Indigenous Groups.' FAO Legal Papers Online. Viewed 1 February 2007 at http://www.fao.org/ Legal/prs-ol/years/1998/list98.htm

———, 2004. 'Is Papua New Guinea Viable *Without* Customary Groups?' *Pacific Economic Bulletin* 19(2): 96–103.

——— (ed.), 2005. 'Privatising Land in the Pacific: A Defence of Customary Tenures.' Canberra: Australia Institute (Discussion Paper 80).

GoPNG (Government of Papua New Guinea), 1973. 'Report of the Commission of Inquiry into Land Matters.' Port Moresby: GoPNG.

———, 1988. 'Land Mobilisation Programme: Programme Description.' Port Moresby: Department of Lands and Physical Planning.

———, 1995. 'Manual on Land Group Incorporation.' Port Moresby: Papua New Guinea Forest Authority.

Hasluck, P., 1976. 'A Time for Building: Australian Administration in Papua and New Guinea 1951–1963.' Carlton: Melbourne University Press.

Hughes, H., 2004. 'Can Papua New Guinea Come Back from the Brink?' Sydney: Centre for Independent Studies (Issues Analysis Paper 49).

Koyama, S.K., 2004. 'Reducing Agency Problems in Incorporated Land Groups.' *Pacific Economic Bulletin* 19(1): 20–31.

Lea, D., 2005. 'The PNG Forest Industry, Incorporated Entities and Environmental Protection.' *Pacific Economic Bulletin* 20(1): 168–177.

Levy, D., 1989. 'Customary Land Registration.' Port Moresby: Department of Lands and Physical Planning (unpublished report).

Lynch, C.J., 1969. 'Legal Aspects of Economic Organization in the Customary Context in Papua and New Guinea and Related Matters.' Port Moresby: Legislative Draftsman's Office (unpublished manuscript).

Oram, N.D., 1979. 'Grass Roots Justice: Village Courts in Papua New Guinea.' In W. Clifford and S.D. Gokhale (eds), *Criminal Justice in Asia and the Pacific*. Canberra: Australian Institute of Criminology.

Sahlins, M., 1976. 'Historical Metaphors and Mythical Realities: Structure in the Early History of the Sandwich Islands Kingdom.' Ann Arbor: University of Michigan Press.

Taylor, M. and K. Whimp, 1997. 'Report on Land Issues and Hydrocarbon Framework Study.' Port Moresby: Asian Development Bank for Department of Mining and Petroleum.

Weiner, J.F., 2000. 'The Anthropology of and for Native Title.' *The Asia Pacific Journal of Anthropology* 1(2): 124–132.

Chapter Three

Land, Customary and Non-Customary, in East New Britain

Keir Martin

The Gazelle Peninsula of East New Britain (ENB) Province has for many years been regarded as one of Papua New Guinea's (PNG's) most 'developed' regions, with the village of Matupit being seen as one of the most forward-looking Tolai villages. It was the village closest to the town of Rabaul, and by the 1970s was regarded by many as one of its suburbs. Matupit was one of the most prosperous villages in PNG, where Tolai people enjoyed a peri-urban lifestyle and, by PNG standards, a comfortable standard of living. This prosperity was paid for by wage labour in town and the cash cropping that the Tolai had successfully developed on their customary land. This paper builds on previous anthropological research that has addressed business and change in the Gazelle (T.S. Epstein 1968; A.L. Epstein 1969; Salisbury 1970; Bradley 1982; Fingleton 1985), by describing tendencies that have emerged or come to new resolutions in the resettlement and reconstruction process following the volcanic eruptions of 1994. It will examine how ongoing debates about customary land within recent economic conditions were re-framed by Tolai in the new environment that they found themselves in after the eruption. In policy debates over the reform of customary land tenure in Melanesia, definitions of 'custom' are often left unclear or do not cover all of the potential meanings of the word. But what even a brief overview of patterns of land disputes at Matupit demonstrates is the number of different ways that the word 'custom' or its Tok Pisin equivalent *kastom* is used at a grass-roots level, forcing us to pay attention to the uses we make of key concepts in the course of such debates.

Despite the prosperity, pressures were already developing in the time leading up to the volcanic eruption. In contrast to the situation recorded by Smith and Salisbury (1961), in which intra-Tolai land litigation was rare, by the early 1990s ENB was among the leading provinces in the country in terms of the number of registered land disputes. In particular there was a growing tension between the matrilineal landholding clan and the increasingly important nuclear family.[1] Fathers wanted to ensure that investments made on clan land passed to their

---

[1] See Bradley (1982: 191–200) or Fingleton (1985: 58–9) regarding the increasing importance of the nuclear family in Tolai life.

children rather than to their clan nephews. Customary land came to be seen in many contexts as a problem, and people were reluctant in many cases to build new developments on it. When the ENB Provincial Government offered up five agricultural blocks for lease to individuals before the eruption in 1994, they were amazed to find that there were thousands of applicants. The problem, according to John Brown, the then Advisor to the ENB Lands Division, was that 'people felt as if they had no rights to customary land' (*Post-Courier* 12 August 1999).

Free from Custom? Land at Sikut

Matupit, as the Tolai village with the highest population density and the most extensive economic development, suffered more than most from these problems. Many people described the eruption to me as a 'blessing from God', as the village was about to explode under the pressure of disputes. It is this irony that drew my attention — namely, that a disaster could be a divine intervention that would transform conflictive social relations. The disaster is said to be the main reason for the decrease in disputes, as many Matupi moved to a resettlement area at Sikut, an area of government land alienated from the Baining people during the colonial period. Around 200 Matupi families were each given blocks of around three hectares. The government is adamant that this land is not 'customary' land, meaning that it is to be owned by individual families, not by clans, and that each block will be inherited as property by the children of the title holder (in most cases the husband in a nuclear family unit). This position is, on the surface, supported by the majority of those Matupi who have relocated to Sikut. I was struck by the number of occasions on which Sikut residents told me that the land at Sikut was 'better' than Matupit land, not because it was more productive or plentiful, but because it was not 'customary' land. They described themselves as being 'free' from problems associated with customary ground. On these blocks they could work hard and pass on the benefits to their children.

However, just because the land at Sikut is not 'customary', this does not mean it is free from dispute. Rather, most disputes at present have a new character, causing divisions between some blockholders and those still waiting for blocks. Those waiting for blocks are housed on a small area of land euphemistically referred to as the 'care centre', living in shacks that have been erected out of old pieces of corrugated iron, wood, and even cardboard. People awaiting blocks have been temporarily allocated just under one hectare of land per family for gardening, but have been forbidden from planting cash crops because this land has been earmarked for future use as a centre for commercial activities and government services. The government is wary of the potentially costly and time consuming claims for compensation that would arise if cash crops had to be removed. Many blockholders have returned to Matupit and their blocks remain virgin rainforest. This has led to increasingly vocal demands for these blocks to be forfeited and given to those still waiting in the care centre.

In my experience a majority of the Sikut community supported the forfeit policy, as in theory did the Provincial Government Lands Division. Towards the end of my time in Sikut a concerted effort was made by the Resettlement Committee to get the Lands Division to authorise a mass forfeit of around 40 of the undeveloped blocks. When these undeveloped blocks were allocated to families living in the care centre, a series of stormy meetings took place at Sikut during which blockholders and their supporters living at Matupit would descend *en masse*. Blockholders who had been threatened with forfeit by the Resettlement Committee turned up to 'work' on the block for a few weeks, as a warning to the person to whom the block was to be allocated, before returning to Matupit. Many other people had hoped that the official position of the Lands Division would make this tactic impossible, but political leadership at all levels was divided. The elected Resettlement Committee was largely in favour of the forfeit policy, but they were opposed by most of the councillors, who went to the Rabaul District Government to declare the Resettlement Committee null and void. No one knew whether the Rabaul District Government or the Provincial Government' Land Division held authority over the land, meaning that any forfeit policy was likely to be held up by several years of legal wrangling.

An additional problem was that no one had previously secured title to the Sikut blocks. Most of the blocks were allocated in early 1995, with the expectation that title would be issued to individual title holders within a year. Yet at the start of 2004, no titles had been issued because the Provincial Government and the Gazelle Restoration Authority did not have the money to complete the necessary surveys. According to the Authority, this was because World Bank regulations had consistently led to delays in funding being made available. As a result of this situation, a lawyer who was sympathetic to the forfeit policy informed a Sikut meeting, shortly before I left, that the forfeits issued by the Lands Division would not stand up in court as the initial one-year temporary titles had not been renewed. Consequently, every blockholder at Sikut, whether resident or not, is legally regarded as a squatter, remaining on government land with tacit approval. Only when title was issued would the government be able to attach conditions such as block development to the continuation of that title. In spite of this situation, the Resettlement Committee went ahead with the forfeits and started moving people on to the blocks. In my last week of fieldwork in ENB in February 2004, the inevitable fights were breaking out as the original blockholders arrived to remove the newcomers.

On the surface, the current situation at Sikut may not appear to be a dispute over custom, as both sides accept that Sikut is 'non-customary' land. But the debate over forfeits has inevitably become, at least in part, a debate about the role of custom in land matters. Often in debates about the appropriate use of land at Sikut the phrase 'it's not customary ground' would be used as counter-claim. It was argued by supporters of the forfeits that their opponents (deliberately) failed to understand the difference between land that was given by state licence, whose continued ownership was contingent upon development of that land, and customary land that was held by clans by virtue of an inalienable right, or *kakalei* (Epstein 1969: 131). In these arguments the word 'custom' was used in an entirely negative sense as the alleged recourse of those who were too 'lazy' to develop their state land. The opponents of the forfeit policy did not ever claim to consider Sikut to be customary land, but some of their counter-arguments did draw on practices that most people would consider to be customary. Part of the rationale of the resettlement program was the anticipation that blocks would be developed in the bush at Sikut so that, in the event of another eruption, the displaced people of Matupit would be able to go and stay on blocks at Sikut that they had developed, or with kin who had developed blocks. This was because it was custom among the Tolai to go and stay with kin and seek assistance from them in times of need. The original distribution of Sikut blocks followed the council ward divisions of Matupit, meaning that there was a tendency for members of certain clans or people who had other close customary kinship relations to be situated near to each other. This pattern was arguably put at risk by forfeits that gave priority to residents of the care centre, and this is what prompted objections from some opponents of the forfeit who argued that breaking such patterns jeopardised customary networks of assistance in case of emergency. They argued that if forfeits were truly necessary then the blocks should be given to relatives of the original blockholders to preserve these networks. Although it is accepted that the land is not customary, according to this argument it is still important to take custom into account in the governance of this land.

This kind of argument was not just made by opponents of the forfeits. The wave of forfeits that occurred towards the end of my first fieldwork period was spearheaded by ToPirit, the chair of the Resettlement Committee. At the meeting in Sikut at which he announced that the forfeits were going ahead, Pirit raised another issue, namely the need to correct the inequity that had occurred in the case of large families, where the men had all been given blocks but their sisters had not. Later Pirit told me that the purpose of trying to ensure that sisters also received blocks was to keep clans together. In addition, he was concerned that the young men of the clan would become angry if there were no road open to them to inherit land. More important, however, was his concern to keep the clan together as a kind of social security network. He acknowledged that some people at Sikut said that the clan should become a thing of the past, and that individual families should be self-sufficient. However, he believed that this kind of 'Western' self-sufficiency would never be an option for most Papua New

Guineans, and that even those people who had told me they would not help their nephews would still feel obliged to do so if pushed. Pirit felt that the continuation of this kind of custom was still going to be essential for years to come, and he saw tweaking the land tenure system as a means of encouraging its survival. He argued that this would ensure that people lived close to at least some members of their own clan and to other people who had been 'fathered' by their clan, thus ensuring that these relationships were of daily importance to them and strengthening the bonds of reciprocal assistance. Again, although the non-customary nature of the land is asserted, it is combined with a concern that the way non-customary land is administered can help to preserve at least some elements of what is considered to be customary.

Does Custom Hold Back Development, or Is It 'Fading'?

The widespread enthusiasm of Sikut residents for the new land as 'freeing' them from the obligations, constraints and disputes inherent in customary land, is taken by some politicians and government officials as evidence that a more general reform of customary tenure would act as a spur to development. There has indeed been significant investment and development in some of the blocks. Some blockholders have planted thousands of cocoa trees and are anticipating an income of several thousand kina a month (dependent of course on price fluctuations and crop success). Yet we must add some caveats to this development success story. Individual tenure requires the state to have the resources and will to support it if tenure is to be more than a piece of paper. The inability of the state in ENB to provide title even after 10 years, and the lack of clarity as to which of the competing arms of government has jurisdiction at Sikut, has directly led to the under-utilisation of large amounts of Sikut land. People who have been allocated blocks more recently are wary of putting too much effort into developing the land as they have seen others lose their blocks to the original landholders.

An example that illustrates the shaky basis of government jurisdiction is the road access to the blocks at Sikut, where one of the two main roads is only sealed half way. This is because, in 1995, despite warnings to the contrary, one of the blockholders planted cocoa seedlings close to the edge of his block. When the time came for the road to be sealed, he demanded several hundred kina in compensation from the Division of Works, which was going to remove his seedlings so that the road could be sealed. Exasperated by the prospect of wasting years and thousands of kina on legal action, the Provincial Government reallocated the money to another resettlement scheme. As a consequence, the blocks further away from the centre of Sikut are now serviced by a dirt track. Buses refuse to traverse the dirt track as the damages result in prohibitive costs for spare parts. Blockholders cannot afford to hire vehicles to take their cocoa to selling points, with the result that these blocks are among the least developed in the resettlement area. In theory, as this was government land, not customary land, the government could have removed the cocoa seedlings and continued with the road development. In reality, however, they could not afford the legal costs nor have the police tied up in resolving this situation. This example illustrates the difficulties facing the government in enforcing requirements for project development on land over which they have title, and that leaves serious doubt over the government's ability to enforce tenure reform on customary ground.

It is also worth bearing in mind that individual title, in and of itself, does not free one from the demands of kin or from customary obligations that many see as a disincentive to development. While extensive development has occurred at Sikut, no one has planted their entire three hectares with cash crops and food; the maximum planting level has been around two hectares. The reason frequently given for partial block plantings is the need to avoid constant requests for assistance or the risk of being victimised as a result of jealousy. With increased plantings, relatives calculate the future gains from produce sold and hence increase demands for assistance. As one blockholder put it, 'if they see me harvesting all the time and I don't give to some people they can do some things to my block and my cocoa won't bear fruit'. Although this problem is not as bad as it was 20 or 30 years ago, several informants told me that people who consistently refuse requests can end up dead or injured because of sorcery that is nearly always inflicted by jealous siblings or cousins. The previous chair of the Resettlement Committee (before Pirit) was one of the few who consistently attacked this belief about family interference, yet his credibility in the village in this respect was undermined by chronic arthritis in his left leg, which was seen by many as being caused by the jealousy of someone having magical power.

Most important of all, the granting of individual title will not guarantee against the re-emergence of tenure practices that many would describe as 'customary'. There is a precedent for this in ENB. In the 1950s, the Australian Administration released several large blocks of land at Wudal for lease to individuals from Tolai villages near Rabaul. These leases came with the guarantee of individual title and a policy that the land was to be inherited by the next of kin — ideally the children of the blockholder. In most cases, however, the land stayed within the blockholder's clan, often passing on to his sisters' sons, as would be the case with customary land. Although the majority of Tolai are adamant that this is 'new land', and it is morally right that the children of the blockholder who had put in all the hard work of development should inherit it, the strength of kinship ties makes it hard to refuse nephews of one's own clan when they ask to be allowed to help out on the block and plant a section of it for themselves. In such situations, when there are many working the land, it is even harder to remove them. In most cases the nephews have ended up in possession of the block after the death of the original blockholder. In theory, they could be legally removed. In practice, however, it is a process that can take decades and cost thousands of kina, which is not a realistic option for most Tolai. A plaintiff would probably have to wait several years before the case was heard by a local land court, and any case heard in a local land court would be liable to appeal in a higher court. There are three blocks at Wudal that were given to Matupi. Of these, two are now inhabited by nephews of the same clan as the blockholder. In only one case have the children managed to assert their legal right to inherit the title.[2]

Many Sikut residents will argue that Tolai society has changed since the 1960s. They argue that the nuclear family is stronger today, and that the large numbers of people at Sikut (compared to Wudal) will make it possible for a culture to emerge in which demands by clan nephews will be easier to resist. Although people never refused to recognise their nephews, I observed many occasions on which clear boundaries were drawn around the relationship — especially the nephews' rights to come and stay on the block for extended periods. This is important as traditionally, in the matrilineal system, the relationship between a boy and his maternal uncle was seen as being in many contexts more important than a boy's relationship to his father, and uncles and nephews were expected to spend as much time as possible together. Now the fear of a land grab means that uncles try to limit this relationship and the amount of time that nephews spend on their block. Many people held strong views about this, including one Sikut blockholder working at one of the big mines elsewhere in PNG:

> Now custom is fading away. What happened at Wudal won't happen here. Sometimes the nephews do just take over. But that can't happen now. You've got no right to come and just grab the land from my family. Why do I have to grow my kids? Why do I have to settle some place? This custom from the past is no good. Our ground is clan ground, but my ground is my ground automatically. I will never give it to the clan — no way. This kind of thinking is just for the old or the ancestors, now we've been to school we've got better ideas. If I develop this ground with my children? With my sweat? I'm just going to come and let the nephews kick them off?! No way. Not now! Why should I bother getting married? This kind of thinking is bloody rubbish and bullshit from before ... The nephews won't be able to put demands on the kids just because the father was the same clan. It's different now. The kids will be able to get a bush knife and chase them away! My kids haven't seen a cousin come and help, and if they come and ask, I'll tell them no way. If the nephews take over, the people today see it's no good. You're

---

[2] Fingleton (1985) gives a fuller discussion of the emergence of this tendency in the resettlements of the 1960s.

making the man's family suffer. If I behaved like this on clan land, of course there would be talk, and yes at Wudal it happened, but this generation we've seen it's not good. Because the father raised the children. The father planted the cocoa. It's not the nephews'. It's not the clan's.

I was continually struck by the strength with which these feelings were expressed at Sikut. Although there were some who felt that customary tenure would re-establish itself as it seemed to have done at Wudal, they were a clear minority. Although it is early days, in the majority of cases where blocks have been transferred as a result of death or choice it has gone to the original holders' children or other relatives outside the clan. Perhaps the most vitriolic dispute that I encountered at Sikut was between a sister and brother. The block was in the name of the mother, who initially allowed her daughter to live on the block. Several years later she decided to remove the daughter and give the block to her son. This action was believed to be motivated by an intense dislike of her daughter's husband. As the daughter and her husband had planted hundreds of cocoa seedlings and erected a permanent house, the mother's actions led to a very heated dispute. Without going into the details of the dispute, many Sikut residents remarked that the mother's original arrangement would have ensured that the land stayed in her clan for the next two generations. By attempting to remove her daughter and replace her with a son, she was, in one person's words, 'giving the land away'. Many Sikut residents saw her actions as evidence of a new attitude developing towards kinship and land tenure on state land.

Buying and Selling Land at Matupit: Can Customary Land Be Alienated?

If the allegedly individual and discrete nature of blockholdings at Sikut is potentially complicated by the tendency of customary ways of thinking and acting to creep back in, then it is perhaps also the case that ownership of customary land back at Matupit has also been complicated by Tolai responses to new economic circumstances. Debates around land tenure in this part of ENB have long centered on the issue of patrilineal versus matrilineal transfer of rights, with many associating patrilineality with a positive move towards 'modern' land tenure systems. Most of PNG, however, is classified by anthropologists as having 'patrilineal' customary land tenure. What is fundamentally at stake in these debates is an argument about the alleged economic advantages of removing interests in land from cycles of ongoing customary obligation and reciprocal social relations, and instead making land the alienable property of individual persons or household units. In the matrilineal Gazelle, the distinction between matrilineal and patrilineal inheritance has understandably largely come to stand for this debate, with a shift to patrilineality representing the removal of clan-based reciprocal obligations. However, the ways in which Matupi negotiate these tensions today show that characterising land as customary or non-customary is a far from simple matter.

At Matupit today a large proportion of houses are built on purchased land. It is particularly common for fathers to buy land from their own clan to overcome the problems that will arise between their children and their nephews if they build permanent houses on their own clan land. The buying and selling of customary ground is in theory illegal in PNG, unless the buying and selling can be shown to be a customary practice. The custom of 'buying' ground is known among the Tolai as *kulia*. However, Bill Epstein, who conducted fieldwork at Matupit in the early 1960s, was keen to stress that *kulia* does not neatly equate with the Western idea of an alienable commodity transaction, noting that, '[t]he indigenous concept of *kul* then is translated by the term purchase only at the risk of serious misrepresentation' (Epstein 1969: 132). Epstein devotes some attention to what distinguishes *kulia* from Western ideas of buying and selling, as for him the different nature of this transaction is key to illuminating the ways in which Tolai customary land tenure differs from Western property regimes.

> In the indigenous system land was not a commodity. Transfers of land were not conducted according to the principles of the market; rather they were effected between parties who saw themselves as already linked by social bonds, and when land was exchanged in return for *tambu* it was usually in recognition of the obligations of kinship or other customary claims … the payment demanded in *tambu* was also small. This remains the position today in regard to 'sales' of land within the village, where the sums involved in cash and *tambu* fall very far short of the market value (ibid).

Two reasons are given here for why *kulia* should not be considered equivalent to Western commodity transactions. First, there is the nature of the bonds preceding the transaction, implying that *kulia* should be seen as a part of an ongoing cycle of customary obligation rather than as a stand-alone purchase of alienable property. Second, the low level of payment, 'short of the market value', is provided as evidence that the payment is 'in recognition of … customary claims' rather than an outright purchase.[3]

The conclusion that Epstein draws from this state of affairs is that the *kakalei* or 'claim' to the land 'remains vested in the vendor lineage' (Epstein 1969: 104). This non-alienability of claims in the land is a key difference between Tolai customary land and Western landed property.[4] I have been told that in the past

---

[3] These two observations are backed up by Fingleton in his (1985) study of land tenure at the nearby Tolai village of Rakunat during the mid 1980s.

[4] See Mauss (1970) and Gregory (1982) for key discussions of the central importance of the non-alienability of objects in Melanesian societies in contrast to Western conceptions of alienable property.

there would often be expectations that the land might return to the vendors at some point after the death of the buyers, that they would be considered to have an ongoing relationship with the piece of ground, and that if the 'purchasers' failed to be suitably attentive to their ongoing customary obligations to the vendors then it would be commonplace for the vendors to find a way to reclaim the land. However, even by the early 1960s, Epstein had identified trends that were taking *kulia* away from this customary ideal. First, the increasing number of land deals with the colonial administration and the large amounts of money involved meant that the clan elders who controlled the land were 'now encouraged to think of land increasingly as a commodity' (Epstein 1969: 132). The young men who protested at many of these deals were essentially claiming that the elders 'had no power to dispose of the land so as to remove it from the sphere of Tolai social relationships and customary obligations' (ibid). Second, cash cropping meant that 'many Tolai are beginning to find it necessary to think of land as a commodity even in transactions among themselves' (ibid). Epstein cites the example of a young man who bought a plot of customary land in the village of Napapar to plant cocoa. When his cocoa was ready to bear fruit, they reclaimed the land. Epstein concludes that '[f]or him, as for many Tolai, the traditional system of land tenure was beginning to reveal its limitations in meeting the needs of contemporary situations' (ibid: 133).

Today, I would argue that although *kulia* retains features that distinguish it from the purest ideal of commodity transaction, it has continued to change in many respects. Radin (1996) suggests that what is referred to as 'commodification' is necessarily an incomplete process, and whether a thing, transaction, or relationship should be viewed as a commodity is therefore a matter of degree, rather than an 'either/or' distinction. In my opinion, changes to *kulia* over the past 40 years can be usefully looked at in this way. Parties to the transaction will tend to be involved in ongoing customary relationships, as almost everyone at Matupit is involved in customary relations with everyone else anyway. Fingleton notes that the flexibility of relations in the village makes it easy to construct customary ties that legitimise a *kulia* transaction: 'no land transaction may be mounted without a pre-existing link between the parties, but the relativity of Tolai concepts of group corporateness and kinship facilitates the establishment of a connection between willing people' (Fingleton 1985: 211). This means that even outsiders with no history of relationship to the community can buy land in the village through the creation of customary ties. Although I was unable to observe the purchase of any land during my time at Matupit, I was told that it was not hard to accomplish. Even as early as the 1960s a number of settlers from the Sepik area had bought land on the edge of Matupit, and their descendants were still living there when I was doing fieldwork. Fingleton makes a convincing case that this plasticity of customary relations is an example of the inherent flexibility of customary tenure that makes it better adapted to rapidly changing social relations than fixed Western property law. From a theoretical angle however, this inexhaustible flexibility can be problematic, because if customary culture is so flexible that it can encompass any kind of relationship then it is at risk of becoming a tautological concept that defines and prescribes nothing.

I found that there were regular disputes as to how customary some manifestations of custom really are, the most frequent examples being criticisms of economically powerful 'big-shots' for 'commercialising' custom. Custom is at least partly judged by whether or not one's actions are considered to be embedded in and constitutive of the kind of customary reciprocal relations that Epstein's young men accused the elders of abandoning by selling land to the Australians. Even if one performs custom as a set of rules perfectly, one's actions can be considered to be fundamentally non-customary when judged on this basis. This contrast between custom based on ongoing reciprocal obligations, and Western social life as being based on business transactions, although far from exhausting the multivalent possibilities of the word 'custom' or *kastom*, was an often repeated and important part of the definition. If Radin is correct to say that commodification is a necessarily incomplete process, and Gregory (1982: 23), drawing on Sahlins, is correct in arguing that, 'the distinction between gift exchange and commodity exchange should not be seen as a bipolar opposition but rather as the extreme points of a continuum', then the networks of social relations that go into making up a transaction can be viewed from more than one angle, and indeed often are viewed as part of a process of assessing the morality of these transactions.

The danger in simply describing the ease with which customary relations can be created to make *kulia* possible is that this can assume what it seeks to demonstrate — namely, the fundamental difference between *kulia* as a customary practice and standard Western property transactions as an empirical 'bipolar opposition'. Just as it is possible for Matupi to view the involvement of big-shots in custom from an angle that declares it to be non-reciprocal and therefore not truly customary, it is also possible that customary links which are so easily and flexibly contracted can be seen from certain angles as a kind of preparation for a *kulia* transaction that now looks more like a purchase. *Kulia* may be formally the same as before, but its increasing relative weight and degree of finality may make it appear, in certain indigenous descriptions at least, more like a commodity transaction for which the preceding transactions are preparatory work, rather than part of an ongoing cycle of customary reciprocity. Certainly the description of how custom can 'hide' the true value of a transaction suggests that this is one possible indigenous perspective from which *kulia* can be described today. Some transactions sit so clearly towards one or the other of Gregory's two poles that the scope for different perspectives to be taken on them is severely limited, but others are more ambiguous. I would not argue, against Fingleton and others, that *kulia* is a commodity transaction and therefore that Tolai think of land in the same way as Australians. Rather, my argument is that *kulia* is not *simply* an uncomplicated customary transaction, but can also be viewed as embodying other, less customary, more commodity-oriented ethics. Changes over the past 40 years, while not totally 'commodifying' the transaction (and by implication Tolai attitudes towards land), have moved it further towards that pole of the spectrum by creating more situations in which Tolai find it fruitful to describe land in property/commodity terms. This is perhaps the very process by which partial commodification occurs.

Epstein and Fingleton (especially the latter) do not just stress the importance of establishing customary connections prior to *kulia*, but also the maintenance and continued recognition of these links after the transaction. For example, after noting the flexibility with which customary connections legitimising *kulia* may be created, Fingleton goes on to say that:

> the connection, however, whether direct or indirect, forms the basis of the land transaction. It characterises the tenure thereby gained, so that its security remains indefinitely dependent upon maintenance of the formative connection (Fingleton 1985: 211).

Although it is the case that there is still a tendency for *kulia* to be transacted between persons or groups who were already strongly linked — as when a man buys from his own clan on behalf of his children — I found no evidence that *kulia* transactions tend to strengthen the connections, and in some cases there is little or no ongoing relationship.

One of my closest acquaintances built his house on land that he bought from the last male representative of one of Matupit's major landholding clans. This purchase was made in 1983, and to my knowledge the purchaser has had no ongoing customary relationship with the vendor, and would give him very short shrift if he came to ask for favours or gifts on the basis of his ancestral links with the land upon which the purchaser has built his house, which is something that vendor is wont to do with some people to whom he has sold land. What is interesting is the attitude of the majority of Matupi to requests such as this. Most people say that it is dishonest as it is an attempt to get money 'twice for land that you have already sold'. In many contexts in contemporary PNG, such as negotiations with a mining company, landowners are keen to demand the establishment of an ongoing and more customary relationship that goes beyond single payments because of the other party's long-term presence on the land. Amongst Matupi, however, the idea that a transfer of land can be a way of legitimising such demands is treated with near-universal incomprehension or repulsion. It is clear that Papua New Guineans do not view land transfers according to a logic of inexorable commodification, or according to an unchanging cultural logic of inalienability, but instead are as capable as any other group of people of judging (or disputing) that different kinds of transactions are morally appropriate in different contexts.

Registration of Landownership and Transfer

How do Tolai people now respond to the statement made by Epstein that *kakalei* remains with the vendor clan even after *kulia* (sale). In 2002–04, the response was universally one of incredulity. People would assert that of course *kakalei* can be transferred, there would be no point in buying something if you didn't receive the *kakalei*. This would sometimes be followed by the suggestion any statement to the contrary must be the work of crooked old men who want to get money twice for the same piece of land. Epstein notes that sale by *kulia* never gives secure ownership as it only takes one member of the vendor clan to stand up a couple of years later, and claim not to have been consulted, for the sale to be undone (Epstein 1969: 131–2). Epstein implies that this is one of the ways in which *kakalei* remains with the vendor clan, like the case in which the purchaser is remiss in maintaining an ongoing customary relationship with the vendor after the *kulia* transaction. Today, this 'problem' has been partially resolved by a practice that has evolved over the past 30 years, of witnessing the purchase with a statutory declaration which all adult members of the vendor clan must sign before the deal is finalised.

The practice of witnessing purchase with a statutory declaration started in this part of ENB under the Australian Administration in the early 1970s, although T.S. Epstein's fieldnotes include government records of land purchases in the much less 'developed' Tolai village of Rapitok during the late 1950s.[5] According to Jessep (1980: 123–4), the recording of land sales in ENB was 'apparently valued for the documentary evidence of the sale and the publicity of the payment made at the office'. Fitzpatrick (1983: 19) cites Tolai evidence in support of a wider argument about PNG in the 1970s:

> Unofficial and semi-official land registers … had emerged … [U]nofficial transfers of land as a commodity were taking place between members of different groups. Various operative strategies had developed to restrict the range of obligations effective in succession to land, to increase individual control over the process and to confine transmitted rights more to the nuclear family or a favoured son. Nor were these trends without suggestive precedent in the customary base … With the extension of cash-cropping after the second world war … there emerged a greater awareness of land as having a reified value and greater, and effective, pressure for more clearly defined individual rights in land.

---

[5] T.S. Epstein's fieldnotes are held in the Mandeville Special Collections Library at the University of California, San Diego.

I was often told that if you have 'the paper' (meaning the statutory declaration), then you are safe. One old man explained to me that 'before we did not know how to buy and sell properly; now that we have the paper, we have more *save* (knowledge)'. This clearly indicates the perception that the nature of *kulia* has changed over the years. In this context, as one person described it to me, 'papers' do have power to 'strengthen' the practice of buying ground, and this is part of the process that Tolai have developed in response to their perceived need to secure land that they were buying for their children. Hence, paper 'kills the talk' on a piece of ground — at least between the selling clan and the buyer — although there is always the option for a third party to claim that the vendors never had the right to sell the ground in the first place.

I have no personal experience of the selling clan reclaiming land from a buyer who had a statutory declaration. Of course a registration can be misleading to the outside observer, conflating a number of reciprocal customary obligations into one simple transaction (Fingleton 1985: 184–6). However, registration of the purchase transaction, in Matupit at least, does seem to set a kind of seal on the land transfer, making it harder for alleged oversights in the recognition of ongoing obligations to be used to overturn the transaction. Even if, in many cases, land transfers are unimaginable without a preceding history of relationships and anticipation of ongoing relations, the act of registration does seem to give the transfer a degree of separation from these relations.

The use of statutory declarations is now semi-officially recognised by the Provincial Government: the Lands Division keeps copies of all land purchase statutory declarations and has also put in place official guidelines for the practice. All reports of the origin of this practice claim that its impetus came from the village not the government. According to Fingleton (1985: 181-2), the practice began in Rakunat as a continuation of an aborted attempt by the colonial government to register land in the 1960s, and was carried out by the villagers themselves in order to secure land transfers, not as part of a government plan to reform customary land practices. As he puts it, '[t]he most important changes in ... land tenure ... are those which occurred internally, in transactions within the village community which continued the process of adjustment to changing land demands' (ibid: 178). This is an important point because great attention is often paid to a history of unsuccessful state-driven changes in land tenure imposed upon an unwilling population, as it was in the case of the Gazelle Peninsula (ibid: iii). This ethnographic description fits into what has become a wider theoretical concern in recent years, namely the ways in which the state needs to organise its subjects and their practices in ways that enable it to 'see' and therefore govern them more efficiently (Scott 1998). It is understandable if this history is emphasised to counter the misguided arguments of those who suggest that Western nations should use their disproportionate economic power to force Melanesian nations into land tenure reform. But it is also important to acknowledge that, in an engagement with the global economy in certain contexts, Melanesians are bound to explore the possibility of different ways of transacting land, and that sometimes they will seek the support of the state in making these more secure. To acknowledge that it is just as possible for the state's subjects to be recognised in a manner that fits their needs, as it is for the state to demand that its subjects be organised in a manner that makes it possible for the state to 'see' them, should in no way be taken as an endorsement of overarching schemes to revolutionise village life through legislative action. Quite the opposite: it shows the importance of a careful ethnographic attention to the different details of processes of contested commodification as they occur in different circumstances.

Land that is transacted by this process is still legally considered to be customary land, and although the purchaser, if a man, has the right to pass it on to his children, in the next generation it must follow matrilineal principles.[6] For this reason Matupi will tend to refer to even 'purchased' land at Matupit as customary land, largely in contradistinction to their land at Sikut. However, they are also clearly aware that the custom of *kulia* and its relationship to wider networks of customary obligation has changed in some respects in the past 40 years. Land disputes at Matupit are not as widespread as they were in the years leading up to the volcanic eruption of 1994, but it was notable that not one of the cases I observed was an attempt by vendors to overturn a land sale that had been registered, and I was told by most Matupi that any such attempt would be fruitless. The Lands Division and the majority of Matupi clearly view *kulia* today as a transaction that implies the complete alienation of all rights in a piece of land from one group to another. Epstein's claim that 'the estate vested by a *"purchase"* is *always* regarded as inferior to a *kakalei*' (Epstein 1969: 131, my emphasis) has, at the very least, been complicated by changes to Tolai *kulia* over the past 40 years.

With regard to 'market value', I conducted a village household survey and discovered that the average 'price' paid for a house had hardly risen at all in the past 40 years. This was in contrast to the prices of other essentials, such as imported foodstuff and materials used to build permanent houses, which had risen dramatically. Although what constitutes 'market value' is hard to ascertain in an environment such as Matupit, prices as low as K50–100 (equivalent to the cost of two cartons of beer) seems good value for the outright purchase of a plot of land on which one is going to build a house that will cost thousands of kina. This stability seems to bear out Epstein's original observations about the non-commodity nature of customary land transactions at Matupit, and to cast

---

[6] This means that it will most likely go to the children of the purchaser's daughters, so if a man buys land from his own clan for his children, the land passes from his own matriline to a section of his wife's matriline.

doubt on his prediction that trends were emerging in village life that were going to push land transactions in a more commodified direction. Matupi offered a number of explanations for the relative stability of land prices. One was that land had for a long time been a part of the customary system, although that answer was always accompanied by a caveat that this was changing and that prices for land were starting to rise. Indeed, I was often told that the volcano had stopped an anticipated explosion in land prices, just as it had stopped the explosion of land disputes. Another response was that many of the prices that I had been given during the course of my village survey were most likely exaggerated as many of the prices were much higher than I had been led to believe. People would publicly 'buy' the land for a small amount of money, but behind the scenes, hundreds or even thousands of kina (or equivalents) would change hands. The larger amounts would be kept secret. It is worth pointing out that there were some at Matupit who angrily denied that such a thing could happen, but the very suggestion demonstrated an awareness on the part of some Matupi that there was something of a contradiction here. On the one hand, the legal registration of a seemingly commercial transaction can mask a web of customary obligations; on the other hand, the low monetary value of a seemingly customary transaction can mask a commercial exchange of greater value. Indeed, a few people told me that custom was a means for 'hiding' the value of a land purchase, once again demonstrating that seemingly customary transactions are capable of being viewed from a commercial perspective if one wants to cast them in a certain moral light. We are familiar, in Melanesian ethnography, with a position that stresses how relationships that have seemingly been Westernised or commodified are, on closer examination, still based on a customary ethic of reciprocity. This is undoubtedly often true, but perhaps in stressing such moments we sometimes lose sight of the logical corollary — situations in which what on the surface appears customary and reciprocal can simultaneously embody the opposite ethical values. The ways in which Matupi discuss the 'commercialisation' of custom demonstrates that they have certainly not lost sight of these possibilities.

As well, there are tendencies emerging at Matupit today that suggest a more openly commercial attitude towards land sales. During my last visit to Matupit I interviewed a village councillor about land sales in his ward. He told me of a woman who had sold three separate plots of land for houses in the village on behalf of her clan section in the past year. Instead of the one- or two-hundred kina standard land sale price on my village survey, she had sold land for K2–3000, a price much closer to the amount that similar plots would receive on the commercial market in Rabaul. The councillor stressed that such price rises were the result of land registration, and that meant that the purchase was secure. From the point of view of the state and Matupi themselves, although the land remained customary, in contradistinction to the land at Sikut for example, it clearly does not live up to certain ideals of custom as these are expressed in many ethnographic and indigenous accounts.

The performance of customary ritual has always been of great importance to people's rights to reside on certain pieces of land. A man wishing to stay on his father's clan land after his death would pay close attention to helping his father's clan in custom, in particular distributing large amounts of customary shell-wealth on his death. Even someone residing on his own clan land would not expect residence by right, but would be expected to help in custom. Someone remiss in their customary obligations would bring shame on the clan and would likely be given the worst pieces of ground to live and garden upon. Today the picture is slightly different. The declining power of the big men in the clan means that complaints about young men simply building a house on clan land without consultation with elders of the clan are not uncommon. Members of the Matupi community at Sikut have begun performing customary practices from Matupit, such as the *namata*, a kind of initiation for the first-born son of a family. One of the minority of Matupi who hoped for a return to openly full-blooded 'customary' land tenure at Sikut told me that this emergence of custom at Sikut was a sign that his hopes would be realised, just as had happened at Wudal. He was also of the view that the Provincial Government's attempt to remove customary clan relations from land tenure at Sikut was a continuation of the Australian Administration's attempts to 'turn us into white men' when they tried to enforce patrilineal nuclear family inheritance at Wudal. For most Sikut residents, however, the extent to which the performance of custom heralds the re-emergence of customary land tenure is not clear. As one young male resident at Sikut explained to me in October 2002: 'When you do custom at Matupit you are concerned with land. When you do custom here it is custom only (*tasol*).' He further argued that many Matupit residents who had been heavily involved in custom before they got blocks at Sikut were now involved in the bare minimum required for social respectability. Now that they had their own land, they no longer felt the need to keep the clan happy by performing custom.

Whatever the future holds at Sikut, these examples show that there are problems in defining land as customary or non-customary, and that these may sometimes be overlooked in policy debates. The land at Wudal is still formally regarded by the state as non-customary land, yet it is widely acknowledged to be land where 'custom has come back in' to the extent that many people describe it as 'like customary land' or even *as* 'customary land'. The increasing performance of custom at Sikut, along with trends to acknowledge the importance of customary relations on non-customary land, may well have effects on land use and occupation. The question is how much effect will it have, and how much will be necessary for the inhabitants to acknowledge that the land has become *de facto* customary. Conversely, the land bought and sold by *kulia* at Matupit is still in the eyes of both the state and Matupit 'customary', yet it is described in ways that make it appear less customary, according to certain glosses of the word 'custom', than would have been the case 40 years ago. Custom is as much a position taken on the morality of certain transactions as it is an empirical description of a juridical process to be preserved or reformed in the interests of national development.

References

Bradley, C.B., 1982. Tolai Women and Development. London: University College London (PhD thesis).

Epstein, A.L., 1969. *Matupit: Land, Politics, and Change among the Tolai of New Britain*. Canberra: Australian National University Press.

Epstein, T.S., 1968. *Capitalism, Primitive and Modern: Some Aspects of Tolai Economic Growth*. Canberra: Australian National University Press.

Fingleton, J.S., 1985. Changing Land Tenure in Melanesia: The Tolai Experience. Canberra: Australian National University (PhD thesis).

Fitzpatrick, P., 1983. 'The Knowledge and Politics of Land Law.' *Melanesian Law Journal* 11: 14–34.

Gregory, C., 1982. *Gifts and Commodities*. London: Academic Press.

Jessep, O., 1980. 'Land Demarcation in New Ireland.' *Melanesian Law Journal* 8: 112–133.

Mauss, M., 1970. *The Gift: Forms and Function of Exchange in Primitive Societies*. London: Cohen and West.

Radin, M., 1996. *Contested Commodities: The Trouble with Trade in Sex, Children, Body Parts and Other Things*. Cambridge: Harvard University Press.

Salisbury, R.F., 1970. *Vunamami: Economic Transformation in a Traditional Society*. Melbourne: Melbourne University Press.

Scott, J., 1998. *Seeing like a State: How Certain Schemes to Improve the Human Condition Have Failed*. New Haven: Yale University Press.

Smith, S.S., and R.F. Salisbury, 1961. 'Notes on Tolai Land Law and Custom.' Unpublished report to the Native Land Commission, Kokopo.

Chapter Four

Clan-Finding, Clan-Making and the Politics of Identity in a Papua New Guinea Mining Project

Dan Jorgensen

At Independence in 1975 the famously diverse peoples of Papua New Guinea (PNG) became citizens of a country without any particular sense of national identity apart from an unevenly shared colonial history. Creating such an identity was one of the tasks the state felt obliged to shoulder from the beginning, and adopting the language of tradition was one means of doing so. While there is a rhetoric of localised 'custom' (*kastam*) in popular discourse, the state takes care to package its version of tradition as a bundle of values specific to no particular place but putatively shared by all. Dubbed the 'Melanesian Way' (Narokobi 1980), this generic tradition forms the basis of a post-colonial ideology that seeks to consolidate or overlook differences in the interests of creating a national culture (Philibert 1986, Otto 1997).[1]

Much has been written about the formation of national cultures in the Pacific (for example: Keesing 1989; LiPuma 1995; Wanek 1996: 111–33), and I do not intend to add to this literature here. Instead, I am more interested in examining what happens when the state's ideas about tradition enter into policy and its implementation. In particular, I wish to show how the articulation of the ideology of tradition with local practices turns on the twin issues of legibility and recognition, and how this conjunction plays out in the formation of local identities.

In his book, *Seeing Like a State*, Scott (1998) argues that a precondition for the implementation of state plans is the establishment of what he calls 'legibility'. Legibility enables systematic state intervention in the affairs of its citizens, and creating legibility entails state simplifications of social practices in the form of a standard grid whereby these can be recorded and monitored. Originating from above and from the centre, legibility requires the invention of units — citizens, trees, houses, villages, and so on — that are rendered visible in the interests of

---

[1] In this respect the official discourse on PNG tradition differs from the notion of *adat* (custom), as elaborated by the Dutch in Indonesia, by taking pains to avoid features that would distinguish one set of citizens from another — a fact that has an unexpected relevance for the matters discussed here.

control. The reciprocal of legibility from the point of view of those affected by state projects is recognition. Recognition turns upon the ways in which a state's citizens make themselves visible to the state in a way that gives them some purchase on the state's decisions and operations.

With the issues of legibility and recognition in mind, I begin this paper with a brief account of tradition as formulated in PNG national discourse, drawing attention to certain of its more important ideological characteristics. I move from this to a consideration of the ways in which official tradition takes shape as policy with regard to the resource development projects that have become such a prominent feature of recent PNG history. I then turn to the examination of the dynamics of legibility and recognition in the context of a particular mining project and how these figure in the production of new identities. Finally, I conclude with a short survey of what we know about similar processes elsewhere before offering some observations on what this tells us about the role of state-formulated tradition as a guide to determining rights in land for the purpose of concluding mining agreements.

Development, The Melanesian Way, and The Eight Aims

Whatever PNG lacked by way of common tradition at Independence was more than made up by an enthusiasm for development (*developmen*) in all regions of the country, and many of the new state's claims to legitimacy were based on promises that all Papua New Guineans could expect development to come their way. If one were to ask *where* the Melanesian Way led, the answer would be, *to development*, but on authentic Papua New Guinean terms. While short on specifics, the notion of a Melanesian path to development did more than simply espouse an essentialised identity based on values of community and the continued viability of tradition: it claimed modernity as a Melanesian project. Thus the end of Australian rule did not mean the end of the prospects of development that had figured so prominently in Australia's own justification of its tenure in PNG, and dreams awakened in the colonial era would not vanish, even if the colonialists did.

In attempting to reconcile generic notions of tradition with modernist hopes,[2] the ideology of the Melanesian Way also grappled with one of the worries that preoccupied planners and politicians in the state's early days, namely, the tension between egalitarian goals and the reality that development often produces inequality. A solution adopted by the Constitutional Planning Committee was to turn the platitudes of the Melanesian Way into policy guidelines in the formulation of the 'Eight Aims' (or Eight Point Plan). Widely publicised (for example, Somare 1974) and incorporated into the Constitution, the Eight Aims set forth principles meant to guide development through the use of 'Papua New

---

[2] What Geertz (1973: 240–1) described as the essentialism-epochalism dilemma.

Guinean methods'. Espousing a populist egalitarian ethos, the document calls for

> more equal distribution of economic benefits, including movement toward equalisation of incomes among people and toward equalisation of services among different areas of the country ... [and] an emphasis on small-scale artisan, service, and business activity, relying where possible on typically Papua New Guinean forms of organization (CPC 1974 cited in Fitzpatrick 1980: 203).

Critics have been quick to point out the romanticised myths underlying this ideology (Filer 1990: 9), and many have noted its tendency to mask growing inequalities between rural people and the national elite (Fitzpatrick 1980: 202ff). It is, however, fair to say that the early post-Independence era was marked by an attempt to realise the romantic ideal by implementing these principles in terms of a 'small is beautiful' development policy.

Under the aegis of this commitment to agrarian populism, the state launched a series of schemes promoting rural smallholder production. Such policies did little to generate the revenues needed to finance government programs, however, and a World Bank report in the late 1970s laid the groundwork for a major shift towards capital-intensive enclave projects to develop the country's mineral resources. From the beginning of the 1980s onwards, the state's development strategy mandated the inauguration of numerous mining projects that were to become the mainstay of the national economy.[3]

Mining, Tradition, and Legibility

The shift to large-scale mining development marked a departure from the egalitarian program of the Eight Aims, and fostered regional disparities between prosperous mining enclaves and an increasingly impoverished rural sector. Despite this, traces of the ideology of the Melanesian Way remain in key aspects of the state's dealings with its citizens in areas affected by such projects. The role of the state in mining projects is a dual one in which it strives to deliver a secure contract environment while safeguarding local interests.[4] It is in this latter capacity that the ideology of tradition enters into the picture by providing the outlines of a template for establishing legibility.

PNG law declares subterranean mineral rights to be a state prerogative, but this doctrine has had to come to terms with the fact that virtually all land in

---

[3] The major exception to this pattern is the Bougainville mine at Panguna, which had already become a key revenue earner by this time. Problems surrounding this mine later led to a rebellion and war that resulted in closure of the mine and caused a range of other problems still being addressed through the Bougainville Peace Process.

[4] In recent years the state's role has been further complicated by the fact that it has acted as an equity partner in mining projects, giving rise to more than a suspicion of conflict of interest.

PNG is held under customary forms of tenure — a situation that obliges the state to broker negotiations with local people in order to identify 'landowners'. In this climate the state has been at pains to formulate a template of customary land tenure informed by its ideology of tradition. The logic underlying this approach is best summed up in a recent review under the imprimatur of PNG's Law Reform Commission. After sketching the principles of segmentary lineage systems familiar to most anthropologists, the author concludes that:

> In Papua New Guinea landownership is vested in descent groups — tribal or clan segments. All clan members are co-owners. This gives individuals the right to use land but not to alienate it. Thus, land ownership is part of the identity of a group. It is an inalienable right, passed from the ancestors into the guardianship of successive generations (Toft 1997: 14).

This generic model of clan-based land tenure guards against worries over land alienation by calming fears that local people will be dispossessed by transnational capital because it ties land rights to traditional groups. Ideologically, it fosters a manageable contract environment while affirming tradition, and that means development in the Melanesian Way. The strategy is to mediate between two kinds of corporate entities — mining companies and landowning clans — and its technical prerequisite is to establish the legibility of customary tenure by making clans visible.

Legibility and Recognition in Nenataman

As Filer has pointed out, a popular ideology of landownership has become a general idiom through which local people make claims against the state for everything from compensation to the provision of government services (Filer 1997, 1998; see also Ballard 1997). Where mining projects are contemplated or are already underway, the discourse of landownership has provided local people with a powerful bargaining chip in demanding the restoration or extension of dwindling government services, by raising the possibility that they can block projects by withholding consent until at least some of their demands are met. In such a context discussions that at first sight appear to be about property must be understood to be at least as much about the broad political relationship between the state and its disgruntled citizens (Jackson 1989, 1991).

This point brings us to an important feature of mining negotiations, for landowners' issues are often less about threats to their enjoyment of land than securing recognition that will confer access to benefits that — it is fervently hoped — will flow from mining operations once they are underway (King 1997; Filer 1998). The stakes for local people increase when possible royalties, compensation payments, employment and business development are added to the mix of anticipated benefits.

This context sets up a situation in which there is a tension between the state's need to identify clearly legible landholding units and local people's efforts to establish recognition of their claims to a share in the wealth generated by mining operations. That tension can be illustrated with reference to the proposed Nena/Frieda mining project.[5]

Situated on the boundary between the East and West Sepik provinces, the Nena/Frieda prospect is located in a valley known locally as Nenataman — a thickly forested valley in the rugged foothill ranges south of the Sepik River (Figure 4-1). As with many other mining projects, the mineral deposits at issue are found near the top of local mountains, some of which lie along border zones between adjacent ethnic groups (Figure 4-2).

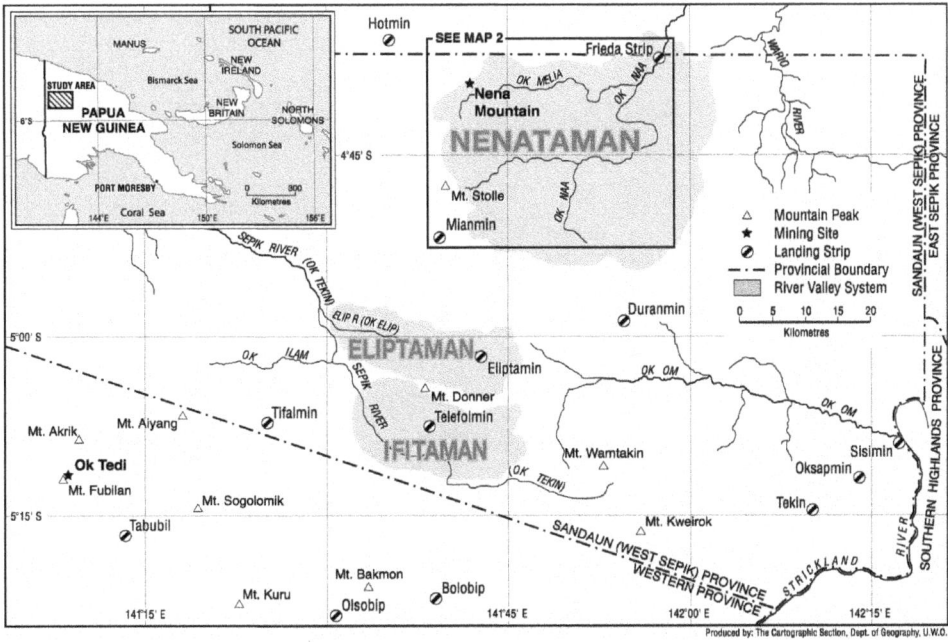

Figure 4-1: Nenataman location map.

Not surprisingly, this location has given rise to disputes about whose land this is — a situation intensified and complicated by the pattern of land use and the history of settlement in the region. Nenataman is inhabited by a scattered and ethnically mixed population of shifting cultivators who supplement gardening with wide-ranging hunting, collecting, and sago making. The valley has been the site of dramatic shifts in settlement and population for at least 150 years, when Telefolmin from the south began expanding into Nenataman at the

---

[5] This project is presently (2006) on hold, and its future is unclear. In this regard it is in fact very much like most other mining projects whose course is rarely certain, especially at the outset. Despite the fact that a mine has yet to materialise at Nena, the dynamics of the present case are instructive in understanding other projects currently on line.

expense of the original inhabitants, the Untoumin. Over a span of about 50 years the Untoumin were raided by Telefolmin and the nearby Miyanmin with the result that most were annihilated and the remainder either scattered or incorporated as captives into Telefol and Miyan settlements. After the destruction of the Untoumin at the turn of the century, Telefolmin and Miyanmin raided each other intermittently until just before pacification around the end of the 1950s. At present, the main settlements in the Nenataman area include: the Telefol villages of Wabia and Ok Isai; Miyan hamlets belonging to Wameimin parish; Bapi, the sole surviving Paiyamo village; and a handful of small Owininga hamlets to the northwest.

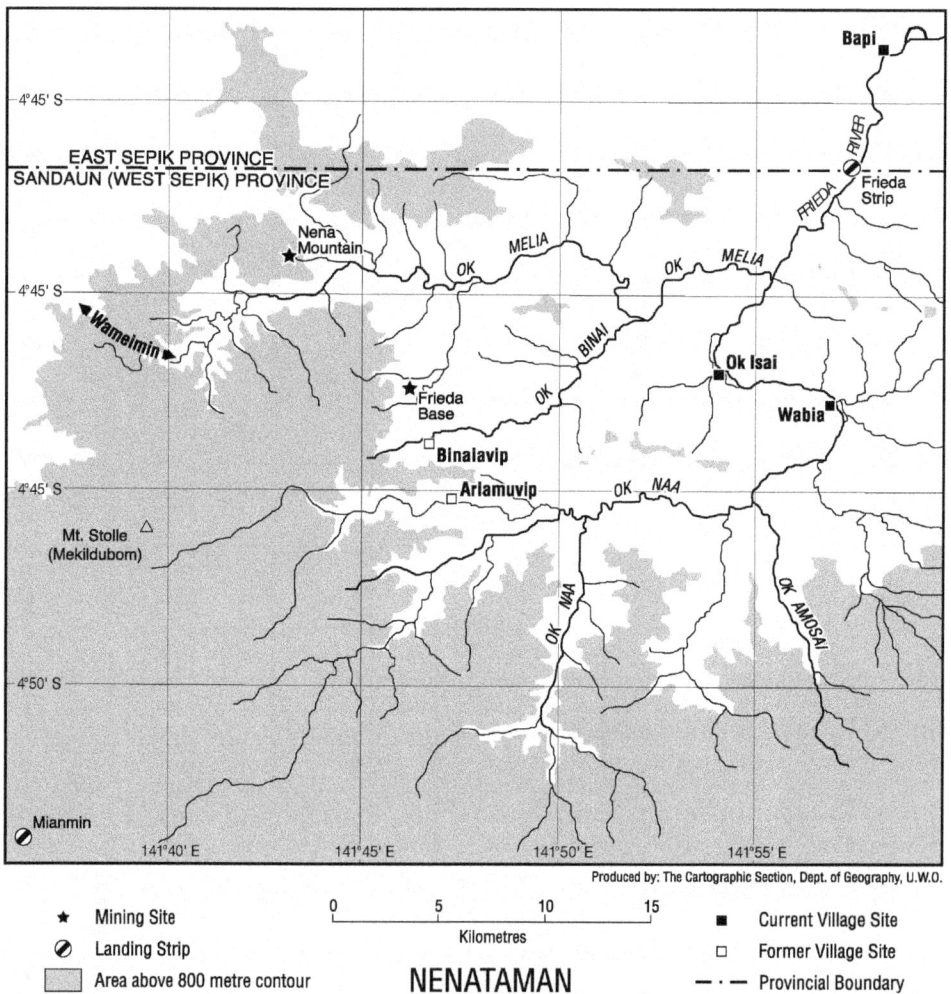

Figure 4-2: Topographical and site map of Nenataman.

The fact that Nenataman has been a contested zone for most of its known history, and the location of the main mineral deposits along its borderlands, are only two of several factors blurring attempts to demarcate territorial boundaries. For Telefolmin of Wabia and Ok Isai, the situation is further complicated by the fact that they settled the valley as colonists assisted by Telefolmin from the Eliptaman and Ifitaman valleys to the south (Figure 4-1). Local ideas of entitlement permit claims of access to the descendants of those who fought to clear the valley's previous inhabitants, and Telefolmin in Eliptaman and Ifitaman now invoke these principles to press their interests.

This general fluidity is accentuated by aspects of Miyan and Telefol social organisation, for although relatively fixed villages provide the structural backbone of settlement, these villages competed for personnel and were relatively open in their recruitment. Kinship is reckoned cognatically, and as it was always possible for individuals to claim affiliation along a diverse range of ties, it is arguable that this kind of organisation facilitated a kind of demographic warfare that was endemic to the region before contact (Jorgensen 1997; Gardner 1998, 2004). Finally, men employed in mineral exploration sometimes tended stands of sago in the prospect area, and Telefolmin recognise such activity as entitling one to claims in the area worked.

Although this untidy picture is probably not unusual for a number of areas in PNG, it represents a nightmare for those interested in drawing lines, circumscribing claims and identifying landowner groups. When it became clear that the prospects of mining in the area were good, the government, the developer (Highlands Gold, now Highlands Pacific), and the recently formed Frieda Mine Landowners' Association[6] sought to clarify the situation by mobilising the apparatus of legibility: making maps, conducting censuses and collecting genealogies.[7]

Both the government and the developer were hoping for some sort of solution to the apparently intractable problems associated with determining claims, but local fears of failing to gain recognition fuelled an increasingly contested atmosphere as the prospect of being excluded from a benefits settlement loomed larger on local horizons. What emerged in response to attempts to create legibility was a strategy of seeking recognition through a series of experiments in clanship. Here it is important to underscore the novel nature of the enterprise, since Telefolmin have no clans.

---

[6] The name of the association draws upon the official name of the main river draining the Nenataman valley, the Frieda River. Highlands Gold subsequently opted to change the designation of the site to Nena in an attempt to recognise local usage.

[7] Don Gardner, George Morren, Rune Paulsen and I worked as consultants on this project (Jorgensen 1997).

Telefolmin from Eliptaman and Ifitaman pressed their claims by virtue of genealogical ties to the current inhabitants of Nenataman, driven in part by the obvious significance genealogical material held for the developers and the government. Some Nenataman Telefolmin began talking about 'clans' (*klen*) defined by 'pure'[8] patrilineal ancestry, and others went a step further by insisting that only those claimants with an unbroken line of descent from the original raiders on *both* paternal *and* maternal sides should qualify as landowners.

These local attempts at gaining recognition through clanship failed for a number of reasons, not the least of which is that these solutions would have excluded sizeable numbers of Nenataman's current inhabitants from any settlement. In the end, however, a novel resolution was proposed: the resurrection of the Untoumin as a clan. Spurred perhaps by the exclusionary claims of the partisans of 'pure' Telefol descent and invoking their own claims of prior occupation, a coalition of people descended from Untou captives declared themselves to be a 'clan' and successfully gained recognition as the registered landowners in the Nena/Frieda prospect. The resulting grouping embraces people otherwise identified as Telefolmin, Miyanmin, or Paiyamo.[9] As such, the Untoumin might be said to comprise a peculiarly 'international' sort of clan, since they include speakers of three different languages drawn from two unrelated language families.

The reinvention of the Untoumin has several incongruities, not the least of which is that as a putatively customary group, the Untoumin have no distinct body of shared custom nor any sense of common identity prior to the search for landowners at Nena. Further, with the apparent exception of claims to land upon which mineral deposits have been identified, the Untoumin seem to have no property in common.[10] While common descent names were sometimes recognised across ethnic boundaries, these never formed the basis for any kind of group and entailed no sense of common interests.[11]

Whether or not the Untoumin are to be regarded as a 'traditional' entity, their recognition as landowners poses more immediate political problems in the project area. The reincarnated Untoumin are dispersed among several villages

[8] The English word 'pure' had become adopted into the local vocabulary of discussions about land and mining — an interesting development in its own right.

[9] The latter resided in Bapi village (Figure 4-1) and were putatively related to the Untoumin.

[10] It is important to note that claims over land for purposes of mining have had no discernible effect on land use for traditional purposes such as gardening.

[11] For example, the Miyan Temselten are said to be 'the same' as the Telefol Atemkayakmin, a claim based on a perception of cognate features of the names themselves (from *atem*, a kind of frog) and suggestions that these commonalities derive from shared ancestry in the remote past. In warfare it was permissible for Telefol Atemkayakmin to kill and eat Miyan Temselten, and vice versa. By contrast, Telefol custom categorically rejected the possibility of cannibalism among Telefolmin or, indeed, bloodshed (though this occasionally took place). The notion that Temselten and Atemkayakmin shared common land rights by virtue of a shared name would have been as unthinkable in pre-colonial times as it is today.

but form the whole of no community. Put differently, the postulated Untou clan asserts differential claims by inscribing a division between 'members' and their co-villagers.[12] As a consequence, this version of clanship runs the risk of destabilising any broad consensus on mining agreements by excluding neighbours and kin from entitlements in each of the communities where so-called Untoumin live — thus ensuring that each village in the project area is internally divided between 'haves' and 'have-nots'.

Despite these difficulties, however, the Untou solution offers definite attractions from the point of view of mining developers and the state. It promises to transcend the ethnic divisions between Telefolmin, Miyanmin and their neighbours — divisions that have shaped contention over claims to Nenataman. Further, the fact that membership in the clan is genealogically fixed eases worries about the vagueness of defining landowners and beneficiaries. From the corporate point of view, limiting entitlements is necessary to limit liabilities. Finally, while PNG land courts have failed to settle on whether conquest or original occupation should receive priority in land claims (Zorn 1992; Westermark 1997; Marco 2000), the Untou solution has the appeal of respectable antiquity by reaching back to a past pre-dating the arrival of any of the currently extant groups — a notional 'Nenataman Ground Zero'. Viewed from the perspective of anxious developers in the present, this holds out the prospect of locating a solution to the distribution of benefits in the distant past — an impulse that clearly owes much to the desire to avoid the unpredictable hazards of contemporary mining politics.

Clanship as Legible Tradition

One of the ironies of the Untou solution is that it is more likely to meet the needs of some claimants for recognition than it is to ensure a secure contractual environment for the mine: far from recognising something one might be tempted to call 'customary land law', it tacitly endorses the creation of politicised identities and attendant drawing of factional lines. This is ultimately the unintended outcome of policies conceived in the light of the ideology of the Melanesian Way. As a version of the Melanesian Way writ small, the search for 'traditional landowners' imagines a depoliticised world in which disagreements about mining entitlements have already been settled in advance through the customary usages of the ancestors.

---

[12] Although I lack the space to develop the point here, one of the muddles nouveau Untou identity poses is this: the claim that they are the original landowners is countered by the view of others that Untoumin were hosted and sheltered by Telefol and Miyan victors, whose readiness to incorporate Untou women and children into their families enabled their survival. The point is obviously a contentious one.

Whether as national ideology or as doctrine governing mining agreements, such ideas have a distinctly mythical quality.[13] Components of this myth are the notion that the various parties entering into such arrangements do so with a minimal disruption of local cultural and social forms. But the state's commitment to customary tenure is framed in terms of the state's own ideas of what customary tenure looks like. This is the presumption of clanship — the idea that land is traditionally held by descent groups identified as clans — and this is the crucial part of the template that renders local land tenure legible (Filer 1997: 165; Gabut 2000). Finding landowners thus becomes a matter of *finding clans*. For local people success in the mining game depends upon transforming the fluid history of occupation in Nenataman into legal recognition of legitimate customary title. This is an exercise in the creation of legal fictions fulfilling the state's need to delineate landowners for the purposes of concluding mining agreements, and a solution hinges upon formulating identities in a way that satisfies the state's interests in legibility by *making clans that the state can 'find'*.

In Nenataman local people invented clans — indeed, they invented several varieties of them — in a way calculated to match the expectations of the government and the mine developer, albeit in ways far removed from traditional ideas about the relation between land rights and collective identities. But the Nenataman case is not an isolated anomaly, as a reading of other instances in similar circumstances reveals (see Golub, this volume).

Official preferences for defining land rights through clanship show a remarkable ability to elicit local responses that produce landowning clans on demand. For example, among the Onabasulu of Mount Bosavi, Ernst found that previously fluid identities had been crystallised in objectified 'clans' tailored to the needs of the state and multinationals engaged in resource development. Designed to position their members advantageously vis-à-vis rival claimants to benefits arising from the Kutubu oil project, these clans are 'largely an artifact of a certificate-based incorporation process' and do not predate the era of petroleum development (Ernst 1999: 88). Writing of the Foi, who are also candidates for benefits arising from the Kutubu oil project, Weiner discusses the effects of the same incorporation process:

> The Foi were … forced to adhere to the convention of incorporation in order to be in a position to deal with both the government and Chevron Niugini. The effect of this is to rigidify the boundaries of a social entity whose most centrally important feature was its porousness and flexibility (Weiner 1998: 10–1).

Such processes are even more striking in cases where there is no system of traditional descent groupings of any kind. For example, from within the Nena

---

[13] See Filer (1990) on popular myths surrounding the Bougainville rebellion.

project impact area, the Sawiyanoo of the Left May River traditionally have no clans, lineages, or other such groups (Guddemi 1997: 634). Yet Guddemi reports that among the Sawiyanoo a flexible land tenure system built around a diverse range of cognatic and other relations has been reframed in less than a decade in terms of principles of patrilineal descent: in response to mineral exploration, rival claimants have produced new kinds of arguments about land and are generating ad hoc patrilineages in the process (ibid: 636). While he is careful not to suggest that such views are illegitimate, Guddemi points out that the emphasis on patrilineality represents a hardening of lines and a closing off of a spectrum of claims that were customarily recognised in the pre-mining era, and he argues that a key role in this shift is played by government officers whose preference for patrilineal descent is all too evident. In the words of one man, 'I used to run around on the land of my wives, but I stopped doing that when the government explained that it was rubbish' (ibid: 640). So it is that while there have been no formal negotiations concerning mining and land rights in the Left May, the Sawiyanoo formulation has changed 'as official ideologies begin to intervene in the ways land is used and thought about' (ibid: 641).[14] The competition to have one's claims to potentially lucrative compensation arrangements recognised has tipped the scales in favour of the creation of corporate descent groups where none had existed before.

Further afield, Hviding (1993) describes a system of 'representational kinship' concocted by New Georgians around Marovo Lagoon in negotiations with a mineral exploration company. Consciously departing from their flexible pattern of land rights through 'highly pluriform principles' (ibid: 803), local people produced simplified models of descent-based landownership in the interests of facilitating recognition of their claims (see also McDougall 2005). Similarly, Burt (1994) reports that among the Kwara'ae of Malaita, local people found themselves under strong pressure to formulate land tenure in terms of membership in unilineal descent groups, despite a fundamentally cognatic kinship orientation. Although no mining activity was at issue in this case, it seems clear that in the Solomons too, governments prefer clans.

In these and similar cases it seems evident that the state-mandated machinery of legibility calls into being what one might call 'special purpose clans'. Yet surely there is something strange in all this. Much of what we know from detailed land tenure studies in Melanesia suggests that an untidy jumble of multiple overlapping claims is at least as common as clearly demarcated clan estates with similarly unambiguous lists of members (Lawrence 1967; Ogan 1971; Burt 1994). Despite this, I would argue that the state favours an image of clan-based tenure because such a view combines the ideological virtues of the Melanesian Way

---

[14] Guddemi makes reference to a paper on mining and land rights by the East Sepik Province's Assistant Secretary for Lands, who claims a generality for the practice of 'Patriarch lineage' (ibid: 641).

with the attractions of a lawyerly desire for clarity. As part of the matrix of legibility, the presumption of clanship embodies a fantasy of a world in which once-and-for-all determinations of rights and commitments are possible without the need for continual readjustments to shifting political alignments.

It is not hard to understand the appeal of such an imagined world, particularly in view of PNG's rocky history of landowner-developer relations in the mining sector. But the presumption of clanship and its simplifications have not always made things easier, as witnessed by the daunting problems of distribution at Kutubu (Weiner 1998), Hides/Gobe (Kameata 2000; Marco 2000) or Porgera (Biersack 1999: 276–7).

Conclusion

Papua New Guineans have proven to be adept at fulfilling the expectations of legibility, and seem quite capable of inventing clans if they turn out not to have any to begin with. While such expedients can give rise to tensions with potentially explosive results, as I have suggested in the case of Nenataman, it must be admitted that dissension over the distribution of mining benefits can arise in any number of ways. Unsystematic tracking of the PNG mining scene suggests to me that those left out of formal settlements seem to have a way of making their needs felt (for example, Mount Kare), and are often capable of pursuing alternate avenues of redress. Likewise, Golub (this volume) argues that insisting too doggedly on fidelity to traditional organisational forms may, at Porgera at any rate, miss the point, since the real problem may be how to forge an effective bridge between the needs of local people and developers (see also Goldman, this volume). Taking such factors into consideration suggests that invented clans may be serviceable as an element in a kind of organisational Pidgin for PNG's mining industry. It does, however, seem prudent to caution against forgetting that such exercises may produce bridges that are too rickety and jerry-rigged to bear much weight, particularly if the cost of cutting a deal is the creation of a pool of dissatisfied neighbours who are unlikely to view their exclusion as legitimate. Invoking notions of tradition or custom will carry little weight if we lose sight of the fact that clan-finding is often ineluctably bound to clan-making.

In an important paper hearkening back to the days of anthropological debates on loose structure, Roy Wagner challenged the notion that there are social groups in any meaningful sense in the New Guinea Highlands.[15] Instead, he argued that local people use names as a form of social creativity to generate sociality, shifting their application as circumstances warrant. He also said that:

---

[15] See also Keen (1995, 2000) who provides an excellent critique of Western group-based metaphors for identity in an Australian context. See Gumbert (1981) for an early discussion of the mischief anthropological models of groups caused in terms of Indigenous land claims.

If we approach the matter with the outright intention of finding groups or with an unanalyzed assumption that groups of one sort or another are essential to human life and culture, then nothing will keep us from finding groups (Wagner 1974: 102–3).

Insofar as he is right, we can count on two things: it will always prove possible to find clans (or other such groups) if one tries hard enough, particularly if local people have a stake in making this possible; and such entities are likely to prove less stable and substantial than government officials (or mining executives) might like. Reconfiguring identities may turn out to be more traditional than we are likely to credit, but this lesson should not be misread: as the history of Nenataman demonstrates, traditional times were times in which identities, communities and whole populations came and went with breathtaking rapidity. This is scant comfort for those who hope that looking to the past will resolve disputes about who is entitled to what, for nobody knows better than Melanesians that the past is almost infinitely arguable. To the extent that local people are able to achieve recognition by fabricating new versions of who they are, the Melanesian Way may indeed be alive and well, but in a way guaranteed to raise questions, rather than settle them.

References

Ballard, C., 1997. 'It's the Land, Stupid! The Moral Economy of Resource Ownership in Papua New Guinea.' In S. Toft (ed.), op. cit.

Biersack, A., 1999. 'Porgera — Whence and Whither?' In C. Filer (ed.), *Dilemmas of Development: the Social and Economic Impact of the Porgera Gold Mine 1989–1994*. Canberra: Asia Pacific Press.

Brown P. and A. Ploeg (eds), 1997. *Change and Conflict in Papua New Guinea Land and Resource Rights*. Special Issue 7(4) of *Anthropological Forum*.

Burt, B., 1994. 'Land in Kwara'ae and Development in Solomon Islands.' *Oceania* 64: 317–335.

Ernst, T., 1999. 'Land, Stories and Resources: Discourse and Entification in Onabasulu Modernity.' *American Anthropologist* 101: 88–97.

Filer, C., 1990. 'The Bougainville Rebellion, the Mining Industry and the Process of Social Disintegration in Papua New Guinea.' *Canberra Anthropology* 13(1): 1–39.

———, 1997. 'Compensation, Rent and Power in Papua New Guinea.' In S. Toft (ed.), op. cit.

———, 1998. 'The Melanesian Way of Menacing the Mining Industry.' In L. Zimmer-Tamakoshi (ed.), *Modern Papua New Guinea*. Kirksville (MO): Thomas Jefferson University Press.

Fitzpatrick, P., 1980. *Law and State in Papua New Guinea*. London: Academic Press.

Gabut, J., 2000. 'Land Tenure and Land Registration in Papua New Guinea.' Paper presented at the conference on 'Problems and Perspectives on Customary Land Tenure and Registration in Australia and Papua New Guinea', University of Queensland, 10–14 September.

Gardner, D., 1998. 'Demographic Raiding and Social Relations in the Northern Mountain Ok Region in Historical Perspective.' Paper presented at the annual meeting of the American Anthropological Association, Philadelphia, 2-6 December.

———, 2004. 'A Proctological History of Miyan Identity.' In T. van Meijl and J Miedema (eds), *Shifting Images of Identity in the Pacific*. Leiden: KITLV Press.

Geertz, C., 1973. *The Interpretation of Cultures*, New York: Basic Books.

Guddemi, P., 1997. 'Continuities, Contexts, Complexities, and Transformations: Local Land Concepts of a Sepik People Affected by Mining Exploration.' In P. Brown and A. Ploeg (eds), op. cit.

Gumbert, M., 1981. 'Paradigm Lost: An Analysis of Anthropological Models and Their Effect on Aboriginal Land Rights.' *Oceania* 52: 103–123.

Hviding, E., 1993. 'Indigenous Essentialism? "Simplifying" Customary Land Ownership in New Georgia, Solomon Islands.' *Bijdragen tot de Taal-, Land- en Volkenkunde* 149(4): 802–24.

Jackson, R., 1989. 'New Policies in Sharing Mining Benefits in Papua New Guinea: A Note.' *Pacific Viewpoint* 30: 86–93.

———, 1991. 'Not Without Influence: Villages, Mining Companies, and Government in Papua New Guinea.' In J. Connell and R. Howitt (eds), *Mining and Indigenous Peoples in Australasia*. Sydney: Sydney University Press.

Jorgensen, D., 1997. 'Who and What is a Landowner? Mythology and Marking the Ground in a Papua New Guinea Mining Project.' In P. Brown and A. Ploeg (eds), op. cit.

Kameata, R., 2000. 'Evolution of Land Group Mechanism, Huli Agnatic Descent and the Implications of the ILG Act.' Paper presented at the conference on 'Problems and Perspectives on Customary Land Tenure and Registration in Australia and Papua New Guinea', University of Queensland, 10-14 September.

Keen, I., 1995. 'Metaphor and the Metalanguage: "Groups" in northeast Arnhem Land.' *American Ethnologist* 22: 502–527.

————, 2000. 'A Bundle of Sticks: The Debate over Yolngu Clans.' *Journal of the Royal Anthropological Institute* 6: 419–36.

Keesing, R., 1989. 'Creating the Past: Custom and Identity in the Contemporary Pacific.' *The Contemporary Pacific* 1: 19–42.

King, D., 1997. 'The Big Polluter and the Constructing of Ok Tedi: Eco-imperialism and Underdevelopment Along the Ok Tedi and Fly Rivers of Papua New Guinea.' In G. Banks and C. Ballard (eds), *The Ok Tedi Settlement: Issues, Outcomes and Implications.* Canberra: Australian National University, National Centre for Development Studies and Resource Management in Asia-Pacific (Pacific Policy Paper 27).

Lawrence, P., 1967. 'Land Tenure Among the Garia.' In I. Hogbin and P. Lawrence (eds), *Studies in New Guinea Land Tenure.* Sydney: Sydney University Press.

LiPuma, E., 1995. 'The Formation of Nation-States and National Cultures in Oceania.' In R. Foster (ed.), *Nation Making: Emergent Identities in Postcolonial Melanesia.* Ann Arbor: University of Michigan Press.

Marco, J., 2000. 'Kirapim Dust Tasol.' Paper presented at the conference on 'Problems and Perspectives on Customary Land Tenure and Registration in Australia and Papua New Guinea', University of Queensland, 10-14 September.

McDougall, D., 2005. 'The Unintended Consequences of Clarification: Development, Disputing, and the Dynamics of Community in Ranongga, Solomon Islands.' *Ethnohistory* 52(1): 81–109.

Narokobi, B., 1980. *The Melanesian Way.* Boroko: Institute of Papua New Guinea Studies.

Ogan, E., 1971. 'Nasioi Land Tenure: An Extended Case Study.' *Oceania* 42: 81–93.

Otto, T., 1997. 'After the Tidal Wave: Bernard Narokobi and the Creation of a Melanesian Way.' In T. Otto and N. Thomas (eds), *Narratives of Nation in the South Pacific.* Amsterdam: Harwood Academic Publishers.

Philibert, J., 1986. 'The Politics of Tradition: Toward a Generic Culture in Vanuatu.' *Mankind* 16: 1–12.

Scott, J., 1998. *Seeing Like a State: How Certain Schemes to Improve the Human Condition Have Failed.* New Haven: Yale University Press.

Somare, M., 1974. 'We Bilong Yusim Et Poin Plen.' Konedobu: PNG Government Printer.

Toft, S., 1997. 'Patrons or Clients? Aspects of Multinational Capital-Landowner Relations in Papua New Guinea.' In S. Toft (ed.), op. cit.

————(ed.), 1997. *Compensation for Resource Development in Papua New Guinea*. Boroko: Law Reform Commission of Papua New Guinea (Monograph 6). Canberra: Australian National University, National Centre for Development Studies (Pacific Policy Paper 25).

Wagner, R., 1974. 'Are There Social Groups in the New Guinea Highlands?' In M.J. Leaf (ed.), *Frontiers of Anthropology*. New York: Van Nostrand.

Wanek, A., 1996. *The State and Its Enemies in Papua New Guinea*. Richmond: Curzon Press.

Weiner, J.F., 1998. 'The Incorporated Ground: The Contemporary Work of Distribution in the Kutubu Oil Project Area, Papua New Guinea.' Canberra: Australian National University, Resource Management in Asia-Pacific Project (Working Paper 17).

Westermark, G., 1997. 'Clan Claims: Land, Law and Violence in the Papua New Guinea Eastern Highlands.' *Oceania* 67: 218–233.

Zorn, J., 1992. 'Graun Bilong Mipela: Local Land Courts and the Changing Customary Law of Papua New Guinea.' *Pacific Studies* 15(2): 1–38.

Chapter Five

From Agency to Agents: Forging Landowner Identities in Porgera

Alex Golub

And this, for me, is the heart of the drama: I'm intensely aware you see that people are wrong to think of themselves as just one person. Each one of us is lots and lots of people. Any number, because of all the countless possibilities of being that exist within us. The person you are with me is quite different from the person you are with somebody else. But we go on thinking we're exactly the same person for everybody, the person we think we are in our own mind and in everything we do. But this isn't the case at all! It comes home to us best when by some ghastly mischance we are caught out in an untypical act. We suddenly find we are sort of dangling from a hook! I mean we can see that the act isn't 'us', our whole self isn't in it. And it would be a savage injustice to judge us on that act alone, never to let us off the hook, to hold us on to it, chain us up for our life on the strength of it for all to see, as if that one action summed up our whole existence! So now do you see how treacherous this girl is being? She caught me out in an unrecognisable situation, in a place where for her I should never have been and doing something which in her eyes I should not have been able to do; and now she insists on seeing this undreamed-of contingency as my reality, identifying me with a single fleeting shaming moment of my life (Pirandello 1995).

In Luigi Pirandello's 1921 play *Six Characters in Search of an Author* the characters in a nineteenth-century story of family conflict are cast out of their creator's imagination and wander in search of an author who will allow them to complete the telling of their story. The bourgeois melodrama they embodied was exactly the sort of play that Pirandello was reacting against, but the deeply reflexive theatre that resulted when the family conversed with directors, actors, and each other about the nature of artistic production is a supreme example of Pirandello's modernist art. In this space of meta-theatre he could explore the thematics which 'tormented' him:

> The delusion of reciprocal understanding hopelessly based on the hollow abstraction of words; the multiple nature of every human personality, given all the possible ways of being inherent in each one of us; and finally the tragic built-in conflict between ever-moving, ever-changing life, and the immutability of form (Pirandello 1995: xvi).[1]

In this chapter I would like to explore Pirandello's thematics in an arena far removed from the Italy of his day. I will examine identity and landownership at the Porgera gold mine in Enga Province, Papua New Guinea (PNG), and what lessons we might learn from it regarding registration schemes in Melanesia and, more broadly, 'indigenous identity' in general.

In PNG today it is a matter of settled legal and popular opinion that indigenous groups have special claims to the ownership of customary land (Rynkiewich 2001; Curtin et al. 2003; Weiner and Glaskin, this volume). This entitlement is both firm and abstract: firm in the sense that customary land is owned by customary groups, but abstract because the criteria for membership in landowning groups are often ambiguous. In cases of land registration for resource development, the boundaries of the land and the ethnonym of the collectivity said to 'own' it are often quite clear. What is controversial is who, in any given situation, gets to be a member of a landowning group. The dilemma of aspiring landowners is similar, then, to that of the characters in Pirandello's play — both seek to be acknowledged by the director (here, the state) and, in doing so, get their turn on stage as a real character in PNG's national drama.

In the past, policy makers and theorists have applied an optical metaphor to customary land registration. On this account, local identities pre-exist state interest in them, and identifying the members of a customary group can be done simply by 'viewing' 'customary' or 'traditional' or 'group' tenure (these are considered synonymous) and translating these arrangements into Western legal form. This is the approach, for instance, which underpins James Scott's (1998) work *Seeing Like A State,* in which the state's pathological misrecognition of pre-existing grass-roots life leads to technocratic tragedies which, he suggests, could be overcome through accurate discernment of conditions on the ground whose shape and form pre-exist its gaze. While his neoliberalism is politically orthogonal to Scott's leftist populism, Hernando de Soto (2000) agrees with Scott that the failure of Third World countries to 'escape the bell jar' of economic stagnation and partake of First World economic prosperity can be traced to the government's inability to recognise people's grass-roots economic activity and the stable 'extralegal social contracts' they generate. A mixture of these approaches has informed policy work on land registration in PNG. Policy makers such as Tony Power and Jim Fingleton combine Scott's fear of disempowerment

---

[1] I acknowledge that the translation used here, by Felicity Firth, takes some liberties with Pirandello that others do not. However, for the purposes of this chapter I find it to be the most evocative.

through the individuation of tenure with de Soto's enthusiasm for grass-roots entrepreneurship in a vision of 'Melanesian capitalism' inspired by Third-Worldism (Power 1996; Fingleton 2005; Chappell 2005; Golub 2006: 385–406).[2] In this instance, as in many others, registering customary landowners relies first on clear discernment of local situations and second on an accurate translation of them out of the realm of custom and into the realm of law. This 'viewing and cataloging' approach assumes that there *are* such things as customary groups. Such an assumption, as Pirandello might put it, hangs indigenous peoples upon a hook by fixating on only one aspect of what we shall see is a many-sided identity.

By now there is a large literature on what we might call the 'poetics of indigeneity' in Southeast Asia (Li 2000), Amazonia (Carneiro da Cunha and Almeida 2000), Australia (Povinelli 2002), and Native North America (Nadasdy 2003) which strongly suggests that indigenous identities are not pre-existing and 'found' intact by Western legal regimes, but are complexly shaped by Western law's elicitation of them (Weiner 2006). This shift from 'viewing' to 'eliciting' is partially due to an increasingly rich body of ethnographic data about both pre-contact social organisation and the land registration process itself. But it is also due to wider developments in political philosophy and socio-cultural theory. In political philosophy authors such as Patchen Markell (2003) have drawn on an Arendtian re-reading of Hegel to argue, contra earlier works on recognition (for example, Taylor 1992), that 'identity can only be reliably known in retrospect' (Markell 2003: 14) as the *results* of action and speech in public' (ibid: 13). As a result, Markell suggests it is inappropriate to speak of the 'recognition' of pre-existing identities and prefers instead a 'politics of acknowledgment' in which we pay attention to the mutual constitution of actors in moments of recognition. This means that we should not only examine the making of landowner identities, but also the concession of authoritativeness to certain disciplines (such as anthropology) and of wisdom (or the lack of it) to the small group of expatriates who have been so influential in the history of land policy in PNG.

In additional, advances in political science have converged with the development of a more 'poetic and pragmatic' turn in anthropology (Ortner 1984; Sansom 1985; Silverstein and Urban 1995; Wedeen 2003; Silverstein 2004).[3] This approach focuses less on a 'museological' description of the cultural inventory of distinct groups, and more on a 'semiotic praxology' (Silverstein 2003) in which 'we now worry about how the image of *a* language or *a* culture

---

[2] For critiques of this position, see Weiner (this volume).

[3] Processual accounts of indigenous identity have a long history in anthropology and certain aspects of Western social thought more generally. I mention the 'poetic-pragmatic' approach not to emphasise its novelty, but simply because it represents a particularly recent and coherent (and, to my mind, fruitful) body of work.

are themselves constituted as meaningful realities within the scheme of normative subjectivity of a population' (ibid: 116) such that 'cultures' are seen as an

> emergent phenomenon of sociocultural process, unstable and sociohistorically contingent as they are themselves invoked by 'the natives' [indigenous or otherwise] as a contributory part — a moment — of a dialectical process of politicoeconomically and historically specific meaning making' (ibid: 115).

In other words, both policy scientists and Pirandello increasingly see indigenous peoples (and everyone else) as living 'ever-moving, ever-changing' lives which are hung on the hook of the 'immutable form' of corporate land registration.

Local forms of sociality in PNG seem particularly suited to this method of analysis due to their tendency to lack clear corporate groups (Barnes 1962; Wagner 1974). Indeed, a focus on the lack of a clear demarcation of the identity of landowners of resource-rich areas of PNG is notable. At Tolukuma (Golub 2006: 399–402), Hides (ibid: 394–7), Mount Kare (Filer 1998: 161–6), Frieda (Jorgensen 2001), and Kutubu (Weiner 2001), politicking over who gets to be a landowner has prevented compensation from resource developments from reaching local people, and in some cases it has halted resource development altogether. A museological approach to viewing and registering supposedly static customary groups must explain this dynamism away as a 'corruption' of a state of pre-existing purity.

But in fact many fine 'pragmatic-poetic' ethnographies of PNG have been produced (Lederman 1986; Merlan and Rumsey 1991). Indeed, some of the most fruitful work produced by Melanesianists involves not merely describing Melanesian approaches to sociality, but adopting them as useful theoretical constructs — the concept of the 'elicitation' of landowner identities being a prime example. Despite the fact that these approaches explain, rather than explain away, the failure of museological approaches to registration, there has been little uptake of this work by policy scientists. In PNG, as in Australia, anthropologists continue to attempt to disabuse the policy community of their notions of static corporate groups existing 'from time immemorial' without reverting to analytically crude notions savagery, 'Africanisation', barbarism, 'instability', dysfunction, and so forth. The question then becomes: How, concretely, can one understand the translation of landowner identities into Western legal forms in a poetic-pragmatic mode rather than an optical and museological one? How do we capture the fact that indigenous cultures innovate and change over time, and that much of this change is elicited by an entity such as the state which demands that the object of its gaze remain static? The concept of the 'invention' of tradition, despite its attempted re-workings by many authors (Otto and Pedersen 2005), continues to carry the critical sting that its original framers (Hobsbawm and Ranger 1983) meant to deploy against British imperialist pretensions. As a result it is not only disempowering to indigenous people (Briggs 1996) but, more importantly, its use of the term 'invention' does a poor job of conceptualising the relationship between practice and structure that has been so fruitfully illuminated by the pragmatic-poetic turn in analysis.

More promising seems an approach which sees custom as a *'modality of action* rather than persistence of the concrete and material substance' (Merlan 1995: 164). Like Markell, Merlan and Sansom suggest focusing on the process, rather than the content, of translation, and echoing Markell, urge us to see this process as one of the reflexive, mutual constitution of indigenous group and state (see also Merlan 2006). In this chapter I will focus on the creation of an official schedule of the Ipili owners of the Porgera gold mine in Enga Province, PNG. This involved the translation of customary forms of sociality into a legal system of corporate clans. I will describe this not as a process of 'invention' but one of 'forging', and I will argue that the trope best used to understand Ipili flexibility and willingness to innovate is not 'instability' or 'barbarism' but 'modernity.' The larger import of this example, I argue, is that modernity might profitably be used as a trope to describe the phenomenon of indigenous accommodation to land registration schemes more generally.

I use 'modernity' in the sense of a distinctive mode of historical consciousness. It is, as Habermas put it, a 'reflective treatment of traditions that have lost their quasi-natural status' (1987: 2). Modernity 'cannot and will no longer borrow the criteria by which it takes its orientation from the models supplied by another epoch; *it has to create its normativity out of itself*' (ibid: 7). The modern world is thus 'distinguished from the old by the fact that it opens itself to the future, the epochal new beginning is rendered constant with each moment that gives birth to the new' (ibid: 6). Seeing modernity as an openness to the new allows us to develop an account which 'dissociates modernity from its modern European origins and stylises it into a spatio-temporally neutral model' which might be applied to a variety of groups (ibid).

In addition to Habermas, I also draw on Sahlins' recent (1992, 2000a, 2000b) writing on *developman*, which has also been an inspiration for much of the recent literature on 'local' or 'alternate' modernities. I diverge from these approaches because I feel that they treat modernity museologically, as a process in which individual items move are either removed from, or incorporated into, an inventory of cultural traits.[4] Bruce Knauft, for instance, defines modernity as 'images and institutions associated with Western-style progress and development in a contemporary world' (2002: 18), while the contributors to a recent volume on *Modernities in Melanesia* (Robbins and Wardlow 2005) focus on modernity as being identical with Christianity, humiliation, and so forth.

---

[4] An example of removal would be the secularisation of Europe, while an example of incorporation would the adoption of Christianity by Pacific Islanders.

To me the true insight of Sahlins' work is that 'tradition' is a distinctive mode of appropriating novelty — a process rather than an inventory to be preserved.

> [It] is not the dead hand of the past. On the contrary, 'tradition' is precisely the way people always cope with circumstances not of their doing and beyond their control, whether acts of nature or of other peoples. Hence tradition has changed in the past, and, by encompassing the goods and relations of the market in its own terms, it would continue to do so (Sahlins 2000a: 21).

Sahlins' understanding of tradition allows us to understand how the creation of landowner identities in the context of land registration can be understood as both 'modern' and 'traditional' when examined from the viewpoint of process.

Finally, I will argue that Ipili identities were 'forged', taking my cue from Daniel Miller's use of the term in his ethnography of modernity in Trinidad.

> In the first place forged is intended to connote the process by which intractable materials are, in the forge, turned into something new, useful, solid and fine. But the term forged is also a verb pertaining to the act of forgery as an act of faking (Miller 1994: 321).

Miller's wonderful evocation of the ambiguity of this word here captures the way in which Ipili seized the moment of novelty introduced by mining and attempted to remake themselves in light of the mine's elicitation of their identity in a way that was both 'modern' and 'customary'. It is to this regime of identification that I now turn.

Porgera's 'Seven-Clan System'

The Ipili are an ethnic group located in the Porgera 'district' in the far west of Enga Province in the highlands of PNG (Biersack 1980).[5] Since contact with the Australian Administration in the late 1930s, Porgera's gold deposits have been central to Ipili history as well as to the wider fate of PNG as an independent nation. PNG relies on taxes and royalties from extractive industry for a substantial proportion of its budget (Banks 2001), and the Porgera gold mine, operated by the Vancouver-based transnational Placer Dome,[6] became a major source of revenues in 1992 (its second year of production), when it produced 1,485,077 ounces of gold, making it the third most productive gold mine in the world (Jackson and Banks 2002). The Porgera mine continues to be a national priority today, even as it matures.

---

[5] The Porgera 'district' is now officially part of the larger Porgera-Lagaip District, which includes a much larger population speaking the Enga language. Speakers of the Ipili language numbered around 5,000 in 1980, but the current population is hard to calculate because of the more recent wave of immigration and intermarriage.
[6] Placer Dome was recently taken over by another Canadian company, Barrick Gold.

The Porgera mine is unusual not just because of the size of its operations, but because of the impact that it has had on the valley where it is located (Banks 1997; Filer 1999; Golub 2001, 2006; Jacka 2003). While people outside the valley often damage the road and power supply into Porgera, and migrants threaten the valley's stability (Patterson 2006), the mine does not have the landowner identification problems faced by other resource developments. Although Porgera is ridden with conflict, social inequity, civil unrest, and a fair amount of resentment for the company, there has been little or no questioning regarding who the 'real landowners' of Porgera are. A 'successful registration' of landowners is one of the reasons for Porgera's success relative to other mines. How, then, did this registration occur?

Throughout the 1980s Placer Dome compensated individual Ipili on a case-by-case basis for land damaged by exploration work. However, in the late 1980s, when Porgera proved to be a feasible site for a mine, Placer Dome was obliged to convert its existing exploration licence into a Special Mining Lease. Under the *Mining Act*, it is the National Government which has the power to issue such a lease, but in order for the lease to be issued the company must sign a compensation agreement with the customary landowners. As it turned out, the mine also required land on which Ipili people were currently living, and an agreement specifying where and how they were to be relocated also became necessary. Finally, for complex political reasons, Ipili landowners, the Provincial Government and the National Government also signed agreements with each other specifying their duties and obligations to each other after the lease was issued. In sum, in order for the mine to open it was necessary that the government and company negotiate, not just with Ipili people, but with 'the Ipili' as a collectivity.

Negotiations with all of the 3,000 or so inhabitants of the future mining lease were obviously impractical, and so government officials used a mechanism of agency described in PNG's *Land Act* whereby Ipili people chose 'agents' to represent them in negotiations. This produced a pool of 300 or so agents, a group composed essentially of the most prominent persons from each of the extended households in the Special Mining Lease area. This number was still too large, however, and so these agents delegated their agency to a set of 23 'agents of agents' or 'super agents'. These people formed the Landowner Negotiating Committee, and it was they who provided legitimate consent to the creation of a mine by putting their signatures (or thumb-prints) on official agreements with the company and the government.

This structure of delegation matches the segmented lineage system which the Porgera Land Study found to be present in Ipili custom. According to this study, land in Porgera is owned by seven landowning clans. Each clan is composed of one or more 'sub-clans.' There were found to be a total of 23 sub-clans within the Special Mining Lease. These sub-clans are themselves composed of a number of 'house lines' (an English gloss of the Tok Pisin *haus lain*) which took the form of extended families. Land was similarly divided: extended families live on individual plots which are parts of larger named territories which are owned by sub-clans, which are themselves part of even larger named units which are owned by clans (GoPNG 1987a).

The result was a happy coincidence — the social structure of the Ipili 'discovered' by outsiders fitted very neatly into a hierarchical Western model of organisation. Thus the land study and system of delegation in Porgera represents a clear example of a museological method of landowner registration, because this Western organisational system is congruent with the segmentary lineage system of Ipili clans. Each level of social segmentation has its own representative who delegates power to the agent representing a higher-level segment of the clan until one reaches the 23 'apical' negotiators of the Landowner Negotiating Committee. This committee speaks for all 23 clans and thus the entire ethnic group.

At first glance, then, the success of Porgera's land registration regime seems to be an example that could be used to bolster a 'view and translate' approach to registration. However, a close analysis of the land study and the meetings that produced it will demonstrate that the seven-clan system was forged in the course of the events of the late 1980s. The seven-clan system is not 'untrue' to Ipili sociality because Ipili ways of being, like Pirandello's characters, have several potential ways of appearing. What made Porgera's system of land registration resilient, I will argue, is that Ipili had the choice of how they were to be apprehended. But before I explain how Ipili identity was 'hung upon a hook' in the late 1980s, we must first examine the many-sided nature of Ipili sociality.

Ipili Sociality

An examination of Ipili sociality, both within Porgera and in relation to people outside the valley, quickly indicates that the seven-clan system that exists in Porgera today was *not* — as a 'view and translate' approach would have it — a method of social organisation which pre-existed the mine and the government's views of Ipili. I will discuss first the difficulties in identifying 'the Ipili' as a discrete ethnic group in the wider Enga/Southern Highlands region. Then I will discuss the difficulty of understanding sociality within the valley as being composed of clans.

First, there is considerable evidence to suggest that the idea of discrete, clearly bounded ethnic groups was not common to the wider region in which the Ipili lived (Biersack 1995). The focus of Iplili local organisation was on regional embeddedness and connections with — rather than divisions between —

different areas of settlement. Like those of their neighbours, the Huli and the Enga, Ipili genealogies run deep, typically beyond ten generations, and terminate with an eponymous apical ancestor. These genealogies frequently trace the migration of ancestors across the region, leaving genealogically connected communities dotted across the landscape. These mythological accounts of ancestral movement seem to correspond, at least in Enga, to actual prehistoric migrations of clans from one area to another (Wiessner and Tumu 1998: 119–55). The result is what might be called 'clan diasporas' — a network of related groups which spread across the Southern Highlands and Enga provinces and which cut across the ethnic boundaries of what are today considered to be the three distinct ethnic groups of the 'Huli', 'Enga' and 'Ipili.' In the past, these ties were used to facilitate long-distance trading (Mangi 1988), to gain access to valuable resources like salt springs (Wiessner and Tumu 1998), and to request hospitality when ecological hardship such as drought or frost meant temporary migration from one's home (Wohlt 1978). Today Papua New Guineans continue to use these ties to conduct business along the Highlands Highway, to find hosts at areas near mines and hydrocarbon projects where work is plentiful, and to travel safely through areas where tribal fighting occurs.

Thus ethnicity in this area is based on grades or continua of cultural difference in a population criss-crossed by flows of people. It is for this reason that Burton argues that the existence of these clan diasporas

> throws into question whether the Ipili people even 'exist' in the same way as, say, Motuans or Hageners do … They begin to look far more like the local representatives of regionally dispersed 'genealogical groups', lumped together under one name only because they live in one place as neighbours. (Burton 1999: 284).

Porgerans are and were, as Aletta Biersack (1995: 7) puts it, 'centered not on themselves as geographical isolates but on culturally diverse fields in which their mythology, trade routes, and marriage practices embedded them'. As a result, 'syncretism is not just an artifact of colonialism; syncretism is *the ordinary state of affairs* … Ipili peoples have always been *cosmopolitan*' (ibid: 6). Of course, it is undoubtedly the case that there are coherent and culturally specific practices which characterise people who live in Porgera as being distinctive from their neighbours and entitle them to be considered customary owners of the land surrounding the Porgera mine. But it is important to note that these differences were not sufficiently clear-cut that they could easily be used as a ready-made charter by a government to exclude people from membership in resource-rich groups. So while it is tempting, as Burton (1999: 284) puts it, 'to uncover as many of them as possible and map them out', clan diasporas lack precision beyond the mythical level, and even mythological associations were unclear and subject to confusion. Thus Wohlt (1978: 42) recounts that while everyone 'know[s] the gist of the myth', in fact, 'if one asks a dozen informants over [the] age of 40 the particulars of genealogical connection … one gets a dozen different versions'. He concludes that 'beyond the unity maintained through oral tradition and the ceremonies described above, relationships among tribal members entail little else than hospitality, and that only in need' (ibid: 54). In sum, what we see is a situation in which individuals justified long-distance travel with reference to genealogical relationships which were enduring but whose meaning was ambiguous. In other words, this was a system in which people had agency to construe the connection between them given a culturally specific form of connection which nevertheless under-determined the exact nature of the relationship between them.

But perhaps these genealogies are the basis of a corporate, descent-based system of clans in Porgera? Not according to John Burton, who argues that 'we can abandon any pretence at trying to fit the Porgeran lines of descent to the orthodox clan model. *In fact, there are no corporate groups we can call "clans" in Porgera*' (Burton 1992: 138). Most researchers agree with him — the Ipili are overwhelmingly described in the literature as 'cognatic' (Biersack 1980, 1995; Jacka 2003). Models of Ipili sociality as clan-based run into several problems.[7]

The first problem with the clan model of Ipili social organisation is that the Ipili do not have a word for 'clan' in the sense of a corporate group defined by descent. It is true that the term 'clan' is often used to gloss the Ipili word *yame*. But *yame* simply means 'group of people' or 'organisation', and has no connotation of descent, consanguinity, or kinship whatsoever. Ipili use the term indiscriminately to refer to Security Guards, descendants of Tuanda, and Lutherans.[8] If anything, *yame* simply means the centre, reason, or principle around which coalitions of people coalesce, a perception of likeness or commonalty among a group of persons. Even in cases where it does refer to cognatic stocks (the technical term for what are often called 'clans' in Porgera),[9] association with such a stock is not exclusive in Porgera, and these stocks do not in and of themselves form the basis for exchange or collective action. Ipili consider themselves to have a 'portfolio' of eight stocks to choose from — one from each of their grandparents. They demonstrate their relationship to these stocks by reciting *malu* (genealogies) that connect them to the apical ancestor after whom the stock is named.

Not only is stock affiliation non-exclusive, it is telling that Ipili do not consider it a virtue to identify strongly with only one of them. Individual Ipili strategies of social placement focus on the interstitial spaces between groups,

---

[7] A complete account of Ipili sociality would require a discussion of descent, affinity, and the role of non-kin-based friendships. Here I focus only on the role of descent in Ipili sociality.

[8] The 'eight *tata* system' reported by Jacka (2003: 107–10) for Tipinini does not appear in the Special Mining Lease area.

[9] 'Stock' here has technical sense used in the literature on cognatic kinship (Freeman 1961).

using multiple affiliations to be 'in the middle' of things — to be 'at the border' as Biersack (1980) describes it. The ideal politician is a *tombene akali* — a 'middle man' (and it is typically a man) who works the interface between two groups and is thus to the Ipili 'at the center of the action', even though in Western terms we would consider him marginal to both. Thus, when mining executives doubt indigenous people's claims to being 'real landowners', they are mistaking their own ideologies of lineal purity for those of the Ipili. For instance, it was occasionally said by mine employees that a group of people descended from a prominent alluvial miner were 'not really Maipangi' because their father was originally from Enga and was related to the Maipangi 'clan' in Porgera through an embarrassingly tenuous set of connections. When I tried this out on one of my informants he looked surprised and remarked that if anyone was Maipangi it was these people, since they had no other groups to claim affiliation with. As far as he was concerned those people were Maipangi because they had used their agency to activate and maintain ties to that stock-cum-residential group, and this singular affiliation was thus seen as an unfortunate impoverishment of a potentially much richer and wider set of relationships rather than a positively valued 'pure' and exclusive group membership.

We can agree, then, with Sturzenhofecker when she writes of the nearby Duna that 'what is articulated in *malu* genealogies is a principle not of group recruitment but of individual entitlement' (1993: 79–80). In Porgera, as in Wohlt's Yumbisa:

> The cognatic nature of groups in practice is the product of the interaction of a 'vertical' agnatic ideology and 'horizontal' ideologies concerning cognation, affinity, and, particularly, exchange, as these are played out against limitations and emergent opportunities in the existing physical and social environment (Wohlt 1995: 215).

Vertical, descent-based relations often come to be used to label coalitions of people mobilised through collateral or other means.

As Burton (1992) has pointed out, despite having an ideology of lineage, Ipili social organisation resembles that of the Garia as described by Lawrence (1984), although they lack the Garia attachment to territory described by Leach (2004). When viewed in this light, Porgeran kinship is less a matter of corporate groups than of a large mesh of egocentric personal networks. An individual's 'security circle' is composed of 'persons with whom he has safe relationships and towards whom he should observe stringent rules governing marriage, diet, and political obligation' (Lawrence 1984: 28), of which consanguineal ties are merely a part. This realisation helps to clarify the meaning of the term *yame*. 'Daniel *yame*', for instance, does not refer merely to the descendants of Daniel; it refers to all those people whose mutual affinity is a result of his presence in their social networks. So while you can refer to Pulumaini *yame* to mean 'everyone whose apical ancestor is Pulumaini', you can also use it to mean 'those five people who use a common tie to Pulumaini as an excuse to go out drinking on Thursdays', even though the five people in question do not include all of Pulumaini's descendants.

For Ipili, finding and mobilising these connections is thus an art, and Ipili are networkers not only in a social-structural sense, but also in the more prosaic sense of the term: they are inveterately social, always on the lookout for new allies and potential ways to expand who they know and where they know them. Ipili enjoy discussing the twists and turns of their *malu* and those of prominent people in the valley in the same way that Americans dwell on the statistical minutiae of professional baseball players. In both regional movement and local sociality, then, the situation in Porgera was one of entrepreneurial agency.

Forging Landowners: the Porgera Land Study

We can see now that the seven-clan system that exists in Porgera today is only tenuously related to the sociality that existed prior to the arrival of mining in the valley. The question then becomes how the entrepreneurial agency of Ipili network building was transformed into the segmentary descent groups of the seven-clan system. How, in other words, did the mine's interest in the Ipili elicit this transformation on their part? A full answer to this question would have to take into account the long history of medium- and small-scale gold mining in Porgera which served as a crucial backdrop for the creation of large-scale mining in the 1980s. Here I will focus on one key moment in this process — the period from late 1985 to 1989. This period begins with the official decision to create an authoritative list of 'who the Porgera gold mine landowners are' and ends with the signature, on their behalf, of the Porgera Agreements by their 23 authorised agents.

In 1983, exploratory work at Porgera uncovered a zone of particularly rich ore, and the following year an ultra high-grade area within this zone was discovered. This work, as well as developments in metallurgy and financing, made the creation of a large-scale gold mine in Porgera seem increasingly likely (Jackson and Banks 2002: 119–38). Much was still unknown about how, concretely, the mine would be created, financed, and regulated. The late 1980s were spent attempting to clarify how these issues were to be dealt with. One of these clarificatory projects was the Porgera Land Study.

In order for a mining lease to be issued, the owners of the land in question had to be identified and compensated. To this end, on 26 September 1985, the Secretary of the Department of Enga issued an order for public servants to begin a land study to generate a list of customary landholders. The PNG Department of Minerals and Energy created a position of 'Porgera Coordinator' with responsibility for liaising with all relevant ministries regarding the mine. John Reid, a former *kiap* (government official), was appointed to this position. He in turn oversaw a group of Papua New Guinean *kiaps* who conducted censuses of the area. Their guideline for conducting the land study was a thin photocopied booklet produced by a senior public servant in the national department. This specified that they were to record the names of adult men as 'landowners', and that each of these men could be associated with one and only one clan.

By December 1986, the land study had collected 15,000 names of Ipili in their schedule of ownership. This was an astonishing feat considering the fact that, by their own estimate, there were only 3,000 Ipili living in the valley at this time. The land team was flummoxed: areas of two or three hectares were being claimed as the customary land of more people than could ever live on the land or, in the case of very small plots, even physically stand there. It appears that individual Ipili were responding to questions by being maximally inclusive and listing their entire kindred.

Both Ipili and government representatives were unhappy with this state of affairs. At a meeting held in December 1986, government officers complained that people were registering themselves multiple times on multiple plots of land, and suggested that Ipili 'select one or two members of a family to represent them in other Landownerships [sic] in the other clans/sub-clans'.[10] For instance, even if a man was married to a woman in another group, his claims to that group's land (through his affinal status) would be represented by his father-in-law or wife. This proved completely unacceptable to Ipili, who saw this as a radical reduction in their portfolio of relationships. As one man put it, 'Porgera people have Landownership Rights in more than one clan. Therefore we want all our names to be enrolled or registered in all the clans that we own Lands'. Another ominously noted that 'if any names are excluded, there will be troubles'.

Eventually a proposal was put to the meeting by Kurubu Ipara, a Porgeran who had previously worked as a *kiap* and was at that time working for the mine's exploration team. He suggested a solution that would 'make it easy on the *kiaps*'. Instead of proceeding by visiting a piece of land and eliciting the names of all the people associated with it, the land study would instead proceed on a 'clan by clan' basis. The result would be a series of seven 'schedules of owners' that would be attached to the land study. This would allow the government to retain the idea that there was a set of distinct 'clans' which owned land. However, each individual Ipili would be allowed to list themselves in as many of these 'clans' as they considered themselves to be part of. This would allow Ipili to retain the inclusivity that they desired. Indeed, in some ways it was *more* inclusive than previous practice, since Ipili could now be fully 'in' clans to which they had previously only a potential and possibly tenuous claim.

---

[10] This quotation and the following account are taken from the minutes of the meeting held on 3 December 1986, held in the Porgera SML Landowners Association Folder in the Porgera District Archives.

John Reid, who was at the meeting, objected that a count done in this way no longer tracked the actual population of the Special Mining Lease and would result in the sort of thing that the meeting has originally been established to avoid: a list of 10,000 people that described an actual population of 3,000. Ipili assured him that redundancies would not over-inflate the list because 'in the previous investigation we have included all our *wantoks* (people who speak the same language) who are living outside Porgera and therefore the population increased. Now we are cutting it down or restricted to landowners living within the Porgera valley'. The Ipili present at the meeting suggested that, in exchange for the government's recognising multiple 'clan' affiliation, they would limit claims to membership — out-marrying women, their husbands, and their children could be included on the list, but all other affines would not be entitled to membership in landowning 'clans'. As a result of this agreement the cognatic stocks which had previously been an important part of Ipili sociality now became 'clans' and these became the sole form of sociality recognised as appropriate for true 'landownerhood'.

As a canonical account, the social organisation of the seven landowning clans composed of 23 sub-clans has shaped life in Porgera for roughly two decades. It exists as a taken-for-granted fact about the valley. The original land study is not only rarely consulted; it is quite difficult to find. Close examination of the original document, however, reveals the traces of the more unruly arena of entrepreneurial agency which, on paper, it replaced.

For example, in the case of the Waiwa 'clan', the schedule of owners lists *two* sub-clans — Waiwa Yaliape and Waiwa Lunda (GoPNG 1987c). This in itself is not a surprise, as the Lunda are a large group who are associated with a piece of ground known as Upalika, whose members include several prominent Porgerans and the wife of one of the key coordinators of the land study. The Lunda are not, however, the 'owners' of any land within the Special Mining Lease; Upalika lies outside it. It is not clear, then, why they ought to be included on a list of owners or have an agent who signed the Porgera Agreements of 1989, as the agents for Waiwa Lunda did. Furthermore, it is not clear who actually ought to be agent for Waiwa Lunda — the agent for Waiwa Lunda listed in the land study is William Gaupe, but the agent who signed the Porgera agreements is listed as Pospi Karapis (Derkley 1989). Did Gaupe delegate his authority to Pospi? There is certainly no record of that fact, and during the time that I knew him William certainly did not make any such claim.

A similar situation pertains with regards to the Tuanda. The Tuanda are divided into two 'sub-clans', Ulupa and Yapala, which are represented by two agents, Sole Taro and Ambi Kipu (GoPNG 1987b). One of the Porgera Agreements, however, lists Aiyope Yawane as the signatory for Yapala rather than Sole Taro, and to confuse matters even more, the 'signature' on the document is a thumbprint with the word 'Sole T.' written over it (Derkley 1989). This is unusual, since Sole is proud of his education and is one of few agents who could sign his own name.[11] In the agency delegation document authorising Sole as agent for the Tuanda (as well as in other documents), he uses a florid and elaborate signature (GoPNG 1987b).

Furthermore, there is no coherent account of the segmentation of the Tuanda. The terms 'Ulupa' and 'Yapala' do not appear in the 'sub-clan' entry on the top of each page of the schedule of owners of Tuanda. Instead we have 'Kareya' and then a series of what are presumed to be sub-subclans in parenthesis — Kareya (Aiyengi), Kareya (Amini) and so forth — as well as a handful of other names. Most tellingly, the sub-clan 'Marinaka (Lio)' is included, and its 'address' is listed as 'c/o Catholic Mission Kasap, Yangiyangi Village, Mulitaka Patrol Post — Lagaip District'. 'The Marinaka' are in fact part of the larger clan diaspora of which the Tuanda are also a part. They come from Mulitaka, an area east of Porgera which is today considered ethnically 'Engan' rather than 'Ipili'. The schedule lists 94 Marinakas: 87 in Laiagam (the township near Mulitaka), and seven people who live in Porgera proper, including one Marinaka man, his wife, and three children. In other words, the schedule of owners purports to list a segmented series of sub-clans, but embedded within it is a specific form of regional sociality — a small group of Engans from Marinaka had moved to Apalaka on the basis of their diasporic ties to Tuanda, recorded themselves as landowners, and then enumerated their kin in Mulitaka as landowners too. Given the agentive nature of kinship in this region, it is not surprising that these people are included in the schedule of owners — as we have seen, the Waiwa Lunda are included on the schedule of owners as well as in the land study itself, despite the fact that (like the Marinaka) they have no land within the Special Mining Lease. But given the imperatives of the system of agency, it is no surprise that no Marinaka agent was appointed and that the Marinaka do not appear as one of the sub-clans in the land study or the Porgera Agreements. Between the compilation of the schedule of owners and the completion of the land study they had lost their status as landowners — a point that the Marinakans living in Porgera during my fieldwork have not forgotten.

Examples of this sort could be given in many of the other clans.[12] In closing I will consider only one of these — the land study's attempted segmentation of the Pulumaini. Some individuals living on Pulumaini lands did not feel comfortable with the idea of agents at the 'sub-clan' level and instead opted for a more granular level of representation, but others made a different choice. The result was a mix of different-sized groups and delegations of agency which

---

[11] The agreement between the National Government and the Porgera Landowners includes nine signatures and 21 thumbprints, and I am interpreting 'signature' as 'any mark made with a writing utensil'.
[12] For instance, two sub-clans of Anga are listed in the land study (GoPNG 1987a), but only one is listed in the agreements (Derkley 1989).

simply could not be subsumed under a lineage model. In the agreement between the National Government and the Porgera Landowners, there are six Pulumaini 'clans' — Ambo-Wagia, Ambo-Amu, Ambo-Endewe, Ambo-Gai, Ambo-Paramba, and Ambo-Yuga (Derkley 1989). Based on these names, each of these groups appears to be a subset of a larger 'Ambo' group. In the agreement between the Porgera Landowners and Enga Province, there are only five sub-clans, none of which are subordinate to Ambo. The clan groups Amu, Endewe, Gai, Paramba, and Yuga are listed, and one of these, Amu, has been added at the bottom of the document in pen (Derkley 1989). Neither of these two agreements match the land study itself, which lists the Pulumaini as being composed of Ambo-Wagia, Ambo-Amu, Tokome, 'Pulumaini Sub-clan Yamawe' (with the word 'Ambo' pencilled in between 'Pulumaini' and 'Sub-clan'), Ambo-Napali, Ambo-Endeme, Ambo-Gai, Yamili-Wapini, 'Pulumaini Sub-clan — Paramba' (with the word 'Yamili' written in pencil between 'Pulumaini' and 'Sub-clan'), Pariwana, and Yunga (GoPNG 1987a). In other words, these documents have never presented a coherent model of the Pulumaini as a clan.

Discussion and Conclusion

Advocates of a 'view and translate' approach might examine the material I have presented here and conclude from it simply that the Porgera Land Study was itself flawed, and that a less sloppy approach would have revealed the coherent corporate groups they expected. After even this brief presentation, however, I think it is clear that the incoherence of the land study and other works from this period are not the result of myopia, but rather of a process through which corporate entities like 'clans' creatively emerged in response to the land study's elicitation of them. We have seen that the land study was indeed 'forged' — it is neither a direct translation of a pristine, timeless Ipili social structure, nor a travesty in which Ipili culture was misapprehended. The land study in Porgera was instead a creative augmentation of Ipili social organisation according to government requirements and Ipili predilections.

We see reflected in the land study not the lineages or segments of a clan with exclusive membership, but a world of malleable corporate identities that took shape around a few prominent 'middle-men' or *tombene akali*. They reflect the fact that everyone 'on the ground' in Porgera knew who had to sign to make an agreement feasible that would protect the mine and allow it to operate. The situation was like that which Evans-Pritchard (1940) describes in *The Nuer*, and even more like that which Pirandello (1995) creates in *Six Characters in Search of an Author* — not 23 sub-clans in search of an agent but 23 agents in search of a sub-clan. Like Pirandello's cast, marooned on stage with no author to valorise or direct their action, the *tomebene akali* used their agency to become 'agents' through the forging of a newly corporate collective subjectivity that valorised their actions as its representatives. The remarkable reflexivity exhibited in these meetings — 'our custom is X, so we will agree to Y' — reveals an openness to the new and willingness to generate new normative frameworks which is, I have argued, quite modern. Porgera was successful because the people involved in the land registration process used the past less as a blueprint which dictated future behavior, and more as a resource in creatively coping with what was going to come. In the course of the land study, Ipili peoples managed to be both modern and traditional.

The land study was meant to be a document which settled once and for all who was and was not entitled to be considered a 'landowner' and an 'agent' in Porgera. What actually happened, however, was that the land charter became the raw material for a creative semiotics of landownership which enabled a wide variety of claims to be made, just as in the pre-colonial system already described. The result is what I have called 'bounded arenas' for contests of Ipili identity (Golub 2006). Interested parties range from Porgerans seeking to use their grass-roots security circles to become recognised and hence powerful agents to Australian mine representatives who strategically label claims of landowner identity true or false in order to widen or contract the field of the mine's legitimate interlocutors. What exists in Porgera today is not a system of agents which replaced a system of agency, but a repertoire of agents and clans within which Ipili continue to exercise their agency. This environment is flexible in that it constrains the forms in which claims to identity must be articulated but does not determine the success of any particular claim. The land study was forged in the sense that it solidified a fluid and — in Levi-Strauss's (1966) sense — 'hot' mass of sociality into a durable system of agents which provided a social context stable enough to host a gold mine. Thus, ironically, even though the land study got the sociology of Porgera wrong, in the end it allowed an Ipili mode of sociality to continue, albeit in transformed circumstances.

Many indigenous people who seek recognition from settler-dominated governments often feel like the son in Pirandello's play, who says that 'it isn't possible to live in front of a mirror which not only freezes us with the image of ourselves, but throws our likeness back at us with a horrible grimace'. Ipili were lucky enough to undertake the registration process at a time when they themselves would decide what sort of reflection they would cast in the looking glass of official policy.

Any politician who has ever had to hammer out the details of a piece of legislation might well find that metaphors of forging come naturally to them. It would seem unnatural, however, for us say that Australia's 1993 *Native Title Act* was 'invented' by the Australian Parliament since, as a quintessentially modern institution, liberal democracy generates new decisions on the basis of consensus formation arrived at through a deliberative process which responds to new situations with legislation which (ideally) expresses the will of its constituents. In this chapter I have suggested that we ought to understand indigenous communities in similar terms. Indigenous traditions are no more 'invented' than are parliamentary laws, and for the same reason. Ipili responses to the Porgera gold mine are, I have argued, just as novel as newly passed laws, and yet just as acceptably a product of their culture as laws are. In both cases, I have argued that this is because of a distinct process, adherence to which constitutes genuineness, rather than because of some specific content. Modernity is a mode of response to temporality rather than a set of things to confront.

For this reason I would go even further. For Europeans and members of their settler colonies, the act of forging oneself and one's society can be unsettling. To a certain extent, James Clifford's concern with the predicament of culture in 'a truly global space of cultural connections and dissolutions' where 'local authenticities meet and merge in transient ... settings' (1998: 4) is merely one of the many concerns that Europeans have had in the face of a world where the authority of the past cannot be taken for granted. But this is 'our' problem, not 'theirs'. As Marilyn Strathern has noted:

> Melanesians have never needed salvage ethnography. Their vision of the world had no problem with how parts fit together. There were no bits and pieces that had to be put back together again, for the sake of a culture restore, a society to conceptualize. Saved Clifford's predicament, I doubt nostalgia for either culture or society figures in their present cosmopolitanism (1992: 99).

Indeed, I would argue that Melanesians are even more modern — more willing to attend to novelty and avoid stereotypic reproduction — than are European organisations and bureaucracies for whom stereotypic reproduction is a condition of existence.

> [T]he relative open-endedness of possible meaningfulness leaves ever more to be experienced and discovered ... [and hence a] rapacious desire to experience and explore the novelty for what this might make manifest about possible difference ... [an] uncovering of new, heretofore covert possibilities' (Merlan and Rumsey 1991: 231).

We might hear in highlanders' 'expectation of the potential revelation' of objects echoes of Baudelaire's (1972: 402) painter of modern life who aims 'to extract from fashion the poetry that resides in its historical envelope, to distill the eternal from the transitory'. This is a view of highlanders who are not 'alternately' or 'heterodoxically' modern (Knauft 2002), but simply 'modern'.

This image of the Melanesian-as-dandy may strike some as an overly-optimistic portrayal of the situation in Melanesia today, so it is important to note that the trope of modernity need not be merely celebratory. Indeed, as Colin Filer (1998) has pointed out, this level of Levi-Straussian 'heat' can lead to a fluidity of social relations that 'menaces' a resource industry predicated on the bureaucratic, stereotypical reproduction of action necessary to keep large resource extraction projects up and running. My point here is that we can understand this openness to innovation as a disposition to action which can have a variety of outcomes. Just because 'menace' is all about fluidity does not mean that all fluidity is menacing.

The Porgera case thus suggests that we should examine the way indigenous claims and Western legal forms are mutually constituted, and suggests that we direct our attention to the process of that constitution in which elaborating tradition (as much as legislation) is a reflexive process. As Merlan (2006: 101) points out, 'the notion of the "mutual constitution" that reflexivity implies has long been one of the strongest potential alternatives to the concept of temporally deep continuity as the source of difference'. If this is the case, then we might in closing return to Patchen Markell's 'politics of acknowledgment' — a sense that justice requires that 'each of us bear our share of the burden and risk involved in the undertaking, open-ended, and sometimes maddeningly and sometimes joyously surprising activity of living and acting with people' (Markell 2003: 7) rather than indulge in a comfortable assumption of 'sovereign invulnerability to the open-endedness and contingency of the future we share with others' (ibid: 15). For the final step of recognising the contingent nature of 'their' identity means a symmetrical recognition that 'we' do not know who we are until after the fact — and that 'they' may be the ones to tell us.

References

Banks, G., 1997. Mountain of Desire: Mining Company and Indigenous Community at the Porgera Gold Mine, Papua New Guinea. Canberra: Australian National University (PhD thesis).

———, 2001. 'Papua New Guinea Baseline Study.' London: Mining, Minerals and Sustainable Development Project (Working Paper 180).

Barnes, J., 1962. 'African Models in the New Guinea Highlands.' Man 62: 5–9.

Baudelaire, C., 1972. Baudelaire: Selected Writings on Art and Literature . New York: Viking.

Biersack, A., 1980. The Hidden God: Communication, Cosmology, and Cybernetics Among a Melanesian People. Ann Arbor: University of Michigan (PhD thesis).

———, 1995. 'Introduction: The Huli, Duna, and Ipili People Yesterday and Today.' In A. Biersack (ed.), op. cit.

——— (ed.), 1995. Papuan Borderlands: Huli, Duna, and Ipili Perspectives on the Papua New Guinea Highlands. Ann Arbor: University of Michigan Press.

Briggs, C., 1996. 'The Politics of Discursive Authority in Research on the Invention of Tradition.' *Cultural Anthropology* 11(4): 431–469.

Burton, J., 1992. 'The Porgera Census Project.' *Research in Melanesia* 16: 129–156.

———, 1999. 'Evidence of "The New Competencies"?' In C. Filer (ed.), op. cit.

Carneiro da Cunha, M. and M. Almeida, 2000. 'Indigenous People, Traditional People and Conservation in the Amazon.' *Daedalus* 129: 315–338.

Chappell, D., 2005. '"Africanization" in the Pacific: Blaming Others for Disorder in the Periphery?' *Comparative Studies in Society and History* 47: 286-317.

Clifford, J., 1998. *The Predicament of Culture: Twentieth-Century Ethnography, Literature, and Art.* Harvard: Harvard University Press.

Curtin, T., H. Holzknecht and P. Larmour, 2003. 'Land Registration in Papua New Guinea: Competing Perspectives.' Canberra: Australian National University, State Society and Governance in Melanesia Project (Discussion Paper 2003/1).

De Soto, H., 2000. *The Mystery of Capital: Why Capitalism Triumphs in the West and Fails Everywhere Else.* New York: Basic Books.

Derkley, H. (ed.), 1989. 'The Porgera Agreements (Annotated).' Wabag: Department of Enga, Office of the Secretary, Legal Services Unit.

Evans-Pritchard, E.E., 1940. *The Nuer.* Clarendon: Oxford University Press.

Filer, C., 1998. 'The Melanesian Way of Menacing the Mining Industry.' In L. Zimmer-Tamakoshi (ed.), *Modern Papua New Guinea* . Kirksville (MO): Thomas Jefferson University Press.

——— (ed.), 1999. *Dilemmas of Development: The Social and Economic Impact of the Porgera Gold Mine, 1989–1994.* Canberra: Asia Pacific Press.

Fingleton, J. (ed.), 2005. 'Privatising Land in the Pacific: A Defence of Customary Tenures.' Canberra: Australia Institute (Discussion Paper 80).

Freeman, J.D., 1961. 'On the Concept of the Kindred.' *Journal of the Royal Anthropological Institute* 91(2): 192–220.

Golub, A., 2001. *Gold Positive: A Brief History of Porgera 1930–1997.* Madang: Kristen Press.

———, 2006. Making the Ipili Feasible: Imagining Local and Global Actors at the Porgera Gold Mine, Enga Province, Papua New Guinea. Chicago: University of Chicago (PhD thesis).

GoPNG (Government of Papua New Guinea), 1987a. 'Land Investigation Report: Porgera Joint Venture Special Mining Lease, Land Instruction 19/103: Final Report.' Porgera: PNG Department of Lands.

————, 1987b. 'Land Investigation Report: Porgera Joint Venture Special Mining Lease, Land Instruction 19/103: Schedule of Owners, Tuanda Clan.' Porgera: PNG Department of Lands.

————, 1987c. 'Land Investigation Report: Porgera Joint Venture Special Mining Lease, Land Instruction 19/103: Schedule of Owners, Waiwa Clan.' Porgera: PNG Department of Lands.

Habermas, J., 1987. *The Philosophical Discourse of Modernity: Twelve Lectures.* Cambridge (MA): MIT Press.

Hobsbawm, E. and T. Ranger (eds), 1983. *The Invention of Tradition.* New York: Cambridge University Press.

Jacka, J., 2003. God, Gold, and the Ground: Place-Based Political Ecology in a New Guinea Borderland. Eugene: University of Oregon (PhD thesis).

Jackson, R. and G. Banks, 2002. *In Search of the Serpent's Skin: The Story of the Porgera Gold Project.* Port Moresby: Placer Niugini Ltd.

Jorgensen, D., 2001. 'Who and What is a Landowner? Mythology and Marking the Ground in a Papua New Guinea Mining Project.' In A. Rumsey and J. Weiner (eds), *Mining and Indigenous Lifeworlds in Australia and Papua New Guinea.* Adelaide: Crawford House Publishing.

Knauft, B. (ed.), 2002. *Critically Modern: Alternatives, Alterities, Anthropologies.* Bloomington: Indiana University Press.

Lawrence, P., 1984. *The Garia: An Ethnography of a Traditional Cosmic System in Papua New Guinea.* Manchester: Manchester University Press.

Leach, J., 2004. *Creative Land: Place and Procreation on the Rai Coast of Papua New Guinea.* New York: Berghahn Books.

Lederman, R., 1986. *What Gifts Engender: Social Relations and Politics in Mendi, Highlands Papua New Guinea.* New York: Cambridge University Press.

Levi-Strauss, C., 1966. *The Savage Mind.* Chicago: University of Chicago Press.

Li, T.M., 2000. 'Articulating Indigenous Identity in Indonesia: Resource Politics and the Tribal Slot.' *Comparative Studies in Society and History* 42(1): 149–179.

Mangi, J., 1988. Yole: A Study of Traditional Huli Trade. Port Moresby: University of Papua New Guinea (MA thesis).

Markell, P., 2003. *Bound by Recognition.* Princeton: Princeton University Press.

Merlan, F., 1995. 'Vectoring Anthropology: A Critical Appraisal of Basil Sansom's Work. *Anthropological Forum* 7(2): 161–178.

————, 2006. 'Beyond Tradition.' In J. Weiner and K. Glaskin, (eds), op. cit.

———— and A. Rumsey, 1991. *Ku Waru: Language and Segmentary Politics in the Western Nebilyer Valley, Papua New Guinea.* Cambridge: Cambridge University Press.

Miller, D., 1994. *Modernity — An Ethnographic Approach: Dualism and Mass Consumption in Trinidad.* New York: Berg.

Nadasdy, P., 2003. *Hunters and Bureaucrats: Power, Knowledge, and Aboriginal-State Relations in the Southwest Yukon.* Vancouver: University of British Columbia Press.

Otto, T., and P. Pedersen (eds), 2005. *Tradition and Agency: Tracing Cultural Continuity and Innovation.* Aarhus: Aarhus University Press.

Ortner, S., 1984. 'Theory in Anthropology Since the Sixties'. *Comparative Studies in Society and History* 26(1): 126–166.

Patterson, K., 2006. 'A Deadly Clash of Cultures: The Ipili Tribe Vaulted Out of the Stone Age in a Generation, Propelled Partly by a Canadian Mining Company that Gave Them Health Care, Housing, Roads and More in Return for the Gold on their Land.' *Ottowa Citizen*, 4 June 2006.

Pirandello, L., 1995. *Six Characters in Search of an Author.* New York: Penguin Books.

Power, A., 1996. 'Mining and Petroleum Development Under Customary Land Tenure: The Papua New Guinea Experience.' In D. Denoon, C. Ballard, G. Banks, and P. Hancock, (eds), *Mining and Mineral Resource Policy Issues in Asia Pacific: Prospects for the 21st Century.* Canberra: Australian National University, Research School of Pacific and Asian Studies, Division of Pacific and Asian History.

Povinelli, E., 2002. *The Cunning of Recognition: Indigenous Alterities and the Making of Australian Multiculturalism.* Durham: Duke University Press.

Robbins, J. and H. Wardlow (eds), 2005. *The Making of Global and Local Modernities in Melanesia: Humiliation, Transformation, and the Nature of Cultural Change.* Burlington (VT): Ashgate Press.

Rynkiewich, M., 2001. 'Myths We Live By: Traditional Land Tenure in Melanesia.' In M. Rynkiewich (ed.), *Land and Churches in Melanesia: Issues and Contexts.* Goroka: Melanesian Institute.

Sahlins, M., 1992. 'The Economics of Develop-Man in the Pacific.' *Res* 21: 12–25.

————, 2000a. 'On the Anthropology of Modernity; or, Some Triumphs of Culture over Despondency Theory.' In A. Hooper (ed.), *Culture and Sustainable Development in the Pacific.* Canberra: Asia Pacific Press.

————, 2000b. '"Sentimental Pessimism" and Ethnographic Experience: Or, Why Culture is not a Disappearing Object.' In L. Daston (ed.), *Biographies of Scientific Objects*. Chicago: University of Chicago Press.

Sansom, B., 1985. 'Aborigines, Anthropologists, and Leviathan.' In N. Dyck (ed.), *Indigenous People and The Nation State: Fourth World Politics in Canada, Australia, and Norway*. St Johns: Memorial University of Newfoundland, Institute of Social and Economics Research.

Scott, J.C., 1998. *Seeing Like a State: How Certain Schemes to Improve the Human Condition Have Failed*. New Haven: Yale University Press.

Silverstein, M., 2003. 'Languages/Cultures Are Dead! Long Live The Linguistic-Cultural!' In D. Segal and S. Yanagisako, (eds), *Unwrapping the Sacred Bundle: Reflections on the Disciplining of Anthropology*. Durham: Duke University Press.

————, 2004. '"Cultural" Concepts and the Language-Culture Nexus.' *Current Anthropology* 45: 621–652.

———— and G. Urban (eds), 1995. *Natural Histories of Discourse*. Chicago: University of Chicago Press.

Strathern, M., 1992. 'Parts and Wholes: Refiguring Relationships in a Post-Plural World.' In A. Kuper (ed.), *Conceptualizing Society*. London: Routledge.

Sturzenhofecker, G., 1993. *Times Enmeshed: Gender, Space, and History among the Duna*. Stanford: Stanford University Press.

Taylor, C., 1992. *Multiculturalism and the Politics of Recognition*. Princeton: Princeton University Press.

Wagner, R., 1974. 'Are There Social Groups in the New Guinea Highlands?' In M. Wax (ed.), *Frontiers of Anthropology*. New York: Van Nostrand.

Wedeen, L., 2003. 'Conceptualizing Culture: Possibilities for Political Science.' *American Political Science Review* 96(4): 713–738.

Weiner, J., 2001. 'The Foi Incorporated Land Group: Law and Custom in Group Definition and Collective Action in the Kutubu Oil Project Area, PNG.' Canberra: Australian National University, State, Society and Governance in Melanesia Project (Working Paper 01/2).

————, 2006. 'Eliciting Customary Law.' In J. Weiner and K. Glaskin (eds), op. cit.

———— and K. Glaskin (eds), 2006. *Custom: Indigenous Tradition and Law in the 21st Century*. Special Issue 7(1) of *The Asia Pacific Journal of Anthropology*.

Wiessner, P. and A. Tumu, 1998. *Historical Vines: Enga Networks of Exchange, Ritual, and Warfare in Papua New Guinea*. Washington (DC): Smithsonian Institute Press.

Wohlt, P., 1978. *Ecology, Agriculture, and Social Organization: The Dynamics of Group Composition in the Highlands of Papua New Guinea. Minneapolis: University of Minnesota* (PhD thesis).

————, 1995. 'System Integrity and Fringe Adaptation.' In A. Biersack (ed.), op. cit.

Chapter Six

Incorporating Huli: Lessons from the Hides Licence Area

Laurence Goldman

According to Stirrat (2000: 31), the practical or pragmatic impact of reports written by anthropologists working as development consultants 'is in many ways irrelevant' because such reports are assessed on aesthetic criteria generated by the culture of modernity and their structure is pre-ordained by the interests of the client who commissions them. If the point is to attain 'closure' rather than 'dialogue' (Henton 2000: 586), then the author of such reports may come to feel that they are being used much as a drunk uses a lamp-post — for support rather than illumination. For their part, clients often suspect that the consultant anthropologist is more interested in pickling and preserving 'cultures' than in addressing the practical problems of 'development'. The result for both parties may be a portrait of the consultant as 'someone who borrows your watch to tell you the time' (Stirrat 2000: 44). Reticent to adopt the mantle of the social engineer, the anthropologist falls back on the strategy of telling developers or development agencies what they already know or can work out for themselves.

Nevertheless, resource developers currently operate in a political climate where sensitivity to indigenous cultures, rights and voices has never been so acute, and so they frequently and desperately seek answers from anyone who appears to exhibit confidence or experience in such matters. Much as they might wish to ignore the complexities of local social organisation and culture, engaging such issues is the only way to demonstrate their corporate social responsibility in respect to the design, implementation and monitoring of their projects. This chapter examines some of the issues faced by all stakeholders involved with indigenous lands rights and customary land group registration in the context of oil and gas development in Papua New Guinea (PNG). It suggests some of the rethinking that may be necessary for the anthropologist and other stakeholders to sustain a relationship that works in the best interests of any community affected by this kind of resource development.

Retrospective on Incorporated Land Groups

Development of petroleum reserves around Lake Kutubu in the Southern Highlands Province of PNG began in the late 1980s. The original developer, Chevron Niugini Ltd (CNGL), established a system of Incorporated Land Groups

(ILGs) in the project area with the approval and support of the then Department of Minerals and Energy. These ILGs were established under the *Land Groups Incorporation Act 1974* (*LGIA*) — a law that was meant to empower customary groups to manage the acquisition, use and disposal of their own customary land and regulate their internal affairs and disputes in accordance with 'custom' (see Fingleton, this volume). As a piece of legislation, the Act is deliberately general in nature so as to reflect the diversity of customary social organisation found across PNG. For example, it often comes as a surprise to those who consult the Act that it does not contain the word 'clan'.

There is no legal compulsion on landowners to form ILGs, nor are developers under any corresponding obligation to perform the function of ILG registration. Under Section 47 of the *Oil and Gas Act 1998*, the holder of an exploration or development licence is only required to produce 'Social Mapping and Landowner Identification Studies' for the information of the Minister and the Department of Petroleum and Energy. However, other sections of the Act make further reference to ILGs. Section 169(2)(b) states that the Minister shall determine by instrument

> the incorporated land groups or, if permitted in accordance with Section 176(3)(f), any other persons or entities who shall represent and receive the [landowner] benefit on behalf of the grantees of the benefit.

Section 176(3)(f) states that

> unless otherwise agreed between the State and the grantees of the [landowner equity] benefit or prescribed by law, the beneficiaries of the [landowner equity benefit] trust shall be incorporated land groups on behalf of the grantees.

The *Oil and Gas Act* therefore seems to imply that ILGs should be seen as the default system for landowner benefit distribution in the absence of some other agreed upon system.

From a strictly legal point of view, the registration of ILGs is a responsibility of the Registrar of Titles (ROT) in the Department of Lands and Physical Planning. However, because ILGs are also one of the vehicles by which accredited landowners receive financial benefits from resource development projects, other government departments, such as the Department of Petroleum and Energy (DPE), are also involved in the process of registration and the management of issues that arise from it. Recognition of an ILG depends on the preparation of a certificate that includes a detailed constitution for each group (see Fingleton, this volume). Although resource developers have no legal responsibility for the production of these documents, CNGL had little option but to accept some of this responsibility because of the limited capacity of government agencies such as the ROT.

There are currently some 600–700 ILGs representing the customary owners of Petroleum Development Licence (PDL) and Pipeline Licence areas in PNG. While CNGL could reasonably argue that the ILG system 'has worked' and the 'benefits have flowed', the systemic and persistent factionalising of ILGs has interfered with the process of registration and validation, and has delayed the distribution of landowner benefits. As I noted in one social mapping study:

> The pattern that has emerged during the course of fieldwork is one where multiple sub-clans, and sometimes lineages, are constituting themselves as separate units for ILG status … [I]n this regard it seems an appropriate juncture to pause and take stock of current ILG work to pose the question whether this trend is one that is cohesive or divisive of the communities and their fundamental structural bases … [T]he fear with the present trajectory of ILG work is that it may promote and institute a pattern of division which breaks down clan mores and implants fissionary tendencies that are counter-productive in the long run (Goldman 1997: 20).

The consensus is that groups have been opportunistically massaging their oral histories and manipulating the lands officers employed by the resource developer in order to maximise their financial benefits. This can be done by splitting ILGs to reduce the number of 'members' attached to any given landholding. In effect, the ILG system has become yet one more mirror to reflect the kind of shifting politics endemic in PNG's wider society. The question is whether these 'resource project cultures' are moving from a predominantly clan-based form of social organisation to one of nucleated families whose members only recognise the wider principles of common descent in a very loose way and whose claims for 'separate' landholding status merely express these generic tendencies and trajectories. My argument would be that these are not broad-based changes but rather a manifestation of the narrower opportunistic concern of each group to maximise its financial gains from the system. The ideology of group membership is unchanged and still expresses the way that people relate to each other, to the supernatural world, and to the ground beneath their feet.

The troubled history of ILGs in PNG is also discussed by Fingleton, Weiner and Filer in this volume. Succinctly stated, whatever system has been put in place eventually falls prey to the process of constant fissioning whereby ILGs break up into smaller and more exclusive units. There is opportunistic registration, de-registration and re-registration, all of which signals a more general failure of ILGs to function as anything more than conduits for the distribution of resource project revenues (see Weiner, this volume). While all parties bemoan the parlous state of customary group registration, and acknowledge the problems posed by the process, solutions have so far been conspicuously thin on the ground.

The origin of these problems is frequently attributed to a number of circumstances. Project operators were compelled to usurp by default the functions of the national government in establishing ILGs in the first place because of a lack of government capacity and resources, but while they did not abrogate their responsibilities under this ad hoc arrangement, the operators were not willing in the first instance to do any more than the minimum necessary to ensure that the project met its own milestones. In effect, the operators identified the beneficiary ILG groups, prepared the paperwork, submitted the forms to the ROT, and managed the process of disseminating the outcomes. This procedure was known as ILG 'facilitation'. The ROT conferred with the DPE to seek initial endorsement of ILG applications since these pertained to existing PDLs. Once DPE staff were satisfied, the ROT usually just endorsed the applications that had been received. There appears to have been little formality to this process: for example, there were no joint committee meetings or decision-making forums involving both government agencies.

While developers took on the burden of creating ILGs, they did not have an exclusive monopoly on this activity, either in law or practice, so even in a new operational area, their efforts could be matched by local people taking their own initiatives, travelling to Port Moresby and filing their own certificates of registration with the ROT. As we have seen, local people's empowerment was precisely the objective of the 1974 Act, but the lack of coordination between the stakeholders was not conducive to a sustainable outcome. In effect, the project operator soon lost control of which, and how many, groups were actually registered within the licence areas. Groups sought to increase their share of project benefits by establishing their own independent ILGs, both as a marker of structural autonomy and as a reflection of the dynamic political shifts and entrenched factionalism that has always characterised indigenous social organisation in both lowland and highland societies of New Guinea.

Once registered, the ILGs received little support by way of training, monitoring, or assistance that might have enabled them to develop their corporate functions and meet their obligations as modern organisations. In effect, the beneficiary ILGs simply became conduits for cash distributions. Since Landowner Companies and Landowner Associations were simultaneously established to cater for the political and economic representation of landowner interests, no further role for ILGs was envisaged by any stakeholder. A succession of studies has shown that ILGs simply do not function as micro-corporations of the kind envisaged by the *LGIA*. They do not cooperate in the management of their resources and only rarely reinvest their cash receipts in business ventures; they do not regulate their membership lists or manage land disputes; they do not have functional Dispute Settlement Authorities as required by the Act; and they have not received any infrastructure support or training over the course of the last decade (Goldman 2005). Social impact assessment data collected since 1998 shows that landowners' dissatisfaction with the performance of ILGs has been increasing, while their dissatisfaction with the performance of Landowner Companies and Landowner Associations, although still high, has been falling (Figure 6-1).

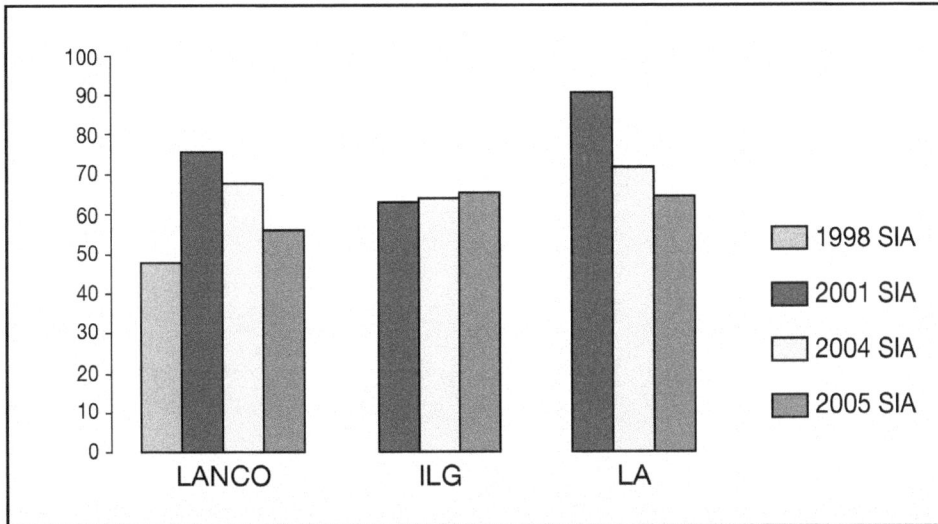

Figure 6-1: Percentage of landowner households dissatisfied with different types of landowner organisation, 1998–2005.

Source: Goldman 2005.

While it seems that landowners do not want ILGs to do anything more than distribute benefit streams, many are still dissatisfied with the current regime. Often ILG members do not get their cash benefits because these are stolen by the ILG's bank passbook holder — usually a male household head. But there are broader systemic problems that pose substantial risks for any further resource development in the affected areas, and therefore seem to demand a new kind of solution. Briefly stated, the problems are common to each of the PDL areas established since the early 1990s — Hides (PDL 1), Kutubu (PDL 2), Gobe (PDLs 3+4), and Moran (PDL 5) — as well as the route of the oil pipeline to Kikori (see Figure 6-2). However, the community affairs teams dealing with landowners in each of these areas have lacked a unified vision or strategic plan for managing such problems. Customary landowner registration has not been carried out in a way that was sensitive to the impact which programs in one area may have on other areas, and different principles for ILG formation and benefit distribution have been applied in different areas. Serious questions have therefore been raised about the need for a common approach to customary landowner registration across the extractive industry sector, most especially when dealing with landowners who belong to a single 'culture area'.

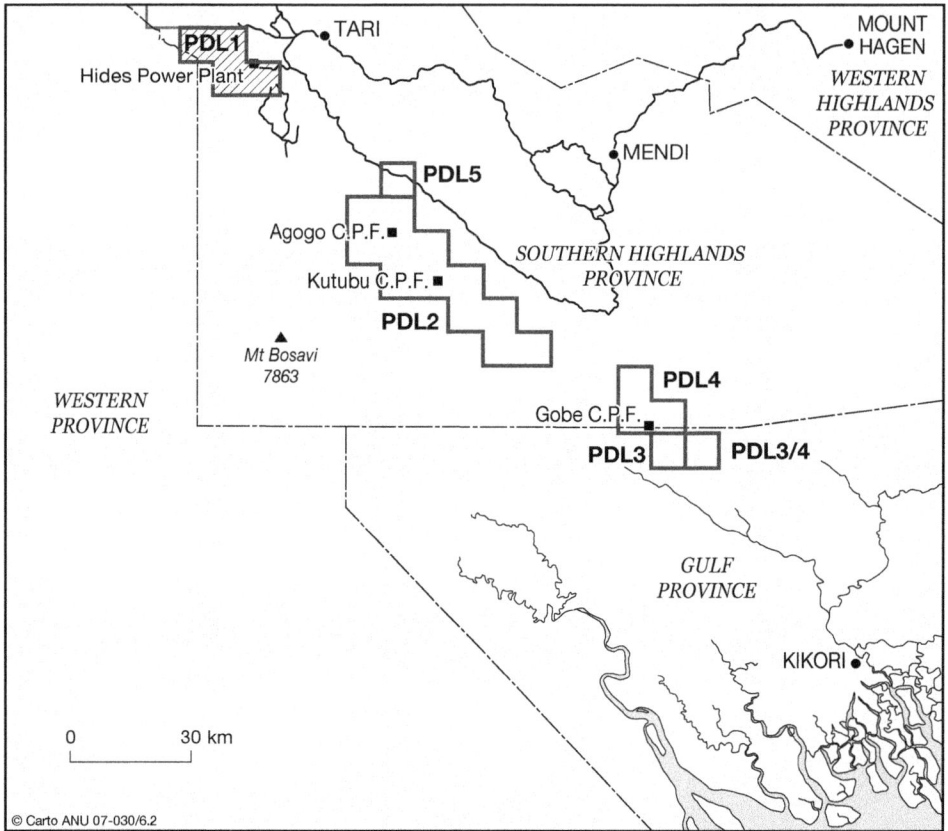

Figure 6-2: Petroleum Development Licence areas in PNG.

Making an accurate count of the number of existing ILGs in the licence areas is problematic because the DPE and the ROT do not have an electronic database containing this information, and no audit of relevant ROT files has yet been conducted. Furthermore, records inherited by the current project operators from CNGL are incomplete, and it is likely that landowners have registered many ILGs on their own account without the knowledge of the operators. Table 6-1 presents an approximate count based on evidence available in October 2004. In Gulf Province alone (along the route of the oil pipeline), it would appear that the number of registered ILGs doubled over the three years from 1997 to 2000. By the end of this period, there were at least 318 ILGs representing approximately 2500–2900 people, which meant an average of 7.8 persons per ILG in this region, as compared with an average of around 350 persons per ILG in the Hides Gas Project area (PDL 1). However, less than 50 per cent of ILGs known to exist in 2000 were in receipt of project benefits in that year. Table 6-1 indicates some of the problems of ILG proliferation (see also Weiner, this volume), but if these are considered as 'operational' quandaries, the anthropologist can see that the whole ILG venture is diseased in quite another sense.

Table 6-1: ILGs in petroleum licence areas, October 2004.

	Hides (PDL 1)	Kutubu (PDL 2)*	Gulf (pipeline)	Gobe (PDL 3+4)	Moran (PDL 5)
Registered	21	241	318	21	33
Deregistered	–	26	–	–	–
Pending	9	–	–	3	5
Applied	–	32	–	3	–

* Includes pipeline landowners in Southern Highlands Province.

ILG registration proceeded on a 'user-convenience' basis. There appears to have been no principled determination in any of the areas as to what unit of social organisation is appropriate for ILG registration. The evidence of systemic splitting of ILGs within a short period suggests that the ILG system is participating in, if not directly impacting on, the wider breakdown of customary social groups. The unchecked tendency for smaller and smaller social units to register as ILGs is a force for division, not cohesion. Although clans and sub-clans in the Kutubu region were always in the process of splitting, the pace and level at which this is now happening far exceeds what has previously been recorded as a 'customary' process.

The ethnographic evidence shows that, in some areas, the ILG system has also created new social units not previously recognised in custom. In the case of the Onabasulu people living to the west of the Kutubu production facility, the project operator's enthusiasm for ILGs created 'clans' which are an artefact of a 'certificate-based incorporation process and which did not pre-exist the era of petroleum development' (Ernst 1999: 88).

> The people identified as 'Onabasulu' are incorporated into 17 clans. This, incidentally, bears no exact relationship to the number of kinship groups, which are called *mosomu* in the Onabasulu language, that are a part of everyday social practice. Rather, the number 17 is important in Onabasulu cosmological beliefs and figures importantly in a cosmogonic myth. This myth has become, in the thinking of people at Walagu, at least, an important discursive tool for creating an exclusive people and category 'Onabasulu' analogous to the category 'Fasu' ... The '17 clans' corresponds to an Onabasulu identity in relation to the cosmogonic myth of Duduma, not necessarily empirical extant kinship groups. But it does so by providing, 'in law', a fixed number of incorporated groups that are called clans (ibid).

In other words, the application of the *LGIA* induced social structural changes quite unforeseen and unanticipated by the developer. In place of 'custom', the application of the Act introduced newly adapted forms of social organisation and ethnic identity in a process which Ernst calls 'entification'.

The historical lesson from the Onabasulu ILG program is that it is important for developers to understand the culturally specific nature of local social organisation before embarking on programs of incorporation if sensitivity to culture is to be a guiding operational principle. The Huli, Fasu and Onabasulu people have vastly different kinship and descent systems, and their complexity should compel caution when attempting to apply a 'clan'-based calculus to an ILG registration system. Nevertheless, the current trend in all areas is towards the formation of nucleated family groups constituting themselves as 'clan segments' in a manner that would not have occurred in the pre-development era. In part this may be because the family is the level at which on-the-ground property rights are actually held and exercised, but the ramifications for genealogical structure and descent group fission still have no precedents in the pre-colonial period.

Whilst the argument for change has ringing endorsement from all participants in the ILG process, the form that this should take is still opaque and the analysis of precisely 'what went wrong' is yet to produce any clear consensus. The argument I want to pursue here is that the ILG 'problem' is precisely the kind of rich landscape in which anthropological expertise of both a pure and applied kind can assist in the development of sustainable representative bodies for project landowners in a manner that also helps resource projects to pursue their business objectives.

Approaches to ILG Formation

The anthropologist may perhaps be forgiven, when faced with the task of advising on a new ILG program, for commencing with the obvious question: What unit of social organisation within this culture or region can we identify as being appropriate and feasible for the constitution of an Incorporated Land Group? Even accepting that an ILG system is fundamentally an attempt to organisationally freeze what anthropologists have long argued is a fluid, dynamic and ever-changing landscape of social relationships,[1] we need to unpack and spell out the preconceptions which might obscure our answers to this question and the legal constraints (arising from the *LGIA*) which might impinge on our considerations.

Developers and anthropologists both commonly seek out what Keesing (1971: 121) called the 'primary segments' of local society. These are building blocks — localised descent groups or primary residential/proprietary units — that provide a focus for economic, political and ritual interests. When faced with a directive to form ILGs, their common inclination is to identify discrete corporate units with separate territories at some level of social organisation. The idea is that the ILG system should become a mirror of a pre-existing social structure, and that ILGs should merely give another form of external recognition to what is already there. This belief is referenced to that catch-all term 'customary', and its legal

---

[1] Structure is always a 'becoming' not a 'being' (Goldman 1993: 23).

expression is the stated intention of the *LGIA* 'to recognize the corporate nature of customary groups'. However, since there is no occurrence of the word 'clan' in any part of the *LGIA*, we are entitled to ask whether the Act constrains us to identify social units which are 'already there'. Can we not take a more liberal interpretation of the term 'customary' so that it not only reflects the principles and visions which underpinned the Act itself, but equally takes cognisance of the fact that 'custom' itself is never a static phenomenon?

My argument is very simple: if anthropologist and developer would both forsake their natural inclination to search out 'primary segments', thus allowing for more lateral solutions to the basic problem, then more progress might be made with customary landowner registration in PNG. I am mindful that such a suggestion is easier to make than it is to instantiate, so what I want to do in the remainder of this chapter is to demonstrate the potential way forward once we loosen our ties to both the 'primary segment' model and its exemplification of 'customary groups'. The case in point will be the problem of incorporating the Huli landowners in the Hides Gas Project area, as shown in Figure 6-2.

The Hides Experience

The Hides Gas Project has been supplying gas to the Porgera gold mine since 1991 and has paid royalties to local landowners since 1994. The initial mechanism for benefit distribution was the so-called 'agency' system allowed under the *Land Act*. In effect, this meant that landowners appointed agents to represent their customary groups (mostly clans or sub-clans), to receive monies allocated to these groups, and then distribute these monies to their own group members. The system served the first and second operators of the project (British Petroleum and Oil Search) until 1999, when the proposed development of a new 'Gas-to-Queensland' Project raised the question of whether the 'agency' system should henceforth be brought into line with the ILG system used in the oil licence areas where CNGL had been the operator.

The task of finding a viable route to ILG registration for Huli landowners in the Hides area was encumbered by the complexity of the Huli land tenure system, in which there are three categories of people resident on any notional 'clan' territory, each with a different portfolio of land rights. Whilst land is notionally owned by clan and sub-clan 'corporations', individual members have rights in perpetuity to do with the land what they want — they are effectively the landholders. Individuals can sub-let land to anyone for a fee or for a fixed term, and can grant others use right or title to garden and hunting tracts by gift, deed or inheritance. In other words, who uses any particular piece of clan territory held by a clan member is at the discretion of that clan member and not subject to any group consensus or decision-making process. The only limitation on such discretion is that clan land can never be permanently and irrevocably alienated — the corporation holds the ultimate title and collective interest.

Two processes operate to cause the Huli clan groups on the ground to have a more complex and cosmopolitan make-up than the one envisaged in a simple 'one clan one piece of land' schema. These processes are at the heart of all problems encountered by lands officers attempting to grapple with the Huli land tenure system.

For all sorts of reasons — warfare, severe flooding or drought, the search for better access to hunting areas, or simply personal preferences — individuals often moved out of their natal clan territories to take up residence on a permanent or temporary basis with relatives or friends elsewhere, and they could do this without necessarily losing any of their rights to land in their 'home' territories. Huli distinguish two categories of migrant: those who are related to their hosts through descent from a female clan member (sisters' sons, for example) are known collectively as *yamuwini* (literally 'born of woman'), while those who have no direct blood tie, but are linked by marriage or friendship, are variously known as *wali haga* ('where women stayed'), *igiri yango* (male friends), or *tara* (others). To distinguish themselves from these other categories of resident, the patrilineal clan members living on their own clan territory refer to themselves as *tene*, which means 'source', 'origin', or 'main stem'. On any tract of clan land (or parish) there will therefore be three distinct classes of residents.

In practice all of these residents are indistinguishable in their everyday behaviour, but the *tene* are regarded as primary members in the sense of holding a sort of freehold title, while the others are secondary members holding a sort of leasehold title. Another way of conceptualising this relationship is to think of the agnates or primary residents as hotel owners and the secondary residents as guests who occupy hotel rooms, often with open-ended bookings, who could in theory be evicted by their hosts (Goldman 1993).

The second process which produces changes in the 'one clan one piece of land' model is in effect the repercussion of the first process over a period of generations. As secondary members migrate from various Huli clans and stay as guests on their hosts' land for several generations, the result is a complex mosaic of Huli clan segments scattered across wide distances. Migrant groups may eventually account for anything up to 99 per cent of the total population of a clan parish, but each of these groups will still retain some knowledge of, and share a sense of identity with, their natal clan. The members will still be *tene* of Clan A while they count as *yamuwini* or *wali haga* for Clan B whose territory they now occupy. Thus any one Huli clan may have several segments scattered outside its own ancestral land (see Figure 6-3).

CLAN A   **CLAN B**

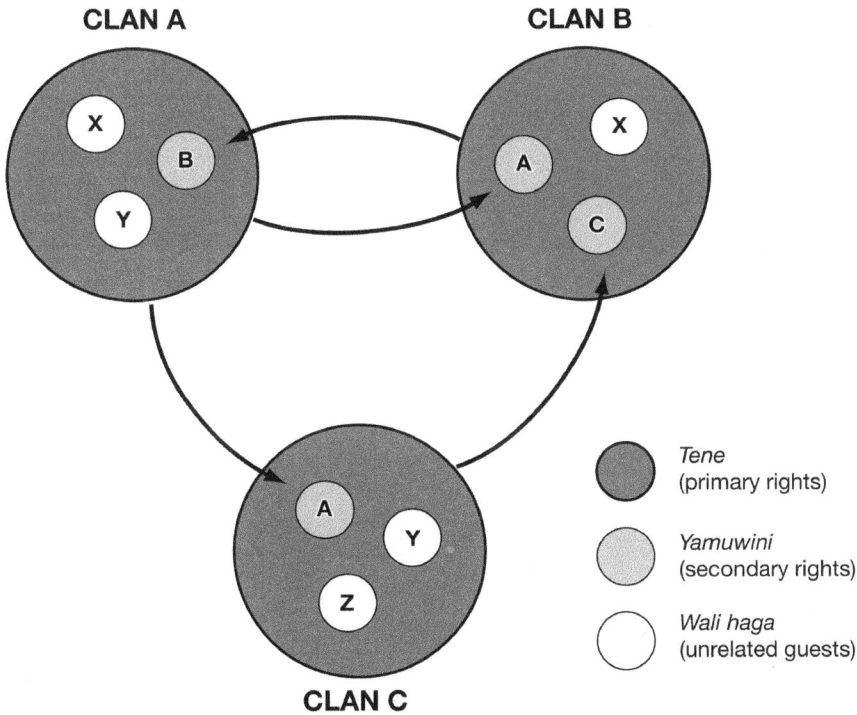

●	*Tene* (primary rights)
◐	*Yamuwini* (secondary rights)
○	*Wali haga* (unrelated guests)

CLAN C

Figure 6-3: A simplified model of the Huli descent and residence system.

The experience of CNGL in the Moran area (PDL 5) had shown that resident groups in each category would try to assert their right to a discrete ILG status, and this meant disputing their relative status as owners, guests, or guests of guests. To make matters even more complicated, Huli people generally have gardens in many different named parish areas, so a person would claim membership of more than one potential ILG and thus claim entitlement to multiple benefits on the basis of this customary practice.

The process of clan boundary demarcation in the Moran area took more than two years and identified approximately 15 per cent of the land as being under dispute. There is still no agreement on the part of the landowners about the number and names of the ILGs that need to be recognised. After initially identifying more than 200 possible social units for registration, CNGL introduced the concept of a 'stock-clan' in order to prioritise some groups for registration as ILGs. Each ILG was to be named after one of these 'stock-clans', which angered those resident groups with different descent affiliations. Initially, 12 groups were registered, and then a further 14 groups were added to the list but without the due process of gazettal having been followed. This created another wave of discontent and a further demand for recognition of 17 more groups that was eventually met by the DPE and the ROT. Project benefits have been distributed in proportion to the area of land within PDL 5 that is held by each of the claimant groups. Although PDL 5 is only one-sixth the size of PDL 1, closure has still not been achieved on a lengthy and costly process of land boundary demarcation and ILG registration.

The proposed development of the PNG Gas Project posed new questions about the need for stable and democratic landowner representation in the negotiation of new benefit-sharing agreements, as well as the actual distribution of cash benefits to project beneficiaries. Government agencies and the project proponents both began asking themselves whether a special model was needed to deal with the organisation of Huli landowners, and if so, whether it should be retrospectively applied to existing 'brownfield' licence areas as well as to new 'greenfield' areas on which development licences had yet to be granted.

More than 400 Huli clans had so far been identified, and satellite segments from each of these clans might be represented in any one licence area. Moreover, these satellite groups might not be confined to discrete segments of land, but might be scattered across several locations within a licence area. The predictable outcome for a developer attempting to locate and register 'primary segments' would be a system under constant challenge from groups dividing into subgroups of ever-diminishing size. At the same time, land boundary work would presage a series of land court claims which would be protracted, costly and counter-productive for all parties.[2] Providing solutions was very much a matter of finding the satisfactory interface between culture and commerce. In consultation with Oil Search community affairs managers, the search began with an effort to isolate and remove each of the variables in the equation that would constitute a subject for disputation. For example:

- Not using a 'clan'-based name for an ILG would remove the appearance of assigning precedence or priority to one social unit over another or signaling the allocation of a tract of land to the sole custody or ownership of that clan.
- Not performing land boundary demarcation would sidestep the problem of trying to pinpoint something which may never have been there in the first place, and which in any event might best be left 'unspoken' or unrepresented.
- Raising awareness of the implications of trying to register more than 400 ILGs in light of the Moran and Gobe experiences would help the landowners to gain some insight into the dilemmas confronting the developer.

The 'Zone ILG' Concept

What was eventually proposed as a result of these discussions was a system of 'zones' conceived as loosely drawn territorial areas occupied by an aggregated set of clans and clan sections which sustained long-term relationships based on intermarriage and exchange (see Figure 6-4). These relationships are more densely

---

[2] In the case of the Gobe licence areas (PDLs 3 and 4), the resolution of landownership issues took 10 years and legal proceedings cost millions of kina.

clustered within each zone than they are between neighbouring zones. In essence, the zone ILG was devised on the basis of customary behaviour patterns rather than principles of land tenure, albeit with a recognition that there has to be a certain degree of arbitrariness in the construction of zone boundaries. The best analogy is to be found in the customary exchange of pigs: If I give you a pig, with which of your neighbours are you compelled by custom to share it? The answers to this question provide the basis for defining a zone.

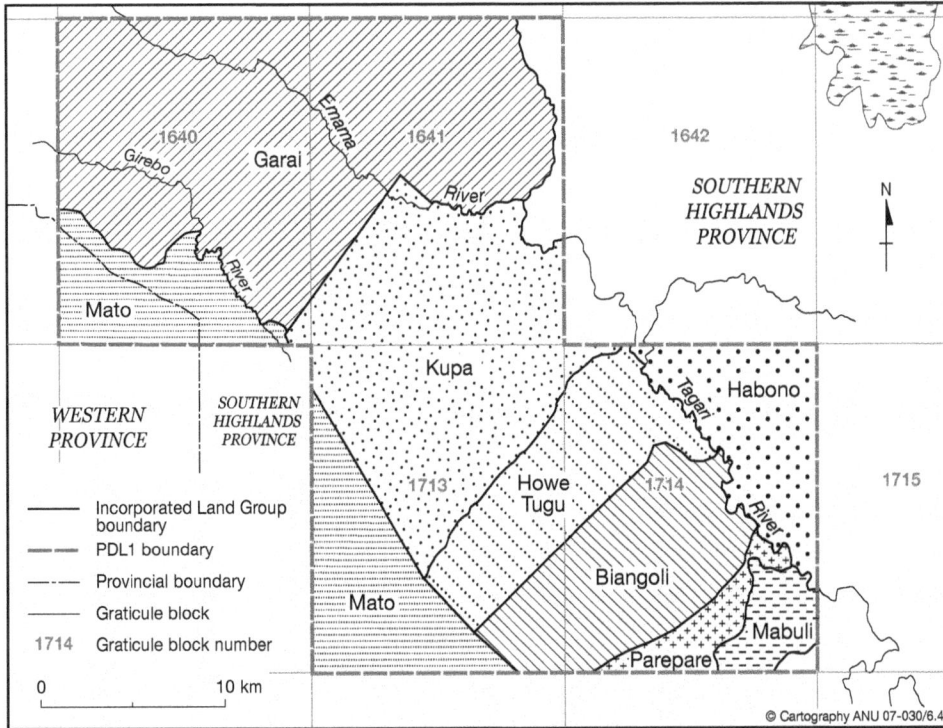

Figure 6-4: Zone ILGs proposed for the Hides licence area (PDL 1).

Each zone would in effect be an umbrella entity capable of subsuming or incorporating ILGs which have already been registered without the need for deregistration or disenfranchisement (see Figure 6-5). Its members would be empowered through their own Dispute Settlement Authority to decide who is or is not a legitimate landowner or landholder within the zone. Neither the resource developer nor the relevant government agencies would be required to adjudicate on competing genealogical footprint claims or make the final decision on who is and who is not an accredited project beneficiary. The actual make-up of any zone which might be established in other licence areas would necessarily reflect local circumstances in light of variations in social organisation across the wider region.

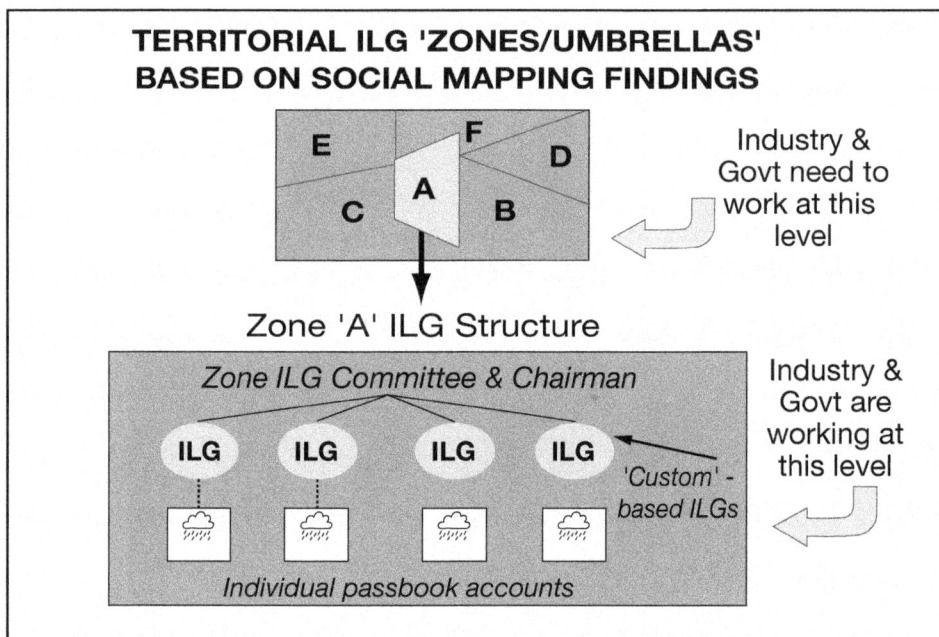

Figure 6-5: Zone ILG structure proposed for the Hides licence area.

The zone ILG system has several advantages over the present ILG system:

- it provides a means of 'registering' interests without upsetting the status quo of the constituent groups in terms of their present ownership or usage of land;
- it obviates the need to undertake land boundary demarcation at a fine scale and thus avoids land disputes;
- it avoids giving priority in land ownership to any one clan at the expense of another (which is also a source of dispute between clan-based ILGs) because zones are not named after clans;
- it allows for non-resident claimants to be incorporated in a zone even if they are members of another ILG elsewhere, which particularly suits the multiple residential affiliations characteristic of Huli society;
- it discourages the process of ILG fragmentation because an existing ILG would gain no financial advantage by seceding from a zone;
- it facilitates a more transparent and efficient form of landowner representation in the negotiation of benefit-sharing agreements because there is a much smaller number of higher-order ILGs representing the landowners in each licence area;
- and this also makes it easier for a developer or an aid agency to build ILG capacities.

Zone ILGs would be formed in practice by a consensus of the component member units informed by social mapping and landowner identification studies undertaken in accordance with Section 47 of the *Oil and Gas Act*, and their social constitution would in that sense be guided by anthropological research. Zone ILGs would allow local-level politics to continue through the proliferation of smaller social units, but would contain the ramifications of this process within a set of higher-level boundaries. The message conveyed by this higher level of organisation is that closely related people need to 'cooperate' to mutually benefit from resource development rather than continue to argue and fight amongst themselves. Zone ILGs would to some extent be artificial entities, but would still be less artificial than the rectangular petroleum licence areas to which they are related. In each area, the licence holders (and government agencies) would only need to deal with a committee made up of the elected chairpersons of each zone, in much the same way as the mining company at Porgera deals with 'super agents' under the agency system (see Golub, this volume).

It is readily acknowledged that any system of this kind is subject to the risk of political manipulation and social strain. While the representative structures in a zonal system should provide constraints on benefit abuse by individual leaders, they would probably alienate the representatives of existing Landowner Associations who would be fearful of being marginalised in project negotiations. Equally, a reformed and rationalised ILG system would still need to provide the community with the level of benefit disaggregation they clearly desire — which means that benefits should end up with individual recipients and not the 'representatives' of larger social units.

Whether or not the zone ILG system needs to be justified in terms of local 'custom', there remains the question of whether it is consistent with the letter and spirit of the *Land Groups Incorporation Act*. Section 5(3) of the Act states that:

Recognition shall not be refused to a group simply because —

(a) the members are part only of a customary group or are members of another incorporated land group; or

(b) the group includes persons who are not members of the primary customary group, if the Registrar is satisfied that those persons regard themselves, and are regarded by the others, as bound by the relevant customs of the primary customary group; or

(c) the group is made up of members of various customary groups, if the Registrar is satisfied that the group possesses common interests and coherence independently of the proposed recognition, and share or are prepared to share common customs ...

The zone ILG is precisely an entity of the type described in clause (c) if we understand 'common customs' to mean agreed principles of behaviour. It should therefore be evident that the *LGIA* does not oblige the developer or consultant anthropologist to chain the constitution of ILGs to some 'primary segment' model. Moreover, Section 5(5) even allows for an ILG to be constituted 'as a group consisting only of incorporated land groups'. The notion of aggregated units is thus specifically and explicitly allowed for in the Act, and if the zone ILG system places the onus for decisions about membership squarely back in court of the ILGs themselves, this is also consistent with the spirit of the Act.

If one does imbue such units with what Ernst (1999) called 'entivity', this may in fact be a positive factor for change in the community. The principles of Melanesian *kastom* are not inconsistent with the creation of a social artifact tailored to the interests of a state and a developer which also benefits the population of local landowners. Under the terms of the *Organic Law on Provincial Governments and Local-Level Governments 1995*, zones actually resemble the local government wards which are also aggregates of local clans and clan segments.

How the 'Zone' Concept Fared

In 2000, Oil Search instituted a 'zone' ILG system for PDL 1 and two adjacent Petroleum Retention Licence areas in anticipation of the PNG Gas Project. This exercise had written endorsement from the DPE and the ROT. Seventeen zones were proposed, and eight were actually registered with the ROT.[3] However, following representations by some individuals from one of the adjacent licence areas (known as Hides 4x), further registrations were halted under instructions from the DPE. Zone ILGs have not yet had an opportunity to function as representative or beneficiary bodies because there is as yet no PNG Gas Project. However, zone ILG agreements about the distribution of future benefits between member sections within each zone are enshrined within the ILG constitutions.

PNG government agencies such as the DPE and the newly established Gas Office are still considering what is the best mechanism for the distribution of potential cash benefits to local landowners. Cash benefits from the existing oil project have either been divided equally between the number of ILGs in a licence area (as in PDL 2) or in accordance with the acreage held by each ILG (as in PDL 5). Whilst the retention of a 'clan'-based system has some attractions because of its apparent consistency with their understanding of *kastom*, government officials are also sensitive to the results of various surveys which indicate that people in some of the licence areas want benefits to be distributed on a per capita basis. This preference is evident in a household survey conducted as part of the

---

[3] The eight zone ILGs registered by 2004 (Biangoli, Kupa, Habono, Obai Tangi, Kamia Gere, Mato, Mindirate and Ayagere) are included in the total number of Hides area ILGs shown in Table 6-1, while the other nine are shown as 'pending' in that table.

Gas Project Social Impact Assessment in 2005 (see Figure 6-6). However, this survey also shows a much greater preference for per capita distribution in Huli areas (Moran and Hides) than along the route of the current oil pipeline which follows the course of the Kikori River. This may reflect the already splintered nature of the ILG system in Gulf Province, where many individuals or families already have their own private ILGs. In all other areas, there is clear evidence of continuing dissatisfaction with the present benefit distribution regimes and support for the move to a more equitable system in which individual group members have their own passbooks and accounts, rather than having to rely on the decision made by ILG chairmen who look after the accounts of their respective groups.

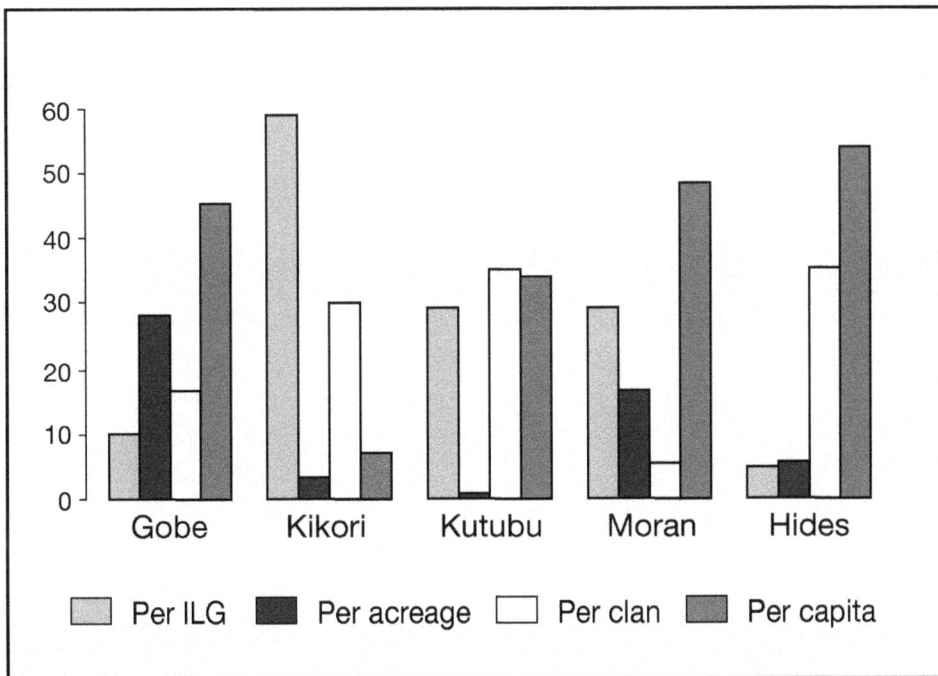

Figure 6-6: Landowner preferences for benefit distribution, 2005.

Source: Goldman 2005.

Despite these findings, PNG government agencies are still saddled with the task of deciding how best to derive a system of landowner representation, given the factionalised nature of local politics in Huli society, and how best to derive a list of 'landowners' that will be acceptable to local people, given the complex nature of Huli land tenure. Government officials seem to think that the social mapping and landowner identification studies required under Section 47 of the *Oil and Gas Act* should extricate them from this minefield by painting a frozen landscape whose 'landowners' could then be vetted or endorsed by the Minister of Petroleum and Energy as 'entitled project beneficiaries'. This position is at variance with the best advice of all consultant anthropologists who have worked in the licence areas over the last decade, who say that the task of providing a definitive beneficiary list based on people's status as individual 'landowners' is nigh impossible, and in any event is a task best left to local people to undertake in accordance with the wide range of factors that make up *kastom*. In the many meetings on this subject in which I have been a participant, the 'zone' system has been firmly rejected by government officials because of its 'non-customary' nature. Debate therefore continues on how to reconcile the equitable principle of per capita distribution with the perceived inequity of a 'clan' system that relies on clan leaders to 'cut up the pig'. This ongoing debate is enmeshed with considerations exogenous to the merits of a zone ILG system, such as the requirements of international financial institutions, the personal agendas of current landowner 'leaders', and misapprehensions or indecision on the part of the policy makers. The final scenarios have yet to be played out.

Conclusion: What Hides Reveals

The 'zone' system was conceived to address problems already experienced with ILGs elsewhere, and it anticipated what might happen with the formation of ILGs in the context of Huli culture and social organisation. From long-term research on dispute resolution and economic exchange in Huli society, a set of scenarios could be foreshadowed which would pose intractable obstacles to the progress and stability of a major resource development project. In one sense the 'zone' system was engineered to allow local-level politics to continue unimpeded: as local groups traditionally argued over the way in which pork should be distributed at ceremonial pig kills, so do these same groups now compete for increased portions of the 'project pig'. The solution was to establish a system with a built-in firewall such that these utterly conventional but highly localised competitive encounters would not necessarily hamper development activities.

At the same time, the solution seemed attractive to this consultant because it offered an opportunity to build a new form of 'community' within a socio-cultural environment which lacked village-like settlements or any aggregated form of residential pattern. Thus supra-local community would be a grouping of clans and clan segments sharing different parts of the 'benefit pig', with a democratically elected leadership committee that could then seek to expand its activities by applying for development grants from suitable aid donors.

It is important to add that a three-month process of consultation with landowners in the Hides licence area (PDL 1) found unanimous support for the system, partly because the problem associated with the previous formation of ILGs in the neighbouring Moran licence area (PDL 5) and the more distant Gobe licence area (PDLs 3 and 4) were already well known in the Hides area. Indeed, the success of the implementation process which followed the consultation process reflected the real and historical relations of intermarriage and exchange between zone members.

Perhaps this shows how the anthropologist as consultant is able to 'gate-keep' a practical solution to a widely acknowledged problem by engineering a new social system that is not only consistent with the realities of economic development and the expectations of the developer, but also helps to manage 'custom' as a basis for sustainable innovation. According to Stirrat (2000), development consultancy work is commonly based on the mistaken belief that consultants can somehow penetrate to the 'truth' or 'essence' of what is going on in the world. But the consultant anthropologist who counts as an acculturated observer of one particular society is more like a translator who knows enough to anticipate social trajectories and provide constructive solutions to the problems they contain.

References

Ernst, T., 1999. 'Land Stories, and Resources: Discourse and Entification in Onabasulu Modernity.' *American Anthropologist* 101(1): 88–97.

Goldman, L., 1993. *The Culture of Coincidence: Accident and Absolute Liability in Huli*. Oxford: Oxford University Press.

———, 1997. 'Moran Social Mapping Report.' Unpublished report to Chevron Niugini Ltd.

———, 2005. 'PNG Gas Project Social Impact Assessment.' Brisbane: Exxon Mobil.

——— and S. Baum, 2000. 'Introduction.' In L. Goldman (ed.), *Social Impact Analysis: An Applied Anthropology Manual*. Oxford: Berg.

Henton, D., 2000. 'Singing Songs of Expectation.' In P. Buchanan, A. Grainge and R. Thornton (eds), *Proceedings of the Fourth PNG Petroleum Convention*. Port Moresby.

Keesing, R., 1971. 'Descent, Residence and Cultural Codes.' In L. Hiatt and C. Jayawardena (eds), *Anthropology in Oceania*. Sydney: Angus and Robertson.

Stirrat, R., 2000. 'Cultures of Consultancy.' *Critique of Anthropology* 20(1): 29–46.

Chapter Seven

The Foi Incorporated Land Group: Group Definition and Collective Action in the Kutubu Oil Project Area, Papua New Guinea

James F. Weiner

In this paper I examine the genesis and progress of the Incorporated Land Group (ILG) in the Kutubu oil project area of Papua New Guinea (PNG). The ILG is a legal entity empowered by legislation passed in 1974 to give legal and formal recognition, protection and powers to customary landowning groups in PNG (see Fingleton, this volume). In the Kutubu oil project area, at the instigation of Chevron Niugini Ltd (CNGL), the previous managing partner of the Kutubu Joint Venture, the Foi, Fasu and Lower Kikori River clans became incorporated under PNG's *Land Groups Incorporation Act 1974* (*LGIA*) and now receive royalty payments from the sale of petroleum. The ILG mechanism was employed by the developers in the belief that it would 'give powers to landowners so that they could manage their affairs in a businesslike way' and 'provide recognition of the land group [that would] enable the village landowners to act in a way that outside people and agencies must recognize' (Power 2000: 29). The advocates of the ILG mechanism asserted that 'the ILG constitution guarantees that decisions regarding clan resources are made by the correct authorities in the clan' (ibid).

But since the original round of ILG registrations, there have been numerous applications for new ILG status from subgroups within these original ILGs incorporated in the early 1990s. In 1998, 13 new Fasu ILG applications were lodged, all of them by subgroups within already incorporated clans. This proliferation is in the context of the most common complaint concerning these ILGs: that the income is not being satisfactorily shared by those members of the executive committee designated by the ILG to distribute its income. These new ILGs wish to have their own passbooks and receive their income payments directly.

The previous project operator, CNGL, interpreted this trend in two ways: as a sign that local clan leaders are dishonest, and as a sign that local people themselves have not yet sufficiently understood the nature of contemporary managerial procedure. They stop short of admitting the possibility that the clans themselves are not 'customarily' either corporate or collective units that exist for the common interest of its members.

But the *LGIA* is based on a quite erroneous assumption of the communal nature of landholding and transmission within the Melanesian 'clan' and of its essentially 'collective' interest. As Evans-Pritchard reminded us — and this became a founding approach of the Manchester school of African social anthropology in the 1950s and 1960s — the whole concept of the segmentary lineage system around which the attributes of corporateness were first empirically examined was founded on the notion of enduring and regular structural relations of conflict and consequent group fission as the mode of societal reproduction. Acts of legislation such as the *LGIA* have not understood this aspect of social structural formation in PNG, resulting in problems such as those CNGL has encountered in applying the *LGIA* to customary 'landholding' units. The companies and government departments who have attempted to implement the *LGIA* have made an ethnographically indefensible apportionment of the 'political' to external relations among landholding units, and consequently see the resulting conflict and competition *within* them as adventitious and subversive of the 'customary' landholding units themselves. This arises from the tendency to assume that the *internal* affairs and composition of landowning social units are both practically and ontologically prior to their external relations.

The ILG and the Petroleum Industry in PNG

In the early 1990s CNGL undertook a census of all villages with clans who owned land in its Petroleum Development Licence (PDL) area and incorporated the recognised landholding groups at the same time. A total of 54 Foi ILGs were registered as PDL landowners with the aid of CNGL's Lands Department between 1992 and 1994.

In an unpublished paper circulated amongst CNGL and other petroleum industry and government personnel, Tony Power, one of leading architects of this process, stated:

> The Land Groups Incorporation Act was the most significant outcome of the 1973 Commission of Inquiry into Land Matters (CILM). The Act embodied a constant refrain in the CILM reflecting the desire of the Commissioners that Papua New Guinean ways be employed to maintain the integrity of custom in the management of land. The Commissioners soundly rejected all forms of land tenure conversion. At the same time the same concepts were being developed by the founding fathers and found their way into the Constitution exhorting the use of Papua New Guinean ways. *The mind of the legislator was clearly that modern management mechanisms can and should be applied by customary groups*

to manage their affairs in relation to land and related matters (2000: 52, emphasis added).

The administrators trying to come to terms with the task of protecting customary PNG landholding units today are engaged in the same epistemological exercise that their structural-functionalist predecessors were during Radcliffe-Brown's time (Weiner and Glaskin 2006: 1–2).

> The more emphatically the investigators insisted on the importance of definitions, rationality, and their own conceptions of law and property, the more substantial and strictly bounded the groups became. They became, in short, much more like the consciously organized, planned, and structured groups of Western society in spite of a lack of any kind of evidence that natives actually thought of them in that way. 'Groups' were a function of *our understanding* of what the people were doing rather than of what they made of things (Wagner 1994: 97).

Anthropologically, it might seem ironic that just as global industry is (re-) discovering the wisdom of Colonial Codification, anthropology has focused its attention away from the normative, the collective and the bounded in social life. In more recent years, a variety of theoretical developments have caused the pendulum to swing away from an acceptance of the collectiveness and corporateness of indigenous landholding units, and towards an understanding of the unstable, porous, nomadic, centripetal and fluid characteristics of such groups.[1] Yet the increasing contemporary struggle over control of land and resources has produced a movement in the opposite direction: towards some evolution of universal principles for the protection of property rights, and the codification and legal protection of indigenous customary law around the world. The present panoply of laws (increasingly subject to international codification and recognition, most notably through the United Nations and other international agencies) that define a wide range of indigenous customary institutions is consequential for the future of indigenous custom, practice and self-understanding. Although aspects of this have received relatively recent public exposure,[2] Australian anthropologist Kenneth Maddock put the matter succinctly somewhat earlier:

> It is important to distinguish, in principle, between rights originating in modern statute law and rights having some other origin. Otherwise, *anthropologists will smuggle into their accounts a legal view that, intended to express a traditional reality, has been shaped in its original formulation*

---

[1] Sutton (2003) comments on the similar effects of Fred Myers' (1986) Pintupi ethnography on the interpretation of Australian Aboriginal group structure.

[2] Notably the Coronation Hill and Hindmarsh Island Bridge sacred site claims in Australia, the Ok Tedi pollution case in PNG, and the Exxon Valdez compensation case in Alaska.

and subsequent development by the exigencies of legal policy and reasoning
(Maddock 1989: 173, emphasis added).

The first problem in PNG law is that nowhere does it contain a definitive definition of what a 'landowner' is. As Filer has convincingly argued in the PNG context, the issue of 'landownership' as such is largely an artifact of the recent mineral exploitation in PNG:

> There is a sense in which Papua New Guineans have only *become* landowners over the course of the last 10 years ... the question of whether 'clans' exist as 'landowners' in the fabric of national identity is the question of how 'clans' *have actually become* groups of landowners claiming compensation from development of their own resources (Filer 1997: 162, 168).

The genesis of the concept of the landowner can partly be traced to the various preambles and explanatory addenda to the *LGIA*:

> Developers of resources in PNG must by necessity involve the owners of land because all land where resources are located is privately and communally owned. Developers are concerned that the landowners in the project area fully support their project. In order for this to happen landowners must manage the physical, social and economic impact of the resource development. A critical element of impact management is the distribution of direct cash benefits arising from land use, royalties, and equity. If the impact of the project is so great as to destroy the social fabric then the security of the project will be greatly eroded. The ILG system is not just [an] exercise to distribute cash benefits. The ability to fairly distribute cash benefits, though important, is only one outcome of a successful ILG system (Power n.d.(a): 1).

This points to the second problem: there is a critical ambiguity in the above statement. Is, or is not, the chief function of the ILG system to distribute benefits from commercial developments such as petroleum extraction, mining and logging, or should it have some wider and more synergistic function with the traditional social units in PNG, specifically with respect to the protection of land rights and their customary form of transmission? Having worked with the Foi, both before and since the advent of the oil project, there seems no doubt in either my mind or theirs: the ILG is perceived solely as a petroleum benefit-receiving body, and all of the uses to which it has been put by the Foi (and other people within the petroleum project area) have been exclusively related to this function. It has not yet been put to use to attend to matters pertaining to ownership of land *per se*, as it was originally designed to do. PNG's Land Titles Commissioners made this same point in one of their judgments on a dispute about landownership in one petroleum project area:

The issues contested in the hearing is [sic] not only limited to customary landownership. There are arguments on public policy considerations, application of the *Land Act* and the *Petroleum Act* for purposes of settling claims of rights of parties owning land affected by the petroleum project (Kanawi et al. 1998: 11).

Rather than the ILG mechanism serving to legally 'modernise' the existing system of land proprietorship, the Foi and other oil project area peoples have employed it as the unit of political struggle over petroleum benefit sharing, much to the consternation of CNGL's External Affairs Office, the PNG Department of Petroleum and Energy and the PNG Department of Lands, which deal with landowner relations in petroleum licence areas.

The Proliferation of 'New' ILGs

Tony Power, who was working for the CNGL External Affairs Department when the initial registration of oil project area ILGs was first carried out in 1992, recently wrote the following account:

> Since the beneficiaries are Incorporated Land Groups, vetting of lists that have developed since dividends began to be paid must be done to prevent possible fraud. In the early 1990's before there was any clear incentive to form new land groups all the population within the project area belonged to the original land groups assisted by Chevron to incorporate via the Land Groups Incorporation Act. All of these people were also censused and recorded in the Village Census Books. Nobody forced these village people to record their genealogies in this manner and hence it must be assumed that the original groups were for the most part accurate. Since the original land groups were incorporated a number of 'new' ILGs have emerged. As new groups will dilute the benefits to the original groups it is necessary to examine all new ILGs to see if they are justified. This could be done in the field by a team including Chevron, DPE and a Provincial Lands Officer, after consultation with the Registrar of Titles and PRK (Power n.d.(b): 1).[3]

As I have said, the ILG is simply seen by the Foi as a strategic device whose purpose is primarily political-economic rather than one of customary land management *per se*. Leaders among the Foi are using the creation of new ILGs to leverage additional shares of the petroleum revenue for their supporters since, as a result of the initial memoranda of agreement, each ILG owning land in the PDL area would receive the same share of the revenue, regardless of population size or absolute amount of PDL land owned. PDL landowners are also enhancing

---

[3] PRK (Petroleum Resources Kutubu) was a company established by the State to hold equity in the oil project on behalf of the customary landowners.

their own support amongst non-PDL landowners by offering to make them 'PDL landowners' in a variety of ways.

An example of how this is working itself out can be found in Lower Foe. The leader behind the landowner company called Muiyoke Pty realises that he represents only a small population, and what is more, compared to the larger and more central Foi villages, he commands few educated, literate men who can help him form the core of an effective political and economic organisation. He thus uses Muiyoke to attract men from the more populous Upper Mubi. This is achieved by promising them that if they buy shares in the company, not only will they receive oil revenues, but by forming their own ILGs, through their shares in Muiyoke, they can become, by definition, PDL landowners. This is illustrative of a distributive mechanism that is not based on the assumed behaviour of the liberal sovereign individual who is viewed by many as the basis of the governance system empowered by the *LGIA* (Weiner 1998; see also Rowse 1998; Lea 2000).

In the same way that the *LGIA* requires (without enshrining) this autonomous, sovereign individual, the same urge that characterised early social anthropology — towards achieving a clear, unambiguous 'sharp-edged' definition of indigenous social units and their territorial property — is evident in the thinking behind the *LGIA*:

> If an original land group divided into two or more then the members would have to demonstrate the following:
>
> - That the two or more land groups have distinct land and do not have cross claims or interests in each other's land.
> - That they followed their ILG constitution when dividing the original ILG.
> - That they have the support of their ethnic group who recognize their separate identity.
>
> *Where new ILGs have no customary basis for division* they would divide their original one share between them [emphasis added]. This is exactly what happened with the Foi beneficiaries for royalties. 24 ILGs representing 8 clans shared 8 shares of dividend …
>
> A primary consideration must be that recognition of new groups will dilute the benefits to existing beneficiaries. In that case any new groups would have to be approved by the existing beneficiaries. A mechanism will have to be devised to seek approval of existing beneficiaries by means of consultation at general meetings with the members of landowner associations or shareholders of companies. Once this vetting takes place a definitive list of beneficiaries can be recognized by DPE and forwarded to the Trustee (Power: n.d.(b): 1).

But the previous examples indicate that the ILG (as understood by its architects) has been uniformly misunderstood and misapplied by the great majority of ordinary Foi. By 1999, there were at least 48 cases requiring 'land group maintenance': that is, the alteration, re-registration, or splitting and new registration of previously incorporated land groups. In mid-1999, 26 original ILGs had been deregistered by the Lands Department in Port Moresby, and about 80 new ILGs had been registered claiming distinct and separate status (and separate petroleum revenues as well). Additional new ILGs were applying for and receiving ILG certificates from the Lands Department in Port Moresby in June 2000. The reasons given for these proposed alterations have been varied:

- groups fear that money has not been distributed equitably within the ILG and therefore wish to establish their own income stream and passbook;
- disputes have emerged over the land borders originally registered, and over the membership of groups already registered;
- there have been uncertainties as to the kinship and clan membership of component groups within the ILG;
- finally, and commonly, there were accusations of improper behaviour levelled at ILG chairmen.

At a broader level, regional leaders tried to register as many ILGs under their own political 'association' as they could, to claim as large a proportion of the fixed petroleum royalty as possible, and to enhance the appearance of their numerical support. In all of these cases, the codification of customary ownership of *land* figures hardly at all.

This progressive fragmentation of 'traditional' landowning groups has been perceived to be against the spirit of the ILG program. The philosophy of the ILG is that the corporate group will act in the interests of a body corporate. When it does not do so, it is common to blame the failure on the self-interest of its leaders or on the ignorance of local landowners — although the frequent and regular emergence of such 'self-interested' leaders should itself act as a critique of the assumption of the landowning group's 'collective interest'.

I have argued, however, that the fragmentation of Foi ILGs is consonant with more deep-seated oppositional behaviour that governed to a marked extent the shape of political life and the resulting composition of local residential groups in Foi and indeed throughout the societies of the petroleum project area (Weiner 1998). The company, on the other hand, has mistakenly taken the appearance and rhetoric of collective *action* as evidence for the existence of a collective *interest*.

The proliferation of 'splinter ILGs' represents the response to the pressure on the Foi system of pervasive social differentiation caused by the influx of petroleum revenues. The 'names' of Foi social groups, like those of their Daribi counterparts, 'only group people in the way that they separate or distinguish them on the basis of some criterion' (Wagner 1974: 106). Usually, this criterion is territorial in the Foi case. Hence, subdivisions of clans are referred to as, for example, Mubiga So'onedobo ('the So'onedobo who live near the head of the Mubi River'), as opposed to Baibu So'onedobo ('the So'onedobo who live near Baibu Creek').

Individual lines within a Foi clan are conventionally differentiated in one of two ways. The most common is to label them according to their land. For example, in Hegeso village, the elder men Abosi and Haibu were 'Hesa Orodobo' and Midibaru and Tari were 'Yebibu Orodobo'. Midibaru's son Kora cannot build a house or garden on Hesa Orodobo land without permission; and Abosi's son Dobo cannot do the same without permission from Yebibu Orodobo, even though they maintain they are of a single clan and act collectively in other matters. The other manner of distinguishing lines within a clan is by way of their clan of origin. For example, Sobore, a Fo'omahu'u man, was taken in by the Orodobo clan of Hegeso, was given resources and protection, and kinship ties were extended to him. His descendants, though functionally full Orodobo clan members, are more precisely referred to as Fo'omahu'u Orodobo.

As Wagner has observed, these names are significant 'not because of the way they describe something, but because of the way in which they *contrast* it with others' (Wagner 1974: 107, emphasis added). These distinctions are for the most part contingent and emergent — they appear in the context of some specific incident of oppositional behaviour, and can easily disappear once that opposition is defused or brought to some resolution. Most often, Foi men of the same local clan find themselves in dispute over one issue or another — the division of bridewealth, the use of specific spots of land, accusations of adultery or theft, and so on. These can lead to factions emerging that look 'as if' the clan is fissioning. But such acts of fission are not necessarily either irreversible or even long-lived, though they can be both. They merely reflect the territorial fluidity of such groups, in a manner strikingly reminiscent of the way Evans-Pritchard described the Nuer:

> Nuer tribes are an evaluation of territorial distribution and tribal and intertribal and foreign relations are standardized modes of behaviour through which the values are expressed … Moreover, it is not only relative because what we designate a tribe to-day may be two tribes to-morrow, but *it can only be said to determine behaviour when a certain set of structural relations are in operation, mainly acts of hostility between tribal segments and between a tribe and other groups of the same structural order as itself, or acts likely to provoke aggression.* A tribe very rarely engages in corporate activities, and, furthermore, the tribal value determines behaviour in a definite and restricted field of social relations

and is only one of a series of political values, some of which are in conflict with it (Evans-Pritchard 1940: 149, emphasis added).

More generally, what Schieffelin (1976) calls the 'opposition scenario' in this part of PNG can have a more positive rendering — that is, the customary understanding that land boundaries and landownership are what neighbouring clans acknowledge them to be. In a judgement pertaining to disputed ownership of the Hides gas project licence area,[4] and in one of the judgements pertaining to the Gobe dispute, it was recognised that 'a land [sic] is said to belong to a group when the land boundary is acknowledged by the neighbouring clans' (Kanawi et al. 1998: 17).[5] It is this recognition of the *relational* aspect of property, and of land in particular, that leads Cooter (1989: 13) to contrast 'market property', appropriate to the non-kin-based societies of the modern West, with 'relational property', characteristic of the kin-based societies of nations such as PNG.[6]

The Local Clan Versus the ILG

There is thus a fundamental conflict at the heart of the ILG mechanism which crops up constantly. This conflict can be stated as follows: the *LGIA* was purportedly designed to enshrine the *traditional landowning group as a legal landowning corporation*. The purpose of this was to give *legislative protection* to the traditional landowning units in any given area of PNG. Take the following list prepared by Power under the heading of 'Measurable Indicators of Incorporated Land Group Effectiveness':

> The most important deliverable of the land group incorporation process is the identification and training of a cadre of village land workers, being villagers, old and young, keen to become involved in the learning process in the transition from an oral to a written society. These are the contacts in the villages that can relate to government and developer extension officers in developing management for the ILGs. Answers to the following questions will illustrate the degree of progress made.

> - Does the ILG have a recognized 'custom expert'?
> - Does the ILG recognize a 'custom expert' from another clan in the village?
> - Does the ILG have a literate facilitator?
> - Does the ILG have access to a literate facilitator within the village?

---

[4] *Re Hides Gas Project Land Case* [1993] PNGLR 309.
[5] The 'opposition scenario' can have the opposite effect as well — lines without genealogical connection have formed a single ILG by banding together in both the Gobe and South East Gobe licence areas. The Land Titles Commission opined that this was an improper use of the *LGIA* (Kanawi et al. 1998).
[6] Of course all property is relational in the sense that things are 'owned' *in rem*, that is, only as against other people.

- Have any of these ILG functionaries ever attended a training workshop to help them develop their skills?
- How many outstanding land disputes over either ownership or use rights between resident clans are in the village?
- How many outstanding land disputes over either ownership or use rights are there with outside clans?
- Does the village recognize a Dispute Settlement Authority (DSA) empowered under the *Land Groups Incorporation Act*?
- How many times has the DSA met since the formation of the village ILGs?
- Does the ILG have a Minute book?
- Does the ILG have a corporate seal?
- How many formal decisions have been made by a given ILG in the last 12 months?
- Were these decisions recorded in a minute book, signed off by the Committee and kept for future reference?
- Does the Village Development Committee take an active interest in ILG functions, activities and responsibilities?
- Is there a formal member of the VDC responsible for ILG matters?
- Enumerate any ILG related activities pursued in the village.
- Does the ILG have any customary obligations to outside clans that should be addressed by the ILG Committee or are these obligations more on a family basis?
- Does the village have any permanent residents from other villages?
- Which ILG(s) has responsibility for managing these people?
- What land rights do these guest residents have?
- When did the guest residents first come to the village?
- What is the status of guest residents in regard to land management? (Power 2000: 99).

These questions invoke the Western terms of *corporation*. A corporation is a group that is legally treated as a single individual. The *LGIA* assumes that the landowning unit acts collectively in its collective interest. It assumes that the decisions that a landowning unit makes are similar to the decisions a corporation makes.

This is not the case, at least not among the Foi. It is not demonstrable that the local clan acts collectively to further the interests of the clan as a collective unit. What anthropologists such as Roy Wagner (1974), Marilyn Strathern (1985), Simon Harrison (1993) and myself have described as the 'givenness' of connection and obligation in PNG sociality has been mistaken by the architects of the *LGIA* as evidence of communal, corporatist ownership and decision making. If this is so, then the act of incorporation cannot protect the customary status of the local

Foi clan — it can only force it into new forms which can take on the functions that the *LGIA* assumes such units will undertake.

The conclusion we must face is that traditional custom cannot be protected by an act of legislation. The legislation is composed and empowered by a cultural and legal system very much at odds with the way local 'traditional custom' arises and is implemented. To again quote from Power:

> The [*LGIA*] actually spells out this relationship between land and group in the opening words: *'Being an Act —*
>
> a.   to recognize the corporate nature of customary groups; and
> b.   *to allow them to hold, manage and deal with land in their customary names and for related purposes.'* [Original emphasis] ...
>
> Thus the purpose of the Act is to empower groups owning land *communally* to manage their land. NB The Act does not narrowly confine itself to the aspect of managing benefits coming to the owners, though it clearly accommodates this.[7]

In their judgment on the Gobe dispute, the Land Titles Commissioners said that:

> Where claims arise in that [sic] a certificate is issued under the provisions of the *Land Groups Incorporation Act* amount to title in land, such claims are not valid on the basis that [sic] the characteristics of the 'title' referred to in the provisions of Section 1 of the *Land Groups Incorporation Act* is [sic] not the same title to land ownership in that it [sic] relates to 'title to name' of the customary land owning group ... (Kanawi et al. 1998: 31).

And again:

> Sowolo clan members by their own admissions have allied with the Haporopakes and have formed a common clan unit sharing social values, protecting and using various common land marks. This traditionally binds the persons as a clan unit and therefore one cannot retract from [sic] those customary obligations for the sake of some monetary benefits derived from the land at this time (ibid: 64).

Thus, insofar as the ILG is acknowledged by the Commissioners to have been utilised primarily as a unit receiving petroleum benefits, it must constantly work against what they perceive to be the interests of the traditional customary landowning group.

---

[7] 'Definition of Land Groups and Group Lands.' Chevron Niugini File note A.P. Power 6 February 1998.

What is Customary Law?

Power has also written about what constitutes the 'law-like' in customary law:

> The corporate nature of the land group makes allowance for a constitution to govern the management of the group. This is analogous to the constitution or articles etc of companies and business groups. A very significant weakness in implementation of the *LGIA* to date has been the failure of the groups to appreciate the importance of their constitution and hence their inability to manage their affairs accordingly. Thus when issues arise that could be dealt with by the group under the leadership of their management committee, the group fails to act. This leads to dissension in the group and moves to split up into smaller groups. Splitting into smaller groups may completely distort the responsibilities and effectiveness of the land controllers and should be avoided at all costs since it is totally contrary to the purposes of the Act (Power 1998: 39).

The intent of the audit of the Kutubu ILGs which I carried out in 1999–2000, and the policy of the CNGL Lands and External Affairs officers, was to make sure that the ILG program preserves the customary landholding units in the oil project area. However, to repeat, the *LGIA* is based on Western notions of property ownership and collective, corporate decision making that are not Melanesian principles as such. Therefore, the *LGIA* already works to some extent against traditional custom, by making a concrete 'thing' out of land and of the landowning group (Weiner 1998). But 'customary law is not a statement of practice. It is a normatively clothed set of abstractions from practice ...' (Hamnett 1977: 7). Bohannan says that:

> Whereas custom continues to inhere in, and only in, these institutions which it governs (and which in turn govern it), law is specifically recreated, by agents of society, in a narrower and recognizable context — that is, in the context of the institutions that are legal in character and, to some degree at least, discrete from all others ... (1967: 45).

> Law has the additional characteristic that it must be what Kantorowicz calls 'justiciable,' by which he means that the rules must be capable of reinterpretation, and actually must be reinterpreted, by one of the legal institutions of society so that conflicts within nonlegal institutions can be adjusted by an 'authority' outside themselves. (Bohannan 1967: 45–6).

I think the issue of justiciability and its relation to the work of 'interpretation' more generally is what is critical here — a point to which I return at the end of this chapter.

The Foi landownership system was highly flexible in traditional terms and groups varied dramatically in size, from the large clans of Damayu and Fiwaga which had over 100 adult male members, to Kuidobo clan of Hegeso which in the 1980s had a single adult male. There simply were no guidelines or ideal parameters governing what a local clan 'should' consist of. Clans and individuals alienated land frequently and commonly, and gained exclusive ownership over new parcels of land constantly. It must also be repeated that no local clan was in any absolute sense disadvantaged over others in terms of access to all types of land.

In fact, the evidence is that customary land law is human cataloguing of a land redistribution mechanism that has evolved over a very long time in the development of interior New Guinea agricultural systems (Weiner 1988b).

> Customary law in the highlands redistributes land involuntarily in response to changing power relationships among groups. Weak groups that are dispossessed of land by their enemies get absorbed by others [voluntarily in nearly all cases] to bring power back into balance. *By keeping groups small and constantly re-aligning them, no group gains complete dominance over others* (Cooter 1989: 69, emphasis added).

Another important feature of the fragmentation of Foi clans through the ILG mechanism is that adopted lines are singled out, either for second-class status within the clan or for expulsion as outsiders. However, the process can work the other way around — the impetus can come from the descendants of immigrants themselves who use that justification of foreign origin to set up their own ILG. In either case, the *territorial* dimension of 'clan', that is, *local group* organisation is being eroded by the inextricable link between the ILG mechanism and the distribution of resource benefits. In either case, the full status of descendants of immigrants is subject to erosion of full clan rights. While it is true that foreign origins were never forgotten in the past, there was virtually no distinction in status within the clan because of it. It appears that the Foi are on the way to developing their own model of infra-indigeneity, whereby 'original' people are contrasted with 'immigrants'.

But the fact that PDL land is valuable in a way that traditional land was not means that the system threatens to 'set in concrete' a division of the clan into PDL and non-PDL landowners (Weiner 2001), although — as the example of Muiyoke indicates — there are indications that the Foi are indirectly redistributing even PDL land more widely. These points have already been summarised more effectively in the course of Cooter's earlier observations:

> The courts that hear cases in customary law — village courts and land courts — are better placed than parliament to make authoritative findings about customary law ... Melanesian legal principles are to be discovered by deciding cases in customary law. The 'common law process', which

refers to the courts working custom into formal law, involves litigation, not legislation (Cooter 1989: 19).

The Fragmentation of Foi Clans

Many of the new ILGs at Lake Kutubu are the result of large clans such as Wasemi Fo'omahu'u Orodobo or the large Damayu and Fiwaga clans splitting into constituent subclans and lineages. These new applications are defensible in terms of population growth alone, which was the most common precipitating cause of clan fission. In Foi, *ira* ('tree') is the term applied to three generations of male descendants of a single man. Practically, it takes the form of a group of full brothers whose land is normally contiguous — in other words, they live near each other as well as being closely related. The ILGs that were audited at Wasemi were all 'trees' of the Orodobo and So'onedobo clans — the two biggest clans at Wasemi. I have previously identified the *ira* as the property managing and work-related cooperation group within the Foe social system (Weiner 1986, 1988a), and so there is nothing non-traditional about this kind of division — it merely gives formal ILG recognition to a unit that is already explicit and visible in the Foi social system.

The ILG, though based on principles by which clans are defined as landowning entities, is not the same as the clan *per se*. The Foi themselves are clear about the different functions of ILGs and their traditional clans. For example, a single clan may consist of two or more subclans for the purposes of ILG recognition and land stewardship. But the entire clan still acts as a unit, for example, in the collection and receipt of bridewealth for its female members.

A singularly appropriate feature of the *LGIA* is that it defines the land belonging to a landowning group not in terms of a discrete unbroken border, but in terms of a list of specific sites over which its constituents exercise what for all intents and purposes are the prerogatives of ownership. In this context, ownership is defined as control of access to the site or ground in question. Among Foi the local clan exercises a sort of nominal communal dominion over its territorial resources, but effective *ownership*, that is *control of access*, is always exercised by specific individuals or, at most, a set of full male siblings and their father (Weiner 1986, 1988a).[8]

The issue at stake is not just *control of resources* but also *the mechanism and locus of decision making at the local level*. As a result of there now being two social units, the ILG and the clan, clan-wide decisions concerning things such as bridewealth and ceremonial will be split off from decisions concerning resource management and distribution. It is an open question whether, in terms of

---

[8] This is similar to Sutton's (1998) distinction between proximate and underlying title in Australian Aboriginal landholding practices.

traditional custom, the control of land was seen as distinct from all these other clan functions.

The local Foi group reached consensus not by convergence upon a common interest but by the temporary rhetorical abeyance of the fissive mechanism that really 'founds' group formation (Goldman 1983). In traditional times, the local clan rarely acted as a single unit, except ceremonially, as in bridewealth distributions for example. Land decisions were the affairs of those directly involved. Although disputes over land within the clan were commonly adjudicated, they did arise. Disputes over distribution of bridewealth were also common.

Some Comparative Observations and Conclusions

I wish to conclude by making the following observations:

- customary law cannot be made into justiciable law without turning it into something altogether non-customary;
- the landholding clan, at least in regions like the Kutubu oil project area, is neither solidary, corporate, nor bound by collective sentiment;
- but I agree with the architects of PNG post-Independence land reform that the relation to land is central to the PNG person's being and social identity.

As is the case with the Nuer, social units, though phrased in the language of consanguineal kinship, are also equi-primordially territorial relations. But land is only one part of what a local clan exists to 'control', or to put it another way, the allocation of rights to land is only one of the social conditions through which the clan is elicited as a social entity — for the most part, rhetorically. Yet this is what is required from an ILG by the local 'External Affairs' requirements of the resource companies, which tend to phrase their concern for achieving a manageable local decision-making process in terms of clear guidelines for the allocation of authority over land matters.

Wagner (1988: 60) has characterised the so-called solidariness of Daribi social units in the following way:

> Vengeance raids, nasty fights over a pig or domestic situation, and factional standoffs are not so much accidents of the critical social structure as social structuring within the larger accident of the critical social mass. They carry the same weight as social norms and rules or family-values, only in a different mood. The social charter of the Sogo people is the fight of their split from Noru; that of Weriai is the fight of its fissioning from Iogobo, and so forth. Fights, in this context, are the elementary structures of kinship.

Bamford (1998: 30), writing about Kamea inheritance through clans, makes a similar and more general statement:

Land, paternal names, and modes of ritual competence are all transmitted through men, typically from a father to his son. Yet it is important to note that gaining access to these and other resources is not an automatic concomitant of patrifiliation — instead, it is constitutive of it.

Smith (1974: 43) observed much earlier that:

Evans-Pritchard's distinction between the types of corporateness of local and lineage units among the Nuer implies a recognition of distinctions between the ideological and organizational aspects of social units, and as such, between corporateness evidenced by group action, and corporateness postulated as such.

And Evans-Pritchard (1940) originally observed that:

Nuer lineages are not corporate localized communities, though they are frequently associated with territorial units, and those members of a lineage who live in an area associated with it see themselves as a residential group, and the value or concept of lineage thus functions through the political system.

Finally, if we are to take the critique of the self-evidence of internal and external relations seriously, then neither can we long sustain the fiction that CNGL is *radically external* to the land groups themselves. Through its own attempts at educating landowners about the relevant PNG legislation, its own acts on behalf of the State in registering the ILGs in the first place, and its commitment to monitoring, evaluating and maintaining the ILG system in 'good repair', the company is a critical force for the transformation of group dynamics in the oil project area. The anthropological study of indigenous culture and society in a resource extraction environment cannot limit itself to the indigenous people as such. A complex, non-local 'culture' comprising government, resource companies, and local landowners is developing in every mining enclave in PNG, and this non-local and non-traditional culture deserves monitoring in its own right. In order to reveal this culture as an object of anthropological scrutiny, it will be necessary to view the PNG 'clan' not chiefly as an age-old and resilient feature of 'traditional' society but also as a strategically elicited form of social and political self-presentation in the highly charged intercultural encounters of PNG's resource sectors.

References

Bamford, S., 1998. 'Humanized Landscapes, Embodied Worlds: Land and the Construction of Intergenerational Continuity Among the Kamea of Papua New Guinea.' In S. Bamford (ed.), op. cit.

——— (ed.), 1998. *Identity, Nature and Culture: Sociality and Environment in Melanesia*. Special Issue 42(3) of *Social Analysis*.

Bohannan, P., 1967. 'The Differing Realms of the Law.' In P. Bohannan (ed.), *Law and Warfare: Studies in the Anthropology of Conflict*. Garden City (NY): Natural History Press.

Cooter, R.D., 1989. 'Issues in Customary Land Law.' Port Moresby: Institute of National Affairs (Discussion Paper 39).

Evans-Pritchard, E., 1940. *The Nuer*. Oxford: Clarendon Press.

Filer, C., 1997. 'Compensation, Rent and Power in Papua New Guinea.' In S. Toft (ed.), *Compensation for Resource Development in Papua New Guinea*. Canberra: Law Reform Commission of Papua New Guinea (Monograph 6). Canberra: Australian National University, National Centre for Development Studies (Pacific Policy Paper 25).

Goldman, L., 1983. *Talk Never Dies: The Language of Huli Disputes*. London: Tavistock.

Hamnett, I., 1977. 'Introduction.' In I. Hamnett (ed.), *Social Anthropology and Law*. London: Academic Press.

Harrison, S., 1993. *The Mask of War*. Manchester: University of Manchester Press.

Kanawi, J., B. Noki and C. Malaisa, 1998. 'Gobe South East Gobe Customary Land Ownership Dispute Appeal: Reasons for Judgment.' Port Moresby: Land Titles Commission.

Lea, D., 2000. 'Individual Autonomy: Group Self Determination and the Assimilation of Indigenous Cultures'. Canberra: Australian National University, North Australia Research Unit (Discussion Paper 18).

Maddock, K., 1989. 'Involved Anthropologists.' In E. Wilmsen (ed.), *We Are Here: The Politics of Aboriginal Land Tenure*. Berkeley: University of California Press.

Power, A., 1998. 'Land Groups: The Foundation for Nation Building in Papua New Guinea'. Unpublished manuscript.

———, 2000. 'Land Group Incorporation: A Management System.' Canberra: AusAID.

———, n.d.(a). 'Incorporation of Land Groups.' Unpublished Chevron Niugini Limited file note KJV9740X.

———, n.d.(b). 'Trustee Arrangements to Deliver Royalty and Equity Benefits to Landowners'. Unpublished Chevron Niugini Limited file note KJV9734X.

Rowse, T., 1998. 'Appropriate Forms of Indigenous Organization.' Canberra: Australian National University (unpublished seminar paper).

Schieffelin, E., 1976. *The Sorrow of the Lonely and the Burning of the Dancers.* New York: St Martin's Press.

Smith, M.G., 1974. *Corporations and Society.* London: Duckworth.

Strathern, M., 1985. 'Discovering "Social Control".' *Journal of Law and Society* 12(2): 111–134.

Sutton, P., 1998. *Native Title and the Descent of Rights.* Perth: National Native Title Tribunal.

———, 2003. *Native Title in Australia: An Ethnographic Perspective.* Cambridge: Cambridge University Press.

Wagner, R., 1974. 'Are There Social Groups in the New Guinea Highlands?' In M. Leaf (ed.), *Frontiers of Anthropology.* New York: Van Nostrand.

———, 1998. 'Environment and the Reproduction of Human Focality.' In S. Bamford (ed.), op. cit.

Weiner, J., 1986. 'The Social Organization of Foi Silk Production: The Anthropology of Marginal Development.' *Journal of the Polynesian Society* 85(4): 421–439.

———, 1988a. *The Heart of the Pearl Shell.* Berkeley: University of California Press.

——— (ed.), 1988b. *Mountain Papuans: Historical and Comparative Perspectives on New Guinea Fringe Highlands Societies.* Ann Arbor: University of Michigan Press.

———, 1998. 'The Incorporated Ground: The Contemporary Work of Distribution in the Kutubu Oil Project Area.' Canberra: Australian National University, Resource Management in Asia-Pacific Project (Working Paper 17).

———, 2001. 'Afterword.' In A. Rumsey and J. Weiner (eds), *Emplaced Myth: The Spatial and Narrative Dimensions of Knowledge in Australia and Papua New Guinea.* Honolulu: University of Hawai'i Press.

——— and K. Glaskin, 2006. 'Introduction: The (Re-)Invention of Indigenous Laws and Customs.' In J. F. Weiner and K. Glaskin (eds), *Custom: Indigenous Tradition and Law in the 21st Century.* Special Issue 7(1) of *The Asia Pacific Journal of Anthropology.*

Chapter Eight

Local Custom and the Art of Land Group Boundary Maintenance in Papua New Guinea

Colin Filer

A variety of agencies engaged in the business of developing (or even conserving) the natural resources which are located on, in, or underneath the huge swathe of customary land in Papua New Guinea (PNG) must also deal with the absence of any systematic record of the social or territorial boundaries of the 'land groups' which are generally thought to be the collective owners of such land. The strategies which they adopt to make amends for this deficiency are shaped, not only by those national laws and policies which apply to the ownership of customary land, but also by those which regulate the distribution of compensation payments and community benefits to customary landowners within specific resource sectors. At the same time, the past experience and future prospect of such deals and dispensations has its own effect on the way that 'land groups', 'land boundaries', and 'group boundaries' are represented in the mental landscape of the actors who negotiate them, whether at the level of the village or the level of the state.

In this chapter, I propose to examine the interaction of law, policy and ideology in the social construction of 'land groups', 'land boundaries', and 'group boundaries' with reference to specific moments in the recent history of 'resource development' in PNG. Here we find a long debate about the significance of 'customary land law' which reveals the existence of at least two distinct forms of agrarian populism opposed to the resource-dependent form of capitalist development which has come to dominate the nation's formal economy. Here we also find that institutional mechanisms originally established to facilitate the growth of an indigenous peasant economy have since been applied to an entirely different business, which is the validation of 'landowner consent', the accountability of 'landowner companies', and the distribution of 'landowner benefits', first in the petroleum and forestry sectors, and much more recently (and only partially) in the mining and agricultural sectors, of this resource-dependent economy.

It was in the petroleum sector that I first encountered the concept of 'land group maintenance', when I was part of a formal policy process whose remit was to rationalise the distribution of landowner benefits to an increasingly disorganised array of beneficiaries. I have added the word 'boundary' to the title of my chapter, because the relationship between land boundaries, group boundaries and benefit distribution was the fundamental point at issue in this process. The art or practice of land group boundary maintenance also counts as an example of the management, manipulation or negotiation of a thing called 'custom' in the name of another thing called 'development'. This, it might be said, is nothing but the art of the impossible, because there is no way of reconciling custom with development, either in theory or in practice. But I would argue that this opposition or antithesis is broken down and reconstructed in those practices of management and resistance which belong to real and specific social relations. It is not a gulf which exists *outside* of these relations, and which can therefore cause them to vanish in that world of wishful thinking where 'custom' is the light by which 'development' is shown to be a false god not worth worshipping.

Land, Groups, and Boundaries as Elements of 'Custom'

When anthropologists reflect on the topic of customary land tenure in Melanesia, their reflections are often configured in terms of the triangular relationship between 'land', 'groups', and 'boundaries', or the tripartite relationship between landowning groups, land boundaries, and group boundaries. The sort of question which arises from this configuration is whether it makes more sense to say that land belongs to groups or groups belong to land. This question can be rephrased by asking whether land boundaries are more or less substantial, flexible, or porous than group boundaries. Should we say that the central feature of the customary 'system' of land (or resource) tenure is the division of the physical landscape into named parts, to which human beings are attached by various means, or through which they move by various routes? Or should we say that the central feature of the system is the division of the social landscape into named social groups, which exercise various kinds of rights over pieces of land or other physical resources? Some anthropologists may think of these as purely *ethnographic* questions about the variable nature of 'local custom', but they are also questions posed and partially resolved in the realm of public policy, where 'local custom' is incorporated into the regulation of a modern economy.

If anthropologists turn their attention to the *Land Groups Incorporation Act* (*LGIA*), enacted by PNG's House of Assembly in 1974, they find that the Act is configured in terms of the triangular relationship between 'land', 'groups', and 'custom', in the sense that it provides an avenue for the legal recognition of customary land groups by means of their 'incorporation'. But the Act makes no mention of 'boundaries'. It makes no provision for the demarcation of land boundaries, and is as vague as any law could be about the nature of the 'custom' which determines the membership, and therefore the boundaries, of the land groups which can be incorporated. In other words, the Act underlines the significance of the questions which anthropologists would normally want to ask about customary land tenure, but carefully refrains from giving any kind of answer.

While the *LGIA* has nothing to say about the demarcation of customary land boundaries or the registration of customary land titles, it does seem to assume that the process of legal 'incorporation' will help customary land groups to 'develop' their land. So if the Act fails to answer questions about customary land tenure, it does raise other questions about the triangular relationship between 'custom', 'law' and 'development'. These are also questions of interest to anthropologists. But when anthropologists try to interpret the significance of a law like this by finding answers to such questions, they often seem to arrive at a dead end, which is a portrait of 'custom' as a distinctly Melanesian way of reflecting on a generic process of modernisation, commercialisation or globalisation (Keesing and Tonkinson 1982; Errington and Gewertz 1995; Foster 1995). Speakers of the Neo-Melanesian language may talk about 'custom' (*kastom* or *kastam*) in ways that sound quite exotic to Western ears, but that does not prevent customary law from being part of a national discourse of development in which Western voices also participate — and these are not just the voices of ethnographers. The *LGIA* was one of a number of laws enacted around the time of Independence which purported to make a contribution to the fifth goal of the National Constitution, which was 'to achieve development primarily through the use of Papua New Guinean forms of social, political and economic organisation' (see Fingleton, this volume). Many anthropologists would argue that any attempt to insert or transform Melanesian custom into state law is doomed to failure, precisely because the state itself is a European imposition on Melanesian custom, and not an indigenous form of political organisation. Some lawyers might agree with them, but lawyers are also adept at the art of making fine distinctions. Robert Cooter, for example, would agree that the State of PNG is not in a position to make effective use of national laws which aim to incorporate customary land groups or register customary land titles, but if local and district court magistrates make sensible judgements when customary land rights are disputed, then Melanesian custom will slowly turn into a Melanesian form of common law, in the same way that ancient English custom evolved into English common law (Cooter 1989).

The point at issue here is not the flexibility of custom, but the form of its relationship to law. My argument would be that Melanesian custom does not really *exist* in a form which would allow us to ask how it could or should be recognised in modern national law, because it was actually born out of the armpit of Australian colonial law. This is not to deny the possibility of reconstructing the form of social practice which preceded the colonial intrusion, but rather to assert that the *concept* of 'custom', as an object of contemporary thought and practice, as a 'road' which is distinct from other roads, is something which only makes its appearance at the end of the colonial period, and which could only make its appearance when 'truly traditional' or pre-colonial forms of social practice had already been consigned to the far horizon of the late colonial imagination (Filer 1990, 2006a). In other words, custom needs here to be conceived as something which develops *out of* law, not something which develops *into* it. And this is simply one aspect of the wider form of 'development' through which colonial capitalism develops into something else — whatever that might be.

We can put this point about custom in another way, if we say that the 'vertical' relationship between landowners and developers has long since subsumed the 'horizontal' relationship between 'traditional' political communities, and then go on to observe that the internal constitution of the 'landowning community', which now reflects this vertical relationship, has likewise overwritten the 'traditional' networks of social reciprocity which once dissected and shaped these local political boundaries.[1] So custom is not the starting point for a journey along the road, or down the river, which is called 'development'. Custom is a diversion from that road, or an island situated in the middle of that river, a subordinate feature of a more general set of social relations. To go further down this road or river, we may think about the construction or negotiation of 'custom' as something which takes place within the *several* forms of 'development' which exist at the intersection of different branches of production (or economic sectors), social formations (which might be construed in either political or cultural terms), and stages or periods in the history of the global capitalist system.

As for customary land tenure, we need to recognise that 'land', 'groups', and 'boundaries' are things which were initially removed, abstracted or alienated from the traditional social landscape by the policy and practice of colonial administration (MacWilliam 1988). The shape of their triangular relationship then became part of the further removal, abstraction or alienation of custom from law in the subsequent process of 'national development'. Instead of thinking about the tripartite social construction of 'land groups', 'land boundaries', and 'group boundaries' as a recoverable form of 'custom', or as a sort of bridge between 'custom' and 'development', I propose to think of it as a pattern which exists *inside* that form of development which is commonly called 'resource development', and thus reflects that tripartite social relationship between Developers, Landowners and the State which I call 'resource compensation' (Filer 1997).

---

[1] The tradition of analysis which regards the superficial appearance of Melanesian social groups, and even Melanesian persons, as the icing on the cake of 'unbounded' social relationships (Wagner 1974) may neglect to consider the extent to which the inherent flexibility or adaptability of these social relationships has enabled them to take the forces of 'development' to their very core.

Compensation and Incorporation in the Realm of Heavy Industry

The trouble with the concept of 'resource development' is that it sounds like a specific form of the general concept of 'development'. But 'development' is just a fairly recent name for what Adam Smith called 'the wealth of nations', which is nowadays measured by a pile of social and economic indicators. We do not have to deconstruct this general concept in order to recognise that 'resource development' is a very different kind of thing. It is a type of *industrial process* which involves the transformation of natural resources into commodities. And the relative preponderance of this type of industrial process within a country's national economy is, if anything, inversely correlated with that country's general level of 'development'. Hence the so-called 'resource curse' or condition of 'resource dependency' which may be seen as an affliction rather than a contribution to national welfare (Auty 1993; Ross 1999; Sachs and Warner 2001; Bannon and Collier 2003). But the concept of 'resource dependency' also has its drawbacks, because it seems to condemn the 'developing countries' which suffer this affliction to a state of backwardness from which they cannot escape, and draws attention away from the struggles which occur between 'resource developers' and other 'stakeholders' in the relations of production which surround this peculiar type of industrial process (Ascher 2005; Banks 2005; Filer 2006b). And that is why I propose to use the term 'resource compensation', which better serves to highlight the tension between dependency and autonomy which is embedded in the heart of these relations of production.

Where Marx formerly discovered the relationship of wage-labour (or employment) buried within the pile of money and commodities which formed the superficial pattern of the capitalist world, I would argue that this relationship of compensation is the partly hidden 'secret' of the much smaller pile of money and commodities which is currently found on customary land in PNG, *insofar as* this pile of money and commodities emerges from the jaws of what I should now like to describe as the Melanesian version of 'heavy industry'. This creature has four legs, or four component branches of production — the oil (and gas) industry, the mining industry, the timber (or logging) industry, and the oil palm industry.[2] The resources transacted through the relationship of compensation are thus rights to extract oil, gas and minerals contained in the ground, the timber contained in the trees which grow on top of it, and the nutrients contained in the soil itself. All four types of heavy industry entail large-scale investment in plant and machinery, but their 'heaviness' can also be ascribed to the problem of managing relationships with customary owners of the land on which these

---

[2] A case could be made for inclusion of the sugar industry, the rubber industry, and even parts of the fishing industry within the same economic complex, but I exclude these from consideration here in order to simplify the broad outline of my argument.

investments are made. And that is why the agencies responsible for managing these relationships in all four branches of production have been obliged to think about the merits of land group incorporation as a management strategy.

The products of heavy industry, as thus defined, have accounted for 80–90 per cent of PNG's annual export earnings over the past decade. While this fact alone provides us with an indication of its significance to the national economy, and more especially to the revenues of the national government, my definition clearly flies in the face of the orthodox argument that agriculture is the real backbone of the national economy because of the vast numbers of people who make a living from it and the sheer volume of land which is devoted to it. But I would argue that the oil palm industry is distinguished from other branches of agricultural production by virtue of its scale, its 'modernity', and the peculiar nature of its relations of production, which cause it to resemble the three terrestrial branches of extractive industry rather more than it resembles the colonial plantation economy (which already lies in ruins) and those forms of export crop production (notably coffee and cocoa) which are dominated by a smallholding 'peasantry'.[3]

Of course, the four legs of this new-fangled beast all have their own peculiar characteristics. But before I touch on these peculiarities, I shall try to establish the general shape of the beast itself, and thus show how Landowners come to be 'incorporated' into it.

As Landowners and Developers enter into their mutual relationship, the State does two things (apart from any role which it may play as a joint venture partner). First, it takes certain rights away from the Landowners, by mutual agreement, not by compulsion, and it hands on these rights to the Developers. This enables the Developers to begin the process of development. Then the State takes a share of the proceeds away from the Developers, by means of taxation, and hands a smaller portion of the proceeds back to the Landowners, in the form of 'benefits' which compensate the Landowners for the previous diminution of their rights.[4] At the same time, the Developers also 'compensate' the Landowners directly, by providing them with a mixture of 'compensation' payments for damage done to their resources and additional 'benefits' which are intended to maintain the relationship in good working order. The Landowners themselves may not recognise the distinction between 'compensation' and 'benefits', nor even the distinction between the benefits which come from the Developers and those which come from the State. The whole package simply represents their share of

---

[3] Palm oil has accounted for something between one quarter and one third of annual agricultural export earnings over the last decade.

[4] The balance of the 'resource rent' is redistributed between different parts of the State, and sooner or later finds its way back into private pockets, by fair means or foul, but this aspect of the relationship does not concern me here.

the income, or their part of the relationship, which comes from the development of 'their' resources.[5]

The Developers equate the 'development' of natural resources with the consumption or extraction of those resources, and thus see 'landowner compensation' in the same light as 'community relations' — as a cost which has to be incurred in order to achieve this form of 'development' (Filer et al. 2000: 3). The Landowners, for their part, equate the 'development' of *their* resources with their own social, political and economic advancement to a level at which they can truly imagine themselves to be the equals of the Developers, so that 'compensation' becomes what one Lihir landowner famously described as 'the state of equilibrium reached when [the] forces of destruction and impact must [be] equal to the forces of compensation ... [so that] the Landowners are forever happy and accept the losses and impact they will suffer' (Filer 1997: 160).[6]

But an 'Integrated Benefits Package' which is intended to achieve this equation of 'compensation' and 'development' also has to be distributed amongst the Landowners who receive it. This is not just a problem for the Landowners to solve by themselves. It is also a problem for which the State and the Developers are obliged to offer their own solutions. That is because their understanding and experience of the process of development on customary land has led them to conclude that they must also do something to manage the 'internal' relationships of the landowning 'community' which has been brought into existence by this process, and even the 'external' relationships between this local community and those other 'landowners' who live around the edges of it.

Where the State attempts to manage these additional relationships, its efforts could be seen as an extension of its efforts to manage the relationship between Developers and Landowners. But there is a further element of complexity here, which arises from the State's diminishing capacity to manage anything at all, and which raises the question of whether there really are three parties to this relationship, or only two. It is often the Developers who have to manage the relationship between the State and the Landowners, as well as their own relationship with the State, even to the extent of 'facilitating' the process by which the State acquires the rights which it later passes on to the Developers themselves. And where the State is unable to manage the relationships within and between local communities in the vicinity of the development, the Developers

---

[5] The laws of PNG declare that subsurface mineral resources are the property of the State, but the State has been forced to deal with Landowners in a manner that seems to deny this claim (Filer 2005).

[6] Once the definition of 'compensation' is expanded to include or subsume the relationship of employment, where Developers employ Landowners within the context of their mutual relationship, then we can say that compensation is truly a relation of *production*, in the Marxist sense, because it combines specific forms of property and work under the same umbrella.

may have to extend their own efforts to manage these relationships to the point of compensating for the State's failure to do so.[7]

Nor are the Landowners themselves purely passive recipients of all this 'management' (or mismanagement). While some Landowners try to manage (or mismanage) the 'compensation package' which is meant for all Landowners, some Landowners also try to counter the management strategies of both the State and the Developers with management strategies of their own, which might better be described as political strategies intended to enlarge their control over the total distribution of wealth, status and power within the development relationship. Indeed, all three parties have a tendency to *interfere* with whatever management strategies or political strategies are adopted by the other two, thus enveloping the relationship in a kind of mutual frustration which tends to defeat the 'rationality' of management itself. And so life goes on.

Now this relationship, with all its complexities, can be construed as a sort of bargain, or a sort of game, which is the way that economists are inclined to see it (McGavin 1994). However, it is not my purpose here to elaborate on the general form of the negotiation which takes place between the agents of each party, but rather to pinpoint the role which is played by the practice of 'land group incorporation' as a method of managing land, groups, boundaries, or benefits.

We can think of 'incorporation', in a general sense, as one of the transformations which are inherent in the social impact of resource development or the social relationship of resource compensation. I am not suggesting that incorporation, in this general sense, is necessarily something which the State or the Developers impose upon the Landowners as a condition of their mutual relationship. Landowners have ways of organising themselves, most obviously through the formation of landowner companies and landowner associations, and many other ways of being organised by politicians who claim to represent their interests. But *land group* incorporation, considered as a specific and variable feature of this relationship within the realm of heavy industry, *has been* promoted by the State and the Developers for reasons which we now need to consider in greater depth.

The Brave New World of Customary Land Law

More than half a century has passed since Paul Hasluck, in his capacity as the Australian government minister responsible for the Territory of Papua and New Guinea, decided that its economic development would necessitate 'a change in

---

[7] Power (2000[1]: 86–7) has given voice to their frustration at this prospect: 'The Government just sits back and expects the developer to make things happen. The landowners expect everything to be done for them because the developer is on their land. The developer is reluctant to take over what they [sic] see as the role of the Government … What is needed is a shift in the way the developer and the Government do business. It requires the taking on of a new mental model where development is part of the package that is traded for resource commodities.'

the basic native concepts of rights to use, occupy or cultivate land' (Hasluck 1976: 126).[8] A legal framework for the registration of 'native' land or 'customary' land had already been introduced in 1952, and the *Land Tenure (Conversion) Act* of 1963 provided a further opportunity for members of landowning communities to secure individual title by mutual agreement with their fellow members. But these measures did not have the effect of 'liberating' large areas of customary land from the constraints of custom, even if that was their intention (Simpson 1971: 7). Instead, many of the traditional owners of land which had been alienated for agricultural purposes during the early colonial period were agitating for its resumption, and their cause was espoused by the more vocal 'native' members of the House of Assembly during the 1960s. One of the first landmarks in the transition to Independence was the establishment, in 1972, of a Commission of Inquiry into Land Matters (CILM) whose membership was entirely indigenous, even though the support staff were all expatriates (Fingleton 1981; Ward 1983). The CILM's reassertion of the primacy of customary title was confirmed by several provisions of the National Constitution, by the *LGIA* of 1974, which was intended to facilitate the resumption of alienated land, and by the *Land Disputes Settlement Act* of 1975, which established a system of Local and District Land Courts to resolve disputes over customary title (see Fingleton, this volume).

At the time when the CILM was making its deliberations, it was calculated that three per cent of PNG's land area had been alienated, while 97 per cent remained under customary tenure. For the last 25 years, these figures have been repeated with such frequency, and circulated so widely, that they now count as 'common knowledge'. If true, this would seem to indicate that the CILM was at least successful in defending customary land from any further acts of alienation, and might even be taken to indicate that the whole system of land tenure has been set in some kind of post-colonial concrete. By 1989, however, the 600,000 hectares of alienated land which could still be found in the records of the Lands Department was more like 1.3 per cent of the total surface area (Larmour 1991; Turtle 1991), which would suggest that a substantial proportion of land formerly alienated to the colonial plantation economy had already reverted to customary ownership or control. And this estimate was made before the plantations on Bougainville were effectively 'resumed' in the wake of the 1989 rebellion.

But the legal instruments established on the recommendations of the CILM seem to have been no more effective in facilitating this process of resumption than the legal instruments of the late colonial administration had been in facilitating the creation of a class of small freeholders. Fifteen years after the passage of the *Land Tenure (Conversion) Act*, less than 10,000 hectares of land

---

[8] Hasluck announced his new land policy in 1960, but this statement was based on the report of a working party which he had established four years previously (Morawetz 1967: 3).

had been subject to legal tenure conversion (Cooter 1989). Fifteen years after the passage of the *LGIA*, only eight land groups had been incorporated under the Act (Whimp 1995). In both cases, the *demand* for conversion or incorporation was much greater than the capacity of relevant government agencies to meet it. One might therefore speculate that the net 'loss' of alienated land was as much a function of the loss of record-keeping capacity in the Lands Department as it was a function of a more substantial social process.

This is not the only respect in which the noble goals of the CILM were subverted by the force of bureaucratic inertia. The *LGIA* placed particular emphasis on the constitution of customary groups, rather than the ownership of customary land, because the CILM had recommended a separate piece of legislation for the demarcation and registration of customary land (Taylor and Whimp 1997; Fingleton, this volume). This was intended to supplant the legal mandate of the Land Titles Commission, whose own attempts to demarcate and register customary titles during the late colonial period had not met with great success (Morawetz 1967; Hide 1973; Jessep 1980). The same recommendation was repeated, 10 years later, by a national government Task Force on Customary Land Issues, and the buck was then passed to the Land Mobilisation Programme, whose achievements included the counting of those 600,000 hectares of alienated land. But the only piece of legislation which ever reached the statute books was in the 'pilot province' of East Sepik, where the provincial government enacted a *Customary Land Registration Act* in 1987 (Fingleton 1991, this volume; Power 1991).

In retrospect, it is worth noting that much of the academic and public debate on the subject of customary land tenure during the first 15 years of national independence, from 1975 to 1990, was constructed around the assumption that agriculture was indeed the backbone of the national economy. A substantial part of the debate therefore concentrated on the ancient question of whether customary tenure was or was not an obstacle to the development of capitalist agriculture, and sought to assess the motives and capacities of those groups or classes — rich peasants and poor peasants, largeholders and smallholders, indigenous and foreign members of the bourgeoisie, or simply 'capital' and 'households' — who were trying to push the boundary between customary and alienated land in one direction or another (Hulme 1983; Donaldson and Good 1988; MacWilliam 1988). Even those commentators who eschewed the language of class struggle were primarily concerned with the question of what the State could or should do, by means of policy or legislation, to meet the material needs and aspirations of landowners whose main economic activity was farming or gardening (Cooter 1989; Ward 1991).

While the territorial expansion of small-scale commercial agriculture has almost certainly been one of the main forces behind the apparent resumption of alienated land, this has not made any impact on the territorial expansion of the four branches of heavy industry. Their occupation of customary land does not entail the liquidation of customary title, but depends on various forms of partial and temporary 'alienation' which are allowed by the laws pertaining to each sector. The mining companies get Exploration and Mining Leases, the oil companies get Petroleum Prospecting and Development Licences, the logging companies get Timber Permits, and the oil palm companies have come to rely on the so-called the 'lease-leaseback' clause in the *Land Act* which was originally meant to facilitate the establishment of 20-hectare coffee blocks in the central highlands (McKillop 1991). Once we escape the blinkers imposed by the technicalities of land law, we can see that the social dynamics of the 'customary' landscape are not determined by the capacity of customary landowners to resist or roll back the process of alienation, but rather by their capacity to enter into, and benefit from, the social relations of compensation which reflect and condition the process of resource development.

If the CILM did not intend the *LGIA* to function as a surrogate for the demarcation and registration of customary land titles, its members also failed to imagine the use which the State and the Developers would eventually make of this law in their efforts to manage 'community relations' in the sphere of heavy industry (Sinaka Goava, personal communication, September 1998). While their report did envisage the possibility that Incorporated Land Groups (ILGs) might serve as a vehicle for landowner participation in the development of forestry projects, it expressed grave reservations about the degree of freedom which was apparently granted to landowners by the *Forestry (Private Dealings) Act* of 1971. This law allowed customary landowners to bypass the provisions of the *Forestry Act* by selling timber rights to a landowner company under the terms of a Dealings Agreement, which only required the assent of the Forests Minister, and allowed the landowner company to enter into a Logging and Marketing Agreement with a logging contractor, who was then able to extract and sell the logs with minimal government supervision.

To the best of my knowledge, no land groups were ever incorporated for this purpose.[9] In 1989, a Commission of Inquiry into Aspects of the Forest Industry (the Barnett Inquiry) found that the *Forestry (Private Dealings) Act* had simply enabled logging companies to cheat local landowners of the benefits promised in the Logging and Marketing Agreements, and recommended that the law should be repealed (Barnett 1992). And so it was, with the passage of a new *Forestry Act* in 1991. The closure of this 'loophole' is significant because it underlines one of the main points of convergence in the social relations of

---

[9] Only eight land groups were incorporated in the eight years following the passage of the *LGIA* (Taylor and Whimp 1997: 77), and most of these were formed to take advantage of the Plantation Redistribution Scheme (Ward 1991: 184).

resource development on customary land, which is not so much the conflict of interest between Developers and Landowners, but the manner in which a steadily disintegrating State continues to interpose itself as a sort of 'middle-man' in the legal form of their relationship. The forest industry was thus restored to its 'rightful place' as one of the four branches of heavy industry which are firmly attached to the trunk of resource compensation.

The new *Forestry Act* also gave a new lease of life to the *LGIA*. However, the forest industry was not the first branch of heavy industry to accomplish this feat, and the process of land group incorporation does not have the same history or significance in each of the four branches. The common point of departure was the criticism levelled, by some individuals associated with some branches of industry, against the provision of the *Land Act* which allowed (and still allows) the Land Titles Commission or a Local Land Court to appoint 'agents' to act on behalf of undefined and unincorporated groups of customary landowners. Once appointed, these agents had (and still have) the power to transfer all manner of rights to the State, and to 'accept any rent, purchase money, compensation or other moneys [sic] or things, and distribute that money or those things to the persons entitled', whoever they might be. The law has assumed that these agents should be 'customary leaders' of some sort, but has never sought to specify the customs which create or regulate their leadership, nor even the type of customary group which they should be taken to represent (Taylor and Whimp 1997). The advocates of land group incorporation regard the process of incorporation as a way of saving custom from abuse by self-appointed leaders whose pursuit of 'rent, purchase money, compensation or other moneys' has no customary sanction. But how has this argument actually made its way through the four branches of heavy industry, why has it made more progress in some branches than in others, and what have been the practical effects of its partial success?

Land Group Incorporation in the Petroleum and Forestry Sectors, 1990–95

1989 was a good year for anyone who had a ready-made solution to the problem of managing the social relations of resource compensation — not just because of the Barnett Inquiry, but also because of the Bougainville rebellion. While Barnett (1989: 368) found that landowners were 'gaining a maximum of dislocation and alienation in exchange for minimum benefit from the harvesting of their timber', Francis Ona and the other members of the new Panguna Landowners Association had come to a very similar conclusion with respect to the harvesting of copper from their land. What I wrote about the 'titleholders' whom the Land Titles Commission had appointed as agents of the Panguna landowners could just as well have been written about the 'clan agents' who had been responsible for signing Timber Rights Purchase Agreements with the

Department of Forests, or Dealings Agreements with the directors of 'their' landowner companies:

> Although the titleholders constitute a relatively small minority within the landowning community, there is no outside interest in the question of whether and how they will use these monies for the benefit and satisfaction of their respective family groups. It has evidently been assumed that 'customary' norms of distribution and consumption will apply to this new form of wealth, and this will raise no special problems for the company or for the government. But the complaints of the new PLA have shown that this assumption is false. The titleholders stand accused of keeping all the money to themselves, not even giving any to their closest relatives. If this is true, it might be taken as a sign of selfishness or greed, but I suggest that it may also be a sign of something else — the simple absence of a custom which prescribes the proper way to redistribute rent (Filer 1990: 90).

Of course, the Bougainville rebellion showed that the stakes were much higher, and the consequences could be far more serious, in the mining sector than in the forestry sector. But it also added some serious weight to the argument that dysfunctional 'clan agents' were only one part of a larger problem, that landowner organisations of all sorts were suffering from a serious lack of democracy, transparency and accountability, that their directors or managers were ripping off the ordinary members, shareholders or beneficiaries, and that the State had better do something about it.

It is therefore somewhat ironic that the first application of the *LGIA* to the problem of managing the social relations of resource compensation was neither made in the mining sector nor made by the State. It began in April 1990, when Chevron Niugini Limited (CNGL) appointed Tony Power as its Business Development Manager, or perhaps in May 1990, when the company formally lodged its application for the Kutubu Petroleum Development Licence and Pipeline Licence, and began to prepare the ground for project construction.[10] Power was able to persuade the Developer, and then able to persuade the State, that the royalty and equity benefits due to the customary owners of both licence areas should only be paid to ILGs, and that these groups should be the sole shareholders of the landowner companies which were due to receive the benefits of CNGL's Business Development Program. In the five years following his appointment, he masterminded the incorporation of more than 400 land groups in the project impact area.

Power had become an advocate of land group incorporation during his previous incarnation as a senior bureaucrat in the Department of East Sepik

---

[10] The licences were granted at the end of 1990, and the oil began to flow in mid-1992.

Province,[11] where he had played a key role in promoting the *Provincial Land Act* and the *Customary Land Registration Act* which were passed in 1987 (Power 1991; Fingleton, this volume). Having departed the ranks of the bureaucracy in 1988, he initially entered the petroleum sector as a consultant to Oil Search and Ampolex, which were both partners in the Kutubu Joint Venture. It was from this vantage point that he began, in his own words, to 'fight bloody hard' to make ILGs into an essential feature of the Kutubu project landscape (Tony Power, personal communication, September 2000). By November 1989, he was able to announce the first signs of his impending victory, and this was done at a forest policy seminar held at the Forest Research Institute (Power and Waiko 1990: 46). That meeting was part of the policy reform process engendered by the findings of the Barnett Inquiry, and Power believes that his own intervention in this process was partly responsible for that part of the 1991 National Forest Policy which requires, as a precondition of any future Forest Management Agreement between local resource owners and the State, that

> Tenure over the resource must be made certain by: title to the affected resource being vested in a Land Group or Groups under the Land Groups Incorporation Act, or title to the resource being registered under a customary land registration law; or where the above two options are impractical — at least 75% of customary resource owners in each clan owning timber affected by the agreement must give their written assent to the Agreement (PNGMoF 1991: 17).

The process of 'resource acquisition' prescribed in Sections 54–60 of the 1991 *Forestry Act* reiterated this requirement.

This meant that the function of land group incorporation in the forestry sector was quite different to the function which it performed in the development of the Kutubu oil project. In one case, a Developer was persuaded to incorporate Landowners as part of a strategy designed to promote the values of equity, transparency and accountability in the distribution of project benefits, and the Developer then had to persuade the State to set its own seal of approval on this strategy, at a time when the *LGIA* did not rate a mention in any of the laws and policies which regulated the petroleum sector. In the other case, the State was persuaded to incorporate Landowners as part of a policy and a law which were intended to produce a certain level of 'informed consent' to the State's acquisition of the right to harvest their timber resources, and to protect Landowners from Developers who had proven adept at manipulating the appearance of such consent to their own advantage.

---

[11] He was appointed as Provincial Planner in 1982, and later became the First Assistant Secretary for Economic Services.

When the new *Forestry Act* was finally gazetted and implemented in 1992, officers of the newly designated National Forest Service were thus confronted with a task which was already taxing the patience and resources of a multinational oil company, and were expected to perform this task in many different parts of the country. If this were not daunting enough, the 1993 National Forestry Development Guidelines indicated that the process of land group incorporation should be preceded or accompanied by a Landowner Awareness Programme which would provide landowners with the information required for them to make their own assessment of 'the likely costs and benefits, impacts and responsibilities associated with a forest development project' and enable them to 'truly participate in the project formulation process and ensure that it is sensitive to their needs and concerns' (PNGMoF 1993: 4). But help was at hand, in the shape of a Forest Management and Planning Project organised by the World Bank as part of the National Forestry and Conservation Action Programme. This project included a 'Landowner Involvement Component' which was meant to strengthen the capacity of the National Forest Service to practice the arts of land group incorporation and landowner awareness (PNGFMPP 1995). In a fitting tribute to his own experience at Kutubu, Tony Power was one of several consultants engaged to implement this project component. His manual of procedure, entitled 'Village Guide to Land Group Incorporation', was printed and circulated in March 1995 (Power 1995).

In the three years which had then elapsed since the function of land group registration was transferred from the Registrar of Companies to the Department of Lands and Physical Planning, 700 land groups had already been registered, and another 500 applications were awaiting the department's attention (Whimp 1995: 71). These figures suggest that officers of the National Forest Service had already completed the fieldwork and paperwork required to register more land groups than had so far been registered through the efforts of their counterparts in CNGL. On the other hand, none of the Forest Management Agreements which resulted from this process had formed the basis of a new timber concession. The first Timber Permit issued under the new *Forestry Act* was granted in June 1995, as an 'extension' of the permit already held by Turama Forest Industries in Gulf Province. And it seems that the logging company played a fairly active role in the process of land group incorporation which laid the ground for the Turama Forest Management Agreement (Hartmut Holzknecht, personal communication, March 1997). At any rate, some local NGOs referred the decision of the National Forest Board to the Ombudsman Commission, which eventually found (in August 1997) that there had indeed been some breach of the procedures laid down in the *Forestry Act*.

This dispute served to confirm the fear previously expressed by the Forest Industries Association, that the long drawn out process of land group incorporation had another, 'latent' function, beside the function of protecting the property rights of innocent landowners. This other function was to implement one of the key recommendations of the Barnett Inquiry, which was to 'slow down' the whole process of resource acquisition and allocation in the forestry sector while new forms and standards of regulation were applied to existing concessions. The very small volume of timber resources which has since been allocated through the production of Forest Management Agreements and the distribution of new Timber Permits would seem to support this interpretation (IFRT 2001, 2004). But this means that hundreds of land groups which have been incorporated through the bureaucratic efforts of the National Forest Service have yet to complete their passage into the social relations of resource compensation in the logging industry, even if they wish to do so. That is because most logging operations are still governed by agreements signed under the previous legislation, and most of the payments or benefits which they yield for local landowners are still distributed to the clan agents and landowner company directors who signed these agreements.

Land Groups in the Oil and Gas Act, 1998

The question of how to regulate the distribution of project benefits, and the question of how local landowners should be organised and represented in the process of distribution, became a major issue for the local petroleum industry in 1997. There were several reasons for this. Firstly, the Chan government had changed the rules of this game in 1995 and 1996, by proposing to grant local landowners 100 per cent of the royalties which the State would henceforth collect from the developers of new projects in both the mining and petroleum sectors, together with a 'free' two per cent share of project equity whose cost would be shared by the other joint venture partners in proportion to their own stakes in the project. At the same time, the 1995 *Organic Law on Provincial Governments and Local-Level Governments* created an entirely new set of financial relationships between the three tiers of the State, but took not the slightest account of the relationships already embodied in the development agreements for mining and petroleum projects. And to make matters even more confusing, the new Organic Law required all resource developers to pay a new kind of tax, to be known as 'development levies', to the provincial and local-level governments hosting their operations, but did not specify the manner in which this liability was to be calculated (Filer and Imbun 2004).

These innovations caused more concern in the petroleum sector than in the mining sector, because the agreements covering development of the Lihir gold mine had already been concluded, and there were no other major mining projects whose development conditions were still subject to active negotiation. In the petroleum sector, by contrast, the stakeholders were still negotiating the division of the spoils from the Gobe project, whose flow of oil was in the process of being added to that of the Kutubu project. The Draft Memorandum of Agreement between the State and Gobe Project Area Landowners, produced in January 1997, was a model of the muddle which now afflicted the social relations of resource compensation in this sector. And to make matters worse, three years of legal disputation had still failed to determine who actually counted as a Gobe Project Area Landowner in the first place.

Under the draft Gobe agreement, landowner benefits were to be distributed between local 'clans' in proportion to the amount of land which they owned within the boundaries of the Petroleum Development Licence (PDL), and then subdivided between a number of ILGs in each 'clan' in proportion to the number of members which they contained (Taylor and Whimp 1997: 81). This principle of distribution was at variance with the one adopted in the Kutubu project agreements, where the benefits were distributed equally between all the land groups which owned any amount of land within the boundaries of the PDL, or any section of the route taken by the export pipeline.[12] But by 1997, the Kutubu principle had already given rise to a predictable problem: the original land groups were splitting into smaller land groups, and some 'spurious' land groups were being manufactured in the process.[13] Hence the call for CNGL to invest more time and money in the art of 'land group maintenance' (see Weiner 1998, this volume; Goldman, this volume).

The final, and perhaps the most important, reason for rethinking and reconstructing the social relations of compensation in the petroleum industry was the existence of two proposals to develop the reserves of natural gas which had been found in association with the oil now flowing down the export pipeline. Both proposals would entail a very substantial amount of fresh capital investment, and both would yield a new 'benefit stream' of unprecedented size (CIE/NCDS 1997; Simpson et al. 1998). The addition of a gas industry to the existing oil industry demanded a new policy framework and a major overhaul of the 1977 *Petroleum Act*. If nothing were done to regulate the flow of benefits, the benefits might never flow at all, because one or both projects might drown in 'political risk'.

The 'interrelationships, roles, responsibilities and authorities of sectoral participants in relation to issues affecting the involvement of landowners in petroleum projects' were scrutinised in some detail by a pair of lawyers engaged under a Technical Assistance grant from the Asian Development Bank (Taylor

---

[12] The benefits were initially divided between language groups, in accordance with the proportion of the PDL area, or the length of the pipeline route, which was thought to lie within the territory of each group, and were then divided equally between the land groups within each language group. This arrangement was apparently the one preferred by landowner representatives in the development negotiations.

[13] This problem arose because the *LGIA* does not require land groups to have mutually exclusive membership lists, and the Registrar of Titles can only refuse to register a land group if it can be shown to be a 'non-customary' group (Taylor and Whimp 1997: 117-8).

and Whimp 1997). Their recommendations were subject to discussion by a number of 'sectoral participants' at a two-day seminar held in January 1998. The main target of their recommendations was the State's manner of dealing with landowners, though it was recognised that any major change to one side of the triangular relationship would necessarily have some impact on the other two. The State's position, or the State's quandary, was rather nicely expressed in the title of the seminar presentation by an official of the Department of National Planning and Implementation: 'Packaging MOA [Memorandum of Agreement] Projects as a Subsidiary or Small Public Investment Programme: A View to Impose and Instill Discipline and Development Consciousness in the Utilisation of Benefits Derived from Natural Resources for Equitable Distribution as Benefits to Landowners' (Lovuru 1998).

The outcome of this seminar was the establishment of an Action Team whose membership was drawn from those private companies and government agencies which had some stake in reformulating the 'benefit regime' in the petroleum sector. The main body of the Action Team held at least 15 meetings between March and June 1998, at which its members talked at length about the problem of establishing principles that would serve to rationalise the distribution of part of the national government's share of petroleum revenues between provincial governments, local-level governments, and local landowners in each project impact area. The fruit of these reflections was a set of drafting instructions for something to be called the *Petroleum (Project Benefits) Act*. Some members of the Action Team joined a smaller talking shop, which came to be known as the 'ILG Breakout Group', and which reflected on the riddles posed by the State's lack of capacity to make effective use of the *LGIA* as a vehicle for landowner organisation and benefit distribution. The conclusions of this smaller body were discussed at another two-day seminar held in September 1998.

Following one of the recommendations previously made by Taylor and Whimp (1997: 109), the Action Team suggested that the design of better models for distributing landowner benefits within a landowning 'community' should henceforth be based on 'social mapping studies' funded by developers as a condition of their prospecting licences. In my own capacity as a member of the Action Team, I drafted a document on this subject which proposed that:

- one of the aims of a 'preliminary' social mapping study would be to 'establish the basic principles of customary resource ownership and group formation in the licence area, with specific reference to the feasibility of incorporating local land groups under the Land Groups Incorporation Act' (Filer 1998b: 1); and
- one of the aims of a 'full-scale' social mapping study would be to 'recommend the principles and procedures to be adopted in the process of incorporating local land groups', *or else* present an argument against land group

incorporation, and 'recommend the most appropriate, and least contentious, alternative forms of representation or methods of distribution, which would be consistent with both: (a) local custom and practice; and (b) the principles established by government policy and national legislation' (ibid: 3).

Despite his unrepentant enthusiasm for the practice of land group incorporation, Tony Power was unable to persuade all other members of the Action Team that this practice should now be granted the force of legal necessity. Within the industry itself, there was a split between CNGL, in its capacity as operator of the Kutubu and Gobe projects, and British Petroleum (BP), in its capacity as operator of the Hides gas project, which had been developed as a source of power for the Porgera gold mine. The BP line was spelt out by one of the company's consultants, George Clapp, who argued that the Huli landowners of the Hides project were recalcitrant traditionalists who preferred to see their leaders divide up large amounts of cash by means of public ceremony, rather than be forced to reflect in private on

> the sad fact that in a PNG context where one has cheques put into accounts and signatories to those accounts, there will be fraud. By far the best method to ensure that some compensation monies trickle down to the grass roots level is to pay in cash and use the agent system. In that way the money is there for immediate division according to custom, the people know when it is going to be paid out and, although the leaders as agents may be entitled to keep some back, at least the larger proportion is divided out according to custom (Clapp 1998: 6).

In this respect, the Hides project simply followed the example set at Porgera, where the Ipili 'clan agents' were also accustomed to dealing with public scrutiny of periodic flows of cash. The Huli people were also seen to resemble the Ipili people in possessing a form of social organisation in which individuals could and did claim membership of more than one 'clan' (Burton 1991; Allen 1995; Golub, this volume), thus confounding the principle of mutual exclusion which had informed the original process of land group incorporation in the Kutubu project impact area.

Tony Power and other members of the ILG Breakout Group thought that the problem of multiple membership could be solved by means of a legal distinction between the 'controllers' and the 'beneficiaries' of each land group, so that individuals could have 'interests' in more than one land group without being members of more than one 'controlling group'. They also proposed a number of other amendments to the *LGIA* that were meant to discourage the registration of 'spurious groups', limit the opportunities for misappropriation of group funds, enable each group to lease parts of its estate to individual members or outsiders for business purposes, and strengthen the mechanism for resolving disputes within and between groups. But even if the Lands Department could be persuaded to persuade its minister to push this raft of amendments through Parliament, a very large question mark would still be left hanging over the State's capacity to supervise, support or 'maintain' an ever-expanding number of land groups.

In the event, no *Petroleum (Project Benefits) Bill* was ever presented to Parliament. Instead, some of the recommendations of the Action Team found their way into the *Oil and Gas Act* that was approved by Parliament in November 1998, while others were treated as matters of policy or regulation, and some were simply laid aside (Filer and Imbun 2004). This is not the place for a detailed discussion of what the new law had to say about the determination and distribution of landowner benefits, the conduct of social mapping studies, or their relationship to the 'landowner identification studies' that are also now required as preconditions for the issue of development licences in the petroleum sector. Suffice to say that the law follows the recommendations of the Action Team to the extent of saying that monetary benefits allocated by the State to project area landowners will normally be paid to ILGs 'unless otherwise agreed between the State and the grantees of the benefit or prescribed by law'. Under Section 169, social mapping and landowner identification studies are two of the bodies of evidence which are expected to guide the Minister in deciding which land groups, or which other 'persons or entities', are to receive these benefits on behalf of the landowners. Section 176 follows another recommendation of the Action Team by saying that these landowner benefits shall be divided between 'incorporated land groups or other representatives … in proportion to the number of project area landowners each represents'. In this respect, the law exhibits a preference for what I have called the 'Gobe model' rather than the 'Kutubu model', because it says that benefits should be distributed between land groups in proportion to the size of their membership, rather than the area of land which each group holds within a licence area.

But the irony of this preference is revealed in the addition of a new section (169A) in the *Oil and Gas (Amendment) Act* of 2001, which expressly relates to the distribution of benefits from 'existing petroleum projects' as well as from new ones. As in the original Section 169, there is a recognition that the identity of the landowners or their representatives may still be undecided or disputed, in which case the Minister is entitled to 'make a determination' in light of

> … any agreements by persons who are or claim to be project area landowners, the decisions of courts of Papua New Guinea as to ownership of land or rights in relation to land in the vicinity of the petroleum project in question, the results of social mapping and landowner identification studies carried out in accordance with this Act, and submissions from affected Local-level Governments or affected Provincial Governments of

the petroleum project in question or from any other person claiming an interest or to be affected by the decision of the Minister.

This long list of different kinds of evidence is itself evidence of the ongoing problems created by the policy and practice of land group incorporation in the oil and gas sector. And anyone reading the national newspapers in PNG will know that these problems remain especially acute in the relationship between the State and the people who claim to represent the Gobe project land groups.[14]

The Beast's Two Back Legs

There is little doubt that newspaper stories about the contested distribution of very large amounts of money to ILGs in the petroleum sector has encouraged a popular belief that land group incorporation is a way for customary landowners to gain access to the social relations of resource compensation, even when the prospect of actual resource development may be quite remote. For example, a crowd of more than 25,000 people is said to have assembled in one Eastern Highlands village to witness the presentation of a certificate of incorporation to a local landowner association whose members thought they had discovered oil in a lake and 'were currently working on formalities to enable them to sign a memorandum of agreement with a possible developer to carry out a feasibility study and exploration in the area' (*Post Courier*, 27 January 2005). According to Fingleton (2004: 101), there were more than 10,000 ILGs registered with the Department of Lands by March 2004, which is an awful lot more than the 700 which had been registered by March 1995. It is hardly possible to attribute the whole of this increase to the diligence of people employed to implement government policies, whether in the forestry and petroleum sectors or any other sector of the national economy. What we do know is that land group incorporation has been deliberately used to promote the expansion of the oil palm industry, but has found little or no favour with the administrators of the mining industry. This should lead us to ask whether the use of land group incorporation as a policy instrument is encouraged or constrained by structural factors specific to each branch of production, or whether its adoption has more to do with contingent historical factors. These contingencies might include the history of decisions and disputes in specific parts of the country, or the influence wielded by individual decision makers in specific policy domains at certain points in time, but they might also extend to the growth of a nationwide 'cult of incorporation' that is not part of any formal policy process.

The mining sector is especially notable for the recent appearance of land groups whose spokesmen seem to be staking dubious claims to projects which

---

[14] See, for example: *Post-Courier* 8, 22 and 26 January 2004, 23 August 2004, 15 October 2004, 17 and 20 December 2004, 10 January 2005; *The National* 1 and 2 March 2004, 24 August 2004, 17 and 20 December 2004, 12 January 2006.

have not yet been developed, as if the act of incorporation were somehow meant to gain them additional leverage in the process of negotiation with the State and the developers.[15]　However, government officials and company managers responsible for the administration of the mining sector have not followed the example of their counterparts in the petroleum sector by advocating the incorporation of land groups as vehicles for landowner representation or benefit distribution. This is not just because the first group have learnt a salutary lesson from the troubles encountered by the second group (see Weiner 1998, this volume; Sagir 2001; Lea 2002a, 2000b; Koyama 2004), even if that explains the sense of caution currently displayed by the Department of Mining (PNGDoM 2003: 28). Back in 1990, when CNGL was adopting the policy and practice of land group incorporation, the mining mandarins could hardly have foreseen the dysfunctional outcomes. Yet they already knew that one of the factors behind the outbreak of the Bougainville rebellion, which they had also failed to predict, was the dysfunctional outcome of the 'clan agent system' as a method of connecting the Panguna landowners to the other parties in the resource compensation relationship (Filer 1990).[16] So why did they persist with this model when an alternative was being actively promoted in both the forestry and petroleum sectors?

One answer would be that the rest of the mining industry was still engaging former *kiaps* (colonial district officers) to manage the corporate relationship with customary landowners, and these individuals saw no good reason to change their own customary practice. The practice of 'land investigation', through which clan agents and clan boundaries were identified, was still part of the land acquisition process prescribed under the *Land Act* (Filer et al. 2000: 32–3) and the dispute settlement process prescribed under the *Land Disputes Settlement Act* (Filer 2005: 913). Rather than blame the clan agent system itself for the outbreak of the Bougainville rebellion, the old *kiaps* were more inclined to blame the premature localisation of Bougainville Copper Limited's Village Relations Office or the unique history of local resistance to colonial rule. Discounting Bougainville as a 'special case' (Griffin 1990), they could maintain that theirs was still the best way to deal with customary land and landowners in other parts of the country. They were also dealing with landowners in the petroleum sector, where George Clapp's arguments in favour of the clan agent system were typical of their position. CNGL's preference for Tony Power's arguments might therefore have been a contingent effect of that company's Texan corporate culture, which had little in common with the values of Australian colonial paternalism, and

[15] See, for example: *The National* 21 May 2004, 14 and 22 September 2004, 26 August 2005; *Post-Courier* 6, 26 and 28 October 2004, 3 November 2004, 5, 6 and 20 April 2005.
[16] The author can vouch for this fact because he was then in regular communication with senior officials in what was then the Department of Minerals and Energy.

CNGL's ability to influence the national policy process was simply a function of its dominant role in the development of the Kutubu project.

However, the influence of old *kiaps* was only one of the factors which kept land groups out of the mining sector in the decade following the Bougainville rebellion. As a result of the mineral exploration boom in the preceding decade, the people responsible for managing 'community affairs' had already established relationships with customary landowners in many different parts of the country — not only in places where new mines had been or would soon be developed, but also in places where no development has yet occurred. In 1990 there was no clean sheet on which to inscribe an unfamiliar process of land group incorporation. But if this was partly a matter of timing, it was also a question of scale. The areas of customary land which had to be 'acquired' for development of the Kutubu project were much larger than those required for development of any mining project, so the Kutubu Joint Venture could not imagine for a moment that it was dealing with a single 'landowning community' with its own unique set of customs and a small number of customary leaders with whom personal 'community relations' could be cultivated through the process of mineral exploration. The differential intensity of the social relations of resource compensation is itself a significant structural difference between the two branches of production.

If that is one reason why the mining companies preferred to trust old *kiaps* to deal with customary landowners, it does not mean that policy makers in Port Moresby saw no reason to change their own approach to the problem of landowner representation. Even before the outbreak of the Bougainville rebellion, they had to deal with an unprecedented set of demands from the Porgera landowners, and those included a demand for greater representation in the development process. The policy response to this demand was the institution of the 'development forum', which would henceforth grant formal negotiating rights to representatives of the customary owners or 'holders' of land required for the development of a major mining project (West 1992). But the policy makers were careful to avoid making any statement about the way that this representation ought to be achieved. The *Mining Act* of 1992 leaves that to the discretion of the Minister. The project coordinators in his department were well aware of the extent of variation in the capacity of landowners in different parts of the country to organise or be organised in any particular way. So, when the closure of the Panguna copper mine bore witness to the deficiencies of the clan agent system on Bougainville, they were not inclined to advocate another model of landowner organisation and inscribe it in the national policy framework. Instead, they began to advocate the practice of social mapping by anthropologists as a way of getting beyond or beneath the simplified representations of local social organisation espoused by the old *kiaps* (Filer 1999).

Needless to say, the anthropologists played their part by revealing the diversity and complexity of the relationship between customary group boundaries and land boundaries in areas of interest to the mining sector.[17] It is therefore somewhat ironic that the need for social mapping studies found legal recognition in the *Oil and Gas Act* of 1998, without ever being enshrined in the mining sector's formal policy framework. Although CNGL conducted one early experiment with social mapping in its own licence area (Ernst 1993), this initially failed to dent the company's enthusiasm for land group incorporation or promote its appreciation of social anthropology. It was the steady accumulation of disputes about land boundaries and group boundaries in the petroleum sector which eventually caused a change of heart, and that was because of the intervention of lawyers providing donor-funded 'technical assistance' to the national government (Taylor and Whimp 1997). It just so happened that these lawyers were familiar with the policy innovations of the mining sector, and government officials from that sector were also involved in framing the relevant provisions of the *Oil and Gas Act*. However, the official lack of enthusiasm for land group incorporation as a model solution to the problem of landowner representation in the mining sector was matched by an appreciation of the need for flexibility in regulating the social relations of resource compensation (Filer et al. 2000; PNGDoM 2003). The results of social mapping studies in this sector had only served to confirm this prejudice, and that is one of the reasons why social mapping studies themselves have not so far been subject to regulation under the *Mining Act*.

While the mining industry has hesitated to follow the model of land group incorporation adopted by the oil and gas industry, the oil palm industry has shown more enthusiasm for the model adopted in the forestry sector without any comparable pressure from government regulators. The reason for this may be found in the relative permanence of large-scale agricultural estates and the relative scarcity of land available for their expansion.

By the year 2000, the five main oil palm schemes occupied more than 110,000 hectares of land in four different provinces (Koczberski et al. 2001). More than half of this land was alienated during the colonial period and then dedicated to the development of nucleus estates and 'land settlement schemes' for smallholders transplanted from other parts of the country.[18] For three decades the industry was able to expand by bringing an increasing proportion of this alienated land into cultivation, raising the productivity of the parts that were already under

---

[17] Most of this work remains unpublished because landowners and developers have normally been wary of potential abuse by competing claimants to ownership of specific licence areas. One exception which serves to illustrate the methodology is Young's (1993) study of an area on Normanby Island in Milne Bay Province.

[18] The resettlement schemes are associated with the Hoskins and Bialla projects in West New Britain and the Higaturu project in Oro Province.

cultivation, and offering incentives for customary landowners to plant 'village oil palm' on their own land. By 1997, however, it was evident that this process of expansion could not continue indefinitely without a mechanism for raising the intensity of production on customary land (Oliver 2000).

Although there have been several proposals to establish new oil palm estates on customary land by clear-felling forests initially allocated to a logging company under the *Forestry Act* of 1992, these have met with disconcerted opposition from the World Bank, the PNG Forest Authority, environmental NGOs, and even customary landowners themselves. That is because they all had good reason to believe that the proponents were using the prospect of long-term agricultural development as a pretext for extracting the native timber resources as quickly as possible (Filer 1998a: 187–97). Nevertheless, the World Bank and the national government have continued to advocate an expansion and intensification of production in areas where nucleus estates have already been established (PNGDNPRD 2004). The mechanism which has been adopted in order to achieve this goal has been a combination of land group incorporation with the rather peculiar arrangement known as 'lease-leaseback' under Division 4 of the *Land Act*.

This arrangement was originally devised in 1978 as a way for customary landowners to secure bank loans and modern managerial expertise for the development of 20-hectare coffee estates in the central highlands without losing their customary title to the land (McKillop 1991). By amendments to the *Land Act*, the Minister was allowed to 'lease customary land [from its customary owners] for the purpose of granting a special agricultural and business lease of the land' to a 'person or persons' or 'to a land group, business group or other incorporated body, to whom the customary owners have agreed that such a lease should be granted'. In effect, this is a way of getting around the legal prohibition against non-citizens dealing in land which has not been registered under the *Land Registration Act*, for when the State leases land back to a person or body approved by the customary owners, the lease is registered under this Act. This has so far proved to be the only way of mobilising customary land for large-scale agricultural development without actually alienating it.

Although land group incorporation is not an essential feature of this process, it has come to be recognised as the best way to limit transaction costs when mobilising fairly large areas of customary land (Jones and McGavin 2000). Even so, the incorporation and registration of land groups is only one of 16 different steps which the oil palm industry had to take in order to access customary land through the lease-leaseback arrangement, and it was necessary to engage a former Land Titles Commissioner as a consultant in order to make sure that all these steps were taken in the right and proper order (Oliver 2000, 2001).[19] The first 'mini-estate' to be created in this way covered 6,000 hectares of land west of the Kulu River in West New Britain Province. Once Special Agricultural Leases had been issued to four land groups representing the customary owners of this area, each land group issued a 40-year sub-lease to New Britain Palm Oil Ltd.[20] In return, each land group received an annual rental payment of K50 per hectare, a monthly royalty payment equivalent to 10 per cent of the farm gate price of harvested fruit, and 10 shares in the oil palm company for each hectare covered under the lease (Oliver 2000: 24).[21]

By the end of 2000, the mini-estates covered roughly 11,000 hectares of customary land, and thus accounted for roughly 10 per cent of the total area planted to oil palm (Koczberski et al. 2001: 6; Oliver 2001: 69). The area devoted to mini-estates in four of the country's five oil palm schemes seems to have doubled by the end of 2004, and another 4600 hectares had been developed under a similar arrangement, known as Community Oil Palm Development, in the vicinity of the fifth scheme (Bourke 2005). Since the other spatial components of the industry have been relatively static, it is therefore likely that industrial production on customary land now accounts for as much as 25 per cent of the total area planted to oil palm. On the other hand, the existing schemes are now encountering physical and demographic constraints to further expansion along these lines (Michael Bourke, personal communication, April 2006). Although Ramu Sugar Ltd (in Morobe Province) has now joined the ranks of the oil palm industry, and has also taken advantage of the lease-leaseback arrangement to expand its operations, there is as yet no evidence that this arrangement could be successfully applied to the development of an entirely new agro-industrial enterprise in an area where there is no alienated land on which to locate its central processing plant.

Conclusion: African Models in the Neo-Melanesian Mindscape

In March 2006, the Secretary for Lands and Physical Planning was reported to have said that 'incorporated land groups were not owners of the land but were people legally recognised as a group' (*Post-Courier*, 10 March 2006). This provoked one member of the public to write a letter complaining that

> The Secretary is fundamentally incorrect to insinuate that the ILGs are not landowners but are a legal group. His very own department subjects

---

[19] Norm Oliver's role in facilitating this process for the oil palm industry was similar to the role previously played by Tony Power in the petroleum sector.
[20] The period of the lease was based on the assumption that oil palm has a 20-year life cycle. At the end of the 40-year period, the landowners would have the option of renewing all the lease arrangements, granting sub-leases to another oil palm company, or allowing all the leases to lapse.
[21] The shareholding was later increased to 50 shares per hectare (Oliver 2001: 67).

clans to prove their ownership of the land the ILGs are incorporated over because clans own the land, not individuals … Most lives are here at the rural areas so the ILGs are well positioned for empowerisation and resourcing now than ever before (*Post-Courier*, 10 March 2006).

It seems that the Secretary was making a distinction between the process of land group incorporation and the process of registering titles to customary land, or between the legal mechanisms for establishing land boundaries and land *group* boundaries, in order to show that 'some of the land legislation needed to change' if these two things were to be combined. His respondent, on the other hand, was articulating an 'ideology of landownership' which both reflects and distorts the social relations of resource compensation (Filer 1997, 2006a). This ideology asserts that 'clans' and 'land groups' are essentially the same thing, and their incorporation only serves to confirm the fact that these 'customary landowning groups' are the basic building blocks of Melanesian society. But when the author of this letter says that the State 'subjects' these groups, he exposes an interesting fault line in this ideology, for it is not clear whether he means to say that the State itself has been responsible for the creation and empowerment of these collective subjects, or whether he means to say that they are traditional subjects which have been subordinated to the power of the State and now need to reassert their relative autonomy.

One of the 'Ground Rules' which the Petroleum Policy Action Team adopted at the behest of the jolly Chevroid who acted as its facilitator was for its members to 'have fun'. And one of the main sources of amusement was the recurrent banter between myself and Tony Power on the question of whether land groups, or groups of landowners, should or should not be described as 'clans' in any statement of national policy. At one of our many meetings, I laid two trump cards on the table, which were photocopies of two pages in a special issue of the journal *Anthropological Forum*. One was taken from an article by Dan Jorgensen, and contained a passage in which he described the type of evidence which his Telefol informants had prepared for his consumption, once they knew that he was coming to evaluate their claims to ownership of land in the vicinity of a proposed copper mine close to the Sepik River.

Most of this came in the form of oral accounts of personal genealogies and land use histories, with detailed listings of the marks they or their ancestors had left on the ground around the proposed mine site. This testimony was backed up with the aid of locally recognised collateral evidence in the form of ancestral relics, war trophies, and the texts of commemorative songs that provide a crucial medium of Telefol oral history. Some came with typescript statements or computer-generated census lists that made an excellent approximation of official village registers. Others, who were familiar with government notions of landholding, began talking of traditional cognatic descent categories (*tenum miit*) as 'clans', complete with patrilineal descent (Jorgensen 1997: 611).

The other page was taken from an article by Philip Guddemi, and included a rather similar observation about the 'invention of clanship' in another community whose members were reflecting on the same prospect.

> The presence of a 'Sepik Ideology' of patriliny is a present-day political reality to which Sawiyanoo make reference as they contemplate the possibility of land compensation. Certainly, the official East Sepik government stance is quite clear: Solomon Hopkis, the Assistant Secretary for Lands for the East Sepik Province, is on record in a Working Paper on the Frieda Mine issue as saying that: 'We commonly practice Patriarch lineage thus very rear materneal [sic] lineage otherwise not at all' (Guddemi 1997: 641).

Guddemi went on to interpret the word 'rear' as one which corresponds to the Sawiyanoo vernacular term for 'following behind', rather than the English word 'rare', which is perhaps what Mr Hopkis had in mind. But Guddemi's allusion to the existence of a 'pan-Sepik' ideology of patrilineal inheritance (if not patriarchal authority) made no mention of the role which my fellow teamster had played in the development of this ideology through his efforts to secure the registration of customary land in East Sepik Province. So I scribbled 'Influence of Tony Power!' in the margin of the photocopy before I passed it over to my target, and by this means was able to banish the word 'clan' from his vocabulary for the next couple of meetings.

But no amount of ethnographic evidence seems likely to affect the way in which this word is used by Papua New Guineans whose thoughts lie well beyond the proven influence of Tony Power. While the Action Team was actively debating the question of landowner organisation, one member of the national intelligentsia published a newspaper article whose title boldly declared that 'The Clan Sits at the Heart of PNG Politics' (Anere 1998). Oddly enough, the evidence deployed in support of this statement comprised the votes cast in the Namatanai Open Electorate in the national election of 1992 — an electorate in which there were only two candidates, and both accumulated substantial numbers of votes in each of the 12 census divisions into which it was divided. Nowhere could the footprint of the 'clan' be seen on this particular trail of numbers. At a seminar held shortly afterwards, I drew this fact to the attention of the author, and reiterated my own argument that 'clans' have only come to be seen as the homogeneous building blocks of national society because they '*have actually become* groups of landowners claiming compensation from development of their resources' (Filer 1997: 168). But the other members of the national intelligentsia who were present at this meeting seemed to be unanimous in their endorsement of the view that 'clans' in all parts of the country are fundamentally alike, have always been the sole collective owners of all natural and cultural resources, and naturally vote as one in national elections. No doubt many national members of the Action Team thought likewise, which might help to explain why Tony Power soon reverted to the argument that 'clans' are not only synonymous with 'land groups', but are also 'very independent of each other, even within one tribal (ethnic, language) group' (Power 2000[1]: 7).

Anthropologists may find it somewhat ironic that they should now be cast in the role of opposing a 'nationalist' ideology that seems to recapitulate the outmoded version of their own discipline which formerly informed the colonial vision of 'native society'. That vision was based on the practical need to establish representations of the native population that would place its component parts in the spatial hierarchy of colonial administration and subject them to the most effective forms of social control (Brown 1963; Strathern 1966; Wolfers 1975). That is why they adopted the 'African model' of segmentary social organisation in which the principle of unilineal descent gave rise to a set of 'tribes' divided into 'clans' and subdivided into 'lineages' whose members were literally lined up in front of the *kiap* when he came to conduct a census. Melanesian ethnography began to recoil from this African model in the early 1960s (Barnes 1962; Wagner 1974; Lawrence 1984), and most practitioners have since abandoned the concept of 'social structure' as a figment of the modernist imagination. But Australian government officials were not content with the application of one African model to the business of aligning customary group boundaries with those of a modern state. After 1960, they also tried to apply the 'Kenyan model' to the registration and privatisation of 'communally owned land' in order to realise Hasluck's vision of an indigenous peasant society (NGRU 1971; Quinn 1981). Indigenous politicians objected to the legal instruments of this 'agricultural revolution' (Ward 1972) because they would 'grant a small number of named members of the [customary] group the power to deal with the land as if they were the absolute owners' (Ward 1981: 250). In other words, they would have used the 'clan agent system' as the basis for a wholesale transformation of landed property relations.

Like the Constitutional Planning Committee, the Commission of Inquiry into Land Matters was attempting to nationalise the body of colonial law by turning 'native custom' into 'customary law' and making this the 'underlying law' that would inform the new laws of the Independent State. If the colonial regime had divided the native population into 'clans' and 'tribes' for the purpose of ruling over them, the new national body of land law was careful to avoid the use of either of these words for reasons that most anthropologists would readily endorse. If a customary 'land group' were to be granted legal status through the process of 'incorporation', local custom would still need to determine the name, shape and size of the group in question. So how is it that the 'clan' has since been reinstated as the heart and soul of the independent nation?

One answer would be that there is no other word in the English language that could be adopted as shorthand for a 'customary social group', and the use of this word does not necessarily mean that the speaker subscribes to any particular model of social organisation or would deny the diversity or flexibility of the Melanesian social groups to which the label is applied. If Tok Pisin speakers now use the word *klan*, instead of the word *lain*, to talk about these customary groups, this might simply show that they have moved beyond the restricted vocabulary of the colonial social order. The creolisation of Neo-Melanesian political discourse might encourage English-speaking social scientists to think that they are hearing the construction of an ideology when a new noun, like *klan* or *kastom*, appears to turn a set of social relations into an object. However, it is not single words but whole conversations which have this ideological effect, and then only because of the way they reveal and conceal what people are talking about. And in the present case, the point at issue is not the way that people vote in national elections, but the way that people get involved in the social relations of resource compensation (Filer 1997; Holzknecht 1997; Ernst 1999; Hirsch 2001).

If 'clans' have become subjects or objects in an ideology of landownership, it might still be argued that this is an ideology articulated by the dominant class or party in these social relations of production. In that case, the 'Neo-Melanesian' mindscape might turn out to be a neo-colonial vision articulated by members of an indigenous political and bureaucratic elite who represent the constitution of their own society when dealing with bodies like the World Bank or a multinational oil company. Their enthusiasm for land group incorporation might then be seen as a betrayal of the values articulated by the CILM, either because it merely replicates the colonial project of subordinating customary social groups to modern political and corporate structures, or worse still, because it has become a backdoor route to the registration and privatisation of customary land.

There is no doubt that some members of the national elite, including the Secretary for Lands, would like to strengthen or streamline the connection between land group incorporation and the registration of customary land. Furthermore, as we have seen, this connection has already been established in the oil palm sector. But this does not mean that land group incorporation and the ideology of landownership are both aspects of a neo-colonial conspiracy to subordinate Landowners to the State or the Developers.

First, we must recall that the CILM and its legal advisers were never opposed to the registration of customary land, but were only concerned to ensure that this was not done in a way that would lead to the dispossession of customary owners and the creation of a landless proletariat (Fingleton 1981, this volume; Ward 1981). Second, land group incorporation finds absolutely no favour with those expatriate commentators who have recently begun to reiterate the demand for individual, transferable land titles as an essential condition of PNG's economic development (Lea 2002a, 2000b; Gosarevski et al. 2004a, 2004b). Third, the white advocates of land group incorporation, who might be said to represent the 'progressive' strand of agrarian populism, no longer have their hands on the central levers of public or corporate policy in PNG. Fourth, there are many national managers of 'community affairs', especially those working in the forestry and petroleum sectors, who have many practical reasons to wish that they did *not* have to practice the art of land group maintenance (Koyama 2004). And finally, the 'reactionary' strand of agrarian populism, which opposes land group incorporation on ideological grounds, is in fact articulated by members of the national intelligentsia (Lakau 1997), while the demand for incorporation now seems to be coming from people who represent 'the Landowners' in the social relations of resource compensation.

These are all good reasons to deny that the ideology of landownership is merely recapitulating the 'native narratives' of the colonial regime. Colonial administrators were content to treat 'tribes' and 'clans' as the *superficial form* of the relationship between the State and 'native society'. They did not seek to lift the 'corporate veil' by modernising, legalising or harmonising the *internal constitution* of these 'customary groups' (Taylor and Whimp 1997: 74), but only tried to establish the social and political responsibilities of the individuals who were appointed or elected as their leaders. The 'clan agent system' implied the existence of 'clans' without granting them any kind of legal status or demanding that they act in any particular way (ibid: 102). While anthropologists were busily discovering the diversity of 'local custom', colonial administrators lost interest in this subject as their project changed from 'pacification' to 'development'. Although they were responsible for initiating several large-scale resource development projects in the final decade of their rule, they barely began to think of ways to 'customise' the social relations of resource compensation.

If nowadays we find a cult of incorporation amongst the Landowners themselves, this suggests that the ideology of landownership is not the property of any one party to the social relations of resource compensation, but is a form of the relationship itself. This new African model asserts the novel, newly rediscovered power of 'custom' and 'customary groups' *against* the powers of the State and the Developers, but because it retains a segmentary structure, it represents a customary shadow of the State that could either be a source of compliance or resistance in the process of resource development. Landowners anticipate their relationship with Developers before the Developers arrive on their land, both in their imagination and in their social practice. They generally want 'development' to happen, and they prepare themselves for it. If the Developers do arrive, they also come with expectations about the Landowners, which are derived from their understanding of national and local custom, national and provincial laws and policies, their own corporate policies and practices, and those of other companies with which they are associated. That is the broad 'mental landscape' within which actual relationships are forged, and that is the reason why the relationship of resource compensation reaches beyond the local context of specific 'development projects'.

The State and the Developers might think they are incorporating land groups as part of a corporate strategy to control the wayward behaviour of clan agents, landowner company directors, or other leaders of the 'resource development cult' (Filer 1998a: 284), but these same land groups may then turn out to be weapons of political intrigue in the hands of these same leaders (Lea 2002a; Gosarevski et al. 2004b). If 'the incorporated land group represents an attempt to deal with the reality of capitalist relations of production through what the legislators have conceived to be the traditional form of property' (Lea 2002a: 83), it may also be one of the main reasons why '[t]he state is like a landlord which cannot get the tenants out of its house' (Taylor and Whimp 1997: 127). At one moment, the process of incorporation is represented as a way of subordinating custom to capitalist relations of production; at the next moment, it becomes the vehicle by which those relations are customised, tribalised, or even demonised.

These are all partial truths or double movements that bespeak the presence of an ideology. What this ideology reveals is a desire to standardise the social organisation of customary landowners as a condition or consequence of their dealing with the social relations of resource compensation. What it conceals is the fact that this desire is nowhere near to being realised.

Much of the debate about land group incorporation seems to assume that land groups are indeed all much alike, just as 'clans' are all much alike, and this view seems to be shared by the most radical proponents and opponents of any kind of land reform. What I have tried to demonstrate in this chapter is that people have been incorporating land groups for different purposes and with different outcomes in different branches of extractive industry. But that is only half the story. For if the ideology of landownership also conceals a real variety of 'local customs in relation to land', we should also expect to find that Landowners in different parts of the country are not all equally willing or able to sustain the incorporation of 'land groups' for any particular purpose, whatever the policies or strategies adopted by the State or the Developers. And that is the point at which the art of land group maintenance invites the need for social mapping studies to debunk the ideology.

References

Allen, B.J., 1995. 'At Your Own Peril: Studying Huli Residence.' In A. Biersack (ed), *Papuan Borderlands: Huli, Duna, and Ipili Perspectives on the Papua New Guinea Highlands.* Ann Arbor: University of Michigan Press.

Anere, R., 1998. 'The Clan Sits at the Heart of PNG Politics.' *The Independent,* 29 May.

Ascher, W., 2005. 'The "Resource Curse".' In E. Bastida, T. Wälde and J. Warden-Fernández (eds), op. cit.

Auty, R., 1993. *Sustaining Development in Mineral Economies: The Resource Curse Thesis.* London: Routledge.

Banks, G., 2005. 'Linking Resources and Conflict the Melanesian Way.' *Pacific Economic Bulletin* 20(1): 185–191.

Bannon, I. and P. Collier (eds), 2003. *Natural Resources and Violent Conflict: Options and Actions.* Washington (DC): World Bank.

Barnes, J.A., 1962. 'African Models in the New Guinea Highlands.' *Man* 62: 5–9.

Barnett, T.E., 1989. *Report of the Commission of Inquiry into Aspects of the Forest Industry: Final Report* (2 volumes). Unpublished report to the Government of PNG.

———, 1992. 'Legal and Administrative Problems of Forestry in Papua New Guinea.' In S. Henningham and R.J. May (eds), *Resources, Development and Politics in the Pacific Islands.* Bathurst: Crawford House Press.

Bastida, E., T. Wälde and J. Warden-Fernández (eds), 2005. *International and Comparative Mineral Law and Policy: Trends and Prospects.* The Hague: Kluwer Law International.

Bourke, R.M., 2005. 'Agricultural Production and Customary Land in Papua New Guinea.' In J. Fingleton (ed.), 'Privatising Land in the Pacific: A Defence of Customary Tenures.' Canberra: Australia Institute (Discussion Paper 80).

Brown, P., 1963. 'From Anarchy to Satrapy.' *American Anthropologist* 65: 1–15.

——— and A. Ploeg (eds), 1997. *Change and Conflict in Papua New Guinea Land and Resource Rights.* Special Issue 7(4) of *Anthropological Forum.*

Burton, J., 1991. 'Local Organisation in Porgera: Ipili Lines of Descent and Central Highlands Clans Compared.' Paper presented to the conference on 'New Perspectives on the Papua New Guinea Highlands', Canberra, 16–18 August.

CIE/NCDS (Centre for International Economics and National Centre for Development Studies), 1997. 'Gaining from Gas: The Economic

Contribution of the Papua New Guinea LNG Project.' Canberra: CIE and NCDS.

Clapp, G.E., 1998. 'Agents: The Case For and Against.' Port Moresby: BP (PNG) Pty Ltd (unpublished memorandum).

Cooter, R.D., 1989. 'Issues in Customary Land Law.' Port Moresby: Institute of National Affairs (Discussion Paper 39).

Denoon, D. and C. Snowden (eds), 1981. *A History of Agriculture in Papua New Guinea: A Time to Plant and a Time to Uproot*. Port Moresby: Institute of Papua New Guinea Studies.

Donaldson, M. and K. Good, 1988. *Articulated Agricultural Development: Traditional and Capitalist Agricultures in Papua New Guinea*. Aldershot: Avebury.

Ernst, T., 1993. 'Kutubu Petroleum Project: Social Mapping and Incorporated Land Groups Project Report.' Unpublished report to Chevron Niugini Pty Ltd.

————, 1999. 'Land, Stories and Resources: Discourse and Entification in Onabasulu Modernity.' *American Anthropologist* 101: 88–97.

Errington, F.K. and D.B. Gewertz, 1995. *Articulating Change in the "Last Unknown"*. Boulder (CO): Westview Press.

Filer, C., 1990. 'The Bougainville Rebellion, the Mining Industry and the Process of Social Disintegration in Papua New Guinea.' In R.J. May and M. Spriggs (eds), op. cit.

————, 1997. 'Compensation, Rent and Power in Papua New Guinea.' In S. Toft (ed.), *Compensation for Resource Development in Papua New Guinea*. Boroko: Law Reform Commission (Monograph 6). Canberra: Australian National University, National Centre for Development Studies (Pacific Policy Paper 24).

————(with N. Sekhran), 1998a. *Loggers, Donors and Resource Owners*. London: International Institute for Environment and Development in association with the PNG National Research Institute (Policy That Works for Forests and People, Papua New Guinea Country Study).

————, 1998b. 'Social Mapping under Licence Conditions or Legislation.' Boroko: National Research Institute (unpublished report to Petroleum Project Benefits Action Team).

————, 1999. 'The Dialectics of Negation and Negotiation in the Anthropology of Mineral Resource Development in Papua New Guinea.' In A.P. Cheater (ed.), *The Anthropology of Power: Empowerment and Disempowerment in Changing Structures*. London: Routledge (ASA Monograph 36).

————, 2005. 'The Role of Land-owning Communities in Papua New Guinea's Mineral Policy Framework.' In E. Bastida, T. Wälde and J. Warden-Fernández (eds), op. cit.

————, 2006a. 'Custom, Law and Ideology in Papua New Guinea.' In J. Weiner and K. Glaskin (eds), *Custom: Indigenous Tradition and Law in the 21st Century*. Special Issue 7(1) of *The Asia Pacific Journal of Anthropology*.

————, 2006b. 'Pacific 2020 Background Paper: Mining and Petroleum.' Canberra: AusAID.

————, D. Henton and R. Jackson, 2000. *Landowner Compensation in Papua New Guinea's Mining and Petroleum Sectors*. Port Moresby: PNG Chamber of Mines and Petroleum.

———— and B. Imbun, 2004. 'A Short History of Mineral Development Policies in Papua New Guinea.' Canberra: Australian National University, Resource Management in Asia-Pacific Program (Working Paper 55).

Fingleton, J.S., 1981. 'Policy-Making on Lands.' In J. Ballard (ed.), *Policy-Making in a New State: Papua New Guinea 1972–77*. St Lucia: University of Queensland Press.

————, 1991. 'The East Sepik Land Legislation.' In P. Larmour (ed.), op. cit.

————, 2004. 'Is Papua New Guinea Viable *Without* Customary Groups?' *Pacific Economic Bulletin* 19(2): 111–118.

Foster, R.J., 1995. *Social Reproduction and History in Melanesia: Mortuary Ritual, Gift Exchange, and Custom in the Tanga Islands*. Cambridge: Cambridge University Press.

Gosarevski S., H. Hughes and S. Windybank, 2004a. 'Is Papua New Guinea Viable?' *Pacific Economic Bulletin* 19(1): 134–148.

————, 2004b. 'Is Papua New Guinea Viable *With* Customary Land Ownership?' *Pacific Economic Bulletin* 19(3): 133–136.

Griffin, J.T., 1990. 'Bougainville is a Special Case.' In R.J. May and M. Spriggs (eds), op. cit.

Guddemi, P., 1997. 'Continuities, Contexts, Complexities, and Transformations: Local Land Concepts of a Sepik People Affected by Mining Exploration.' In P. Brown and A. Ploeg (eds), op. cit.

Hasluck, P., 1976. *A Time for Building: Australian Administration in Papua and New Guinea 1951–1963*. Melbourne: Melbourne University Press.

Hide, R.L, 1973. *The Land Titles Commission in Chimbu: An Analysis of Colonial Land Law and Practice, 1933–68*. Canberra: Australian National University, New Guinea Research Unit (Bulletin 50).

Hirsch, E., 2001. 'New Boundaries of Influence in Highland Papua: "Culture", Mining and Ritual Conversions.' *Oceania* 17: 298–312.

Holzknecht, H., 1997. 'Problems of Articulation and Representation in Resource Development: The Case of Forestry in Papua New Guinea.' In P. Brown and A. Ploeg (eds), op. cit.

Hulme, D., 1983. 'Credit, Land Registration and Development: Implications of the Lease-Lease-Back Scheme.' *Melanesian Law Journal* 11: 91–98.

IFRT (Independent Forestry Review Team), 2001. 'Review of Forest Harvesting Projects Being Processed Towards a Timber Permit or a Timber Authority: Observations and Recommendations Report.' Port Moresby: Unpublished report to the Inter-Agency Forestry Review Committee.

———, 2004. 'Towards Sustainable Timber Production: A Review of Existing Logging Projects' (3 volumes). Port Moresby: Unpublished report to the Inter-Agency Forestry Review Committee.

Jessep, O., 1980. 'Land Demarcation in New Ireland.' *Melanesian Law Journal* 8: 112–133.

Jones, L.T. and P.A. McGavin, 2000. 'Creating Economic Incentives for Land Mobilisation in Papua New Guinea: A Case Study Analysis of the Formation and Maintenance of Institutions that Assist Mobilisation of Land for Agricultural Uses.' Port Moresby: Institute of National Affairs (Discussion Paper 77).

Jorgensen, D., 1997. 'Who or What is a Landowner?: Mythology and Marking the Ground in a Papua New Guinea Mining Project.' In P. Brown and A. Ploeg (eds), op. cit.

Keesing, R.M. and R. Tonkinson (eds), 1982. *Reinventing Traditional Culture: The Politics of Kastom in Island Melanesia.* Special Issue 13(4) of *Mankind.*

Koczberski, G., G.N. Curry and K. Gibson, 2001. *Improving Productivity of the Smallholder Oil Palm Sector in Papua New Guinea: A Socio-Economic Study of the Hoskins and Popondetta Schemes.* Canberra: Australian National University, Research School of Pacific and Asian Studies, Department of Human Geography.

Koyama, S.K., 2004. 'Reducing Agency Problems in Incorporated Land Groups.' *Pacific Economic Bulletin* 19(1): 20–31.

Lakau, A.L., 1997. 'Customary Land Tenure, Customary Landowners and the Proposals for Customary Land Reform in Papua New Guinea.' In P. Brown and A. Ploeg (eds), op. cit.

Larmour, P., 1991. 'Introduction.' In P. Larmour (ed.), op. cit.

———— (ed.), 1991. *Customary Land Tenure: Registration and Decentralisation in Papua New Guinea*. Boroko: Institute of Applied Social and Economic Research (Monograph 29).

Lawrence, P., 1984. *The Garia: An Ethnography of a Traditional Cosmic System in Papua New Guinea*. Melbourne: Melbourne University Press.

Lea, D., 2002a. 'Incorporated Land Groups in Papua New Guinea: Part of the Problem or Part of the Solution?' *Pacific Economic Bulletin* 17(1): 79–90.

————, 2002b. 'Are there Advantages to Maintaining Customary Land Tenure in Papua New Guinea?' *Pacific Economic Bulletin* 17(2): 42–55.

Lovuru, K.A., 1998. 'Packaging MOA Projects as a Subsidiary or Small Public Investment Programme: A View to Impose and Instill Discipline and Development Consciousness in the Utilisation of Benefits Derived from Natural Resources for Equitable Distribution as Benefits to Landowners.' Paper presented to the Department of Petroleum and Energy Seminar on Landowner Issues, Port Moresby, 27–28 January.

MacWilliam, S., 1988. 'Smallholdings, Land Law and the Politics of Land Tenure in Papua New Guinea.' *Journal of Peasant Studies* 16: 77–109.

May, R.J. and M. Spriggs (eds), *The Bougainville Crisis*. Bathurst (NSW): Crawford House Press.

McGavin, P.A., 1994. 'Economic Security in Melanesia: Key Issues for Managing Contract Stability and Mineral Resources Development in Papua New Guinea, Solomon Islands and Vanuatu.' Port Moresby: Institute of National Affairs (Discussion Paper 61).

McKillop, B., 1991. 'Land Mobilisation in the Highlands.' In P. Larmour (ed.), op. cit.

Morawetz, D., 1967. *Land Tenure Conversion in the Northern District of Papua*. Canberra: Australian National University, New Guinea Research Unit (Bulletin 17).

NGRU (New Guinea Research Unit), 1971. *Land Tenure and Economic Development*. Canberra: Australian National University, New Guinea Research Unit (Bulletin 40).

Oliver, N., 2000. 'Land Act No. 45 of 1996, Sections 10 and 102 Lease/Lease Back Provisions: Enabling Access to Customary Land for Commercial Agricultural and Business Purposes.' Unpublished paper.

————, 2001. 'The Lease, Lease-Back Instrument in Agriculture and in the Establishment of Timber Plantations.' In C. Hunt (ed.), *Production, Privatisation and Preservation: New Policy for PNG Forests*. London: International Institute for Environment and Development.

PNGDNPRD (PNG Department of National Planning and Rural Development), 2004. 'The Medium-Term Development Strategy 2005–2010: "Our Plan for Social and Economic Advancement".' Port Moresby: PNGDNPRD.

PNGDoM (PNG Department of Mining), 2003. 'Sustainable Development Policy and Sustainability Planning Framework for the Mining Sector in Papua New Guinea: Green Paper.' Port Moresby: PNGDoM.

PNGFMPP (PNG Forest Management and Planning Project), 1995. 'Working Papers Produced as Part of the FMPP Landowner Involvement Component 1993 to 1995.' Boroko: PNGFMPP.

PNGMoF (PNG Ministry of Forests), 1991. 'National Forest Policy.' Hohola: PNGMoF.

———, 1993. 'National Forestry Development Guidelines.' Hohola: PNGMoF.

Power, T., 1991. 'Policy Making in East Sepik Province.' In P. Larmour (ed.), op. cit.

———, 1995. 'Village Guide to Land Group Incorporation.' Hohola: PNG Forest Authority.

———, 2000. *Community Relations Manual: Resource Industries* (2 volumes). Port Moresby: PNG Chamber of Mines and Petroleum.

Power, T. and J. Waiko, 1990. 'Incorporation of Land Groups for Land and Other Resources Development.' In N. Fernando and T. Nen (eds), *Towards a National Forest Plan: Papers Presented at the National Forest Plan Seminar held at the Forest Research Institute, Lae, 7–10 November 1989*. Boroko: National Research Institute.

Quinn, P.T., 1981. 'Agriculture, Land Tenure and Land Law to 1971.' In D. Denoon and C. Snowden (eds), op. cit.

Ross, M. 1999. 'The Political Economy of the Resource Curse.' *World Politics* 51: 297–322.

Sachs, J. and A. Warner, 2001. 'The Curse of Natural Resources.' *European Economic Review* 45: 827–838.

Sagir, B.F., 2001. 'The Politics of Petroleum Extraction and Royalty Distribution at Lake Kutubu.' In A. Rumsey and J. Weiner (eds), *Mining and Indigenous Lifeworlds in Australia and Papua New Guinea*. Adelaide: Crawford House Press.

Simpson, G., L. Goldman, J. Brooksbank, A. Goie and M. Finlayson, 1998. 'PNG Gas Project Environmental Plan: Social and Economic Impact Study' (3 volumes). Canberra: Project Design and Management Ltd.

Simpson, S.R., 1971. 'Land Problems in Papua New Guinea.' In NGRU, op. cit.

Strathern, A., 1966. 'Despots and Directors in the New Guinea Highlands.' *Man* (NS) 1: 356–367.

Taylor, M. and K. Whimp, 1997. 'Report on Land Issues and Hydrocarbon Framework Study.' Port Moresby: Asian Development Bank for Department of Mining and Petroleum.

Turtle, C., 1991. 'Administrative Reform and Land Mobilisation.' In P. Larmour (ed.), op. cit.

Wagner, R., 1974. 'Are There Social Groups in the New Guinea Highlands?' In M.J. Leaf (ed.), *Frontiers of Anthropology*. New York: Van Nostrand.

Ward, A., 1972. 'Agricultural Revolution: Handle With Care.' *New Guinea* 6(1): 25–34.

———, 1981. 'Customary Land, Land Registration and Social Equality.' In D. Denoon and C. Snowden (eds), op. cit.

———, 1983. 'The Commission of Inquiry into Land Matters 1973: Choices, Constraints and Assumptions.' *Melanesian Law Journal* 11: 1–13.

———, 1991. 'Time to Make a New Start.' In P. Larmour (ed.), op. cit.

Weiner, J.F., 1998. 'The Incorporated Ground: the Contemporary Work of Distribution in the Kutubu Oil Project Area, Papua New Guinea.' Canberra: Australian National University, Resource Management in Asia-Pacific Project (Working Paper 17).

West, R., 1992. 'Development Forum and Benefit Package: A Papua New Guinea Initiative.' Port Moresby: Institute of National Affairs (Working Paper 16).

Whimp, K., 1995. *Representative Resource Owner Bodies for Forestry Projects.* Boroko: PNG Forest Management and Planning Project.

Wolfers, E.P., 1975. *Race Relations and Colonial Rule in Papua New Guinea.* Sydney: Australia & New Zealand Book Company.

Young, M.W., 1993. 'South Normanby Island: A Social Mapping Study.' *Research in Melanesia* 17: 1–68.

Chapter Nine

Determinacy of Groups and the 'Owned Commons' in Papua New Guinea and Torres Strait[1]

John Burton

The means of owning and managing customary land (also known as traditional land) in Australia and the Pacific has been treated in many ways in the century and a quarter since Sir Arthur Gordon's initiatives in Fiji (France 1969) — the first large-scale attempt to accommodate native ownership in the framework of a Western system of administration.[2] In Australia, discussions of the essence of native title, the local vehicle for customary ownership, have been framed in terms of a 'recognition space' where Western law and customary law intersect but remain separate. However, I deal in this paper with cases where this concept is not an especially useful prism through which to view the situation, and I choose not to pursue this line of argument.[3] In the cases I present, indigenous groups have been successful in pursuing their claims to land through various processes of landowner identification, including through litigation, but have found the outcomes extremely difficult to work with afterwards. In several cases, the key problem is that the indigenous system had either to be misrepresented by witnesses or misinterpreted by state officials in order for *any* outcome to be arrived at. This happened in a different way in each case, but the

[1] I would like to thank Jim Fingleton and James Weiner for comments on this paper, and Peter Bennett, Ngawae Mitio, Lengeto Giam, the spokesmen for Nauti, Akikanda, Minava and Yokua villages, the office bearers of Mer Gedkem Le, the Mer Island Council, and the individual persons in all other communities I have consulted for being extremely forthcoming with information. I also acknowledge all the relevant organisations for whom I have worked as a consultant or employee for enabling the field investigations reported in this chapter.
[2] In this chapter I will necessarily have to use terms that are familiar and comfortable in one jurisdiction, but conventionally require qualification in the other. Thus the usages 'custom', 'law', 'customary', 'traditional', 'indigenous', 'landowner' (or 'land owner' or 'land holder' in some discussions), and more have a particular history in the relevant bodies of literature relating to PNG and Australia. But except where I specifically qualify a term, I am trying to use such phrases in such a way that general principles can be derived across the two jurisdictions.
[3] A metaphor that has been used in native title discussions is the intersection of two circles in a Venn diagram (Mantziaris and Martin 1999). The metaphor has the arguably political purpose of disclaiming the intention of state-made laws to connect directly with customary law, and perhaps even to deny the possibility of this. In Papua New Guinea and the Pacific, though, the political agendas of statehood emphasise the emergence of the state from customary forms of society — whether this is accurate or not.

result was essentially the same: landowners have been left to their own devices struggling to make their custom inter-operable with their state's administrative system.

Approaches to Identification of Traditional Owners of Land

The administrative systems of both Papua New Guinea (PNG) and Australia provide a variety of legal mechanisms for recognising the ownership of customary land. In both cases the solution has two steps: the recognition of owning entities, and the description of land estates and the connections that the owning entities have to them.[4]

In both PNG and Australia landowners often emerge in a political context prior to more specific identification. Sutton (2003: 116) suggests that indigenous custom in Australia reflects a dual system:

> The living holders of specific traditional land interests, often now called the 'traditional owners' ... hold title in the proximate sense, while underlying titles are maintained by the wider regional cultural and customary-legal system of the social networks of which they are members.

There is no provision to recognise 'underlying title' in Australia other than politically. It is manifested in the creation of Native Title Representative Body areas based on criteria such as occupation of ethno-geographic regions (for example 'Torres Strait') or modern political regions (for example 'Victoria'). Another illustration is the 12 per cent of Western Australia held by the State's Aboriginal Lands Trust, which was established by the *Aboriginal Affairs Planning Authority Act 1972*. Many of the reserves that this includes are leased or occupied by Aboriginal corporations, but quite a number are not, and might therefore be considered as falling under indigenous commons ownership (see Glaskin, this volume).

In PNG, the equivalent of 'underlying title' is, I suggest, also shown by political representation. One example is the creation of 296 Local-Level Governments that are intended to group together people of ethnic and linguistic affinity or, in Sutton's terms, people who share the same 'cultural and customary-legal system'.

The Handling of Proximate Titles — Papua New Guinea

When land is required for a non-customary use, a Land Investigation Report (under the *Land Act 1996*) must be carried out for each separately owned parcel by a government Lands Officer. A Schedule of Landowners, with attached signatures (or thumbprints), is attached to a survey plan and other descriptive

---

[4] 'Owning entity' is a choice of words here that does not prejudge what kind of body it is that owns land in a particular case: a named person, a family, a 'clan' (defined in some way), a Schedule of Owners, or a made-up legal entity such as a Body Corporate.

details. The Schedule of Landowners is not an 'owning entity' but a list of people who attest to the fact that the description of the land is accurate and that they have interests in it.

A formal kind of body that has the *potential* to be an owning entity for indigenous land in PNG is the Incorporated Land Group (ILG), under the provisions of the *Land Groups Incorporation Act 1974*. The main usage of ILGs has been in forestry, where legislation requires their formation, and in the Southern Highlands oil and gas projects (see Filer, this volume). The key defect in the administration of this legislation is that applicants merely pay a fee to the Registrar General's office to register an ILG. No branch of government exists, or is contemplated, for the purpose of vetting applications, in other words seeing that they are properly formed or even that they really exist.[5] In consequence, there are now believed to be over 10,000 registered ILGs, with the number increasing at 10–15 per day (Fingleton 2004: 117).

Not only is it easy for ILGs to proliferate in terms of absolute numbers, the absence of provisions for the governance of ILGs has created ideal conditions for existing ILGs to undergo rapid fission. Among the Foi and Fasu (Weiner, this volume), members of subgroups within incorporated clans complained that the executives and passbook signatories failed to distribute benefits fairly and they split off to form new groups.

I can suggest here that the checks and balances provided by proper governance — the holding of regular meetings freely attended by members, the keeping of minutes, the election of and submission to accountability of the office bearers — could have counteracted this propensity to fission. As I point out below, in PNG the system is full of owning groups but empty of governance, whereas in Australia the equivalent system is full of governance but empty of owning groups.

The Handling of Proximate Titles — Australia

All the 'title' forms of indigenous tenure in Australia require that some kind of incorporated group be formed first. In the Northern Territory the vehicle used by the *Aboriginal Land Rights Act* is the Aboriginal Land Trust. In the Queensland legislation, a land trust is used with trustees appointed by the Minister for Aboriginal and Torres Strait Islander Policy. The High Court, in the second Mabo decision,[6] was not prejudicial to any particular form of traditional ownership, such that the wording used by the majority (Brennan J at 61) was copied in Section 223(1) of the *Native Title Act* as 'communal, group or individual rights and interests' which are said to belong to the 'common law holders'.

---

[5] See Burton (1993) on the registration of five groups at Hedinia.
[6] *Mabo and Others v Queensland* (2) (1992) 175 CLR 1.

Be that as it may, the Act goes on to makes it clear that the standard means of implementation is for the 'communal, group or individual rights and interests' to be loaded into a Prescribed Body Corporate (PBC) after a successful claim. This is the pointy end of the native title process and there is little provision for anything beyond incorporation (Mantziaris and Martin 1999, Chapter 2 and Figure 2).

Integrity in native title is maintained by at least three levels of vetting. A Native Title Representative Body will in the first instance endeavour to avoid the formation of overlapping claim groups and overlapping claim areas by holding meetings with members of communities in its representative area. Next, the National Native Title Tribunal, through the application of the registration test (Section 190 of the *Native Title Act*) and its Geospatial Services, in checking for overlapping or geographically invalid claims, will screen out invalid claims and claimant groups. Last, contested claims that cannot reach negotiated settlement can be subject to trial in the Federal Court.

Examples of improperly constituted claim groups are groups consisting of only one person, containing non-indigenous people, or containing so-called 'historical' people — for example, indigenous people living in another group's area (Sutton 2003: 19–20). While the Office of the Registrar of Aboriginal Corporations (ORAC), in its acceptance of PBCs, does not have a role in the determination process, it is meant to continue to make sure that PBCs continue to correctly represent traditional owners by holding Annual General Meetings, electing office bearers with correct procedures, and submitting (brief) annual reports. In practice, PBCs often fall behind with compliance, whether they are 'empty' PBCs set up in anticipation of winning native title or PBCs that hold native title following successful determinations. Given that these bodies are unfunded, policy makers have no current answer to this situation — successfully claimed native titles could hardly be forfeited — so the effectiveness of the oversight role of ORAC in the governance of PBCs is moot.

The irony with these arrangements is that, with only 53 successful claims so far, Australia has an elaborate system that is empty of owning groups, while PNG has 10,000 owning groups but nothing like the National Native Title Tribunal to vet applications or ORAC to ensure that each of the groups is properly formed and sticks to its rules.

Determinacy, Bounded Groups and 'Owned Commons'

From the above it can be seen that there is a strong expectation of the group ownership of proximate titles in both jurisdictions and that, at any point, the membership of an owning group is fully determined in the following senses: any reasonably knowledgeable adult member ought, at least in principle, to be able to list all the other adults in the group; no member is likely to contest the eligibility of other members of the group to be in it, except in borderline cases which should be few in number; and, in a landscape of many similar groups, it is not expected that members with full rights in one group could also have full rights in another group, even if it is possible to have lesser rights in another group.

This essentially portrays such entities as *bounded groups*. It contrasts with the fully indeterminate situation in a parcellised landscape where many people each claim rights to many land parcels; an indeterminate number of people claim rights to any one parcel (that is, the information to work out how many claimants there are likely to be is not fully knowable); many of the claimants do not know of one another's claims, or identities, or both; and a large proportion of claimants dispute the claims of others. In the indeterminate situation, 'groups' — collections of people who can take coordinated action — cannot be found in a meaningful sense.

In the Australian context, Sutton foreshadows the possibility of considering more than two layers of title, but after briefly giving examples, he says that the 'usages refer to constructs that are different from the underlying/proximate distinction' he has made (Sutton 2003: 116). The concept he touches on but passes over is that of a 'grant' from a proximate title. It is worth noting here that no provision is made in either jurisdiction for differentiating the internal ownership of titles (or for varying the types of rights across a native title area). In consequence, when ownership is undifferentiated and collective, it can be said to be held as *owned commons*.

In PNG, influential writers seem more than content to go along with the 'corporate clan' or even 'corporate village': 'a village recognises itself as an independent, autonomous social unit ... identity constitutes the unit as a "corporation", an entity' (Narokobi 1989: 21–2). No extant public utterances offer a contrary view to the assumption that village-level social units — usually 'clans' or *wanpisin* in the newspapers — are the title-holding entities and the primary owners of land.

'Owned Commons' Cases: Dauan and Iralim

An Australian example of an 'owned commons' case is the native title determination over Dauan Island in Torres Strait.[7] I have chosen this because of the small size of the island (4.5 km^2) and the easy grounds for saying that the Dauan people, the Dauanalgaw, form a single owning entity. While they recognise totemic divisions among themselves, and families identify with particular areas of gardening land, no 'tribal' divisions were noted as relating to land when the then very small community of 67 people was first visited by a government agent

---

[7] *Dauan People v Queensland* 2000 FCA 1064.

(Captain Pennefather) on 5 December 1879, and none are claimed today. In other words, such internal boundaries that exist are within the single polity represented by Dauanalgaw, and negotiations over access are a matter of discussion between families. In this sense, Dauan fits the owned commons model reasonably happily.

In PNG, a nationally important example is the *Mining (Ok Tedi Agreement) Act 1976* that granted the Special Mining Lease around Mt Fubilan. Hyndman was present at the time and found that main ridges between drainage basins and the Ok Tedi River divided the landscape up in to 'parishes':

> The ... parishes are territorial and social groupings which have claims on and ultimate rights to use named and delimited hamlet, garden and rain forest resources. Thus, the parish is recognized as a clearly bounded, territorially discrete unit (Hyndman 1994: 7).

This led to the identification of the people of the Wopkaimin Iralim parish as the traditional owners of Mt Fubilan. The residents of Bultem and Finalbin villages, within Iralim parish, were treated for all intents and purposes as a single group of landowners (Welsch 1979; Jackson et al. 1981, Table 5.2).[8]

I use this example because it is one of very few in PNG where anthropologists and government lands officers concurred on the *absence* of internal differentiation in ownership rights. For example:

> Wopkaimin land tenure is essentially communal in nature ... everyone in [the] community shares rights to a large tract of undeveloped forest land used for hunting and foraging. (Welsch 1987: 122).

Hyndman's map (1994, Figure 1.4) shows that a parish is further subdivided into bounded 'neighbourhoods', though he does not say if parish members have differentiated rights among neighbourhoods. At all events, there are few impediments to Wopkaimin moving among hamlets that can spring up anywhere within the parish, and Hyndman himself recounts that in 1973–74 his was the first house built at a hamlet called Moiyokabip, in the upper part of the Kam Valley, which had seven houses by the end of his stay. A short time later, most of the Wopkaimin had relocated to new settlements on the Ok Tedi mine access road, and by 1985 only 12 of 700 Wopkaimin were still living anywhere in the Kam Valley where almost all had lived previously (Hyndman 1982, 1994: 108ff.).

---

[8] I am familiar with the case of the Wopkaimin from my time as co-leader of the Ok-Fly Social Monitoring Project, 1991–95, a consultancy project of the University of PNG for Ok Tedi Mining Limited. Field investigations were done in the neighbouring Ningerum and Awin areas in 1991–92 and touched on Wopkaimin matters only in relation to Ningerum and Awin claims to, and legendary associations with, Wopkaimin places.

The Collectivisation of Land at Mer Island

The Mabo case, which concluded in 1992, is widely known for its effect of erasing the concept of *terra nullius* — the idea that Australia had been the 'land of no-one' prior to white settlement (Beckett 1995; Keon-Cohen 2000).

This achievement has overshadowed the effects of the case on the Meriam themselves.[9] The Mabo plaintiffs did not present evidence to the Supreme Court of Queensland in the form of conceptual claims against the government, but as they had done for a century when litigating among themselves in the Murray Island Court. When the case was referred to the High Court in Canberra, and its judgement handed back to the Supreme Court of Queensland, the individual statements of claim were abandoned without resolution.

Subsequently, a PBC, Mer Gedkem Le (literally 'Mer Landowning People'), was created to act as the holder of Mer's native title. This promised to put Meriam customary ownership of land on a sound footing. The problem remained, however, that observations going back to the first moments of the annexation of Mer to Queensland in 1879 did not emphasise corporate or collective rights but personal ones.

In 1879, Captain Pennefather reported of Mer that the islanders 'are very tenacious of their ownership of the land and the island is divided into small properties which have been handed down from generation to generation'.[10] In 1886, John Douglas, the Government Resident at Thursday Island, wrote: 'I do not see how it will be possible to administer these islands under the present laws of Queensland, more especially as touching the land question.' In 1891, Douglas commissioned Captain Owen of the Queensland First Regiment to make a land survey of Mer showing all dwellings labelled by household head — the only island in Torres Strait where such a detailed survey was undertaken (Douglas 1894).[11] Owen's map, it should be added, remained undiscovered during the Mabo case. Wilkin, a member of the Cambridge expedition to Torres Strait in 1898, began his account of land tenure with the statement that 'Queensland [in other words European property law] has not affected native land tenure' (Wilkin 1908: 163). J.S. Bruce, who presided over the Murray Island Court from the

---

[9] I am familiar with the cases of Dauan and Mer from my time as Senior Anthropologist, Native Title Office, Torres Strait Regional Authority 2001–03. In the case of Mer, I spent a further month on the island in 2003–04 as a consultant to the latter body to prepare for a land dispute workshop held in January 2004 (Burton 2005). The native title determination at Dauan predated my tenure.

[10] Captain Pennefather's 'Report of a Cruise in the Islands Lately Annexed to Queensland' is held in the Queensland States Archives at COL/A288/460.

[11] Owen's report, entitled 'Meer Island, the largest of the Murray Islands group, surveyed by Captain Owen, 1st Regiment Queensland, June 1891', is held in the Queensland State Archives at REP (formerly Q9 1891).

1890s, wrote in the 1904 annual report: 'I was present at the hearing of 29 of the [42] cases ... the land disputes are the source of a lot of trouble.'[12]

The dispute cases among the surviving records of the Murray Island Court[13] (1908–83) leave the reader in no doubt that the matters at issue are about the struggles of individuals to assert rights to marked out pieces of land in a system of inheritance:

> S wished to get possession of seven portions of land in the Piadram district which belonged to his uncle E (deceased). His father, I, succeeded to the land at his brother E's death and at his death his mother D looked after the land, at her death G was appointed the guardian of the land for K and S (the sons of E) as they were both minors (Murray Island Court, 25 August 1910).

> M charged G with encroaching on her portion of land at ... by altering the boundary line. M is acting as a caretaker of the portion for her nephew E (Murray Island Court, 25 April 1913).

> B disputed the right of E to a portion of land at ... on the ground that it was part of G's property and should go to her family as heirs. E stated that when she married D in 1901, G gave them the portion from the kapere tree to the point and up as far as the bamboos just on the other side of the street. She had been in possession for 24 years, using the ground for herself, and G had never disputed her right (Murray Island Court, 26 August 1925).

An annual average of 10–15 land cases went before the court up to World War Two and 5–10 thereafter, dwindling to none by the end of the 1970s. The reduction in cases after 1960 is in part a reflection of new life choices being exercised by Meriam. For example, a reduction in the frequency of disputes over garden land parallels the decline in importance of garden cultivation at Mer. Similarly, when Meriam began to migrate to mainland Australian towns in significant numbers in the 1950s, it is likely that pressure on land for family housing in the village area slackened. Meriam land tenure, of course had not changed at all:

> The traditional system of land tenure persists, with ownership rights transmitted by inheritance and generally vested in individuals or a group of brothers. Everyone owns some land, though some are said to be short while others have more than they need (Beckett 1963: 174).

---

[12] Letter to H. Milman, Government Resident, Thursday Island, 27 December 1904 (Queensland Votes and Proceedings 1905).
[13] Records for the years 1908–1983 are held in the Queensland State Archives (Microfilm SRS4117).

The final demise of the Murray Island Court may be laid at two institutional changes. The first is the evolution of the role of the council from mainly political representation in a system of colonial-style indirect rule — including presiding over the court — to acting as a service deliverer in the conventional manner of local government. The second is legislative change in the form of the *Community Services (Torres Strait Islands) Act 1984*, which included provision for a new, more formal island court system presided over by islander Justices of the Peace. This simply had the effect of killing off the previous system without replacing it. No Island Court is believed to have been convened in Torres Strait under this legislation; cases of a civil nature either go unresolved or are reformulated as offences that can be heard in the Magistrates Court on Thursday Island.

At Mer, disputes were put on hold from the inception of the Mabo case in 1982 until the High Court judgement of 1992, and after this until Mer Gedkem Le was registered (in 1999), and then until office bearers were successfully elected (around 2001). In the meantime, the disadvantages of living in a remote part of Queensland were now being addressed in the form of State and Federal grants for new housing, road sealing, reliable power generation, greatly improved access to education at all levels, better health care and care for the aged, new technology services such as electronic banking, and the 'normal' availability of telephones.[14] This has stemmed the exodus of Meriam and it has led to a reversal of the direction of migration in some age groups.

These things have combined to create a heightened demand for housing land and a resurgence in land disputation. In 2002, the Council of Elders tried to hear eight dispute cases using provisions in the constitution of Mer Gedkem Le, but this escalated intra-community tensions when all eight decisions were immediately appealed. A workshop held in 2003, with funding from the Mer Island Council and the Torres Strait Regional Authority, was no more conclusive, but it did at least help to document more fully the backlog of at least 50 cases. A workshop in 2004, with the additional participation of the National Native Title Tribunal, probed the problems again with no greater success. The upshot is that the annual $2–3 million construction program is compromised. Houses are not being built for needy families and building materials are frequently moved from house block to house block, as disputes break out one after the other, until they spoil in the weather and cannot be used at all (Burton 2004, 2005).

---

[14] In his commentary on the Mabo case, Keon-Cohen (2000) pointedly observes that Mer had just one public phone in 1988.

When Owned Commons is a Contrivance: The Case of Nauti

'Nauti' is one of three landowner parties with rights to Hidden Valley, a gold mine prospect on an extension of the Owen Stanley Range near Wau.[15] The Nauti people are Hamtai language speakers, otherwise known as Watuts. The other two parties are 'Kwembu' and 'Winima' in the Biangai language area. The three names, which are the names of the nearest three villages to Hidden Valley, emerged from a 1987 ruling of the Provincial Land Court in Morobe Province.[16] In 2000 they joined formed the Nakuwi Association to negotiate with the mining company (Burton 2001). [17]

For the benefit of the current analysis I want to deconstruct the meaning of 'Nauti' from the point of view of landownership. In the first place Nauti, a village in the Watut Council, [18] is certainly not a 'clan'. Agnatic members of the Yatavo patriline — the descendants of a man called Yatavo — of Equta patronymic, whose spokesmen were the appellants in the Provincial Land Court case, made up no more than 26 per cent of the residents of the village, who numbered 330 in 2000. Their spouses and recently Nauti-born non-agnatic cognates (mainly sisters' children) formed another 26 per cent, and more distant relatives (mainly grandfathers' sisters' descendants) in six other patronymics (together with their spouses) make up the remaining 48 per cent.[19]

The word 'Nauti' is actually derived from the name of the Nautiya patronymic, which currently has *no members resident* in the main part of the village. It was probably first applied by the patrol officer K.W.T. Bridge who took up station at the nearby Otibanda Patrol Post in 1935, as shown in Blackwood's map of the area at the time of her fieldwork in 1937 (Blackwood 1950, Map 1; 1978). This was a correct designation at the time, but the original population of the Nauti

---

[15] I worked on Nauti representational and social impact issues on a consultancy basis to CRA Minerals 1995–96, to Australian Goldfields 1997–98, and as an employee of and consultant to Morobe Consolidated Goldfields 2000–01.

[16] Record of Proceedings, Provincial Land Court, 6–22 May 1987, before Geoffrey Charles Lapthorne, Provincial Magistrate. The parties, incidentally, are alternately referred to in the proceedings as the 'Nauti clan', 'Nauti people', 'Kwembu clan', Kwembu people', and so forth. Space precludes me from deconstructing 'Kwembu' and 'Winima' here, but suffice it to say that, like Nauti, they are neither 'clans' nor do they map cleanly onto group-like clumps of people called the 'Kwembu people' or 'Winima people'. In the text, 'Nauti', in apostrophes, will refer to the court party and Nauti, with no apostrophes, to the physical village.

[17] Nauti + Kuembu (alternate spelling of Kwembu) + Winima = Nakuwi. The mining company was initially CRA Minerals, then Australian Gold Fields, then Morobe Consolidated Gold (and Harmony Gold after the events described here).

[18] The culture area was called Upper Watut by Blackwood (1950) and is to be distinguished from the Middle Watut which is inhabited by unrelated people speaking a different language; today Blackwood's Upper Watut forms the Watut Council, one of several Local-Level Governments in the Bulolo District. Blackwood also used the term Kukukuku; Watuts use this as an alternate today (for example in business group names) deriving it from *Kouka! Kouka!* or 'my boy! my boy!' in the Hamtai language.

[19] See Burton 2003: 207–8 for this usage of the term 'patronymic' and a full dissection of the composition of Nauti.

area — who were of Nautiya patronymic — was almost completely replaced after epidemics of disease swept across Morobe at the end of World War Two.[20]

Because of this complication, a meeting of hundreds of would-be claimants, from perhaps 20 villages in the Watut Council area, was held at a hamlet called Tontomea before the court case. At this meeting it was resolved to endorse the understanding that the Yatavo patriline at Nauti, the nearest village downstream of Hidden Valley on the Watut River, and their close relatives at Yokua, Akikanda and Minava villages,[21] which are located in other parts of the Watut Council, would be designated as *ol man i go pas* ('those who go first'), and the remainder of the Watut claimants would *sanap baksait* ('stand behind them') to receive secondary benefits. This is referred to as the Tontomea Agreement.

The coalition had no name for itself so the spokesmen approached Guyo Saweo, the senior man of Nautiya patronymic living on the forested tracts of Nautiya land where Nauti had been in Blackwood's time (Saweo and Saris 1995). They asked for, and were given, permission to use the name of Guyo's *sit paia* (hearth), the place name 'Nauti'.

There was a strong expectation that the magistrate, whether an expatriate (as he was) or from another part of PNG, would only be capable of dealing with the most straightforward group name possible. The Watut claimants knew that their Biangai neighbours were going to court with two village names of their own, Winima and Kwembu, the nearest settlements on their side of Hidden Valley. The name 'Nauti' would match these for simplicity.

To Watut ears, use of the term 'Nauti' also conveyed the fact that this was a 'hearth', a real place, or, in language, *wa taka*. Strictly, the exact location of the current village was not a *wa taka*, because it was of recent foundation. The name owned by Guyo, though, was a real *wa taka*: that is, it referred to the traditionally founded Nauti that existed in Blackwood's time. When the spokesmen were granted the use of the name, it lent their litigation cultural authenticity.

The Provincial Land Magistrate duly set out a distribution of rights to an *area of common interest* at Hidden Valley among the three parties, and Nauti won 50 per cent of this area (Figure 9-1).

[20] See, for example, J.H.L. Armistead, Wau PR No. 5 of 1943/44 and Wau PR No. 1 of 1944/45.
[21] These are the descendants of two men called Qavaingo and Pakieo.

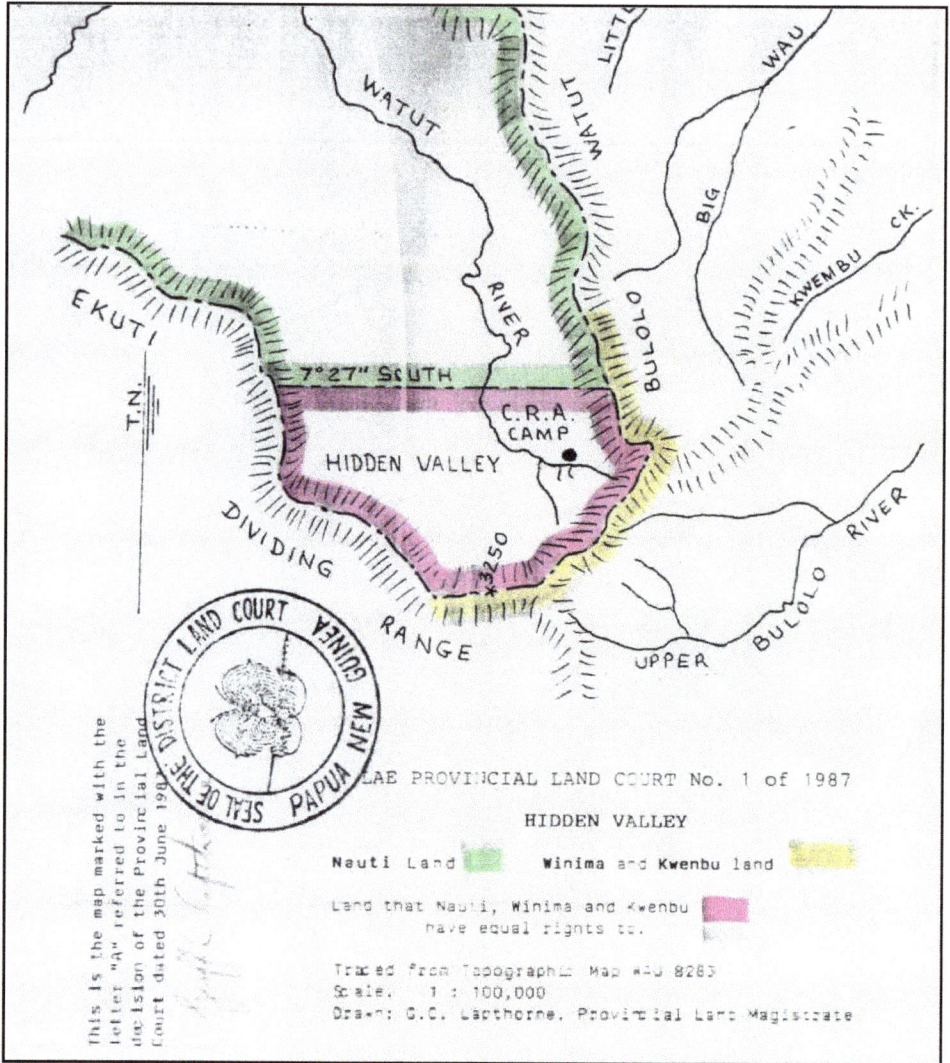

Figure 9-1: Area of common interest at Hidden Valley.

The compression of a multiplicity of Watut interests into the single entity 'Nauti' for the purposes of going to court — and even allowing the court recorder to represent it as a 'clan' — was a contrivance for the purpose of representing Watut rights in Hidden Valley to the outside world. In reality, 'Nauti' was made up of the 332 descendants of closely related patriline ancestors spread among five villages (Table 9-1).

Table 9-1: Distribution of living descendants of the 'Nauti' constituent patrilines of Equta patronymic by village (in 2000).

ANCESTOR	VILLAGE					
	Akikanda	Kaumanga	Minava	Nauti	Yokua	Total
1. Yatavo	1	–	–	87	–	75
2. Qavaingo	43	1	9	1	50	104
3. Sons of Pakieo*	–	–	–	–	–	–
3a. Yandiyamango	–	–	26	–	–	26
3b. Mdakeko	23	–	–	–	–	23
3c. Tupango	23	–	–	1	–	24
3d. Yamaipango	–	–	32	1	–	33
3e. Aqipango	–	33	–	–	1	34
Total descendants	90	34	67	90	51	332
Total residents	198	90	162	330	129	991
Descendants (%)	45.5	37.8	41.4	23.1	39.5	32.2

* In agreements and in the business group name 'Yakaya', Pakieo's descendants area collected together as 'Yandiyamango' though Yandiyamango was strictly the name of the eldest of five brothers.

After the case the solidarity of 'Nauti' wavered. This can be seen in the subsequent evolution of the payment arrangements for occupation fees and bush damage compensation with the mining company. For several years, these cleared legal debts and earlier advances. The few bankable amounts left over were made out to 'Nauti Land Owners' and witnessed by patriline spokesmen.

In 1991, Yakaya Business Group[22] was formed to be a new organisational umbrella. But this also failed to satisfy, and the government's Project Liaison Officer spent most of 1992 brokering a percentage distribution formula among the constituent groups.

From this point, cheques were raised for each subgroup separately. Then the Yatavo and Qavaingo groups fell into dispute and for a period in 1993–94 asked that no payments be made to them. At the same time, the number of signatories proliferated in each village (Figure 9-2).

---

[22] Yatavo + Kavaingo ('Qavaingo', the spelling on their own documents) + Yandiyamango = Yakaya.

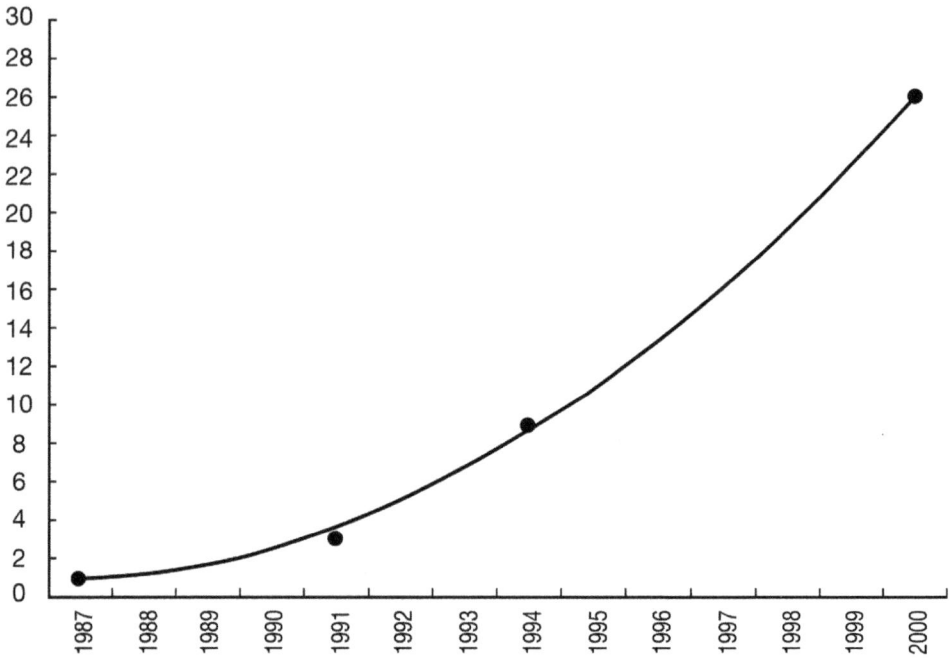

Figure 9-2: Approximate number of signatories for 'Nauti' by year.

This tendency to break down into ever-smaller groups is sometimes taken as evidence of a society fragmenting under the pressure of modernisation. But here we can see that a collection of people with joint rights in a property created a contrived owning entity to win recognition from a court. That accomplished, what is seen is not fragmentation but a reversion to normality.

Discussion

I will now revisit some of the concepts I introduced earlier to produce a more critical analysis of each situation. Table 9-2 provides a summary of the criteria by which the four cases can be differentiated.

Table 9-2: Some attributes related to commons ownership in four cases in Torres Strait and Papua New Guinea.

	Dauan people, Torres Strait	Meriam people, Torres Strait	Wopkaimin of Iralim parish, North Fly District, PNG	'Nauti', Bulolo District, PNG
Area over which ownership asserted	Dauan Island	Mer Island	Mt Fubilan	50% of Hidden Valley
Is the owning entity 'fully determined'?	Yes	Yes	Uncertain	No
Is the owning entity a well bounded group?	No, but Saibai + Dauan are well bounded	Yes	Yes, (with qualifications)	No
'Owned commons' appropriate?	Yes	No	Yes, (say the anthropologists)	No
Ownership determined by Connection Report/Land Investigation Report?	Yes	Yes	Yes	No, litigated outcome
Did community acquire legal title?	Yes	No, litigated outcome	No	No
What was the form of recognition used?	Native Title by consent	Native Title following Mabo No 2	Agreements endorsed by government Lands Officers	Decision of Provincial Land Court magistrate, 1987
Did external boundaries exist?	Yes, the sea	Yes, the sea	Yes	No, 'Area of Common Interest' ruled on by magistrate
Were external boundaries determined by survey?	Yes, long-standing property description (Queensland)	Yes, long-standing property description (Queensland)	In parts only, other sections follow ridges and waterways	Yes, but concealed
Was internal ownership differentiated?	No	Yes, very strongly	No	No
Were internal boundaries surveyed?	No	No (sketch plans part of evidence)	No	No
Were there other primary claimants to the area from the same ethnic group?	No	No, other Eastern Islanders claimed their own islands	No, other Wopkaimin (Wangbin, Migalsim) had claims elsewhere	Many
Was ownership encumbered by other members of the same ethnic group?	Saibai people: close relatives but focussed on their own claim over Saibai Island.	No, although an identity problem resulted in an ambit claim by a family not believed to be from Mer	Other Wopkaimin: uncertain, but focussed on their primary claims elsewhere	Yes, very greatly
Were there secondary claimants to the area from neighbouring ethnic groups?	No	No	Yes, Ningerum, Awin, Faiwolmin, Telefomin preferred for employment (*Mining (Ok Tedi) Act*)	Yes, Biangai claimed the whole area and gave place names in their own language
Were there secondary claimants to the area from distant ethnic groups?	Ambit claims from Papua, but dealt with in Torres Strait Treaty between Australia and PNG	No, claimants all genealogically connected to the Eastern Islands only	Yes, Tari and Kopiago for example, but dismissed as frivolous (see Welsch 1987: 127)	Many, but dismissed as frivolous by residents of the Bulolo District

189

Determinacy of Groups

Were the claimant groups 'fully determined' in the sense I have used? With the Wopkaimin, it is possibly surprising that we cannot say for certain. On the one hand Hyndman (1994: 7) says that a Wopkaimin parish is a 'clearly bounded, territorially discrete unit', but on the other he describes the cognatic Wopkaimin as having far-flung connections of kinship across the wider Min cultural region. Thus the Wopkaimin could be characterised as the 'proximate owners' among an indefinitely extended network of 'underlying' Min owners, all of whom are, at least in theory, secondary right holders anywhere in their cultural region (Welsch 1987: 129). The many informal settlements around Tabubil known as 'corners' and built by immigrants from other Min areas may be a symptom of this. Analysis of the flows of mine-related benefits from the Wopkaimin to non-Wopkaimin relatives, such as occurs between landowners and their relatives at Porgera (Banks 1994, 1997), might also cast light on the situation. Unfortunately we have little information on the subject.

The Dauan and Meriam people are 'well determined' as groups. A short distance beyond their shores there were traditionally no more Dauan or Meriam people. The only ambiguity is posed by drawing a line between them and their neighbours: for Dauan, this was Saibai and Boigu Islands, and for Mer, Erub (Darnley Island) and Ugar (Stephen Island). Beyond these places there were no further speakers of their respective languages, Kala Kawaw Ya and Meriam Mir. Genealogically speaking, the lines were quite easily drawn, with the exception of some families with shared Dauan and Saibai ancestry. The situation did not resemble that of a seamless net of kin extending into a hinterland.

The 'Nauti' are not 'determined' at all, which underscores their problem. The name represents a composite of many descent lines and, while the core lines are arguably 'determined', in the sense that the agnatic descendants of particular apical ancestors are knowable, there are many competing histories which could have placed — or could yet place — an ancestor from a different descent line in the same position.

Boundedness of Groups

The Wopkaimin parish boundaries, as indicated by Hyndman, have the integrity of a local organisational type[23] where main ranges and large rivers form land estate boundaries.

---

[23] To avoid a lengthy discussion, I will use this terminology at face value for present purposes. Two key attributes of the type in question are that it is common in areas of low population density, and 'excisions' (bits of territory excised to another territory along the boundary) and 'pockets' (enclaves of other clans or tribes in the middle of a territory) are uncommon.

Being islands, Dauan and Mer have external boundaries which give the native title areas a ready integrity such as is much harder to come by on the mainland of Australia.

This configuration of land estate is ostensibly found in the 25 km long valley formed by the headwaters of the Watut River above Nauti village where principal ridges and creeks draining from the high ranges form the boundaries of family landholdings. But it is hard to portray this as an absolute boundary of 'Nauti' because of the indeterminacy of the group. The map of the 'area of common interest' at Hidden Valley (Figure 9-1) does show a boundary — it follows the crest of the dividing range for the most part and is completed by a straight line at latitude 7°27" south — but it is an artificial line created by prospecting authority maps in the 1980s. 'Nauti', the entity discussed in court, is not bounded after all.

Were Internal Ownerships Differentiated and Boundaries Surveyed?

In no case were internal boundaries surveyed. At Dauan and among the Wopkaimin, as I have discussed, internal boundaries are purported not to have existed or, if they did (as in the case of Wopkaimin 'neighbourhoods'), they were not seen as relevant to the main issue of community identification.

Around Nauti village, as noted, principal ridges and creeks delineate the family landholdings of residents, but it took me several years to ascertain *which* families matched with *which* ridges and creeks.[24] Nauti leaders were reluctant to disclose information that might enable family heads to bypass them in relation to lease and compensation payments (see Figure 9-2). My view was that maintaining their positions as signatories was a burden upon leaders that stood to poison their relationships with community members and obstructed them from representing community viewpoints effectively. It was also leading them to make extremely inequitable distribution arrangements. Surprisingly, these did *not* always advantage the principal families; in 2000 an obscure cousin lineage of five men shared K17,000 while 62 men in a main lineage had to divide up K20,000. This was just bad arithmetic; I sought to move benefit distribution to a fairer census-based formula along the lines already being used for the mining company's discretionary assistance schemes, such as housing improvement and school fee payments. I devoted a section of my socio-economic impact study (Burton 2001) to how this should be done, but the project was sold to a new company shortly afterwards and neither I nor my PNG counterpart have been contacted since to see how this formula should be implemented.

---

[24] See previous footnote on the circumstances of fieldwork in this area.

At Mer, the internal differentiation of landownership and maintenance of boundaries is a key element of Meriam culture and identity. The colonial response to Meriam landownership was to commission an immediate land survey of the island and to create an island court — both accomplished by 1892. The court's records contain many sketches of land portions and boundaries (Murray Island Court 1908–1983; Sheehan 1987–89). But as time went by, Mer's internal boundary problems were taken less and less seriously by the Queensland Government. Since the 1970s it is probably true to say that hundreds of thousands of dollars have been expended on survey work for infrastructure improvement, but not a single garden, patch of bush, *deup* (traditional boundary bank or line of piled volcanic rocks), or customary house block has been surveyed in the same period. I did sufficient social mapping in 2003–04 to scope out the problems, but my work ran against the trend of a policy blank in the area of assisting PBCs to sort out internal governance issues. At Mer, as I have said, these are severe (Burton 2004, 2005).

Were There Other Primary Claimants from the Same Ethnic Group?

It would be rare indeed if there were not competing claimants to a land estate, but at Dauan, Mer and among the Wopkaimin, the position of the primary claimants is not seriously challenged by others from the same language group.

A qualification at Mer is that a current land dispute concerns whether a disputant's ancestor was from Mer or Erub, a neighbouring island; it is thus about group membership, not whether non-Mer people claim bits of Mer.

Among the Wopkaimin, people whom residents of Iralim parish and outsiders alike might not see as Wopkaimin — because they were born and reside elsewhere — might believe otherwise. Although they would not contest Wopkaimin title, on the grounds that they already believe themselves to be inside the claim group, this is an encumbrance on ownership by people of the same ethnic group.

On the other hand, the 'Nauti' were and are vigorously contested in their rights to land by other speakers of their language. Competing claims take the form of assertions by men of distant lineages that their ancestor preceded any other on the land and that they alone know the hidden history of the area (even though they do not live in it). As with the preceding, this is an encumbrance on ownership by people of the same ethnic group. However, the challengers repeatedly fall down because they cannot — and it does not occur to them to do this — form a claim group representative of a putative resident population 50, 100 or 150 years ago. The 'Nauti' are safe from challenge from a tribe-like or clan-like entity from among other Hamtai speakers because the problem of determinacy besets the challengers as much as it does the incumbents.

Were There Secondary Claimants from Other Ethnic Groups?

At Dauan and Mer there are no effective secondary claimants from neighbouring ethnic groups, mainly because the main candidates living to the north are politically cut off by the international border between Australia and PNG.

The Wopkaimin are subject to political challenge from Ningerum and Awin speakers to the south from time to time. For example, a councillor of Mongulwalawam village, in the Ningerum council area, in 1984 claimed a billion kina a fortnight compensation on the grounds that Mt Fubilan was *not* a Wopkaimin place (Burton 1997: 42). This kind of claim is ineffective, and the Wopkaimin have been defended both by government officials and anthropologists — Welsch said none of the Ningerum 'have any obvious claim ... on Mount Fubilan' (1987: 121).

Welsch discusses the claims to the mine area made by the Faiwolmin, Tifalmin, Telefomin and other northern neighbours with considerable cultural affinity with the Wopkaimin. He says the Wopkaimin did not dismiss the claims in principle, but also did not entertain the idea of sharing their royalties with what would potentially have been another 20,000 people (ibid: 129–130). Politically, these broad area sentiments had a certain amount of traction, because the *Mining (Ok Tedi Agreement) Act 1976* granted the Kiunga (including Awin and Ningerum) and Telefomin people 'preferred area' status for employment and business development. Ambit claims were floated between 1978 and 1980, when Kopiago and Tari people (in another province and separated from Ok Tedi by impassable geographical barriers), and the OPM (Organisasi Papua Merdeka) in West Papua, each claimed ownership of Mt Fubilan (Welsch 1987: 126–7). None of these claims made any political headway for obvious reasons.

I have already mentioned the court settlement reached in 1987 between the 'Nauti' and their eastern neighbours, the Biangai villages of Kwembu and Winima, now joined in the Nakuwi Association. This also now faces new claims. Candidate claimants include the Manki, a relict enclave of distantly related Anga speakers in the Upper Watut; and the Taiak, Galawo, Kapin and Sambio people generally called 'Middle Watuts'. It would seem unlikely that claims from distant places would make political headway, but a salutary lesson is that the Buang Mai-i clan from Mumeng did succeed in claiming Bulolo township in 1999 and continue to grumble over Bulolo and Wau landownership to this day.[25]

---

[25] Recently a Mai-i clan letter writer complained that 'the Nakuwi Association ... are not the rightful owners to that land [Hidden Valley] ... they lost the case several times against the Mai-i clan' (*Post-Courier*, 'Gold signing questioned', 5 October 2005). It is unclear what case the writer refers to.

Conclusion

The purpose of presenting these cases in detail is not to make out that indigenous and Western legal systems are universally incommensurable — I do not believe this to be the case — but to point to two problem areas.

The first area is that which current procedures allow outsiders — whether lawyers, anthropologists, lands officers or various representatives of the State — and traditional owners to map out together in the identification phase of a claim.

In Australia today, pre-litigation investigations and negotiations relating to the configuration of claim groups is often exhaustive but, on the other hand, the law is highly prescriptive about the rights that can be claimed and the kind of legal vehicle that will hold successfully claimed rights. This can subject the claims process to a hegemony of legalism that can be intimidatory to both claimants and anthropologists alike, and stands to defeat the close rapport that may develop between claimants and investigators in the earlier stages of a claim (Martin 2004: 38–41).

In PNG, negotiations prior to litigation or registration have often been perfunctory in the past. Far from taking a firm grip of legal processes and standing over customary owners, the State has become enfeebled and is itself the victim of all kinds of rorts. It is notorious that many cases have been pursued by single litigants or very small groups of litigants acting against other parties without their knowledge.[26] There is no place for anthropologists, or any other professionals, in such actions.

In formal terms the situation has brightened since the 1980s. For example, social mapping is mandated by the *Oil and Gas Act 1998* and, although mining sector legislation does not require it, mining companies have adopted similar practices as part of the social impact assessment process since the mid-1990s. However, in both cases outcomes have been less than satisfactory over the longer term (see Goldman and Weiner, this volume).

How could the 'Nauti' have been helped? That they won at all is admirable, as they went to court without outside help. But they could have been greatly helped if there had been a way of getting the same outcome without having to pretend they were one of Mr Narokobi's 'independent, autonomous social units'

---

[26] The main contribution to the large number of recent actions against the State are the 37 orders made by Papua New Guinea's National Lands Commissioner between July 1999 and September 2002 for the State to pay K80 million compensation to the supposed customary owners of Kiunga, Bulolo, Mt Hagen and parts of various other towns and plantations. In four cases I looked into in Hagen in 1999, the State had been unaware of the actions and the National Lands Commission had met secretly with the claimants. Similarly, the Commission awarded the Mai-i clan of Mumeng K1.2 million in 1999 for parts of Bulolo township without any of Bulolo's customary owners — in the eyes of the majority of the public — being aware of the action. The Deputy Chief Justice ordered the 37 cases to be reviewed in October 2005 (*Post-Courier*, Public Notice, 29 August 2005).

when they were not. As things stand, there is no provision for an alternative way of administering unincorporated rights without incorporating them.

The second problem area concerns the level of assistance to which customary owners can get access to help them properly 'operate' their native title, or recognition of customary title, once they have it.

'Nauti' quickly ran into difficulties because they were unable to devise governance procedures for the very few tasks that they needed to carry out in the years after 1987 — namely, holding simple meetings and distributing very small amounts of lease fees. A government liaison officer was available to them as a mediator, but he had few resources. For example, he had irregular access to a vehicle but his clients lived several hours' drive from town without means of communication with one another.

The Meriam do not need to be told of their litigious reputation and they are well aware of the predicament they find themselves in. In short, it is that the Mabo case says traditional 'laws and customs' should now govern land dealings among themselves, including dispute resolution, but it is not proving easy to adapt traditional ways to the point where any matters can be handled decisively and quickly. In Australia, no money is available to manage successfully claimed native title because PBCs are not funded.

Personally, I was struck by the directness of the question which George Mye OAM, a well-known Eastern Islands elder first elected to Mer Council in 1955 (Beckett 1963), asked me when he found out I had worked in PNG: 'Can people in PNG own land individually?' While I could easily answer 'yes, of course' from the customary point of view, a lengthier response would have been that the *legislative response* to land matters in PNG, as in Australia, places an equally heavy emphasis on the collective ownership of land. This was the gist of Mr Mye's complaint: that Islanders had campaigned for years for autonomy, but when the government had finally given ground in the wake of Mabo, it was to give them something they did not want in the form of the *forced collectivisation* of traditional land.[27]

How can the Meriam be assisted? This is not hard to set out. The Meriam are a case not readily covered by Sutton's two-tier conceptualisation of ownership, if it is 'proximate' ownership that matches with a determination of title.[28] In order for this model to fit their case, a 'family' tier of ownership has to be envisioned. Meriam operated customary transactions perfectly well for the first

---

[27] The antipathy of older Islanders to the threat of over-centralising governments may also be seen in the popularity of membership in the Mer branch of the Australian Legion of Ex-Servicemen in the 1950s (Beckett 1963: 205ff). This was one of several Australian ex-service organisations with a reputation for conservative politics and, in that period, anti-communist leanings.

[28] It could be said that the native title on Mer is an 'underlying title', but the regional system is a wider thing.

100 years after annexation because the Murray Island Court made it as if this tier was recognised by Australian or Queensland law. Native title has confused the situation and the community has yet to find a new institution to replace the old court.

It is not possible to be overly prescriptive about a replacement, but one attribute is easy to set down. Most disputes are inheritance disputes compounded by ambiguities over the intentions of the deceased, the recognition of the rights of adopted children; and the caretaking of land belonging to absentees. In these cases the ability to maintain proper documentation is an excellent aid to straightening out what particular disputes are about.

The Meriam themselves have evinced an avid interest in documentary evidence for a century. Oral testimony has been largely replaced in favour of the presentation of documents — typescripts, photocopies of genealogies that every family knows its place in,[29] and copies of wills and letters. Unfortunately, such official records of new disputes that are made have a typical lifespan of 2–3 years. Supporting documents disappear with the building contractors whose work could not proceed, and council, Island Coordinating Council or Torres Strait Regional Authority correspondence rarely survives beyond this time as offices are moved and files put in storage or just lost. The poor standard of documentation in the post-Mabo period means that there is a weak ability to track current disputes as they arise. A first step towards getting to grips with the 50-case backlog of disputes is to rectify this situation, and the failure to do so is primarily due to the inability of the various tiers of government to grasp the problem (Burton 2005).[30]

[29] These include the 1898 genealogies of W.H.R. Rivers (Rivers 1908).
[30] Contrast this with the institutional reverence with which Eddie Mabo's papers, held at the National Library of Australia, are preserved (Mabo 1943-1992). They are one of only two Australian entries in UNESCO's *Memory of the World Register*, the other being Cook's *Endeavour* journal (http://www.unesco.org/webworld/mdm/register/index.html).

References

Banks, G., 1994. 'Porgera Social Monitoring Programme Economic Modelling Project. Second Report: Gardens and Wantoks.' Canberra: Australian National University, Research School of Pacific and Asian Studies, Department of Human Geography (unpublished report to Porgera Joint Venture).

———, 1997. Mountain of Desire: Mining Company and Indigenous Community at the Porgera Gold Mine, Papua New Guinea. Canberra: Australian National University (PhD thesis).

Beckett, J., 1963. Politics in the Torres Strait Islands. Canberra: Australian National University (PhD thesis).

———, 1995. 'The Murray Island Land Case.' *The Australian Journal of Anthropology* 6: 15–31.

Blackwood, B., 1950. *The Technology of a Modern Stone Age People in New Guinea.* Oxford: Pitt Rivers Museum.

———, 1978. *The Kukukuku of the Upper Watut.* Oxford: Pitt Rivers Museum.

Burton, J.E., 1993. 'Kutubu Petroleum Project Social Monitoring Programme: Commentary of Methodology and Results.' Port Moresby: Unisearch PNG Pty Ltd for Chevron-Niugini Ltd.

———, 1997. 'Terra Nugax and the Discovery Paradigm: How Ok Tedi was Shaped by the Way it was Found and How the Rise of Political Process in the North Fly Took the Company by Surprise.' In G. Banks and C. Ballard (eds), *The Ok Tedi Settlement: Issues, Outcomes and Implications.* Canberra: Australian National University, National Centre for Development Studies and Resource Management in Asia-Pacific (Pacific Policy Paper 27).

———, 2001. 'Morobe Gold and Silver Project: Socio-Economic Impact Study (3 volumes).' Wau and Perth: Morobe Consolidated Goldfields Ltd.

———, 2003. 'Fratricide and Inequality: Things Fall Apart in Eastern New Guinea.' *Archaeology in Oceania* 38: 208–216.

———, 2004. 'Investigation of Land Disputes at Mer Island, Torres Strait.' Canberra: Pacific Social Mapping for Torres Strait Regional Authority.

———, 2005. 'The People Remember and the Government Forgets: The Last 100 years of Land Disputes at Mer, Torres Strait.' Canberra: Australian Institute of Aboriginal and Torres Strait Islander Studies (unpublished seminar paper).

Douglas, J., 1894. 'Report of the Government Resident at Thursday Island for 1892–3.' *Queensland Votes and Proceedings* 2: 914.

Fingleton, J., 2004. 'Is Papua New Guinea Viable *Without* Customary Groups?' *Pacific Economic Bulletin* 19(2): 96–103.

France, P., 1969. *The Charter of the Land. Custom and Colonisation in Fiji.* Melbourne: Oxford University Press.

Haddon A.C. (ed.), 1908. *Reports of the Cambridge Anthropological Expedition to Torres Straits — Volume VI: Sociology, Magic and Religion of the Eastern Islanders.* Cambridge: Cambridge University Press.

Hyndman, D., 1982. 'Population Settlement and Resource Use.' In D. Hyndman, J. Pernetta and D. Frodin (eds), *Ok Tedi Environmental Study — Volume 5.* Melbourne: Maunsell and Partners Pty Ltd.

———, 1994. *Ancestral Rain Forests and the Mountain of Gold.* Boulder: Westview Press.

Jackson, R.T., C.A. Emerson and R. Welsch, 1981. *The Impact of the Ok Tedi Project.* Port Moresby: Department of Minerals and Energy.

Keon-Cohen, B. 2000. 'The Mabo Litigation: A Personal and Procedural Account.' *Melbourne University Law Review* 35. Viewed 20 March 2007 at http://www.austlii.edu.au/au/journals/MULR/2000/35.html.

Mantziaris, C. and D.F. Martin, 1999. *Guide to the Design of Native Title Corporations.* Perth: National Native Title Tribunal.

Martin, D., 2004. 'Capacity of Anthropologists in Native Title Practice.' Canberra: Anthropos Consulting Services for National Native Title Tribunal.

Narokobi, B., 1989. *Lo Bilong Yumi Yet: Law and Custom in Melanesia.* Suva: Melanesian Institute and Socio-Economic Service and the University of the South Pacific.

Rivers, W.H.R., 1908. 'Genealogies.' In A.C. Haddon (ed.), op. cit.

Saweo, G. and J. Saris, 1995. 'History of Nautiya clan in the Thainameo family of Nauti Village (Watut).' Unpublished typescript.

Sheehan, C.G., 1987–89. 'Guide to sources on Murray Islands, Queensland.' Brisbane: John Oxley Library (typescript).

Sutton, P., 2003. *Native Title in Australia: An Ethnographic Perspective.* Cambridge: Cambridge University Press.

Welsch, R., 1979. 'Resources, Land Tenure and Ownership in the Ok Tedi Area.' Port Moresby: Department of Minerals and Energy (unpublished report).

———, 1987. 'Multinational Development and Customary Land Tenure: The Ok Tedi Project of Papua New Guinea.' *Journal of Anthropology* 6(2): 109–154.

Wilkin, A., 1908. 'Property and Inheritance.' In A.C. Haddon (ed.), op. cit.

Chapter Ten

Outstation Incorporation as Precursor to a Prescribed Body Corporate[1]

Katie Glaskin

On my first journey to northern Dampierland Aboriginal communities in 1994, many members of those communities spoke to me about 'making a claim'. I had travelled there to speak with Bardi and Jawi peoples about the native title claim a group of elders had legally instructed the Kimberley Land Council to begin preparing on their behalf.[2] Within a short time I realised that when people spoke to me about 'making a claim', and when I spoke with them about the native title claim, we were referring to different matters. They were speaking about outstations and the process of incorporation under the Commonwealth *Aboriginal Councils and Associations Act 1976* (*ACAA*); I was talking about a claim to native title under the Commonwealth *Native Title Act 1993* (*NTA*). The conflation many people subsequently made, between 'making a claim' to form an outstation group and 'making a claim' for native title, had its basis in their experiences of the outstation movement.

The outstation movement amongst Bardi and Jawi has resulted in a large number of small incorporated outstation groups, while a determination of their native title claim requires the formation of a single larger incorporated group, a Registered Native Title Body Corporate. The latter is defined either as a Prescribed Body Corporate (PBC) or as a body corporate registered on the National Native Title Register.[3] A Registered Native Title Body Corporate holds native title on trust (as in a PBC) or acts 'as an agent or representative of the common

[1] An earlier version of this chapter is embedded in my PhD thesis (Glaskin 2002). For their contribution to the overall development of that work, I am grateful to Francesca Merlan, Ian Keen, and Tim Rowse. To James Weiner for comments on an earlier draft of this chapter, to Bardi and Jawi people who have shared so much of themselves with me since 1994, and to Geoffrey Bagshaw with whom I worked on their native title claim since that time, I am also extremely grateful. The fieldwork on which this chapter is based would not have been possible without the support of the Kimberley Land Council and The Australian National University. I am grateful to them and to the Berndt Foundation at the University of Western Australia, which awarded me a postdoctoral fellowship that enabled me to further develop this work.
[2] This claim was heard by the Federal Court of Australia in 2001 and 2003, and the court delivered its native title determination on 10 June 2005.
[3] See Subsections 193(2)(d)(iii) and (iv) and Section 253 of the *NTA* (reprinted as at 27 July 1998).

law holders in respect of matters relating to native title' (*NTA* Section 58(a)).[4] For the purposes of this chapter, I shall focus on PBCs incorporated under the *ACAA*.

This chapter is concerned with the relationship between two different kinds of incorporation among Bardi and Jawi peoples of Western Australia. Outstations are a means by which people can live on their country; native title is a mechanism by which people seek legal recognition of their relationships to country. Both require incorporation and are concerned at some level with indigenous connections to country. At issue here are not just the relationships between different kinds of Aboriginal corporations formed in response to different legislative requirements, but the consequences for the expression and enactment of property relations amongst those concerned. To what extent are these successive corporatising regimes an expression or transformation of those customary relations to land that they are constituted to represent in some sense, and how might such developments affect or influence one another?

This chapter is based on fieldwork conducted at various times between the years 1994 and 2001, prior to the determination of the Bardi and Jawi native title claim in June 2005.[5] It does not, therefore, address post-determination efforts and discussions concerning PBC establishment; rather, it is concerned with the processual relationship between these kinds of incorporation as they emerged prior to a determination of native title. Notwithstanding this, I would expect that many of these same issues would emerge post-determination, and that the form of the determination itself is likely to have created additional issues with respect to PBC formation.[6]

Background

The area considered in this chapter is located in the northwest Kimberley region of Western Australia. It includes the northern tip of the Dampierland Peninsula (north of the Beagle Bay Reserve) and the islands in the King Sound to the west of Sunday Strait, the area over which Bardi and Jawi made their native title claim.[7] There are three main communities within the claim area — Lombadina, Djarindjin and One Arm Point — which are also incorporated under the *ACAA*. Lombadina was a Pallottine Catholic mission that began as an outpost of Beagle

---

[4] Fingleton (1994: 5–6) identifies the main functions of a PBC under the *NTA*, which include: entering into agreements with the government, whether for the surrender of native title (s.21(1)(a) and (3)), authorisation of future Acts (s.21(1)(b)), or to enter into local or regional agreements (s.21(4)); to participate in negotiations regarding grants of mining rights over native title land (s.29(1) and (2), s.31(1)(a) and (b), s.33); to be consulted about access to native title lands (s.26(4)(c)); to exercise procedural rights with respect to compulsory acquisition (s.23(6)); to deal with compensation issues (s.61 and s.51(6)); and to apply for variation of native title determinations (s.61). See Memmott et al. (this volume) for further discussion.

[5] *Sampi v State of Western Australia* [2005] FCA 777.

[6] As of 10 July 2006 this decision was under appeal before the Full Federal Court of Australia.

[7] The islands were not included in the determination of native title made on 10 July 2005.

Bay Mission to its south in 1910.[8] In the 1980s, local politics within Lombadina led to the formation of Djarindjin community. This is situated immediately adjacent to Lombadina, and the two communities are distinguished mainly by the fence that divides them, separate corporations (and hence community councils), and their own community stores.[9] Sunday Island Mission was originally formed as a non-denominational Protestant mission in 1899, and was transferred to United Aborigines Mission control in 1923.[10] Bardi and Jawi were still coming into these missions up until the late 1920s at least, and even then, many people did not remain sedentary at the missions but moved between them and a number of white pearlers' camps. Such movement meant that the populations at these missions did not become settled until after World War Two (Robinson 1973: 175). Following a period of dislocation in Derby in the 1960s when Sunday Island Mission was closed, Bardi and Jawi who had formerly lived at the island established the community at One Arm Point in 1972.[11]

Bardi and Jawi movements into these missions in the early days had both voluntary and involuntary aspects. 'Coming in', as a number of Bardi people have referred to this movement, initially occurred as news spread that rations were available at the missions, and ultimately became a practical necessity in a changing economic landscape. Once a number of people were congregated at the missions, being near kin provided additional impetus for bush people to 'come in' to the missions. These centralisation movements occurred slowly. The movement of Sunday Island Mission residents to Derby occurred more quickly, and under greater coercion, as the mission was closed and school-aged children from the mission were taken to Derby and were subsequently followed by their parents.[12] Coombs (1974) discussed Bardi and Jawi movement from Derby back to Sunday Island, and the ultimate formation of One Arm Point community, as an early example of the 'decentralisation trend'. Although this movement began as a process of individuals splintering from a centralised group, within a short time nearly all the Bardi and Jawi from Sunday Island Mission, who had been living in Derby, were living at One Arm Point. In that sense, while it was a disaggregation in terms of Bardi and Jawi moving away from other Aboriginal groups in the reserves at Derby, the movement is better understood as a return by those people who had been in exile from their country. All of these movements, however, can be seen as 'symptomatic of an inherent tension in Aboriginal accommodation to European presence' (Sullivan 1996a: 27). The

---

[8] For further information regarding the establishment and founding of Lombadina, see Durack (1997).
[9] They share a school and a health clinic.
[10] For a detailed discussion of the formation of Sunday Island Mission, see Robinson (1973).
[11] See Drysdale and Durack (1974) and Coombs (1974) for further discussion of the early establishment of One Arm Point community.
[12] This was not just the case with respect to Sunday Island. Jebb (2002: 254–5) says that when Kimberley Aboriginal children from pastoral stations were taken to school in Derby by Native Welfare, they were similarly followed into the town by their parents.

outstation movement, a movement away from the major communities, is not dissimilar in this respect.

While the outstation movement can be considered, as it is by Coombs (1974), as a 'decentralisation trend' (and this is true of both its spatial and administrative aspects, since it has resulted in the multiplication of incorporated outstation groups), it also has a centralising aspect. As the processes of incorporation (under the *ACAA*) and the economic means through which outstations can be established originate outside the indigenous community, the apparent dispersal of groups conceals a more complete political centralisation with respect to administrative and incorporative processes. Nevertheless, since one of the effects of the movement is to create multiple indigenous corporations, each with its own chairperson, set of rules and so on, with this caveat in mind, I continue to consider the outstation movement as decentralising in terms of intra-indigenous relationships and political authority.

The Outstation Movement

In parts of the Kimberleys, usually those where outstations are excised from large pastoral leases, Aborigines refer to excisions as 'matchboxes' because of their small size. When speaking in a possessive sense Bardi most commonly refer to an outstation as a 'block'. The outstation or homelands movement has been a visible trend amongst Aborigines in many parts of Australia for at least three decades (Coombs et al. 1980: 1). As well as returning to traditional country, Aborigines have chosen to form small outstation groups to avoid social problems in larger communities.[13] The timing of the trend was concurrent with the provision of welfare benefits to Aboriginal people (Smith 2000: 62), and with government policy shifts, from assimilation to self-determination (later self-management) formulated in the late 1960s and early 1970s (Coombs et al. 1980: 5; Altman 1986: 477).

There are significant differences between outstation movements in different regions of Australia. Sexton (1996) compares the outstation movement in the Northern Territory and Western Australia, concluding that one of the most significant differences is in relation to the tenure of the land available for outstations. In the Northern Territory, the operation of the Commonwealth *Aboriginal Land Rights (Northern Territory) Act* since 1976 has resulted in the return of significant amounts of land to Aboriginal people. Aborigines who successfully claim land under the Act obtain a title that is an estate in fee simple (Sexton 1996: 5). Altman (1987: 1818) similarly identifies 'a correlation between the growth of the outstation movement and security of tenure' gained under

---

[13] For example, Sullivan (1996a: 25) refers to movements by Aborigines from Warmun (Turkey Creek) to set up independent camps on Alice Downs, Frog Hollow and Glen Hill 'without facilities' in the mid-1970s, as moving away from destructive and disruptive social processes in the larger community.

this Act in the Northern Territory. In Western Australia, where there was no land rights legislation prior to the *NTA*, secure tenure of this kind was not available. Many outstations were formed on vacant Crown Land (now called 'unallocated' Crown Land). Some were excised from pastoral leases, in which case the outstation group obtained a Special Purpose Lease for periods of 25–50 years, though these 'guarantee free entry to the holders of a mining tenement' (Sexton 1996: 6). The third possibility was for an Aboriginal group to obtain a 99-year lease from the Aboriginal Lands Trust, although in the northern Dampierland Peninsula these seem usually to be issued in relation to the creation of Aboriginal reserves under the Western Australian *Aboriginal Affairs Planning Authority Act 1972* (such as the One Arm Point reserve), rather than outstations. The consequences of the Western Australian system were that Aboriginal land was 'much more a product of government discretion' than in the Northern Territory, with its statutory regime for claiming land (Sexton 1996: 6).

There are regional differences in outstation movements within states as well as between them. In the Kimberley region, there are marked differences in the outstation movement between Bardi and other nearby groups. While there are outstations south of Bardi in the Beagle Bay Reserve among Nyul Nyul and Jabirr Jabirr peoples, and south of Broome among Yawuru and Karajarri peoples, the density of outstations in these regions is not the same as amongst Bardi.[14] The factors Smith (2000: 450) identifies with respect to variation in the outstation movement in the Coen region — local organisation, the environment and historical factors — are equally salient to the explanation of such differences between Bardi and other nearby groups.

In Western Australia the outstation movement has been in progress since the 1980s, and in 1999 there were some 225 outstations across the state (Muir 1999: 11). The outstation movement coincided with an era in which Aborigines began to receive wages or cash welfare payments instead of rations, and the transition 'from rations to cash' reflected 'a change in the rationalities of government, from tutelary/pastoral to liberal/contractual' (Rowse 1998: 86). In remote communities, integration into the cash economy was accompanied in many instances by the transition from mission-dominated institutions to secular self-governing towns, resulting in a 'dramatic shift in the nature, structure and moral economy of these Aboriginal communities' (Peterson 1998: 109).

Moizo relates the introduction of the Community Development Employment Projects (CDEP) scheme in Fitzroy Crossing to the movement of Fitzroy Aborigines

---

[14] According to a 1994 ATSIC listing of incorporated groups in the ATSIC Kullari region (which encompasses this area), there were a total of 18 incorporated outstation groups in the region extending south of the Bardi and Jawi claim area to Bidyadanga, over a north-south distance of approximately 250 km. In contrast, during the same period, there were at least 33 outstations in the Bardi and Jawi claim area, a north-south distance of approximately 60 km.

out of the town and into smaller (outstation) communities.[15] He says that this movement occurred 'since they had the opportunity to be financially autonomous, an opportunity that did not exist prior to the introduction of CDEP', which was implemented in Fitzroy Crossing in 1988 (Moizo 1990: 36). CDEP provides an important source of income for outstations, and this is augmented by pension monies, one-off grants, and cash earned through various means (Altman 1986: 478; Spicer 1997: 32–3; Smith 2000: 397). In 2005, government debate about the economic viability of remote Aboriginal communities was specifically linked with a view that communal landownership and lack of economic opportunities for remote area Aboriginal people were causally linked (Dodson and McCarthy 2005).

Outstation Establishment

In the Bardi and Jawi claim area, in common with many outstations in Western Australia, living areas are not large areas and do not 'confer much actual land or control on Aboriginal people' (Sexton 1996: 7). The outstations I was able to measure on the basis of land tenure documents are 5223 m², 7782 m², 1.5 ha, and just over 2 ha, and this appears to cover the usual size range.[16] By way of comparison, the communities of One Arm Point and Djarindjin have leases covering areas of 14 339.5 ha and 56 727 ha respectively.[17] Sullivan (1996a: 26) says that, on average, outstations in the Kimberley are of 1 km² (0.405 ha or 4050 m²) in size.

During the latter half of the 1980s, the first of the outstations in the Dampier Peninsula became incorporated under the *Aboriginal Councils and Associations Act.*

> The provisions of the Act relate to a *residential* group in the area, not the *owning* group. They confer control over very limited aspects of the life of the group, are subject to very intrusive intervention prior to incorporation by the Registrar of Aboriginal Corporations and encourage non-Aboriginal procedures for representation and decision-making (Sullivan 1997: 18, emphasis added).

Funding grants through various government agencies were available to incorporated groups to assist with the establishment of outstation infrastructure,

---

[15] Sanders (1998: 145) describes CDEP, a scheme that began in March 1977, as an attempt to 'put in place a more appropriate arrangement for remote Aboriginal communities than standard individualised UB [unemployment benefit] payment. This more appropriate arrangement was justified by an analysis of difference.' The arrangement, as Moizo (1990: 36) describes it, reduces the number of Aborigines on unemployment benefits by requiring Aborigines 'to do several hours of work per week in order to get an amount of money similar to that which they would receive on unemployment benefits'.

[16] One outstation is as large as 8.0089 ha, and the exceptionally sized outstation in the region is 405.3871 ha (Pender Gardens in the southern portion of the claim area).

[17] These are One Arm Point Reserve 20927 and Djarindjin Aboriginal Corporation, Dampier Location 297.

such as bores or rain tanks, energy panels or generators, basic housing facilities, and outstation vehicles.[18] The absence of recognised land rights in Western Australia meant that outstation groups were dependent on government support of this kind, since mining companies were not obliged to make financial contributions or compensation to indigenous landholders (Sullivan 1996a: 29). Regular outstation income then is derived from specific purpose grants, pensions or CDEP funding.[19] Muir's description of the economy on which outstations in Western Australia have generally been built accurately portrays the situation I am familiar with in the peninsula:

> The people moving to outstations were often registered as participants in CDEP projects of the larger communities. These people then remained on the larger communities' CDEP programs, with the outstation allocated as a specific CDEP project. The CDEP wage meant that people had an income and were able to purchase essential capital items ... As outstations developed, became permanent and incorporated under the *Aboriginal Councils and Associations Act 1976* (Cwlth), they were, formally, able to secure separate funding from ATSIC for essential services like water, housing and continued CDEP support (Muir 1999: 11–12).

The outstation economies in this region then are based on a mixture of subsistence through fishing and hunting, with some gathering, social security payments (including pensions) and CDEP monies. Some outstations derive further income from commercial trochus exploitation, aquaculture, and tourism.

A Place of One's Own: The Politics of Land Tenure

Since outstation groups become incorporated under the *ACAA*, applications for incorporation go to the Registrar of Aboriginal Corporations and must include a copy of the proposed rules of the corporation. Sullivan says that 'while the rules may be based on Aboriginal custom (s. 43(4)), they need to address a number of matters ... many of which have no counterpart in Aboriginal custom or may be contrary to it'. These include the requirement for the corporation to make rules regarding meetings (there is a requirement for Annual General Meetings), and to keep a register of members, of which there must be at least twenty-five (Sullivan 1996b: 16–17).

After addressing a number of requisite criteria, including that of incorporation, applications for land to form an outstation are submitted to the Aboriginal Affairs Planning Authority which administers the *Aboriginal Affairs*

---

[18] These are now available through the Office of Indigenous Policy Coordination, and were formerly available through the now-defunct Aboriginal and Torres Strait Islander Commission (ATSIC) and its precursor, the Department of Aboriginal Affairs.
[19] See Sanders (1998) for a discussion of the basis and development of the scheme. The process of incorporation required outstation groups to submit plans for outstation specific CDEP.

Planning Authority Act that established the Aboriginal Lands Trust. One criterion was to demonstrate that the applicants had traditional attachment to the area in question, although the corroborating documentation required was not substantial.[20] Such documentation could include genealogies prepared by anthropologists, by resource agency workers (who generally assisted with all facets of the incorporation process), or by the applicants themselves. Assertions regarding traditional attachment to the area could be augmented by supplying the local language name of the area as well as brief comments about the connections of the applicants to the area. Such requirements have been neither extensive nor prescriptive, and they have not been tested nor made subject to the kinds of proof of connection to country that is ultimately required by the *NTA*. So, while some parallel could be drawn between these two processes on the basis that both involve traditional affiliation with country, the very real differences between the two mean that the parallel cannot be sustained to any great extent.

Local shire councils also scrutinise applications for outstations, because of the implications of service delivery to remote communities.[21] Local community councils also have a role in the approval of outstation areas, where proposed outstation areas fall within their lease jurisdictions. The process of groups seeking community council approval to form an outstation on an area of land seems to occur prior to the more formalised processes associated with incorporation and the Aboriginal Lands Trust application. Even this is likely to be preceded by informal consultations with other Aboriginal people with attachment to the area in question.[22] Once a group has been incorporated and its outstation area has been approved by the Trust (and subject to these other processes), applications for funding the outstation group are submitted to the relevant funding body.[23]

In the absence of land rights legislation in Western Australia prior to the *NTA*, most Bardi family groups have sought to secure an outstation on their country. As a result, numerous outstations now exist within a very small region. Figure 10-1 represents the general locations of outstations within the Bardi and

[20] Under the heading 'Customary Tenure', Section 32 of the *Aboriginal Affairs Planning Authority Act* refers at 32(1) to 'Aboriginal inhabitants of that area, being persons who are or have been normally resident within the area, and their descendants'. At 32(2) the Act says that: 'Regulations made in relation to an area to which subsection (1) applies may provide for the compilation, maintenance, and use of documentary evidence as to the entitlement of persons to any interest in the use of, or benefit to be derived from, specific areas of land or in the enjoyment of natural resources related to customary land use.'

[21] With respect to outstation policy, the 25 June 1992 minutes of the Shire of Halls Creek in the East Kimberley included that 'the applicant is required to provide details as to their traditional association with the land' (Crough and Christophersen 1993: 137). The Shire resolved that they would not 'be responsible for the provision and maintenance of any services' (ibid).

[22] Amongst Bardi, failure to consult with relevant landowners would usually have ramifications, including for community council members who were held responsible for allocating the land.

[23] At the time of my research, this body was ATSIC. As at 2006, such applications for funding would be handled by the Office of Indigenous Policy Coordination.

Jawi claim area.[24] These outstations are all located quite close to the major communities, and to each other, and are typically situated within a small walking distance from the coast. This spatial distribution is reflective of Bardi and Jawi local organisation, which itself also reflects upon the environment — the availability of fresh water sources along the coast, as opposed to the hinterland — and the narrowness of the Dampierland Peninsula at its northernmost end.

Figure 10-1: Approximate location of outstation groups in 2001.

---

[24] The orthography in this figure is that used by the incorporated outstation groups. The most distant outstation is approximately 50 km away from one of the major communities, while most outstations would be roughly within a 20 km radius or less of these communities.

Local Organisation

Bardi and Jawi share a system of local organisation comprised of estate groups centred on freshwater sources on the mainland coast or islands. The interior of the Dampierland Peninsula, which lies between Bardi estate groups, does not contain permanent water and is characterised as *nimidiman* (shared) country, or *nimidiman jugara buru* ('together possessing country') (Bagshaw 1999: 48), analogous to the notion of shared commons (see Burton, this volume). Bardi and Jawi are primarily affiliated with estates through patrifiliation: paternal adoption (*andala*) can similarly confer primary estate affiliation (Bagshaw 1999: 58). An individual's 'own' country (their *buru*) is therefore considered to be the *buru* of their father (and father's father). Individuals also have significant rights in their maternal estate (*ningarlm*) and in their spouse's estate (*gurirriny*). However:

> In all matters pertaining to their respective *ningarlm* and *gurirriny*, individuals are expected to defer to estate-affiliates (i.e. those identified with the estate through patrifiliation). They are also expected to 'back up' the latter on estate-related issues ... (Bagshaw 1999: 62).

Effectively, rights in mother's country (*ningarlm*) and spouse's country (*gurirriny*) are not considered to be of the same primary order as those in father's country (*buru*). Bagshaw writes that while the land component of estates 'is typically quite small' (around 6 and 4.5 km^2 in two mapped examples), 'the offshore areas of a *bur* may ... be quite extensive' (ibid: 49). Tidally exposed areas contiguous with the land are considered part of an estate, as are nearby offshore features such as islands, rocks, sandbanks, reefs and shallow waters (Bagshaw and Glaskin 2000: 5). Bagshaw (1999, 2001a, 2001b) identifies 21 extant Bardi *buru*, four extant Jawi *buru*, and six deceased estates within the Bardi and Jawi claim area. The deceased estates are in various stages of succession. The general locations of these *buru* are represented in Figure 10-2.

Hiatt (1996: 13–35) summarises the anthropological arguments that have historically occurred regarding the concept of clan, horde and band. Clan groups are not the same as residential groups; the latter consist of people related to each other by various means, and common descent in the male line, the criterion of estate (clan) affiliation, is only one of these. Bardi outstation groups frequently reflect and are premised on estate ownership, but similarly, the residential groups formed at outstations do not correlate entirely with them.

Bardi and Jawi consider the main requisite criteria of a person's ability to establish an outstation in a particular location within the terms of their own system of land tenure. Patrifiliates are considered to have every right to build an outstation in their own country, although senior patrifiliates are the people having greatest authority (or 'say') over that country and other members of the estate group should, in principle, defer to them. Outstations within the Bardi and Jawi claim area have largely (though not entirely) been established by estate affiliates within their own *buru*, and consequently some estate affiliates have begun to use the terms referring to their estate (*buru*) and to their outstation ('block') interchangeably.[25] Since there are very few people in the Bardi and Jawi claim area with 'historical' rather than traditional associations to country, historical attachment (as opposed to traditional affiliation) has not been a significant issue in the allocation of land for outstations to date. Some Aborigines who were neither Bardi nor Jawi grew up at either Sunday Island or Lombadina, but these cases are few. Typically, where these cases do occur, the family or person with the historical attachment has approached patrifiliates from the estate where they would like to build their outstation for permission to do so.

Where individuals have a non-Bardi or non-Jawi father, and have not been 'grown up' by a Bardi or Jawi father, they often emphasise other lines of descent in order to reckon their connection to country.[26] Some individuals with Bardi mothers and non-Bardi fathers (who are therefore unable to reckon country through their father) have instead 'followed' their maternal grandfather (*nyami*) 'for country' — in other words, in reckoning matters of descent, and consequently in articulating rights in country. This sometimes produces considerable friction between people claiming rights to the same area through different mechanisms. Where estate affiliates are unable to form an outstation within their own country because the land is alienated, they too have sought to emphasise other means of connection to country in order to make claims within other *buru*. These strategies have implications for the politics of land tenure among Bardi and Jawi peoples, and these politics have become especially apparent within the context of the outstation movement.

> Estate-affiliates are empowered to grant enduring, albeit limited, rights of access, residence and usufruct in respect of their own *bur* to unrelated or distantly related persons. Such rights (and their referents) are known as *nimalj*, a term which I gloss as 'authorized use' ... Birth at a place outside one's own *bur* is also generally believed to confer a range of inalienable *nimalj* rights (including rights of access, residence and usufruct) in that locality (Bagshaw 1999: 61).

---

[25] This was evident in some evidence given by applicants during the 2001 Federal Court hearing of the Bardi and Jawi native title claim.

[26] This is mainly relevant to marriages with non-indigenous people, but can also occur where the father is Aboriginal (but not Bardi or Jawi) but the individual feels more socially connected to Bardi and has therefore followed the mother 'for country'. Trigger (1987: 223) makes a similar comment with respect to choice of linguistic affiliation at Doomadgee.

Figure 10-2: General locations of Bardi and Jawi *buru*.

Source: Bagshaw 1999, 2001b, 2001c.

When estate affiliates grant *nimalj*, it confers particular rights within a specified area of country to a person (the grantee) for the duration of their life.[27] These rights may be as narrowly defined as the right to harvest bush fruit from a particular tree, or to mine ochre or fish at a certain location. As discussed, Bardi have a strongly held view regarding the primacy of the rights of estate affiliates within *buru*, and this is reflected in normative statements regarding principles of land tenure. Giving permission to others to set up an outstation is a contemporary corollary to giving *nimalj* to camp within that *buru* on an ongoing basis. Reflecting modern alterations of indigenous custom, verbal permission is

[27] As Bagshaw (1999: 62) states, 'unless voluntarily relinquished by the recipient'.

in some instances replaced by written permission. Difficulties arising between the respective parties — the grantor and the grantee — have increased the tendency towards written agreements, since conflict can arise when the individuals making the initial agreement pass away and these issues have to be negotiated by their descendants.

Sutton (1978: 125) describes the formation of outstations in the Cape Keerweer region as 'providing a source for an emerging group structure of a corporate type at a higher order of generality than was previously feasible'. Within the outstation movement, traditional land tenure is being articulated within a new political economy, one that involves aspects of 'intercultural production' (Merlan 1998). The nexus between the politics of land tenure and resource acquisition in this area is accentuated by the structural location of these matters within a 'whitefella' domain, involving various government agencies, programs, bureaucratic requirements in relation to procedure and expenditure, accountability measures, spot-checks on outstation groups, and so on. Such mechanisms pit outstation groups within the same region against one another symbolically, and in many instances materially as well. Claims to country in the context of the outstation movement, have, in my view, consolidated notions of the autonomy of these contemporary land-using groups. While there is a broad correlation between these outstations and *buru* (estate groups), that is, between some of the land users and the landowners (estate affiliates), this correlation is not complete; but where the correlation occurs, outstations are, in some cases at least, conflated with *buru*. These transitions could be considered 'a regenerated Aboriginal system of local tenure ... embedded within a different mode of material production', but which demonstrate 'strong continuities of the social and cultural modes of Aboriginal life including its political and territorial aspects' (Smith 2000: 442). Nevertheless, these transformations have implications for the emergence of new property relationships amongst Bardi in general, and within the context of a communal claim to native title.

Prescribed Bodies Corporate

Rowse's discussion of general principles underlying the incorporation of Aboriginal groups is equally apposite to a consideration of PBCs under the *NTA*.

> As a strategy of reform, incorporation assumed an indigenous willingness to change, just as assimilation programs assumed, solicited and even coerced change in their clients. Incorporation must therefore be seen as an instance of continuity between assimilation and self-determination. Corporations, councils and associations are thoroughly 'Western' modes of collective action ... 'Self-determination' begs the question: what self or selves? (Rowse 2000: 132).

Fingleton says that, since native title is a communal title, the rationale underlying the PBC includes it being the '"contact point" for dealings between the native title holders and outsiders', so that:

> The need for bodies corporate is explained partly by legal reasons — the need for a legal entity with its own separate existence — and also by practical reasons (to facilitate dealings), and by a desire to protect the interests of individual members of the native title-holding group (1994: 3).

As Fingleton indicates, PBCs are designed, in large part, to facilitate external dealings between governments (and other interests) and native title-holding groups. Sansom (in Rowse 1993: 54) describes this succinctly: 'Leviathan addresses not Aborigines, but Aborigines Inc.' But, as Rowse says, 'mobs are not "corporations" whose anatomy can be given in terms of a series of offices and functions' (ibid: 55). Aboriginal social formations are not correlates of Western-style corporations. Political life within Aboriginal domains is characteristically dynamic, not particularly commensurate with the static corporate entity they are being asked to maintain.

The relationship between multiple incorporated outstation groups and a larger PBC (as a native title-holding body) is unlikely to emerge without some difficulty. While the outstation movement in this region can be seen, on the one hand, as both an exercise of people's native title and reflective of their traditional attachments to country, on the other hand, the implications of such incorporation in this area have been considerable. Relationships within communities have been impacted significantly as groups vie for allocation of resources, draw artificial boundaries around their incorporated groups, and use 'traditional' concepts to validate particular positions. Since the politics over land have become exacerbated in this context, the incorporation of the wider native title group as a PBC is likely to prove politically difficult, as I briefly describe below.

Towards a Representative Structure

In 1996 the Kimberley Land Council began working with the Bardi and Jawi claimant group on the development of a PBC. The claimant group's involvement in commercial developments on their country (such as tourism and trochus), and in non-commercial development of land through the outstation movement, meant that the right to negotiate under the *NTA* primarily involved negotiations between claimants rather than others outside of the claimant group.[28]

---

[28] Under the *NTA*, prior to its amendment in 1998, once the National Native Title Tribunal had accepted and registered a native title claim, claimants held 'the right to negotiate' in relation to certain 'permissible future acts' within the claim area. Under Section 26, permissible future acts are 'essentially acts relating to mining, the compulsory acquisition of native title for the purpose of making a grant to a third party, and any other acts approved by the Commonwealth Minister'. The right to negotiate under the *NTA* was not the equivalent of a veto; rather, it allowed claimants and proponents of permissible future acts

Accordingly, the claimant group needed to develop mechanisms through which negotiations over land management issues within the communal and legal context of native title could be addressed. This was necessary both for potential dealings with outsiders and for land and sea management issues arising between members of the claimant group. Management issues (such as the further development of outstations or the setting up of aquaculture projects) also held potential legal implications, since they could result in the issue of leases over land (or sea) that was under a native title claim. Since the right to negotiate required communal decisions about land interests which had not previously been negotiated internally in this manner,[29] the development of a working group as a precursor to a PBC was closely related to the right to negotiate in this claim.

Decisions about land use had not previously been subject to this kind of formalised decision making by the broader Bardi and Jawi group. Rather, they had usually been made by the community councils, which were not necessarily or formally accountable to the wider jural public, although informal consultations with senior patrifiliates (where their country was concerned) and with *madja* or bosses (senior ritual leaders) were sometimes held.[30] *Madja* (collectively *madja-madjin*) also frequently intervene in land use decisions in contexts where *ngulungul* (culturally restricted, 'sacred') locations are threatened by development. However, community council decisions have not necessarily taken into account the principles underlying the laws and customs of their peoples, and in this sense, their relationship with the PBC represents a significant issue.[31]

In late 1996 Bardi and Jawi established an interim working group to deal with matters requiring negotiation and to begin the work of consulting with the other native title holders about how their interests might best be represented in the structure of a PBC. The claimant group decided that their representative working group would comprise two representatives from each of the 'clan groups'. 'Clan groups' is a term that, especially since this time, has been increasingly applied by some claimants to the various regional aggregates defined by directional or geographic descriptions (rather than to estate groups).[32]

(the 'parties') to attempt to reach a negotiated agreement regarding the development or acquisition under consideration.

[29] External negotiations have occurred with the Department of Conservation and Land Management (who sought to declare a nature conservation zone over part of the claim area); these negotiations were conducted via community meetings.

[30] *Madja* is an Aboriginalisation of the English word 'master' and is equated with 'boss'.

[31] These difficulties were already apparent in this area prior to 2002, as some of the community councils reacted against what they saw as a potential loss of power to the PBC — long before the latter entity had even been formed.

[32] The working group members were chosen from the following 'clan groups': *Mayala* (which in this instance referred to Jawi from the islands east of Sunday Island); *Iwanyun* (Sunday Island Jawi); *Inalabulu* (islander Bardi); *Ardiolan* (northern Bardi); *Gularrgon* (western Bardi); *Baniol* (eastern Bardi); *Banararr* (north-eastern Bardi) and *Guwarlgarda* (southern Bardi).

Although 'working group' meetings were designed primarily for nominated representatives, as many claimants attended these (between 1996 and 1998) as attended larger-scale native title meetings. There were a number of reasons why this was the case. Bardi and Jawi have a vital interest in anything potentially having bearing upon their country, and native title falls squarely within this ambit. In addition, the notion that members of the group could have their interests adequately represented by others was at odds with internal community politics and competitive status relations (see Trigger 1988). The political nature of social relationships within indigenous groups means that consensual decision making in the context of PBCs (and their formation) will require time. Decisions are likely to remain subject to 'an ongoing struggle over authority, legitimacy and influence between different groups and factions' (Martin and Finlayson 1996: 7). This means that even so-called 'consensual' decisions (Sutton 1984/5: 382) are likely to be subject to revision, especially where they deal with questions of landownership and resource use. Discussing the problems inherent in 'opinion formation and the problem of group consent', Sutton argues that:

> European ideas of collective decision-making fall back naturally, almost unconsciously, on corporate notions which are different from those of Aborigines ... European corporate groups making major decisions, especially those with financial implications, have well-bounded memberships which may be publicly tested in an established neutral context (the courts). Aboriginal corporations, on the other hand, have customarily been reifications reflecting certain states of negotiation, in some cases blurred by chronic disputation for which no referral to external adjudication has been possible (ibid: 383–4).

In the Bardi and Jawi claimant group, politics within the group reflect the historical experiences of the members.[33] These politics has been accentuated by the outstation movement, which has consolidated intensely localised interests and competition over the allocation of resources; they have typically centred upon whom has pre-eminent rights in *buru*, and as corollaries, who has the right to exploit specific resources in a *buru* (such as trochus),[34] or more generally use that *buru* for tourism ventures. Such issues of connection to country, who is seen to have proprietorial rights in country, and hence can derive economic advantages most legitimately from that country, have tended to assume centre stage in negotiations over the formation of a representative working group and in discussions about their PBC.

---

[33] See Glaskin (2002) for further discussion of this point.

[34] The *alngir* (trochus) issue is a volatile resource issue among Bardi and Jawi, and is heavily implicated in the politics of country ownership. Foale and Macintyre (2000: 34) discuss reefs in West Nggela (Solomon Islands) as 'subjects of formal disputes', also as a consequence of the trochus industry.

Local Organisation in the Contemporary Context

The 'atomic approach' (Sutton 1995: 1) to outstations evident amongst Bardi is reflective of their local organisation (density of estate groups), but I argue that this has been augmented in the current intercultural context. Many of the groups gaining outstations in this region have done so within their own *buru*, and they tend to see the establishment of their outstation as an outsider recognition of their traditional connections to that country. While outstation groups often reflect estate groups or their membership, they are not of themselves equivalent to them. The typical unit of outstation incorporation tends to be the extended family group, and Bardi either do not form incorporated groups on the basis of including all estate affiliates within those corporations or, if they do, they are usually unable to sustain such corporations (see Martin and Finlayson 1996: 7; Mantziaris 1997: 9). In these and other cases, as outstation groups have competed over control of outstation resources and the corporation, the groups have fractured and formed further outstations within the same *buru*. Over time, these choices people make about living arrangements (vis-à-vis the statutory arrangements that make funding for incorporated outstation groups possible) have the possibility of becoming naturalised. For example, Rigsby (1998: 35) has observed that 'individuals and groups may sometimes transform secondary rights into primary property rights over time in a variety of circumstances relating to succession, regencies and even land claim actions'. Sutton (1978: 126) makes the point that 'as the nature of secular property changes, corporate life will change, since it appears to be secular property which provides the most powerful constraints on fragmentation and unification'.

The outstation movement is considered as a 'decentralisation trend' (Coombs 1974) in spatial terms, since it involves the movement of people away from larger communities into smaller satellite communities. However, it can also be considered a decentralising movement in terms of the multiplication of Aboriginal corporations it has produced, each negotiating separately the institutional and administrative arrangements that are necessary to fund and develop outstation infrastructure. Although my discussion of native title incorporation has been on the processes preceding such incorporation (since this has not currently been realised among the Bardi and Jawi claimant group), the parallels and juxtapositions between these two processes should be apparent. Both the outstation movement and native title can be considered as providing new conditions of possibility for indigenous relationships to country to be formally expressed and recognised outside the indigenous domain, and both require incorporation.

However, one of the effects of decentralisation within the outstation movement, as I have argued, has been to consolidate notions of autonomy attaching to the outstation groups. This, along with differentiation within the claimant group consolidated by different historical experiences, and exacerbated by economics associated with resource use, has meant that it has been difficult for the claimant group to act as a corporate group. Rather, much claimant attention has focused primarily on either their own *buru* (estate) or on their own outstation. Particular rights in *buru* are embedded within a larger system which gives form to these local entitlements: an estate group could not reproduce itself but is system-dependent. Sutton (1996: 8) describes this as a 'whole-part dependency' in which the dependency is, on the one hand, 'between particular rights and interests and the wider system of jural and cultural practices in which they are embedded', but on the other hand, is 'between the rights and interests held in land or waters by subgroups or individuals, and the communal native title out of which they are "carved"' (see also Rigsby 1998: 24). While patrifiliates are considered to have the 'final say' with respect to estate matters, this is not generally considered to mean that they are able to deny matrifiliates, for example, their existing rights in those same areas. However, to the consternation of many other Bardi, at least *some* outstation groups were, during the period of my research, speaking and behaving as though their outstations were equivalent to private property, erecting fences and gates around them, effectively preventing (and denying) access by other Bardi to these areas. In addition, the persons who were preventing access during this time were not always patrifiliates.

Conclusion

Although Bardi and Jawi reached an agreement about a representative structure for a working group to precede their PBC, during my research, this representation was consistently challenged from within the group. Incorporation within the outstation context resulted in the multiplication of incorporated outstation groups; but in the native title context, the requirement is for a single incorporated group, a PBC. The outstation movement has a centrifugal impetus, while native title, as in the PBC regulations, has a centripetal one. These two forces are invariably in tension with one another, and it remains to be seen, at some later stage, how the relationships between incorporated outstation groups and the PBC will be accommodated.

At issue here is the relationship between these corporate entities that are, in some sense, designed to give some external representation to indigenous landowners, and landownership itself.

> If the core of property as a social institution lies in a complex system of recognized rights and duties with reference to the control of valuable objects, and if the roles of the participating individuals are linked by this means with basic economic processes, and if, besides, all these processes of social interaction are validated by traditional beliefs, attitudes, and values, and sanctioned in custom and law, it is apparent that we are dealing with an institution extremely fundamental to the

structure of human societies as going concerns. For, considered from a functional point of view, property rights are institutionalised means of defining *who* may control various classes of valuable objects for a variety of present and future purposes and the *conditions* under which this power may be exercised (Hallowell 1955: 246).

In his determination of the Bardi and Jawi claim, Justice French commented on the distinction between the workings of property as a social institution at a broader level that is reproduced over time, and the internal differentiation of various rights within a claimant group that are fundamental to the workings of property. In relation to the Commonwealth's position that the determination of native title should be made at the level of the estate group, he said:

> The Commonwealth argued against the applicants' position that the Bardi and Jawi people comprise the proper native title holding group and that the rights of patriclans, lawmen and others are to be determined intramurally [i.e., internally]. This position, it was said, involved a 'deliberate avoidance' of the requirements of the Act. The Act, it was said, requires the Court to specify who has what rights under traditional law and custom and not to delegate that question to the applicants. The Commonwealth position so expressed risked conceptual confusion between native title rights and interests held in common by a particular society and their distribution and exercise according to elements of a unitary traditional law and/or custom which may be ambulatory and responsive to changing circumstances without affecting the integrity of its normative foundations.[35]

Discussions concerning the level at which native title should be recognised in various jurisdictions will no doubt continue. Different levels of incorporation may reflect, to uneven extents, the different levels at which land is traditionally held (and sometimes the internal differentiation of these). The difficulties indigenous groups encounter in forming PBCs may be considerable, and the implications for social relations within indigenous groups have yet to fully emerge or be understood. Regardless of the form in which native title is determined, and the extent of rights and interests such determinations recognise (Glaskin 2003), Aboriginal groups will be required to form PBCs to hold and administer title or to enact agreements, and this will require internal negotiations within native title claimant groups. At the core of many of these internal negotiations are the claimant group's own property relations, that is, the social relations that they have among each other with respect to their exercise of rights in land or to speak for land. These internal property relations are distinct from those native title rights and interests that may eventually be recognised in native

---

[35] *Sampi v State of Western Australia* [2005] FCA 777, at para 983.

title determinations, but as I have argued elsewhere (Glaskin 2002, 2005), participation in the native title process itself (of which determinations of native title and incorporation as PBCs are part) will ultimately have an effect on the articulation and enactment of the internal property relations within those groups concerned.

References

Altman, J.C., 1986. 'Aboriginal Outstation Communities: Some Economic Issues.' Submission to the House of Representatives Standing Committee on Aboriginal Affairs, 20 November 1985. In *Official Hansard Report (Vol III) of the House of Representatives Standing Committee on Aboriginal Affairs*. Canberra: Government Printer.

———, 1987. 'Aboriginal Outstation Communities: Further Economic Issues.' Further submission to the House of Representatives Standing Committee on Aboriginal Affairs, 10 February 1987. In *Official Hansard Report of the House of Representatives Standing Committee on Aboriginal Affairs*. Canberra: Government Printer.

Bagshaw, G.C., 1999. 'Native Title Claim WAG 49/98 (Bardi and Jawi): Anthropologist's Report.' Report prepared for the Kimberley Land Council on behalf of the native title claimants, February 1999.

———, 2001a. 'Bardi and Jawi Supplementary Anthropology Report Parts 1, 2 and 3.' Filed in the Federal Court of Australia, Western Australia District Registry, General Division, in *Sampi v State of Western Australia*, WAG 49/1998, 27 August 2001.

———, 2001b. 'Applicants' Additional Anthropological Report Concerning Distribution and Spatial Extent of Local Estates (Bur[u]) Within the Bardi and Jawi Native Title Claim Area.' Filed in the Federal Court of Australia, Western Australia District Registry, General Division, in *Sampi v State of Western Australia*, WAG 49/1998, 8 February 2001.

——— and K. Glaskin, 2000. 'Anthropologist's Supplementary Report: Aspects of Bardi and Jawi Marine Tenure and Resource Usage.' Filed in the Federal Court of Australia, Western Australia District Registry, General Division, in *Sampi v State of Western Australia*, WAG 49/1998, 30 October 2000.

Coombs, H.C., 1974. 'Decentralisation Trends Among Aboriginal Communities.' *Department of Aboriginal Affairs WA Newsletter* 1(8): 4–25.

———, B.G. Dexter and L.R. Hiatt, 1980. 'The Outstation Movement in Aboriginal Australia.' *Australian Institute of Aboriginal Studies Newsletter New Series* 14: 1–8.

Crough, G. and C. Christophersen, 1993. *Aboriginal People in the Economy of the Kimberley Region*. Darwin: Australian National University, North Australia Research Unit.

Dodson, M. and D. McCarthy, 2005. 'Customary Land as the Key for Future Development: Empower Those Who Want to Use Their Land and Protect Those That Don't.' Unpublished paper presented at the National Land Summit 'Land, Economic Growth and Development', Papua New Guinea University of Technology, Lae, 23–25 August 2005.

Drysdale, I. and M. Durack, 1974. *The End of the Dreaming*. Adelaide: Rigby.

Durack, M., 1997 (1969). *The Rock and the Sand*. Great Britain: Corgi.

Fingleton, J.S., 1994. 'Native Title Corporations.' Canberra: Australian Institute of Aboriginal and Torres Strait Islander Studies, Native Title Research Unit (*Land, Rights, Laws: Issues of Native Title* — Issues Paper 2).

Foale, S. and M. Macintyre, 2000. 'Dynamic and Flexible Aspects of Land and Marine Tenure at West Nggela: Implications for Marine Resource Management.' *Oceania* 71: 30–45.

Glaskin, K., 2002. Claiming Country: A Case Study of Historical Legacy and Transition in the Native Title Context. Canberra: Australian National University (PhD thesis).

————, 2003. 'Native Title and the "Bundle of Rights" Model: Implications For the Recognition of Aboriginal Relations to Country.' *Anthropological Forum* 13: 67–88.

————, 2005. 'Claim, Culture and Effect: Property Relations and the Native Title Process.' Paper presented at a workshop on 'Effects of Native Title', Centre for Aboriginal Economic Policy and Research, Australian National University, October.

Hallowell, A.I., 1955. *Culture and Experience*. Philadelphia: University of Pennsylvania Press.

Hiatt, L.R., 1996. *Arguments About Aborigines: Australia and the Evolution of Social Anthropology*. Cambridge: Cambridge University Press.

Jebb, M.A., 2002. *Blood, Sweat and Welfare: A History of White Bosses and Aboriginal Pastoral Workers*. Crawley: University of Western Australia Press.

Mantziaris, C., 1997. 'Beyond the Aboriginal Councils and Associations Act? Part 1.' *Indigenous Law Bulletin* 4(5): 10–14.

Martin, D.F. and J.D. Finlayson, 1996. 'Linking Accountability and Self-Determination in Aboriginal Organisations.' Canberra: Australian

National University, Centre for Aboriginal and Economic Policy Research (Discussion Paper 116).

Merlan, F., 1998. *Caging the Rainbow: Places, Politics and Aborigines in a North Australian Town*. Honolulu: University of Hawai'i Press.

Moizo, B., 1990. 'Implementation of the Community Development Employment Scheme in Fitzroy Crossing: A Preliminary Report.' *Australian Aboriginal Studies* 1: 36–40.

Muir, K., 1999. 'Back Home to Stoke the Fires: the Outstations Movement in Western Australia.' *Indigenous Law Bulletin* 4(19): 11–14.

Peterson, N., 1998. 'Welfare Colonialism and Citizenship: Politics, Economics and Agency.' In N. Peterson and W. Sanders (eds), op. cit.

—— and W. Sanders (eds), 1998. *Citizenship and Indigenous Australians: Changing Conceptions and Possibilities*. Cambridge: Cambridge University Press.

Rigsby, B., 1998. 'A Survey of Property Theory and Tenure Types.' In N. Peterson and B. Rigsby (eds), *Customary Marine Tenure in Australia*. Sydney: University of Sydney (Oceania Monograph 48).

Robinson, M.V., 1973. Change and Adjustment Among the Bardi of Sunday Island, North-Western Australia. Perth: University of Western Australia (MA thesis).

Rowse, T., 1993. *After Mabo: Interpreting Indigenous Traditions*. Melbourne: Melbourne University Press.

——, 1998. 'Indigenous Citizenship and Self-Determination: The Problem of Shared Responsibilities.' In N. Peterson and W. Sanders (eds), op. cit.

——, 2000. *Obliged to be Difficult: Nugget Coombs' Legacy in Indigenous Affairs*. Cambridge: Cambridge University Press.

Sanders, W., 1998. 'Citizenship and the Community Development Employment Projects Scheme: Equal Rights, Difference and Appropriateness.' In N. Peterson and W. Sanders (eds), op. cit.

Sexton, S., 1996. 'Homeland Movement: High and Low Roads.' *Aboriginal Law Bulletin* 3(83): 4–7.

Smith, B.R., 2000. Between Places: Aboriginal Decentralisation, Mobility and Territoriality in the Region of Coen, Cape York Peninsula (Queensland, Australia). London: University of London (PhD thesis).

Spicer, I., 1997. 'Independent Review of the Community Development Employment Projects (CDEP) Scheme.' Available from: http://www.atsic.gov.au/programs/noticeboard/CDEP/Spicer_Report/contents.asp

Sullivan, P., 1996a. *All Free Man Now: Culture, Community and Politics in the Kimberley Region, North-Western Australia.* Canberra: Australian Institute of Aboriginal and Torres Strait Islander Studies.

————, 1996b. 'The Needs of Prescribed Bodies Corporate Under the *Native Title Act 1993* and Regulations: A Report on the Issues and Options.' In *Final Report: Review of the Aboriginal Councils and Associations Act 1976 — Volume 2: Supporting Material, August 1996.* Canberra: Australian Institute of Aboriginal and Torres Strait Islander Studies.

————, 1997. 'A Sacred Land, A Sovereign People, an Aboriginal Corporation: Prescribed Bodies and the *Native Title Act*.' Casuarina: Australian National University, North Australia Research Unit (Report 3).

Sutton, P., 1978. Wik: Aboriginal Society, Territory and Language at Cape Keerweer, Cape York Peninsula, Australia. Brisbane: University of Queensland (PhD thesis).

————, 1984/5. 'Opinion Formation and the Problem of Group Consent.' *Anthropological Forum* 5: 382–384.

————, 1995. 'Atomism Versus Collectivism: The Problem of Group Definition in Native Title Cases.' In J. Fingleton and J. Finlayson (eds), *Anthropology in the Native Title Era: Proceedings of a Workshop.* Canberra: Australian Institute of Aboriginal and Torres Strait Islander Studies.

————, 1996. 'The Robustness of Aboriginal Land Tenure Systems: Underlying and Proximate Customary Titles.' *Oceania* 67: 7–29.

Trigger, D.S., 1987. 'Languages, Linguistic Groups and Status Relations at Doomadgee, an Aboriginal Settlement in North-West Queensland, Australia.' *Oceania* 57: 217–238.

————, 1988. 'Equality and Hierarchy in Aboriginal Political Life at Doomadgee, North-West Queensland.' *Anthropological Forum* 5: 525–543.

Chapter Eleven

The Measure of Dreams

Derek Elias

Currently, in the Tanami Desert of Australia's Northern Territory, in excess of seven million dollars in mineral royalties may be distributed to Aboriginal communities and individual Aboriginal people each year. This royalty money can fluctuate markedly from year to year depending on variables such as the success of exploration, the price of gold, mining company expenditure, and the rates of production in terms of mass and quality of ore from both the pits and the mining plants themselves. The money, commonly referred to simply as 'royalties', is primarily paid out by mining companies and is subject to legal agreements made with traditional landowners through their representative body, the Central Land Council (CLC). Sections 35 and 64 of the *Aboriginal Land Rights (Northern Territory) Act 1976 (ALRA)* provide for financial payments to be made to the 'traditional owners' of areas associated with, or affected by, mining and exploration.

The advent of the *ALRA* and the land claim process represented a significant shift in the objective relations of Warlpiri cultural conceptions of place. Land claims and the statutory requirements of the *ALRA* combined to place an emphasis on the relationships of Aboriginal people to their land in a new manner. The land claim process required people to articulate and objectify their relationships to place in a tribunal setting that required the definition of which people owned which land in relation to membership of descent groups and the boundaries of their 'estates'. In essence, the *ALRA* signaled a reification of cultural forms that would underscore the fundamental tenets of Aboriginal society, history and culture which were so clearly different from those of Euro-Australians.

In the Tanami Desert, the CLC, as instructed by Warlpiri and landowners from other linguistic groups, has entered into agreements with a large number of companies. These agreements allow for exploration and mining on Aboriginal land. The two most important features of these agreements, as far as Warlpiri people are concerned, centre on the protection of their places of significance and the payment of royalties to the relevant traditional owners of the land affected by either mining leases or exploration licences. The developments associated with the exigencies of mineral exploration on Aboriginal land have forced, and are continuing to force, traditional owners to make many decisions about their land, such as about the relative importance of places and the bases for membership of royalty receiving associations. The objectification of Warlpiri knowledge of place and people's relationships to place is extremely significant. It is at the centre of tensions and politicking between people to identify who is eligible to receive money from specific tracts of land, and the criteria upon which such eligibility is based, contested and upheld.

In the year 2000, an area of 85,250 km^2 in the central Tanami Desert was covered by seven mining leases, more than 160 exploration licences within 53 separate agreements, with a further 100 applications awaiting consideration. Extensive consultations, beginning with seeking consent from the appropriate traditional owners, are necessary before any work by mining companies or other external development interests can take place on Aboriginal land. Then follows the project of mapping places and identifying those to be protected and avoided during exploration and mining work, which is usually carried out by an anthropologist working with the appropriate Warlpiri people. As a result of these activities and other factors, Warlpiri relations to the lands from which they now derive financial benefits have changed greatly since the arrival of land rights. This chapter will specifically address the demarcation of space and place and the ways in which the Warlpiri landscape is dissected by gold exploration and mining, a complicated development that dominates the current modelling of relationships between people and place in the Tanami Desert.

The CLC's submission to the Reeves Review noted that the *ALRA* reversed a long process that had denied recognition of Aboriginal owners' rights and responsibilities for their land, and that as a result, 'for the first time since contact between Aboriginal people and non-Aboriginal people, the balance of power between Aboriginal landowners and mining interests has shifted' (Reeves 1998: 519). The *ALRA* has afforded the greatest opportunity for Warlpiri, who became sedentarised in missions and reserves following the establishment of such settlements,[1] to once more access their places in the Tanami Desert. These opportunities to access remote country have resulted, firstly from the land claim process, and secondly as a consequence of the processes arising from the mining provisions of the *ALRA* (especially Section 42), which vests traditional owners with a decision-making role over access to place. These provisions have given Warlpiri people control of their places in the face of the intense pressure for economic development in the form of gold exploration and mining in the Tanami Desert. The provisions were vigorously contested in some of the submissions to the Reeves Review, and the debate revolved around the extent to which Aboriginal people will be able to have a meaningful say in the development of economic interests over their land and places (Reeves 1998: 520).

---

[1] See Dussart (2000: 36–38) for further details concerning the 'forced sedentarisation' of Warlpiri people.

The competition for the right to control access to Aboriginal land is one that is now familiar in recent Australian history. In the context of the two most famous cases of disputes between government, the mining industry and Aborigines — Noonkanbah (Hawke and Gallagher 1989) and Coronation Hill (Merlan 1991; Keen 1992; Brunton 1992) — Merlan (1991: 341) has made the observation that:

> Such disputes highlight the problems which arise from contradiction between direct governmental support for Aborigines as a traditional and socio-culturally distinctive 'type', and support from the private sector (thus also indirectly, from government) for them to become and to see themselves as modernizing facilitators of economic development. Conflict between these two paths realizes itself partly in conflict over space, and its material and symbolic definition.

How the conflict over the production of space has been manifested in the Tanami Desert is of direct concern. Elsewhere I have considered Warlpiri places as natural, material phenomena that are imbued with symbolic and practical characteristics that demarcate and orientate social space, to which myths and stories are attached (Elias 2001a: 103–16, 2001b). Particularly important here is the concept of *jukurrpa*, which is a term Walpiri use to refer to the creative epoch often referred to as 'the dreaming'. But it is also used to refer to the ancestral beings who formed the country and to their activities or 'dreamings'.[2] One way places are culturally ordered by Warlpiri is in terms of the way that they restrict access to certain people. Such restrictions are based primarily on categories of age, gender and knowledge, and with respect to the different bases upon which people could claim identity with them as both individuals and social groups.

At the present time Warlpiri places are at the centre of interests that seek to determine their location and physical boundaries. This determination is of great significance for mining companies and governments who want to maximise their ability to access space in order to ascertain the extent of mineral reserves. The *ALRA* legislation recognises the Warlpiri right to exercise a considerable amount of power over access to their land. Here is the source of conflict over the material and symbolic definition of place that Merlan referred to earlier, which is most simply explained by the fact that boundaries have different meanings in different societies (Lefebvre 1991). The process of mapping in the Tanami Desert will be shown to have had profound effects on the definition of place and space, and on Warlpiri conceptions of them both physically and socially in terms of the imposition of boundaries between people and place.

---

[2] See Dussart (2001: 17–24) for a detailed description of *jukurrpa*.

The Land Claim Process

Land claim hearings in the Tanami Desert commenced with the Warlpiri and Kartangarurru-Kurintji claim (Peterson et al. 1978). Lodged in 1978, it was the first claim heard by the Aboriginal Land Commissioner in the Central Australian region. The claim itself involved a huge area of land that encompassed a number of 'tribal'/linguistic groups, including the Gurindji, Kartangarurru, Pirlingarna, Kukatja, Ngardi, Nyininy, and all of the Warlpiri subgroups — Warnayaka, Manyangarnpa (Yalpiri), Ngalia and the Warrmarla. From the outset, discussion of landownership was based on the model of the patrilineal clan that involved the identification of people's association with corresponding groups of places related to *jukurrpa*. The presentation of evidence for the early land claims placed greater emphasis upon social affiliation stemming from relations coded within the land than with respect to places within the land itself. The authors of the claim book explained some of the more practical reasons for this situation:

> The least satisfactory aspect is the accuracy of place location on the maps. The principal reasons for this are the extent of the area involved, the lack of roads in the area, the general difficulties of travel and the fact that we have not visited the remoter parts of the Tanami Desert. We have, however, surveyed the area from a light plane in company with a small group of traditional owners. Even where places have been visited the practical difficulties of accurately locating a soakage or other place in an undulating plain or thick stand of mulga are considerable. In consequence only the major places have been shown on the maps where the location has been visited or can be confidently located. This means that many hundreds of names are not included although they are well known to the people and their order along the song lines is known to us (Peterson et al. 1978: 2).

Clearly, when the Central Desert Land Trust was granted very little was known about the location of most major places of significance except those that were easily identified as topographical features. These places were discussed through the claim hearings but the establishment of a successful claim was not reliant on the demonstration of knowledge of the location of places of significance, but rather on the links of traditional owners to the land. This situation was repeated in the Warlpiri, Kukatja and Ngarti claim (Myers and Clark 1983), where hardly any evidence was heard on the claim area at all and the mapping and presentation of located places was virtually non-existent.

Beginning with the Chilla Well claim, the Land Commissioners (under considerable political pressure) increased the demand for the accurate location and identification of place, which then continued in subsequent land claims (Stead 1985). The first reason for this was that accurate mapping of places was facilitated through a combination of factors, including the availability of more financial and logistical support for research, the fact that a shorter time had elapsed since *yapa* (as Warlpiri people refer to themselves) had worked and lived on the land, and the political climate of the time. This climate was created by the establishment of self-government in the Northern Territory in 1978, and most notably the subsequent development of gold exploration and mining in the Tanami Desert. The combination of these influences placed a pronounced emphasis on the importance of identifying Warlpiri places of significance. There continues to be enormous pressure applied to Aboriginal landowners and the Land Councils by industry and government not to hinder economic development by 'locking' up land. These interests have identified the sacred site or place as a 'bogey man'; its mythical status is argued to be a hindrance to a modern, economically responsible country.

The preparation of the Western Desert and Tanami Downs land claims witnessed the injection of more funds for research by the CLC and involved numerous trips undertaken to identify the location of places. These necessitated taking traditional owners on extended country visits mapping different dreaming tracks. During such research the knowledge of senior people, who had walked through these areas before being moved to settlements, was crucial to the authoritative identification of these places. Maps were produced that accurately recorded locations of places to illustrate how claimed areas of land were 'full' of places that were of significance to *yapa*.

The development of the Northern Territory's mineral base has long been identified as a key priority of the Country Liberal Party which held power from the time of self-government in 1978 until 2001. The Northern Territory Government's opposition to land claims by Aboriginal people was a stance taken in order to remove what was perceived as an unnecessary obstacle to the development of economic infrastructure: the defeat of Aboriginal land claims would have allowed mining and exploration to go ahead unimpeded. Not only did the government fail in this respect; its vehement contest of land claims actually assisted *yapa* to rediscover places of significance, thus strengthening the Warlpiri position. Warlpiri, through the CLC, quickly established a number of agreements with mining companies, and through the procedures of exploration and contingent 'site clearances' provided for in these agreements, people were rediscovering and locating many of their places. As more exploration tracks were made in remote areas they provided the means for people to more easily access their places. This process facilitated the preparation of subsequent land claims as people travelled through country more frequently. However, there is a critical distinction to be drawn between the mapping and recording of place data for a land claim and the mapping and recording of place data for mineral exploration. The exigencies of gold exploration and mining require that boundaries be allocated to located places in order for development to proceed with surety. This situation introduced a new dimension to place that had not previously been conceived by Warlpiri or institutional anthropology.

The Mining Provisions

Sections 41 and 42 of the *ALRA* clearly spell out the procedures for consultation and negotiation between Aboriginal owners, defined as 'traditional owners', other interested or affected Aboriginal people, and mining companies. The first meetings that take place are known as 'consent to negotiate' meetings, and in the Tanami Desert these are convened by the CLC. The CLC is responsible for identifying and bringing together the correct groups of traditional owners (as defined by the *ALRA*) to consider the mining company's Exploration Licence Application. The blocks of land that are the subject of such applications are determined by the Northern Territory Government and subsequently offered to one applicant mining company under the *Northern Territory Mining Act 1980*. The 'consent to negotiate' meeting is the point at which Aboriginal people exercise the power of veto over an application. They may reject outright the proposal of a company to explore over a certain application for any number of reasons that do not necessarily have to be disclosed. If an application is approved by traditional owners, an Exploration Licence is granted and an agreement is forged between the CLC on behalf of Warlpiri and the applicant mining company. Such agreements include stipulations regarding protection of Warlpiri land interests (places), financial compensation in the form of royalties, infrastructure development, provision of employment opportunities, and a realistic environmental protection program (Ireland 1996: 2; CLC 1998a). A separate agreement is concluded if the stage is reached where actual mining can proceed and be profitable.

The right of veto through the procedure of consent to negotiate is the key element of the mining provisions of the *ALRA* that enables Warlpiri people to regulate access to, and potential developments on, their land and places. The right of veto was identified by Woodward (1974) during the Aboriginal Land Rights Commission as the means by which Aboriginal people could be given realistic control over their land and help to establish a meaningful economic base by the subsequent negotiation of royalties and rentals from development on their land. The right of veto has been consistently contested by the majority of the mining industry, and also in some political quarters, on the grounds that it potentially locked up resources and that royalties paid to Aboriginal people would shorten mine life and adversely affect the national economic interest (Altman and Peterson 1984). The record of gold exploration and mining in the Tanami Desert has clearly disproved such a contention.

There have been significant social and economic benefits that have flowed to both traditional owners and the mining industry through the CLC's execution of the statutory processes of the *ALRA* in the Northern Territory. In particular, this process has been assisted by the more progressive mining companies that recognise the special nature of the link between Aboriginal people and the land (CLC 1998a: 49). From the more enlightened industry perspective, the success of the agreements made between mining companies and Warlpiri people in the Tanami Desert hinges on a company's respect for this special link and is the foundation of a workable and mutually beneficial relationship (Ireland 1996: 1).

Manning (1997: 26) has noted that during the last decade there has been a dramatic increase in the total area covered by mineral exploration licences in the Northern Territory. This has been primarily due to negotiations over land in advance and the establishment of protocols between Land Councils and mining companies that have combined to speed up and streamline processes involved in making agreements. Whilst this observation indicates the familiarity that Aboriginal people have developed with the procedures for access to exploration on their lands, it is clear that a comfortable relationship did not develop overnight. The relative ease of gaining access to Aboriginal land for mining companies is in contrast to the operational difficulties experienced by both Warlpiri and mining companies that have been encountered in the actual day-to-day workings of agreements. The process of finding a balance between Warlpiri interests in identifying and protecting their places and the desire of mining companies to maximise the amount of land at their disposal for gold exploration was a difficult one. The introduction of both mining companies and Warlpiri to each other and the Tanami Desert has thrown up intriguing questions as to the contemporary definitions of place, space and *jukurrpa* (dreamtime) for Warlpiri.

Gold Mining Returns to the Tanami Desert

The steady process of the transfer of land claimed and won back to Warlpiri hands was followed closely by the rising interest in gold and other mineral exploration that gathered momentum during the 1980s. By the early part of the following decade, the central area of the Tanami Desert was literally being held under the microscope. Both Normandy NFM (previously North Flinders Mines — NFM) and Tanami Joint Venture were allocated exploration licences over The Granites and Tanami respectively that had lain dormant during the 1970s. An exploration licence was granted to NFM in 1975, with subsequent mineral leases offered by the Northern Territory Department of Mines and Energy in 1980, and an agreement was finally reached between the CLC and NFM in 1983. This agreement was necessary because of the need for NFM to secure more land outside of the licence in order to set up its processing plant and other requirements for the proposed mine at The Granites, including a large and steady water supply. In 1987 mining recommenced at Tanami, and by 1991 control of the mine passed to Zapopan. Zapopan held the exploration licences negotiated with the traditional owners and the CLC around the original Tanami Joint Venture mine site at Tanami, where the gold deposits within the existing lease were soon exhausted. By 1995, further deposits were found in close proximity to the mine and Central Desert Joint Venture was formed by Otter Gold Mines Ltd and Acacia Resources.

The continuing attraction that the Tanami Desert region holds for gold exploration has been buoyed by the success of Normandy NFM in the discovery of a remarkable deposit west of The Granites. The effect of the substantial high-grade gold reserves at Callie–Dead Bullock Soak was the catalyst for a dramatic intensification of Exploration Licence Applications that cover the entire survey area: 'the 1992 discovery of Normandy Mining Ltd's 3 million ounce Callie gold deposit transformed the Northern Territory's Tanami region into a sexy exploration address' (Bell 1998: 65). From the early 1990s Warlpiri of the Tanami Desert have been involved in day-to-day consultations regarding access to places that have been prompted by the post-Callie land-rush which is widely considered to be 'one of the great modern-day Australian gold discoveries' (ibid: 67). The total capital expenditure on Callie up until 1998 was $76 million. Normandy NFM's Callie deposit is by far the greatest reserve of gold so far discovered in the Tanami Desert, and is the first gold mine in Australia that has been developed with the consultation and permission of the Aboriginal owners. In 1999 Normandy NFM were completing a feasibility study on the possibility of a new treatment plant, yet as of late 2000 there was no separate mill or treatment plant at Callie, and ore was transported by haul road to The Granites for processing.

Since its inception in 1976, the *ALRA* has certainly not restricted the access of mining interests to Aboriginal land in the Tanami Desert. Annual exploration expenditure in the Northern Territory went from $1 million to $40 million over a period of 20 years, and is showing little sign of slowing (Ireland 1996: 2). Total expenditure on gold exploration in the Tanami Desert alone was in excess of $12 million in 1997 (CLC 1998b: 6). As of the beginning of the year 2000, there were over 100 Exploration Licence Applications in the Tanami Desert awaiting consideration, more than 160 licences had already been granted under the terms of 53 agreements between the CLC and various mining companies, and there were seven actual mining leases.

The Federal and Northern Territory Governments' programs for the economic development of Aboriginal people in remote areas have met with little success. In contrast, mining companies have been active in exploiting the few opportunities for economic development in remote Australia, particularly in the Tanami Desert. The return of mining to this region is of great significance because of the mutually beneficial relationship it affords. The mining companies benefit through the extraction of gold on Warlpiri terms, and the Warlpiri benefit by receiving considerable financial benefits through royalty payments as well as regional and community development and employment (Manning 1997: 33).

The Measurement of Dreams

Through a diverse variety of historical agents and processes, places — or 'sites of significance', as they are often called— have become highly topical. Conservative ideology has consistently argued that the Australian landscape should not be divided into sacred and profane categories, and the basis of this argument has been that Aboriginal places are empty and devoid of significance because Aborigines no longer live a 'traditional way of life'. Countering this narrow view have been the realities of the *ALRA*, continuing academic research into Aboriginal social and cultural life, and the increase of Aboriginal political representation — all of which have combined to raise public awareness that Aboriginal places and land have profound meanings that cannot be simply dismissed as irrelevant.

The project of mapping places in the Tanami Desert attempts to link the eternal Aboriginal 'dreamtime' or *jukurrpa* to the landscape. Places have been widely conceptualised as the interface between the human and cosmological present. The process involved in exploration and mining has served to give boundary and shape to place. The mapping project results in the demarcation of the 'sacred' and the subsequent division of Aboriginal peoples' relations to land into categories of places. The identification of places that are sacred tends to render the remaining land as meaningless or inert place. This division of space from place is termed the 'grounding of significance' by Lefebvre, and can be seen as part of a wider intellectual process where: 'Places are marked, noted, named. Between them, within the "holes in the net", are blank or marginal spaces' (Lefebvre 1991: 118). But the physical demarcation of the extent of influence of a place or *jukurrpa* cannot be reduced to a simple process of two-dimensional mapping; the content of the *jukurrpa* cannot be measured only by a projection of its surveyed borders onto a map.

Consideration of the practicalities of how exploration and mining proceed on Aboriginal land in the Tanami Desert thus reveals how these interests require Warlpiri people to abstract, delimit and impose boundaries on places. Such processes present both *yapa* and resource developers with considerable practical and intellectual difficulties. The reason is that the identification of areas of land as 'no-go areas' is an alien concept in both mining industry and Aboriginal perspectives. Essentially the mining industry, long used to treating the landscape as a potential economic resource, has been forced to recognise that land has other sociocultural values. However, the realities of the process of exploration in the Northern Territory, and particularly in the Tanami Desert, have also revealed another intriguing reality. Aboriginal places have been infused with a previously absent economic dimension because place is imbued with new meanings when it is identified by the mining companies as being of cultural value. Place becomes valued and commodified as a kind of cultural real estate. It is the complexities informing this infusion of economic value emerging from the division of the landscape into place and space that will be examined in the remainder of this chapter. The implications of this alteration of the meaning of place for Warlpiri are compounded by the payment of royalty monies in the form of rent and compensation for gold mining exploration and development in proximity to Warlpiri places. The first question to consider is the manner in which place becomes bounded and the land becomes divided into the sacred and economically significant. This renders the remainder of the landscape empty of meaning, to be subsequently explored and mined with impunity.

Mining and the Creation of Blocks

For Warlpiri one of the most difficult problems initially faced in coming to terms with the exploration process is the fact that they are forced to consider Exploration Licence Applications that have abstract boundaries made up of lines and angles defined by latitude and longitude and the aeromagnetic grid. The borders of these blocks cut across Warlpiri places and dreaming tracks in a haphazard way that is devoid of any meaning or logic readily accessible to *yapa*. From the outset, Warlpiri are forced to abstract their interests in place to a level that has no correspondence with their understanding and experience of place and land tenure. As Glowczewski (1999: 5) noted, 'the institutional structures which are proposed in Australia rarely give control to the Aboriginals in such a way as to allow them to develop what is specific to them in their spiritual relationship with the environment'. Before examining the initial cross-cultural problems brought about by conflicting frames of reference, it is useful to briefly describe how exploration licence blocks are created and offered to companies by the Northern Territory Government.

In Australia the State owns minerals that lie beneath the ground. The government considers that mining of such resources should benefit all citizens as well as the government itself through the payment of associated royalties. In order to maximise potential economic development and benefits for the nation, the State desires that the exploration and mining processes be as rapid and thorough as possible. This ideal is achieved by fostering healthy competition amongst interested parties in areas of known reserves, resulting in a large number of applicants seeking licences. The choice of licensee is based on the assessment of exploration proposals that are submitted to the Department of Mines and Energy. There are a number of mechanisms in place which ensure that the licences issued to explorers are used as productively as possible.

Exploration for gold usually commences with very little knowledge of an area and relies heavily on published geological data (if available), geological maps and aeromagnetic surveys which assist in identifying anomalies that indicate the possible sites of gold-bearing deposits. It is up to the licence holder to design an exploration program involving sampling and drilling in order to identify potential deposits. This process may take some time and is intensive in terms of effort as well as expense. Competition between explorers could not occur if original licence holders occupied their ground for indefinite periods; this would in effect tie up the land and prevent further exploration. To overcome this problem the size of exploration licence areas is reduced over time in order to maximise the use of space available for competitive exploration. Explorers must not hold up the exploration process, and must therefore relinquish part (approximately 50 per cent) of their licence area each year so as not to tie up land unnecessarily. As a result, licence applications are generally made for areas in excess of those actually required for exploration purposes, so that the risk taker can progressively hand back those areas which are not thought to be prospective. Through this process the government achieves its dual objectives of regulating the size of exploration areas and maintaining economic incentives for exploration (personal communication, Trevor Ireland, 2000).

Extensive exploration occurs throughout the central Tanami Desert region, and as ground is relinquished by one company, another is waiting to apply for the licence. This means that Warlpiri must participate in a bewildering number of meetings and inspections throughout the year if they are to monitor mining company activities and the progress of company work programs. Exploration interests in the Tanami Desert are not showing any signs of abating either. In part this is explained by the application of new exploration techniques facilitating the penetration of deeper layers of rock. Hence mining companies continue to apply for land that was previously thought to have been thoroughly explored (personal communication, Simon Henderson, 2000).

Exploration for gold in the Tanami Desert is under the influence of another dual imperative: the location of sizeable gold reserves as against the location and avoidance of Warlpiri places of significance. This requires spatial measurement, in which 'boundaries' must be defined in order to demarcate areas where mining can proceed and areas where such activities are forbidden. The current land tenure model, in response to the interests of exploration and mining, involves a measurement or weighting of dreams, that requires *yapa* to identify and locate their places of significance and to rank and weigh their cultural order of rights in (and affiliation to) place. The remainder of the chapter will explore the manner in which the mining model of land tenure cuts up the landscape of the Tanami Desert into abstract parcels within which Warlpiri identify places and *jukurrpa*, and ultimately negotiate their relationships with these and with each other.

Every year in the Tanami Desert, Warlpiri encounter a new round of exploration licences for consideration. These areas of land are increasingly irregular in shape; conglomerations of 'empty ground' discarded by former prospectors and in the process of being recycled by others as new exploration licences. Warlpiri are continually being faced with new, irregular boundaries of exploration applications and licences that make it difficult for them to keep track of which places these new boundaries relate to in terms of ownership and affiliation. The problems this situation poses for Warlpiri involve making decisions about who can make decisions over these blocks, locating the places of significance they contain, ensuring that development interests do not encroach upon them, and deciding how they are to be protected. A common feature of all of these problems is the speed of exploration and the impediments that are encountered in attempts to define the boundaries of place within the changing parameters of a mining company work program. There are two approaches that have been used to identify the boundaries of Warlpiri places in the context of gold exploration and mining in the Tanami Desert — the site clearance and the work area clearance — and I shall now examine each of these in turn.

The Site Clearance Process

Long before the shift in Federal Government policy that formed the background of the *ALRA* legislation, Stanner (1965) noted that it was no longer possible to map an Aboriginal region in terms of its full resources — be they human, spiritual or economic. Nevertheless, the reintroduction of people and place in the Tanami Desert has witnessed a determined effort to map and detail Warlpiri interests in and knowledge of place. The method of administering development projects up until the early 1990s involved traditional owners' approval of an Exploration Licence Application, and once the licence was granted by the government, a site clearance process was instigated.

Essentially the site clearance process involved a survey by knowledgeable senior Warlpiri and CLC anthropologists. Together they travelled through the licence area recording the location of places, defining boundaries or blocks where mining exploration was forbidden. From the survey recordings, a map was drawn that detailed places of significance to be avoided and areas in which the mining company could pursue exploration. The method of mapping had the primary aim of ensuring that those places which Warlpiri wished to protect would be safeguarded from mineral exploration. A host of complex problems that arose out of the site clearance process will be briefly summarised here. The mapping project implicit in the site clearance project placed Aboriginal knowledge at the disposal of the mining company but was far from effective in detailing the sum of Warlpiri interests in land.

Mapping the location of places by Warlpiri involved significant problems in that it forced people to detail precise locations of places that were often subject to secrecy. One such example is the location of highly restricted men's places that invariably have rather nebulous boundaries. A site clearance survey had the effect of pinpointing the exact location and features of such restricted places.

This caused considerable problems for senior men in particular who, aware of the location of a place, were often reluctant to reveal it due to the fact that the knowledge associated with it was available to only certain persons on the basis of such criteria as age, race, gender and semi-moiety. As a result it was not uncommon for some of the most important places to remain unspecified and hence unprotected. Also, the informants were unaware of the consequences of maintaining secrecy about these places. The mapping of Warlpiri place involved a clear transgression of sociocultural restrictions that caused considerable difficulties and pressures for those people charged with the responsibility of undertaking the site clearance survey in the first place.

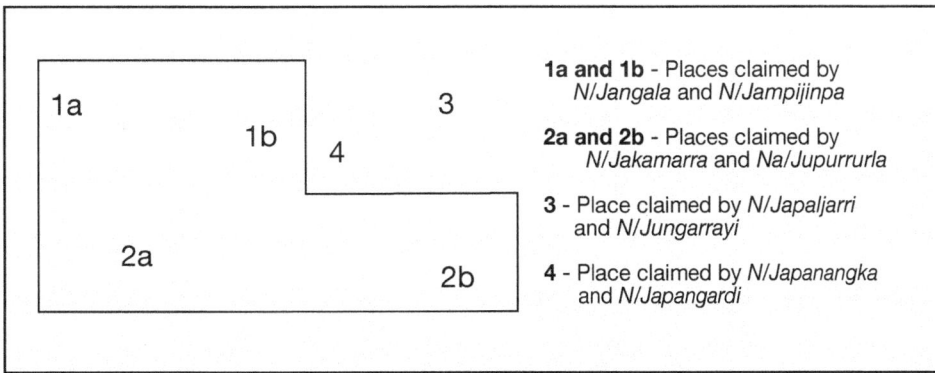

Figure 11-1: Diagram depicting places of significance for the Warlpiri in relation to the licence area in initial year of exploration.

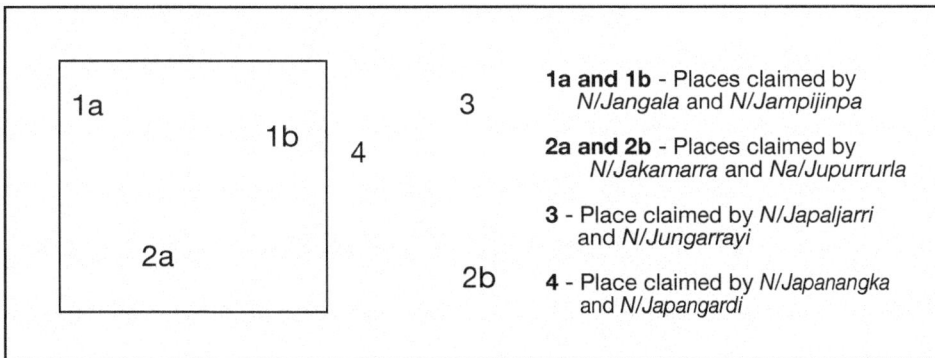

Figure 11-2: Diagram depicting places of significance for the Warlpiri in second year of exploration with reduced licence area.

Figures 11-1 and 11-2 illustrate just how difficult the measurement of dreams can be under the exploration and mining model of land tenure, for both Warlpiri and mining companies. Interpretation of these figures depends on knowledge of the fact that Warlpiri have a subsection system, meaning that they have eight social categories that are inherited through descent. These categories 'potentially allocate all human beings in a universe of classificatory kin, with concomitant obligations and responsibilities' (Bauman 2002: 206). The vernacular terms appearing in the figures refer to male and female subsection names: women and men have similar subsection names, which are differentiated largely by their starting consonant — *Nangala* refers to females and *Jangala* refers to males.

A problem that involved the grounding of the significance of place arose from delineation of the physical boundaries of places. Put simply, the practicalities of drawing a line around a place, as though it possessed a primarily spatial significance that could be bounded, posed difficulties for Warlpiri. This was due to the fact that *jukurrpa* created and left their essence in places, and this presence in the landscape was manifested in complex physical and metaphysical relationships between places (Elias 2001a: 106–12). The mapping of place and the imposition of boundaries required by the site clearance process created serious practical problems for Warlpiri in defining the location of place boundaries.

For example, with respect to Figures 11-1 and 11-2, a comparison can be made between the places 1a and 1b as opposed to places 2a and 2b on the basis of the kind of travel undertaken by the *jukurrpa* related to the two different semi-moieties. For argument's sake, we may think of all four places as important soakages ('native wells') existing in conjunction with some other topographic feature. The *jukurrpa* moving between 1a and 1b travels through the air and so the demarcation of boundaries around these two places is relatively straightforward on the ground. However, in the case of 2a and 2b, the *jukurrpa* ancestors are involved in a number of running battles with each other, so all of the rocks in between the two places represent the bones of people who have been speared and killed, yet this area does not have a name and may not be considered important enough to restrict the activities of a mining company. The way in which Warlpiri demarcate boundaries in such an example is a complex matter and is difficult for a company to map.

Another example might involve an extremely powerful place such as place 4, which exerts influence around a huge area that actually includes the place at 1b, yet place 4 does not even lie within the boundary of the Exploration Licence. The practicalities of issuing instructions to mining companies to effectively manage and protect Warlpiri places of significance were extremely difficult under the site clearance regime and predictably led to miscommunication.

The difficulties faced by Warlpiri in mapping the locations of places within the context of mining exploration was further compounded by the fact that there were deficiencies in the site clearance process that prevented Warlpiri from locating all of their places of interests on their own terms. The site clearance process could be characterised as one that attempted to take a 'freeze-frame' or 'snapshot' of interests in place that was reliant on the imposition of a very restricted timescale that allowed access to knowledge. Conversely, Warlpiri knowledge of place is best understood as one in which layers of knowledge of an area may be revealed slowly over time with the input of various individuals and groups. Places are composites of knowledge that involve uncovering a vast store of layered sociocultural meanings. The site clearance process distilled only one of these layers as though it represented the entire complement of Warlpiri knowledge of places within a region.

The shortcomings of the freeze-frame methodology of the site clearance process can be effectively drawn out when compared to the way that Warlpiri people map their own interests in place. Nash (1998) investigated Warlpiri sand mapping techniques and discussed the ways that they are variously employed to indicate places in an area, the dreaming tracks crossing an area, and how these may be combined. The presentation of subject material displayed in a sand map is dependent on a number of factors including scale, positioning, audience, and the context of the mapping itself. Nash (1998: 3) observed that people would talk about and map *jukurrpa* in order to open up and reinforce memories before travelling to a region, and this was a process that involved a number of talkers and drawers. Such multiple narratives emphasise the fact that the activity of mapping is carried out by individuals and groups of Warlpiri who express different links to country through their expression of rights, knowledge and experience. The themes of knowledge and authority in the mapping of place and the ability of mapping to reveal patterns of interdependence between people within groups have been explored elsewhere in Australia and Canada by Biernoff (1978) and Brody (1986) respectively.

Traditionally, a site clearance survey was undertaken by a limited number of individuals and made no allowance for the fact that land and places contained within an exploration licence area may not have been visited for considerable periods of time. The return to country necessitated by a site clearance survey demanded a reorientation of Warlpiri people to a specific tract of land that was difficult to achieve in only one or two visits. The difficulties involved in assembling the repertoire of place knowledge stem from the fact that a considerable period of time had elapsed since people were in the region, and the fact that the region itself was defined by arbitrary licence boundaries that in no way corresponded with Warlpiri conceptions of regions and meanings. A licence area may cut across land belonging to a wide number of different *jukurrpa*, each with its own interested individuals and groups of people. In visiting a certain area the routes of travel undertaken may have little to do with the previous routes travelled by Warlpiri people or the directions and paths of *jukurrpa*. As wide a group of people as possible was needed to share information, memories, experience and knowledge of places in order to try and define the extent of places contained in a specific area within an appropriate and meaningful cultural framework. The site clearance process could not take such culturally specific parameters into account. The mapping project imposed a temporal and physical boundedness on place that neglected Warlpiri ways of knowing, discussing and experiencing places on their own terms.

Ultimately, the impossibility (for both the mining companies and Warlpiri) of working with a map produced by the site clearance methodology came down to the fact that subsequent visits to a licence area made by Warlpiri would always reveal more places than had previously been identified. There were a number of factors contributing to this recognition that combined to emphasise the vitality of people's relationships to place. These included the contribution made by the knowledge and memory of different individuals, the fact that the area was widely discussed back in communities and among other interested persons after initial site visits, that *jukurrpa* and songs were sung and discussed to check the order and connections of places, the land was often burned to allow easier location of soakages later, and so on. The attempt to locate and bound all Warlpiri interests in place under the site clearance process that attempted blanket coverage of a licence area simply did not work. In Figures 11-1 and 11-2, for example, the places that are mapped in and around the exploration licence area may have taken several visits to locate after a considerable period of time and sustained research had transpired. In addition there may yet be other places to be located such as soakages that are difficult to locate or other places that have not been searched for by knowledgeable informants.

It was not only Warlpiri interests that could not be clearly and definitively mapped after one survey in the site clearance process. The mining companies were also incapable of building a picture of an area in terms of its potential gold-bearing locales through the gathering of information over a short period of time. Sampling, costeaning (trench ripping), and drilling sites, along with camps and access tracks, changed locations quite frequently. It was difficult for both the miners and Warlpiri to keep a track of, and understand, each other's interests in place. The division of land into areas that were important and those that were not, whilst based upon different criteria, was equally difficult for Warlpiri and the mining companies. Lefebvre (1991: 334), observing the commodification of space that attended the rise of capitalism, remarked that under such extractive conditions:

> Space is marked out, explored, discovered and rediscovered on a colossal scale. Its potential for being occupied, filled, peopled and transformed from top to bottom is continually on the increase: the prospect, in short, is of space being produced whose nature is nothing more than raw materials suffering gradual destruction by the techniques of production.

In the case of the Tanami Desert, what constituted space and place ebbed and flowed over time, particularly so when places were continually being encountered during the course of routine exploration. The production of space within the site clearance process sought to divide space into areas organised by introduced scales of economic and sociocultural meanings, using Warlpiri place as the raw material of the system. The process failed to account for the manner in which people were able to identify and locate place, for it was Warlpiri who were the producers of this material not the project of mapping itself. To plot a place on the surface of the land involved trying to remove or extract it from the complicated web of meanings in which it is constituted and negotiated by Warlpiri. To point to a map and say 'there is X at such and such hill' is to take a place and attempt to render it only in its physical dimension in order to confine it in form and boundary. Mapping as envisaged by the site clearance process hinged upon a distortion that did not reflect any other significance of place in both physical and social landscapes. But the significance of place cannot be confined to a purely physical dimension and must be understood in the local, regionalised context of other places, *jukurrpa*, people, affiliations and politics.

The rapid expansion of the number of exploration licences approved by Warlpiri in the Tanami Desert began escalating in the early 1990s, and the site clearance process presented difficult obstacles for them as well as the mining companies. The practical difficulties that prevented an effective working arrangement for both parties also made it hard to see how interests in land and access for the stakeholders could both be protected. The site clearance process was unworkable and was therefore abandoned, to be replaced by the work area clearance method that was designed to communicate and inform both parties of their interests in place as part of an ongoing working arrangement. This new approach achieved considerable success in reducing complications that had arisen from the failure of the site clearance process to effectively identify the complement of Warlpiri places and interests within a particular licence area — and most importantly, within a culturally appropriate frame of reference.

The Work Area Clearance

The development of the work area clearance process cannot be solely attributed to the need to more effectively incorporate Warlpiri ways of knowing and identifying their places. A more successful working relationship between Aboriginal people and exploration companies also required a commitment on behalf of the latter to take a more positive approach to place. This certainly necessitated the incorporation of an understanding of Warlpiri relationships to place, but simultaneously identified and attempted to accommodate the objectives and interests of mining companies. The mechanisms of the work area clearance made the production of space and place more transparent and thus more easily comprehensible to the stakeholders.

The underpinning philosophy of both exploration for and production of gold is straightforward. A company seeks to maximise the amount of land available for exploration in order to increase the chances of finding a prospective gold reserve that will pass on financial benefits to the company and its shareholders. In the Tanami Desert this philosophy had to be adjusted in order to take into account the instructions of Warlpiri people who designated which land was available for exploration. The premise in operation remains the same for both the site clearance and work area clearance process. As the previous exploration manager of Normandy NFM in the Tanami Desert explained:

> Dilemmas are best avoided by the simple commitment to the early identification of sacred sites, and their immediate exclusion from the area subject of exploration — 'If it's culturally important, we don't want to explore there' (Ireland 1996: 11).

The difference between the two clearance processes lay in the manner in which the cultural importance of place was identified and incorporated into a workable relationship between *yapa* and mining interests.

The problems manifest in mapping place in the context of the site clearance has been documented. However the work area clearance process did not dispense with the idea of mapping altogether. The difference was that the attempt to map Warlpiri interests in place under the work area clearance procedure instead focused on the work program objectives of the company. In this way the area under consideration in an exploration licence was substantially reduced and the kinds of activities that were proposed were specifically detailed. The working arrangement became proactive to the extent that Warlpiri people inspected an exploration licence area on a case-by-case basis. Over a more workable time period *yapa* were enabled to make more informed decisions and surveys, the results of which informed subsequent instructions issued to the company. The work area clearance was an approach to place that provided greater scope for Warlpiri management of exploration on their own terms and removed the impediment of designating boundaries of place. The process also allowed different groups of people to identify their interests in places because it provided for a number of visits over the life of the licence area. From the company's perspective, the work area clearance minimized the risk of an unforeseen identification, late in an advanced exploration program, of a place of significance that intersected with a gold deposit. This scenario would present enormous problems for both Warlpiri and the company, but was difficult to avoid in the piecemeal approach of a site clearance.

The Mining Model of Place

The implementation of the work area clearance program in the Tanami Desert had the unintended effect of speeding up the rate of gold exploration in the region. As the work area clearance process was refined, more Warlpiri places were identified, people rapidly reoriented their interests in place, more tracks were built making access easier, and the exploration process itself became progressively demystified in Warlpiri eyes. Indeed, exploration in the central part of the region has become so intense that certain areas have already been the subject of several successful licence applications and exploration programs. The volume of interest in exploration in the Tanami Desert has forced the CLC to convene massive meetings of traditional landowners to consider multiple applications at once. In 1997 two meetings were held to deal with 42 and 62 Exploration Licence Applications respectively (CLC 1998a: 52).

The work area clearance approach of determining access to land was formulated with reference to the dual imperatives of both Warlpiri and mining company interests concerning the demarcation of space and place in the Tanami Desert. The work area clearance process replaced the flawed site clearance process and redressed the fundamental problems the latter caused by failing to effectively locate and identify Warlpiri places of significance. The development of gold exploration and mining has imposed a new model of land tenure in the central Tanami Desert. The first dimension of this model concerns the way that it requires *yapa* to continually divide the landscape into areas of space and place. This measurement of dreams has necessitated that both Warlpiri and mining companies rank and order their interests in land to effectively manage mining related developments.

For a mining company there are a number of different activities that take place over a long period of the time which have variable impacts in terms of levels of disruption caused to the landscape and the extent to which they encroach upon Warlpiri places. In the early phases of exploration these activities include helicopter and four-wheel drive surveys and sampling, camp construction, drilling and costeaning. These aspects of the exploration process have relatively low impacts although they are extensive throughout an exploration licence area. More intensive drilling and costeaning are usually restricted to smaller prospective areas. Exploration requires a small number of specialist personnel and little or no development of infrastructure. Sufficient time is given for the identification of all places of Warlpiri interest before the mining process begins. Mining itself is confined to a relatively limited area. The requirements of a mining venture include the construction of infrastructure such as roads, airstrips, water bore fields, pipelines, gravel pits, offices, accommodation, processing facilities, workshops, tailings and waste dumps, in addition to the ore pits themselves. Exploration and mining are very different activities that variably affect the significance of the local constellation of Warlpiri places and *jukurrpa*. Figures 11-3 and 11-4 illustrate how the interests of mining companies contract over time in order to focus intense development activity in the clearly defined area of a mineral lease. The second dimension for modelling Warlpiri land tenure under the mining regime is the determination of which places are affected by a new mine that has been developed within the original exploration licence area.

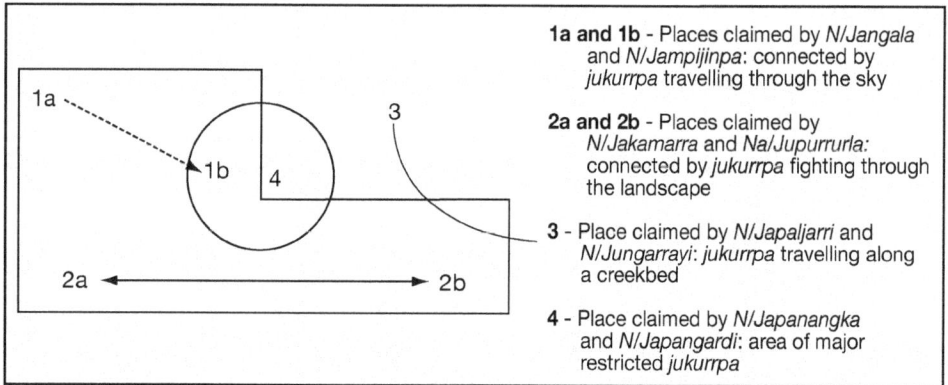

1a and 1b - Places claimed by *N/Jangala* and *N/Jampijinpa*: connected by *jukurrpa* travelling through the sky

2a and 2b - Places claimed by *N/Jakamarra* and *Na/Jupurrurla*: connected by *jukurrpa* fighting through the landscape

3 - Place claimed by *N/Japaljarri* and *N/Jungarrayi*: *jukurrpa* travelling along a creekbed

4 - Place claimed by *N/Japanangka* and *N/Japangardi*: area of major restricted *jukurrpa*

Figure 11-3: Diagram depicting broader areas of importance for Walpiri in relation to the exploration licence area in initial year of exploration.

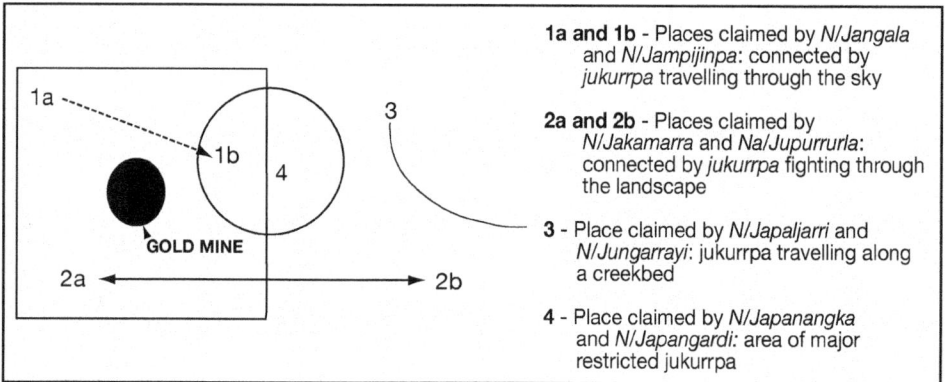

1a and 1b - Places claimed by *N/Jangala* and *N/Jampijinpa*: connected by *jukurrpa* travelling through the sky

2a and 2b - Places claimed by *N/Jakamarra* and *Na/Jupurrurla*: connected by *jukurrpa* fighting through the landscape

3 - Place claimed by *N/Japaljarri* and *N/Jungarrayi*: jukurrpa travelling along a creekbed

4 - Place claimed by *N/Japanangka* and *N/Japangardi*: area of major restricted jukurrpa

Figure 11-4: Diagram depicting mining lease area in relation to areas of significance for Walpiri in the fifth year of mining.

Warlpiri have become increasingly sophisticated in the ways in which they deal with questions determining which places are affected by mining and exploration, how important the places are, and the weight given to them in order to decide the proportions of royalties paid to the appropriate groups of owners. In the exploration example (Figure 11-3) there are clearly four different *jukurrpa* (one belonging to each semi-moiety) related to the licence area, from which people affiliated with each semi-moiety could argue for a role in decision making and a share of proceeds from royalties. To avoid unnecessary consideration of the physical extent of a site, let us say that all four places are fairly important soakages existing in conjunction with some other topographic feature. The most common way that Warlpiri order the interests of each group of *kirda* (patrilineally descended landowners) is as follows (in descending order of importance): 4 claimed by *N/Japanangka* and *N/Japangardi*; 2a and 2b claimed by *N/Jakamarra* and *Na/Jupurrurla*; 1a and 1b claimed by *N/Jangala* and *N/Jampijinpa*; 3 claimed by *N/Japaljarri* and *N/Jungarrayi*.

In discussion of how *yapa* arrive at such a ranking reference will be made to the Warlpiri gradation of place discussed in more depth in Elias (2001a: 106–17). Place 4 is deemed the most important place because it was *yukaka* or *kaninjarra* (inside or below) and is a restricted place where something of consequence was happening (*ngurrjumanu*), even though the physical centre of the site itself lies outside the licence area. It is also the prime place within the local area because there is no other place associated with *jukurrpa* on that level. Places 2a and 2b could be argued to have an equal degree of importance as place 4, even though the *jukurrpa* travelled across the ground (*yaninika-wurna*) and they are not as 'deep' literally or metaphorically by comparison. This argument would be justified on the grounds that there is an area where the ancestors emerged and fought with each other in between the two places (also *ngurrjumanu* as in the previous case), and the entire *jukurrpa* is confined within the licence area, thus elevating its importance. Next in ranking of importance are places 1a and 1b, where a *jukurrpa* simply flew through the air (*kankarlu*) between two places doing nothing of great significance at either place except resting (*ngunaja*). These places are also both entirely contained within the licence area. Finally, the least important place is place 3, where the *jukurrpa* is said to be affiliated with trees along a creek bed which it visited (*ngunaja*) before returning to its place of origin, doing nothing else of significance. At issue in the determination of which *jukurrpa* (and semi-moiety) are included within a licence area on Warlpiri terms are considerations of the power or strength of *jukurrpa*, the proximity of site features, the number of places and the activity of the *jukurrpa* itself.

As indicated earlier, under a mining regime, the emphasis on various aspects of an existing system of Warlpiri land tenure can change rapidly over a short period of time, given that the boundary of a licence area may change according to the success of initial exploration. Figure 11-4 takes up the example five years later when a gold mine is proposed in one part of a new mineral lease and the rest of the licence has been relinquished. In this situation, the case of place 3 is straightforward. It is discarded immediately from negotiations over a role in decision making and a share of proceeds from royalties. What happens with the other places becomes much more interesting. Places 1a and 1b, 2a and 4 all become of equal importance and share authority, with perhaps a smaller proportion of power and authority allocated to place 2b. How does this order change? In the case of places 1a and 1b the *kirda* (bosses) of one patriline and *jukurrpa* become increasingly important because there are two places in close proximity to the site of the mine and their *jukurrpa*. Although travelling through the air, they are still regarded as very close. Place 4 remains at the same high level of importance because it is still the most significant place in the local region. However, in the case of places 2a and 2b a distinction or contrast is drawn between them because, although they share the same *jukurrpa* and are from the same semi-moiety, the patrilineal descent group associated with place 2b is more distant from the mine site and is not within the mineral lease. However, place 2b is still included, albeit on a lesser level, because of the group's close association with place 2a and the fact that their *jukurrpa* is closely associated with the mine, even though their place is not.

This simple example indicates that for Warlpiri the measurement of dreams in terms of *jukurrpa* and place are closely associated with both the boundaries drawn by a mining company and the activity which is undertaken. In reality, the different combinations of *jukurrpa* and place are far more complicated than these illustrations. The important points are that the mapping of responsibility and authority over place is in the first instance mediated the different factors already mentioned, and also the relationships of local descent groups and wider regional considerations. In addition, decisions regarding the affiliation of semi-moieties and *jukurrpa* in a localised region must account of royalty payments and land tenure within a broader sociopolitical context.

Conclusion

The physical reintroduction of people to place in the context of mineral exploration in the Tanami Desert has thrown up complex and challenging issues. The production of boundaries over space and place in addition to the processes of exploration and gold mining have created an enormous amount of work aimed at identifying and maintaining different kinds of boundaries that are physical, social and spatial. Under the *ALRA*, Aboriginal land can neither be bought nor sold, yet the reintroduction of people to place has nonetheless commodified, not only the relationships between people and place, but also those between different groups of people. Mapping was the first part of this process that drew together Warlpiri politicking over rights to places in the face of the institutional requirements of the CLC, the mining industry and the government, in order for them to resolve questions of boundaries and ownership of place. Decisions over the identification and protection of places have, by and large, been the responsibility of senior knowledgeable persons. The identification of the appropriate owners of those places demands that Warlpiri people map their relationships to place with respect not only to their own places and boundaries, but also to those that are created by the development process.

The process of mineral exploration in the Tanami Desert requires Warlpiri to think carefully about their places within different kinds of physical and social boundaries. It has been argued that the mining model of land tenure requires that both Warlpiri and mining companies must carefully weigh how Warlpiri place is constructed with respect to an exploration or mining project. Exploration, mining and royalty payments expand the scope of politicking among Warlpiri by introducing an economic context within which they organise, negotiate and resolve competing claims of ownership and affiliation to place by different individuals and landholding groups.

References

Altman, J. and N. Peterson, 1984. 'A Case for Retaining Aboriginal Mining Veto and Royalty Rights in the Northern Territory.' *Australian Aboriginal Studies* (2): 44–53.

Bauman, T., 2002. '"Test 'im Blood": Subsections and Shame in Katherine.' *Anthropological Forum* 12: 205–220.

Bell, S., 1998. 'SOG pulls out of Tanami Search.' *Australia's Mining Monthly*, December 1998–January 1999.

Biernoff, D., 1978. 'Safe and Dangerous Places.' In L. Hiatt (ed.), *Australian Aboriginal Concepts*. Canberra: Australian Institute of Aboriginal Studies.

Brody, H., 1986. *Maps and Dreams*. London: Faber and Faber.

Brunton, R., 1992. 'Mining Credibility: Coronation Hill and the Anthropologists.' *Anthropology Today* 8(2): 2–5.

CLC (Central Land Council), 1998a. 'Annual Report 1997–1998.' Canberra: Australian Government Publishing Service.

——, 1998b. 'Mines and Myths: The Truth about Mining on Aboriginal Land.' Alice Springs: Central Land Council.

Dussart, F., 2000. *The Politics of Ritual in an Aboriginal Settlement*. Washington and London: Smithsonian Institution Press.

Elias, D., 2001a. Golden Dreams: People, Place and Mining in the Tanami Desert. Canberra: Australian National University (PhD thesis).

——, 2001b. 'Jukurrpa — Golden Dreams.' In I. McCalman, A. Cook and A. Reeves (eds), *Gold: Forgotten Histories and Lost Objects of Australia*. Cambridge: Cambridge University Press.

Glowczewski, B., 1999. 'Dynamic Cosmologies and Aboriginal Heritage.' *Anthropology Today* 15(1): 3–9.

Hawke, S. and M. Gallagher, 1989. *Noonkanbah: Whose Land, Whose Law?* Fremantle: Fremantle Arts Centre Press.

Ireland, T., 1996. 'Exploring for Gold on Aboriginal Land in the Northern Territory.' Paper presented at the Third International and Twenty-First Annual Minerals Council of Australia Environmental Workshop on 'Building International Partnerships in Environmental Management for the Minerals Industry', Newcastle, 14–18 October. Canberra: Minerals Council of Australia.

Keen, I., 1992. 'Undermining Credibility: Advocacy and Objectivity in the Coronation Hill debate.' *Anthropology Today* 8(2): 6–9.

Lefebvre, H., 1991. *The Production of Space*. Oxford: Blackwell.

Manning, I., 1997. 'Native Title, Mining and Mineral Exploration: The Impact of Native Title and the Right to Negotiate on Mining and Mineral Exploration in Australia.' Canberra: Aboriginal and Torres Strait Islander Commission.

Merlan, F., 1991. 'The Limits of Cultural Constructionism: The Case of Coronation Hill.' *Oceania* 61: 341–352.

Myers, F. and B. Clark, 1983. 'A Claim to Areas of Traditional Land by Warlpiri, Kukatja, and Ngarti.' Alice Springs: Central Land Council.

Nash, D., 1998. 'Ethnocartography: Understanding Central Australian Geographic Literacy.' Unpublished manuscript.

Peterson, N., P. McConvell, S. Wild and R. Hagen, 1978. 'A Claim to Areas of Traditional Land by Warlpiri and Kartangarurru-Kurintji.' Alice Springs: Central Land Council.

Reeves, J., 1998. 'Building on Land Rights for the Next Generation: Report of the Review of the *Aboriginal Land Rights (Northern Territory) Act 1976*.' Canberra: Australian Government Publishing Service.

Stanner, W.E.H., 1965. 'Aboriginal Territorial Organization: Estate, Range, Domain and Regime.' *Oceania* 36: 1–25.

Stead, J., 1985. 'A Claim to Chilla Well Pastoral Lease by Warlpiri.' Alice Springs: Central Land Council.

Woodward, A.E., 1974. 'Aboriginal Land Rights Commission: Second Report, April 1974.' Canberra: Australian Government Publishing Service.

Chapter Twelve

Laws and Strategies: The Contest to Protect Aboriginal Interests at Coronation Hill[1]

Robert Levitus

In recent decades, Aboriginal affairs in Australia have been punctuated by disputes over development projects proposed in the vicinity of places attributed mythological significance by local Aboriginal peoples. Noonkanbah, Coronation Hill and Hindmarsh Island have been the biggest of these, attracting intense national political attention. In such disputes, law, party policies and interest group campaigning serially interact through the sometimes prolonged stages of the associated political process. This chapter selects one theme from the management of the Coronation Hill issue, which ran its long and tortuous course from September 1985 to June 1991. It focuses on the early stages of that history, and in particular on the events of 1987, and examines the ways in which two statutory authorities charged with advancing the recognition and protection of Aboriginal interests in land adopted courses of action that in different respects complemented and competed with one another. It further traces the stages through which one of these authorities was able to transform itself from a marginal observer to principal representative of the Aboriginal interest.

The character of the relationship between these two organisations derived from the distinct but overlapping legislative charters under which each operated. There were two Acts involved, and they had a common public policy origin in the recognition of Aboriginal land rights in the Northern Territory in the 1970s. The first and principal Act was the Commonwealth *Aboriginal Land Rights (Northern Territory) Act 1976 (ALRA)*; the second and complementary Act was the Territory's own *Aboriginal Sacred Sites Act 1978 (ASSA)*. Within the overall land rights regime, jurisdiction was divided between the statutory authorities established by these Acts, the Northern Land Council (NLC) and the Aboriginal Sacred Sites Protection Authority (ASSPA) respectively. There were important differences in the way these authorities were empowered to recognise and manage

---

[1] I would like to thank the Aboriginal Areas Protection Authority and the Northern Land Council for access to their records, and those officers of both organisations, past and present, who discussed the history of Coronation Hill with me. I am grateful to David Ritchie and David Cooper for their comments on drafts, and to the editors for their help in producing a shorter and more integrated paper.

the indigenous interest in land. These concerned the extent of the land and the purposes to which it could be put, and the category of Aboriginal people which each organisation was required to consult. This chapter thus relates the contest between them over management of Coronation Hill to the different kinds of indigenous interest that were seen to be at stake.

This analysis therefore does not deal with the most contentious aspect of the interaction between indigenous testimony and organisational strategy during the Coronation Hill dispute. That was the problem of determining whether the Aboriginal custodians genuinely held religious beliefs about that place of a kind that should have precluded mining development. Rather, it is about external history, an interpretation of an aspect of the strategies of the two organisations involved, tracked through consultations, meetings, submissions, lobbying and negotiations from Coronation Hill to Canberra. Connections between these issues, however, will readily be found, as the history given here reveals sufficient incidental details to indicate just how fraught the question of the significance of Coronation Hill was, and why it became the point on which policy, in the end, pivoted (Levitus 1996). That end point ultimately came in 1991 when Prime Minister Bob Hawke, acting from a minority position in Cabinet, insisted that the religious values ascribed by Aborigines to Coronation Hill were of such importance as to preclude mining and justify its incorporation within Kakadu National Park.

Rather, my analysis points to the way the organisations' strategies during this issue flowed in part from the way their understandings of indigenous authority with respect to place were structured both by law and by their own prior histories of practice. In the case of the NLC, that prior history bore the force of precedent from a previous land claim, and in the case of the ASSPA, it took the form of an institutional policy commitment to direct and individualised consultation. Eventually, and after several years of contention, official processes of arbitration and management again called upon local indigenous people to propose their own model of landownership. The model they proposed in response differed significantly from previous representations, most importantly in bringing to salience a structural entity, the patrilineal clan, that had been de-emphasised or left out of account by that prior history of organisational practice.

In the next section, I set out the respective points of departure that grounded the orientations of the two organisations towards Coronation Hill. In later sections, I narrate and analyse the phases of tension and cooperation that developed between them. In the penultimate section I jump ahead to the early 1990s, when the Coronation Hill dispute passed through its final phase and an Aboriginal land claim proceeded over the surrounding area. Here, in an unexpected counterpoint to what had gone before, the local indigenous model of responsibility for country just mentioned achieved recognition in the final political and legal settlements of land interests in the area.

The Land Council and the Sites Authority

The NLC, one of the statutory authorities concerned, was one of two major land councils brought into existence by the *ALRA*. It is a body consisting of Aboriginal people elected from various subregions of the top half of the mainland Northern Territory, and served by a substantial professional bureaucracy divided into branches such as Law, Anthropology and Resource Management. In the period to the late 1990s, now thought of as the first generation of land rights, the NLC's major responsibility was to assist Aborigines to establish their traditional ownership of unalienated Crown land before the Aboriginal Land Commissioner, who could then recommend the granting of inalienable freehold title to an Aboriginal Land Trust (*ALRA* Section 50(1)(a)). More generally, the NLC's functions are to ascertain the wishes and represent the interests of traditional Aboriginal owners of land within the top half of the Northern Territory with respect to any issue relating to ownership or use of that land (ibid. Section 23(1)). Such issues have prominently included the negotiation of conditions under which mining interests will be granted.

Traditional owners are determined by reference to the mythologically sanctioned social structures, such as patrilineal clans or language groups, that mediate relationships between people and land (Keen 1984). In land claims, these structures are described from anthropological research and validated by claimant testimony in a tribunal hearing before the Aboriginal Land Commissioner. Traditional owners thus are members of a group or groups that occupy the appropriate relationship of spiritual responsibility towards sites on the land. While, in a land claim, at least some members of the group will have to show knowledge of the country concerned, those lacking such knowledge retain the status of traditional owners by reason of their membership of the relevant group. Structural entitlement is thus the principal determinant of traditional ownership, and participation in consultations on matters of land management is therefore in principle open to any competent member of the owning group. In accordance with Aboriginal custom with respect to speaking for country and making decisions about land, those with personal attributes of knowledge, relevant life experience, seniority or prestige play the largest roles in deliberations and are those to whom the NLC has most resort for its instructions.

The ASSPA was a Northern Territory Government agency established by the *ASSA*. The ASSPA existed until 1989, when it was reconstituted by new legislation as the Aboriginal Areas Protection Authority. The Authority, consisting of a majority of Aboriginal members nominated by the Land Councils and served by an office of field anthropologists and technical staff, is responsible for documenting and registering Aboriginal sacred sites throughout the Territory.

It registers sites only on a request from local Aborigines customarily responsible for those sites, referred to in its Act as the 'custodians' (*ASSA* Section 3). The custodians generally number between one and a few individuals, and their status derives from a combination of affiliation with the place or area, seniority in age, and knowledge.

Unauthorised trespass upon a site is subject to penalties. Under the original *ASSA*, in force until 1989, the ASSPA could give written consent for access to and works upon a site. It became the practice of ASSPA officers to arrange consultations between proponents of work and the site custodians, and then to seek from custodians their views as to the acceptability of the work, a matter on which they reported to the ASSPA for a formal decision. Since 1989, these procedures have been formalised in law (Ritchie 1996: 214–5).

Other points concerning these arrangements for the protection of Aboriginal land interests need to be made here. The first relates to the intended complementary relationship between the two regimes just described. The *ALRA* provided the definition of a sacred site as, in part, 'a site that is sacred to Aboriginals or is otherwise of significance according to Aboriginal tradition' (Section 3), and further created the offence of unauthorised entry onto a sacred site (Section 69). The Northern Territory's own sacred sites legislation, however, had its policy genesis in a decision by the Federal Government not to provide for all relevant matters within its own land rights legislation, but to allow subsequent 'reciprocal' legislation (*ALRA* Section 73) to be passed by the Northern Territory Parliament, then approaching self-government. Administration of a sacred sites protection process was considered an appropriate area for such reciprocal legislation. This has been an object of criticism by Land Councils who resent the denial of jurisdiction over a matter they perceive as properly a part of land rights, and mistrust the placing of that jurisdiction in the hands of a Northern Territory government dominated, from self-government in 1978 until 2001, by an openly pro-development Country Liberal Party. Consequently, there has been within the NLC persistent doubt as to the ability or the willingness of the Sacred Sites Authority to stand up forthrightly for Aboriginal interests.

The common policy origin of land rights and sites protection also enshrines an underlying difference in the nature of the land interest being recognised. The recognition of a sacred site has different implications depending on whether it is on land claimable by Aborigines or elsewhere. On claimable land, sacred sites are fundamental to the process of proving traditional ownership, because the members of the claimant group have to demonstrate that they have spiritual affiliations to, and exercise spiritual responsibility for, sites on the land (*ALRA* Section 3(1)). Recognition of such attachments in a successful land claim thus founds a legal property right. On land that is not available for claim, such attachments found rights of lesser extent which, though their exact character is open to debate (Ritchie 1996: 211, 217), importantly include a right of entry and a right to deny entry to others.

The land registration regimes administered by the NLC and Sites Authority thus contrast in significant respects, including the areas of land involved, the Aborigines with whom they must consult, and the range of issues on which they are required to consult. Generally, the NLC assists in claiming and managing areas of land, while the Authority assists in the protection of particular places of religious significance, mostly of much smaller size. However, the Authority's charter extends across the entire Northern Territory, while the NLC is restricted to unalienated Crown land with respect to its land claim function, and Aboriginal land for its other functions (subject to an important exception to be mentioned later). The NLC must have regard to the wishes of those identified as traditional owners, while the Authority consults with the site custodians, again a generally more limited group. The NLC must consult regarding the full range of land use purposes bearing upon Aboriginal land, while the Authority specifically manages requests for site registration from the custodians, and requests for site access from others. In summary, then, the laws under which these two authorities operate allow the registration of indigenous land interests of different extent and according to different criteria, and require each organisation to seek instructions from different categories of Aboriginal authority. These differences underlay the divergent and sometimes competing roles of the ASSPA and the NLC with respect to Coronation Hill.

The Regional Context

Coronation Hill is located in the Top End of Australia's Northern Territory. It lies in the upper South Alligator River valley in the northwestern sector of the former Gimbat pastoral lease (see Figure 12-1). In the early 1980s, this area was an object of increasing interest from several quarters, one of which was the mining industry. A previous generation of small-scale uranium mining at many locations along the valley in the 1950s and 1960s had also produced evidence of gold deposits. In the early 1980s the international price for gold rose. Broken Hill Pty Ltd (BHP), the on-site operations company for the Coronation Hill Joint Venture, began drilling at the old open-cut mine on Coronation Hill in 1984, and soon obtained very promising results.[2]

---

[2] See Noranda Pacific Ltd 1985 Prospectus, pp. 16–21.

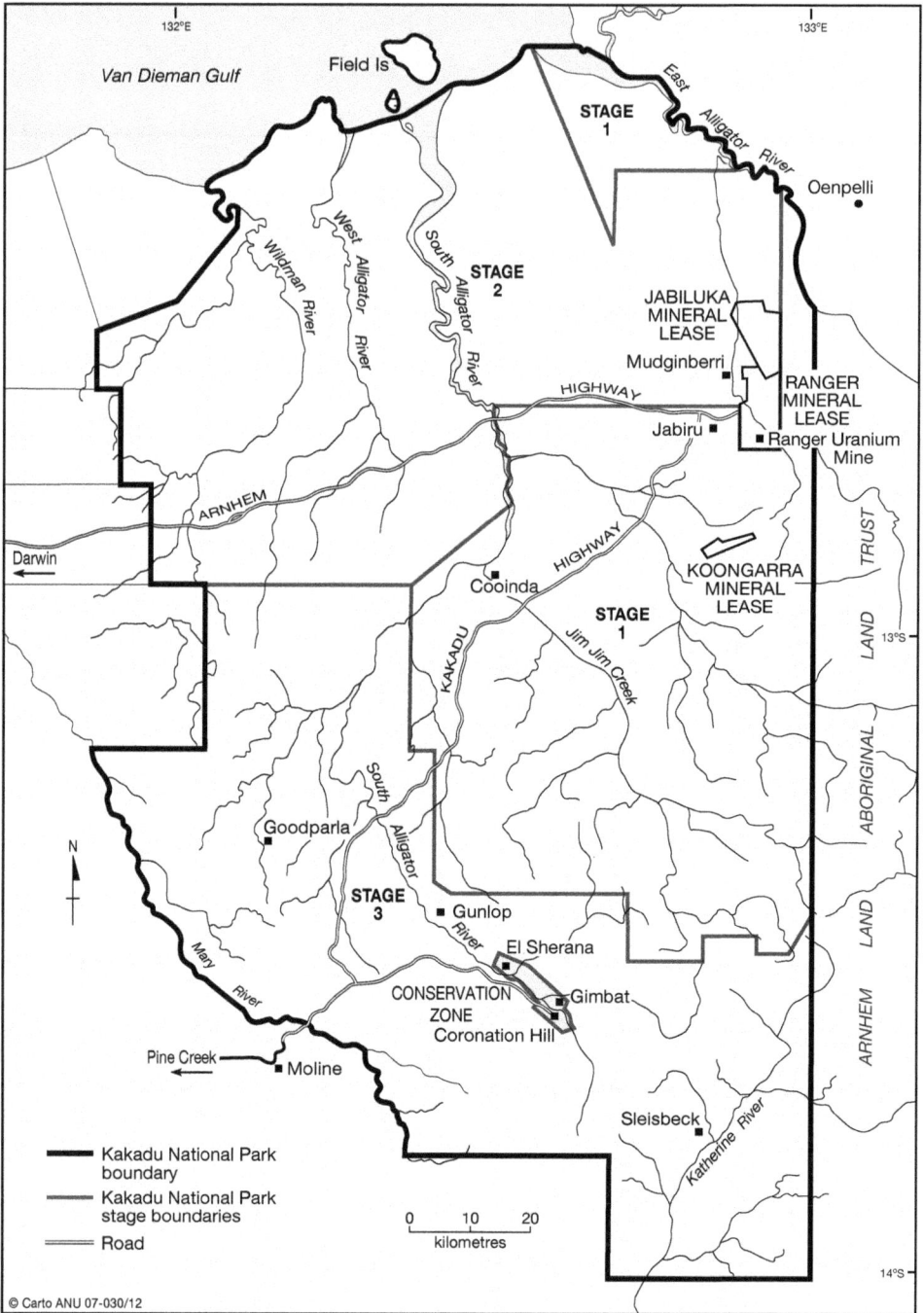

Figure 12-1: Kakadu National Park, showing Coronation Hill and reduced (post-1989) Conservation Zone.

At the same time, the NLC and the environmental movement anticipated that Gimbat would soon become available both for land claim and for declaration as a National Park. In the mid-1970s, the Ranger Uranium Environmental Inquiry (CoA 1977) had put forward a land use framework for the entire Alligator Rivers region. Central to the management regimes it proposed was the establishment of a major National Park to encompass at least one important river catchment. The river selected for protection was the South Alligator (ibid: 288–9), and the National Park was named Kakadu. Declaration of the Park proceeded in stages. Stage I was declared in 1979 and Stage II in 1984, both to the north of Gimbat (see Figures 12-1 and 12–2). By the mid-1980s, declaration of Stage III of the Park was on the Federal Government's agenda, and this was expected to extend Kakadu south into Gimbat and Goodparla stations to protect most of the remaining South Alligator catchment. Prior to the declarations of Stages I and II, opportunities were allowed for Aboriginal land claims to be heard over those areas, after which the successfully claimed lands were leased back by the Aboriginal owners to the Parks Service. The NLC therefore anticipated that, in the time between the stations becoming unalienated Crown land and their declaration as parts of the National Park, there would be an opportunity to claim Gimbat and Goodparla stations on behalf of the traditional owners. Supporters of that scenario were worried that the Coronation Hill development might allow a mining interest to be established before the land could be placed under a new regime that protected its Aboriginal and environmental values.

Gimbat lay within the northerly reaches of the territory of the Jawoyn language group. By the early 1980s there were no Jawoyn resident there, though small numbers had worked and lived there under previous lessees. Now they resided in many directions, but predominantly in a large arc from Pine Creek to the east, in and around the town of Katherine, to Eva Valley Station and Barunga Settlement to the south. The particular significance that Gimbat and its immediate environs retained for a number of knowledgeable senior Aborigines, however, arose from the occurrence there of a number of sites of extreme power and danger associated with the creator figure Bula, not all of which were mapped. While Aboriginal interests could not at that time be asserted through a land claim, research conducted for the ASSPA had led to the registration in 1980 of two Bula sites in Gimbat. Over the next few years, the NLC's research in adjoining or overlapping areas for the Jawoyn (Katherine Area) Land Claim (Merlan and Rumsey 1982) recorded a complex of such sites across Gimbat and into neighbouring areas, and documented the mythology of Bula as the most powerful and dangerous dreaming known to the Jawoyn. The NLC relied on this information in representations to the Federal Government made in the early 1980s, urging the priority of sacred site protection in future land use regimes for the area.

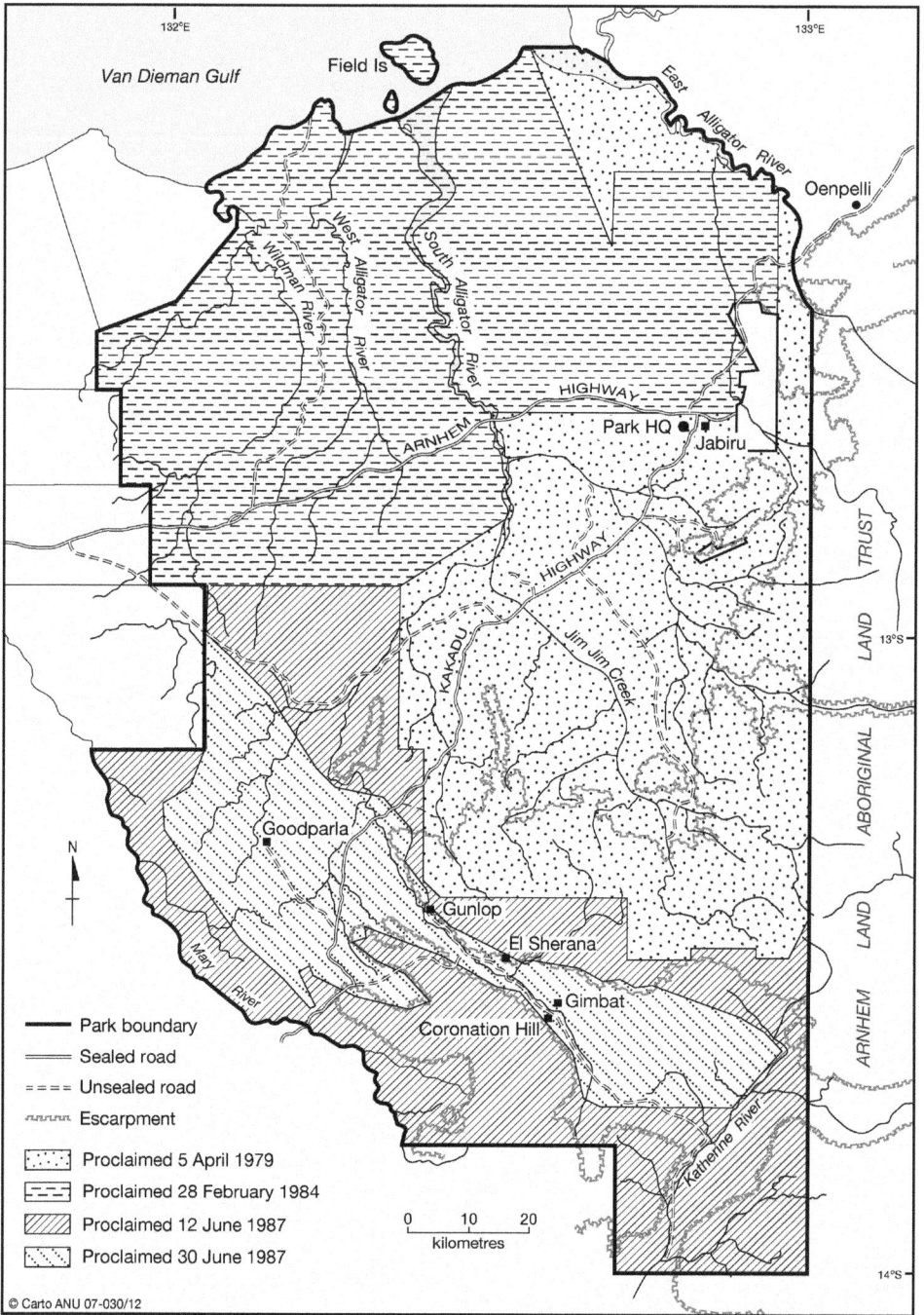

Figure 12-2: Kakadu National Park, showing stages of declaration and the original Conservation Zone.

Source: SSCERA 1988: 2.

During this period the Jawoyn themselves were entering a new phase of political engagement and heightened self-consciousness. A decade after introduction of the new Federal policy of indigenous self-determination, a range of community issues bearing upon some part or other of Jawoyn country demanded the constant attention of senior Jawoyn (Merlan 1998: 89). Among these matters was the preparation and presentation of the Jawoyn (Katherine Area) Land Claim over five parcels of land, the largest and most important being Katherine Gorge National Park, lying between Katherine town and Gimbat Station. The NLC presented this claim in a manner that had a particular bearing upon Jawoyn self-awareness. It argued that the claimants made up a unitary and undifferentiated group of traditional owners, the Jawoyn language group, for all of Jawoyn country (Merlan and Rumsey 1982: 40, 55–6).[3]

That model of traditional ownership also carried implications for the way in which the NLC could approach the policy issues emerging over Gimbat. Though evidence in the Katherine Area claim concluded in 1984, the Land Commissioner's judgment was not received by the NLC until October 1987. Two small parcels of land in northern Gimbat were included in the claim, and the NLC expected the opportunity to lodge a further land claim over Gimbat as a whole on behalf of the Jawoyn. The NLC consequently approached the representation of Jawoyn interests in Gimbat in the mid-1980s under the constraint of that model of landownership already argued before the Land Commissioner. In early 1986, shortly after development works at Coronation Hill had become a public administration issue, the NLC made clear its view of where sovereignty in the matter properly lay. It told a Senate Inquiry that mining development there was a matter for the Jawoyn people as a whole to decide, and that any statement by a site custodian that denied the sacredness of the place should be put before a full Jawoyn meeting for verification (SSCNR 1986: 2331–2).

The ASSPA, by contrast, needed to ensure that it was acting consistently with the wishes of the senior custodians. This group consisted centrally of three old men whose primary traditional attachments lay within Gimbat, though respect was also accorded to the knowledge of a small number of other senior men from other areas. While the ASSPA could accept decisions made at meetings of larger groups, it attempted to verify that the custodians in attendance were in accord with such decisions. Often that would be apparent from the role they played in discussions. The NLC and the ASSPA thus came to the Coronation Hill issue with markedly different conceptions of the locus of Aboriginal authority that should govern its management.

This was of further significance in view of continuing organisational immaturity among the Jawoyn themselves. The Jawoyn Association was

[3] See Rumsey (1989) for a discussion of the concept of the language group and its use in land claims.

incorporated in 1985 to manage royalty and business income from properties in the region. It remained poorly organised and staffed for some years, acting mainly as a public political front during the latter half of the Coronation Hill dispute. In the absence of independent institutional resources, Jawoyn views on Gimbat and Coronation Hill were thus articulated through the channels offered by a continuing and at times intense engagement with external agencies, especially the NLC, the ASSPA, and the BHP project team.

Liaison and Consultation

At the time the new mineral discovery became publicly known in 1985, Gimbat was still a pastoral lease and so not available for land claim, and Coronation Hill itself was not subject to any other form of legal protection for environmental or Aboriginal values. In September 1985, members of the environmental movement alerted the NLC and the ASSPA that a mining company had reported very encouraging test drilling results at Coronation Hill. An ASSPA research officer brought the matter to the attention of a meeting of Jawoyn people, and suggested that the upper South Alligator valley be treated as a priority area for sacred site survey.[4] Following a visit to the valley with three Jawoyn men, including two senior custodians, and supplementary interviews elsewhere, the officer prepared a report for the registration of an area of about 250 km^2 on the southwestern side of the valley, including most of Coronation Hill (Cooper 1985). Registration of that area as a sacred site, the Upper South Alligator Bula Complex, by the ASSPA in October 1985 meant that further testing of the mineral deposit at Coronation Hill could not proceed without permission from the ASSPA.

The process of obtaining such permission involved consultation between BHP's on-site project team and the custodians, mediated by officers of the ASSPA. Those officers had the responsibility of ensuring that the custodians understood and approved of proposals put to them, before recommending to the ASSPA that site access be allowed. At this stage, sacred site registration was the only legal impediment to further mineral exploration, and the ASSPA was the only agency with the power to regulate BHP's access to the deposit according to Aboriginal wishes. Like the NLC previously, the ASSPA also tried, by its representations to Canberra, to insert the Aboriginal interest in the proposed Kakadu Stage III area into the Government policy debate and into regional land-use planning as an independent third voice alongside the mining industry and the environmental movement.[5] In that broader regional context, then, the

[4] File note referring to Jawoyn meeting at Barunga on the 11 September 1985, 13 September 1985, Aboriginal Areas Protection Authority (AAPA) files.
[5] Copy letters Blitner to Holding, 8 June 1983, 28 September 1983, NLC file 87/11; copy letters Ritchie to Holding, Cohen, Evans, 18 November 1985; copy letter Ritchie to Secretary, Senate Standing Committee on National Resources, 2 December 1985, AAPA file 81/208. Access conditions prevent me from providing citations from NLC records for some points in my discussion of the role of that organisation and its officers.

ASSPA shared with the NLC a common view of the extent of the general Jawoyn interest in the future of Gimbat.

Over the following months, the NLC also maintained its interest in the area. It remained satisfied that the Jawoyn opposed mining development at Coronation Hill and represented their position as such. Two NLC officers recorded statements of concern about works at Coronation Hill from a small group of Jawoyn during a visit to the area in November 1985. A Senate Inquiry into the resources of the Kakadu area had by then begun its work (SSCERA 1988), and the first NLC submission to it in December asserted Jawoyn opposition to the mining project.[6] In January 1986 three NLC officers heard anti-mining statements made at a Jawoyn Association meeting, after which the NLC expressed concern for the sacred significance of the area to the Federal Ministers for the Environment and for Resources and Energy. A meeting in March of NLC Regional Members passed a resolution supporting Jawoyn opposition to the project.

This marked the culmination of the first stage of the NLC response to the issue. It was a period in which its officers were able to maintain a role only as observers and informal advisors to the Jawoyn, in which they had no standing to formally oversee land use or site access, but in which their view of Jawoyn interests and wishes with respect to the area, and specifically regarding Coronation Hill, was based on a consistent record of expressed Aboriginal anti-mining sentiment. While they deferred to the ASSPA's jurisdiction, they also noted their first reservations as to its approach. In March, on a joint visit to Canberra, the senior NLC legal officer recorded his concern over hearing the ASSPA director telling government ministers and senior bureaucrats that the Jawoyn custodians might compromise over Coronation Hill.

The BHP project team spent the wet season preparing work plans for the following year, and establishing informal communication with some individual Jawoyn. When in March 1986 its development proposals were rejected by a Jawoyn meeting, it embarked on a broad campaign of informal liaison and information, including field trips, to familiarise small groups of senior Jawoyn people with its personnel and with their work at Coronation Hill, and to ascertain from the Jawoyn the location and extent of sacred places in the upper South Alligator valley. This latter aspect of the BHP team's liaison evoked objections from both the NLC and the ASSPA, both of which wanted communications contained within channels that allowed for proper consultation procedures and representation of Jawoyn interests (Dodson 1986).[7] The NLC during that period recorded further Jawoyn comments opposed to the mine, while the ASSPA director thought mining could be negotiated if communications were handled sensitively.

---

[6] Copy letter Ah Kit to Secretary, SSCNR, 11 December 1985, NLC file 86/36.
[7] Copy letters Ellis to Rush, 3 April 1986, 12 May 1986, AAPA file 85/63.

The BHP project team's initial phase of liaison culminated on 1 July when they organised a Jawoyn meeting that approved the resumption of works at Coronation Hill in those areas already disturbed by past mining. On a report from its officer in attendance at that meeting, the ASSPA gave official approval for conditional and staged development to occur.[8] A second meeting of 4 July, however, conducted by a Jawoyn Association officer and observed by NLC representatives and the ASSPA chairman, reversed that decision. A further ASSPA meeting in Katherine on 11 July discussed this reversal with a number of participants at the two meetings, including the senior custodians, and decided that the approval it had given was valid. The NLC regarded this as a failure by the ASSPA to act on the instructions of traditional owners.

The two decisions of early July were only the first of a long series of contradictions to emerge from Jawoyn meetings and consultations over the ensuing months. These presented a major source of indeterminacy for effective management of the issue and remain an important interpretive problem that is beyond the scope of this chapter (see Keen and Merlan 1990: 67–82; Levitus 2003; Merlan 2004: 259–66). The BHP team proceeded to develop its 'good neighbour' relationship with the Jawoyn, and introduced a Jawoyn employment program on site. In October 1986 a meeting of about 30 Jawoyn, including two site custodians and some other senior people, agreed to BHP's proposals to expand its exploration and development works, this time to areas not previously disturbed.[9] By the end of the year, the results of the drilling program had proven the existence of a commercial mineral deposit. Alongside good exploration results and successful dealings with the Jawoyn, the Federal policy environment was also looking favourable for mining. In September and December 1986, government ministers announced that while Stage III of Kakadu would be declared, 35 per cent of the area would be reserved for a five-year mineral exploration program. Coronation Hill was acknowledged as a project of special economic significance that would be approved subject to proper clearances.[10] In early 1987 the project team maintained continuous direct dealings with the Jawoyn, expanded the employment program, began preparation of an Environmental Impact Study, proceeded with feasibility studies and planned the steps towards a full mining agreement with the Jawoyn. In March the ASSPA confirmed approvals for work proposed late the previous year.

The Role of the Northern Land Council

In the face of this steady progress towards mining, relations between the NLC and the ASSPA were a mix of cooperation and reserve. Among field staff with

[8] Copy letter Ellis to Rush, 4 July 1986, AAPA file 85/63.
[9] Ellis, Minutes of Meeting Held El Sharana 31 October 1986, 3 November 1986, AAPA file 85/63.
[10] Joint Statement by the Minister for Resources and Energy, Senator Evans and the Minister for Arts, Heritage and Environment, Mr Cohen, 16 December 1986.

local experience, there was a shared concern that the Jawoyn were not equipped with the internal community resources and information, nor were they being allowed the time and space, to adequately come to grips with proposals such as Coronation Hill. These officers tried to provide the personal and organisational support they felt was lacking, and were inclined to suspicion of the BHP team's liaison efforts. Formally the two organisations exchanged file materials for mutual information, and the ASSPA director supported the availability of the NLC's Katherine office legal advisor to assist the Jawoyn. Senior NLC people acknowledged that carriage of the issue lay with the ASSPA, but felt, initially, that their reservations with respect to the capacity of the ASSPA to protect Aboriginal interests were being confirmed.

By the end of 1986 a number of inconsistent Jawoyn statements, and the further development works approved at the October meeting, had created new doubts as to the Jawoyn position with respect to mining. Whatever the final position on that issue, the NLC still considered a land claim as essential to protect Jawoyn interests in the area. While such a claim could not be lodged while Gimbat remained a pastoral lease, the NLC hoped in the meantime, by way of Jawoyn requests for assistance, to manouevre itself into the role of protective intermediary. This it achieved in January and February 1987, with formal instructions from the Jawoyn Association to act as the Jawoyn legal representative,[11] and authorisation from the Association to attend all meetings between the Jawoyn and BHP.

By these steps, the NLC sought to overcome any objection to its right to be present and to advise the Jawoyn in all their dealings over Coronation Hill. Shortly thereafter, however, in March and April, NLC officers recorded statements on three occasions, largely from the same senior Jawoyn individuals, in favour, against, and in favour, of mining. The NLC, having finally achieved formal standing as the Jawoyn legal representative, could not effectively advocate its client's position, because it was unable to determine with certainty what that position was. Matters were no better clarified at a Jawoyn Association meeting in May where an NLC officer recorded that those present appeared undecided about the issue.

The NLC encountered further difficulties in having its role acknowledged by the BHP project team. In the midst of the events just described, the senior legal officer wrote to the company advising that 'the Jawoyn Association has instructed the Northern Land Council to act on its behalf on all matters relating to Coronation Hill', and requesting that all communications to the Jawoyn Association should be sent to the offices of the NLC. That letter further offered 'to discuss BHP's current involvement at Coronation Hill in a preliminary manner

---

[11] Letter McDonald to Director Bureau NLC, 21 January 1987, NLC file 86/154.

at your convenience'.[12] The NLC thereby attempted to consolidate its intermediary role by situating itself across the interface of contact between the Jawoyn and the company.

The BHP project team had from the outset been wary of the NLC and suspicious of its motives for intervening, perceiving its tactics as manipulative of the Jawoyn and inimical to successful development of the project. Its Aboriginal Affairs Advisor replied to the NLC that the team had to maintain direct dealings with the Jawoyn on a number of day-to-day matters, but that if the Jawoyn approved, it would deal with the NLC on formal matters.[13] The BHP team thereby refused to defer to the NLC's claim for the priority of its advisor-client relationship, and would allow only limited room for NLC involvement if this was authorised through the team's own communication with the Jawoyn. Approaching the next round of development consultations in June 1987, the BHP team found no support among Jawoyn leaders for NLC involvement. The team proceeded to organise a meeting of about 30 Jawoyn people, including two senior custodians, and ASSPA officers, at which further works on the project were explained and substantially approved, in disregard of the NLC's attempt to establish a formal role for itself.[14]

Events up to mid-1987 thus left the NLC uncertain of its client's views regarding the management of the upper South Alligator valley, lacking confidence in the ASSPA's handling of the central issue of development works at Coronation Hill, and without proper recognition from the mining company as its counterpart in negotiations. At that point, the legal basis of the NLC's participation in the affairs of the region was transformed by a raft of legislative amendments passed by the Federal Government.[15] The *ALRA* was amended to give Land Councils the additional function of assisting Aborigines to protect sacred sites, whether or not on Aboriginal land. Other amendments declared Gimbat and Goodparla stations to be unalienated Crown land and therefore available for land claim, and empowered Aboriginal Land Councils in the Northern Territory to negotiate mining agreements over land under claim, extending their existing power to negotiate only over land already won. In anticipation of these developments, the Jawoyn Association instructed the NLC to lodge a land claim over the area and to invite the company to enter negotiations for an agreement over exploration and mining. The NLC lodged the land claim on 26 June, and wrote to the company on 2 July.[16]

---

[12] Copy letter Gray to BHP Minerals Ltd, 7 April 1987, NLC file 87/104.

[13] Copy letter Rush to the Director NLC, 30 April 1987, BHP/Newcrest correspondence and reports.

[14] Copy note to file, 'Subject: G1/8–67C Aboriginal Community On-Site Meeting, 3/4 June 1987', BHP/Newcrest correspondence and reports; copy letter Ellis to Hewitt, 5 June 1987, AAPA file 85/63.

[15] *Aboriginal Land Rights (Northern Territory) Amendment Acts (2 and 3)*, *Lands Acquisition Amendment Act*, *Environment Protection (Alligator Rivers Region) Amendment Act*, *National Parks and Wildlife Conservation Amendment Acts (1 and 2)*; all of 1987.

[16] Copy letter Gray to Managing Director BHP, 2 July 1987, NLC file 87/104.

The Contest over Aboriginal Interests

The BHP project team delayed negotiations, and instead moved to a new stage in the process of gaining Aboriginal approval for the project. Development approvals to date had covered test drillings and local road works, but there had so far been no use of explosives. The BHP team and the ASSPA arranged a consultation for 18 August 1987 at which the use of small quantities of explosives at Coronation Hill would be demonstrated for the Jawoyn.[17] About 18 Jawoyn were in attendance, including the three senior site custodians. The NLC seized the opportunity of this meeting to radically assert its standing in the issue.

Before the meeting began, two NLC officers arrived and handed to the Coronation Hill project manager a letter drafted the previous day by their senior legal officer. It referred to the NLC's frustration over having 'our clients complain to us about direct approaches by your company', reasserted the privileged nature of its relationship with the Jawoyn, and objected to the company's failure to advise of this meeting and the matters to be discussed.[18] The group then moved to Coronation Hill to observe three successively larger detonations, culminating in a line of four half-sticks of gelignite on a hill-side drilling bench. Before the meeting reassembled for discussion, an NLC officer privately explained to the Jawoyn that the NLC now had the legal power to negotiate a comprehensive agreement with BHP, including exploration works and site protection, and suggested that they should withhold a decision about blasting until after the first of these discussions in a few days time. When, after retiring to consider the matter alone, the Jawoyn announced that their decision would be delayed until the NLC reported to them on the outcome of the proposed discussions, the tensions already evident at this meeting manifested themselves as a direct challenge by the NLC to the positions of both the BHP project team and the ASSPA.

The decision to delay had two implications for the management of the issue. It meant that the progress of the mining project was now contingent upon the BHP team's dealings with the NLC instead of its dealings with the Jawoyn. The project manager attempted to reassert the priority of his team's direct relationship with the Jawoyn, describing it as one of trust that should not be undermined by the imposition of outsiders. He tried to re-establish what he had previously understood to be a separation between the questions of blasting and of dealings with the NLC, arguing that any negotiations with the latter would be directed only towards a final terms-and-conditions agreement for mining and would not cover the exploration stages. Finally, he pronounced a caveat upon any

---

[17] Memo, 'Coronation Hill Joint Venture Fortnightly Site Report to 28 August 1987', BHP Fortnightly Site Report.
[18] Copy letter Gray to BHP Co Ltd, 17 August 1987, NLC file 87/104.

negotiations at all, that they would only happen if the BHP team could be satisfied that the Jawoyn genuinely wished to be represented by the NLC.

Maintaining a separation between the immediate question of whether blasting at the scale demonstrated was an acceptable level of disturbance within the registered site, and the later question of the conditions under which a mining project might eventuate, was equally urgent for the director of the ASSPA. He attempted to impress upon the Jawoyn the legal and functional distinction between what he needed to know — whether the custodians of the site would authorise further exploration works involving explosives — and the larger matter that the NLC wanted to argue out — the material relationship that might finally emerge between the mining company and the prospective Aboriginal landowners. A Jawoyn spokesperson replied that the senior custodians of the site would accept blasting at the level demonstrated but no greater. An NLC officer again tried to dissolve that separation, explaining that the NLC could negotiate everything with BHP, and protect the site better than the ASSPA. When the tenor of the discussion then shifted to adverse reflections on the NLC's past record in local Jawoyn affairs, the ASSPA director concluded the meeting by stating that he would issue a permit for works involving blasting, but would delay it until after the proposed initial discussions between the NLC and the BHP team.[19]

Over the following weeks there ensued a contest between the NLC and the ASSPA over the issuing of the authorisation to the company. The contest turned ultimately on yet another distinction, discussed earlier, that was fundamental to the legitimacy of the ASSPA's claim to an independent role in the issue. That is, whereas the NLC claimed to represent the interests of the Jawoyn people as a whole, the ASSPA was responsible only to the custodians of the sacred site. This distinction between the Jawoyn collectivity and the small group of senior custodians of Bula sites in Gimbat reflected both the contrasting statutory charters of the NLC and the ASSPA, and also the recent land claim history in which the NLC had argued that the entire Jawoyn language group was a single local descent group that satisfied the definition of traditional owners.

In the wake of the consultation of 18 August 1987, this disagreement came to a head in a remarkable scuffle between the two organisations. The ASSPA director began by attempting to re-institute a clear demarcation between their respective roles and responsibilities. He wrote a conciliatory letter to the NLC a few days after the meeting at Coronation Hill in which he offered to discuss a cooperative and coordinated approach to the representation of Aboriginal interests, but also made plain that the ASSPA could receive instructions only from the custodians of the site, not from the Jawoyn Association or from the

---

[19] File Note, 11 September 1987, AAPA file 85/63.

NLC acting as the Association's representative.[20] The NLC responded by having the three senior custodians of the site sign a letter instructing the ASSPA not to issue a permit for blasting pending the outcome of discussions, now postponed, between the NLC and the BHP team.[21] This was an attempt to rescue the position which the NLC had advocated at the blasting consultation, to make progress of development works dependent on progress towards an overall negotiated package. It furthermore positioned the NLC as the channel through which custodians' instructions were communicated to the ASSPA. The ASSPA director advised the NLC that he considered himself bound by the decision of the custodians at the time of the consultation that the blasting was acceptable, and proceeded to issue an authorisation to the project team.

The NLC considered that the ASSPA had again failed to act in accordance with Jawoyn wishes. A meeting of the Jawoyn Association on 1 September was told that the NLC now had the same power as the ASSPA to protect sacred sites. NLC officers took the three senior custodians to one side to explain and have them sign another letter to the ASSPA, this time advising that the Jawoyn Association should henceforth be the source of the ASSPA's instructions. It said in part:

> We want future permit applications to be directed to the Jawoyn Association ... The Jawoyn Association will be expressing our wishes in decisions about permit applications. We would like you ... to accept our instructions in this way from now on.[22]

In response the ASSPA at its next meeting formally noted 'the request of the Jawoyn custodians that future consultation be conducted with the assistance of the Jawoyn Association'.[23]

The ASSPA's legitimacy as a manager of the Coronation Hill issue rested then on its specific responsibility for approving works on a registered sacred site and its obligation to seek instructions from the site custodians. In August and September 1987 the NLC sought to subvert the ASSPA's independence, firstly by trying to subsume sacred site approvals within a general package to be negotiated over all development works at Coronation Hill, and then by trying to subsume the source of the ASSPA's instructions, the site custodians, within the source of its own instructions, the Jawoyn Association. This attempt to assert hegemonic representation of Aboriginal interests was based on a number of perceptions within the NLC: that proper protection of Aboriginal interests in the upper South Alligator valley required comprehensive negotiations over all

---

[20] Copy letter Ellis to Director Bureau NLC, 21 August 1987, AAPA file 85/63.
[21] Copy letter Brown, Barraway and Jatbula to Ellis, 26 August 1987, AAPA file 85/63.
[22] Copy letter Jatbula, Barraway and Brown to Chairman, Aboriginal Sacred Sites Authority, undated, AAPA file 85/63.
[23] ASSPA minutes, 14–15 October 1987.

aspects of BHP's activities, and that removing exploration from the purview of those negotiations constrained real Aboriginal options; that the ASSPA was neither competent nor authorised to handle such negotiations; and that the ASSPA's effectiveness was in any event subject to a political calculus that balanced the protection of Aboriginal interests against the need to demonstrate to its political masters that protection of those interests could be managed in a manner consistent with economic development of the Northern Territory. These perceptions underlay a tactical imperative for the NLC to neutralise the independent role of the ASSPA in the Coronation Hill project. For its part, the ASSPA maintained its concern, first expressed during the contradictory episodes of July 1986, that approvals for works on a registered site should be decided according to the views of the site custodians as bearers of the relevant tradition, and were not properly treated as a negotiating instrument.

The Contest over Policy

While the NLC's intervention on 18 August had failed to achieve its immediate objectives, it had directly challenged the primacy of those relationships that had governed conduct of the Coronation Hill issue up to that point, and had served notice that a new player, strategically aggressive and with a much broader mandate to represent Aboriginal interests, was now in the field. Moreover, that field itself was now much larger than Coronation Hill. Prior to the July 1987 elections, the Federal Government had declared Stage III of Kakadu National Park over the area of Gimbat and Goodparla stations, subject to about one third being reserved as a 'Conservation Zone' in which mineral exploration would be allowed for 5 years. The Australian National Parks and Wildlife Service began preparations to take over management of the other two thirds of the area. The boundaries of the Conservation Zone were drawn tentatively (Figure 12-2), to be refined later in the year, and the Coronation Hill Joint Venture was one of many mining interests expected to compete for exploration rights over the zone. What was immediately clear, however, was that the southern half of the zone intruded into the region of the Bula Dreaming, and included, or lay very close to, a number of powerful sites.

Having established its prominence with respect to Coronation Hill, the NLC in September moved to engage comprehensively with the new complexities of policy in the region. The first requirement was to consolidate its relationship with the Jawoyn. In his report on the blasting consultations of 18 August, one of the NLC officers had noted ruefully that the BHP project team had succeeded in establishing good personal relations with the important Jawoyn decision makers, and that the NLC had now itself to carefully win their confidence. The first step, he suggested, should be to consult with them again to confirm their instructions and clarify their relationship.

The NLC's meeting with the Jawoyn Association on 1 September ranged widely over the problems and possibilities facing the Aboriginal claimants of the area. As most of the Conservation Zone was not protected by sacred site registrations, and as Federal policy at that time appeared to be moving strongly towards allowing at least some exploitation of what was known to be a highly prospective mineral province, the NLC's program had to be broadly concerned with advancing the Jawoyn position within the emerging mix of competing interests. The NLC director pointed out that continued contradictions from the Jawoyn over the Coronation Hill project could ultimately be used against them, and assured them that the NLC would support whatever their final position turned out to be. Following the meeting, the NLC renewed communication with the BHP team to arrange discussions aimed at a mining agreement.

Most importantly, however, the NLC, in concert with the ASSPA and the Australian Conservation Foundation, lobbied the Federal Government to delay any decision on the final boundaries of the Conservation Zone and the allocation of mining tenements until a survey of cultural and natural resources, and the ASSPA's sacred site documentation program, were completed, and the Aboriginal claimants of the area were properly consulted.[24] This renewed lobbying effort showed that the NLC and the ASSPA, even at the height of inter-agency tensions over their respective mandates with respect to Coronation Hill, were still able to act in concert to advocate recognition of Aboriginal interests in the Stage III area at senior policy level. Notably, senior opinion in both organisations regarded Aboriginal acceptance of mining at Coronation Hill as a possibility. The NLC at this point acknowledged both the ASSPA's role in establishing the extent of Aboriginal interests in the Conservation Zone and their joint effort in lobbying the government. However, the request for the government to delay its decision set the stage for a further elevation of the NLC's strategic position in the region.

Five Federal Ministers met on 24 September in Canberra to discuss Conservation Zone policy. Among them, the Minister for the Environment, Graham Richardson, had had previous exposure to Aboriginal disagreements over Coronation Hill, and the Minister for Aboriginal Affairs, Gerry Hand, was also aware that Aboriginal opinion had been unsettled. The Ministers decided that final determination of the Conservation Zone boundaries would be delayed until there had been further consultation regarding Aboriginal concerns. In a policy debate that to this point had been dominated by environmentalists and miners, and in which Aboriginal issues had been seen as a secondary complication, a high-level decision now turned on the Aboriginal interest in the area. More significantly for the strategic disposition of the players, the Minister for Aboriginal Affairs charged the NLC with responsibility for determining

---

[24] Copy letters Ah Kit to Morris, Richardson, Hand, Kerin and Brown, 2 September 1987, NLC file 87/391; copy letter Ellis to Richardson, 9 September 1987, AAPA file 80/25.

Aboriginal views and removing confusion over the Jawoyn position.[25] The NLC thereby became primary advisor to the Federal Government concerning Aboriginal interests in the Conservation Zone. The NLC took this as legitimation of its claim to sole running of the Aboriginal issues in the region. Its senior officers determined that both the Jawoyn and the ASSPA were to be apprised of the NLC's position as representative of Jawoyn interests in the Kakadu Stage III area, and that the Jawoyn should provide the NLC with relevant instructions.

The NLC's position on Coronation Hill, however, was affected dramatically a few days later. After some dilatory communications, the NLC and the BHP team agreed to meet on site on 5 November to inspect the project and begin substantive discussions aimed at a mining agreement. A small Jawoyn group were present to observe and later receive advice from the NLC. This meeting marked the high-water mark of the BHP team's campaign to achieve Aboriginal approval for the project. The following day, 15 members of the newly convened Jawoyn Working Group (established by the NLC to manage Katherine Gorge and Kakadu Stage III issues for the Jawoyn), including two of the senior custodians, met with 10 NLC officers at Barunga and told the NLC that they did not want any mining in the area of influence of the Bula sites, including at Coronation Hill. This declaration sparked significant criticism of the NLC decision to negotiate with BHP, including from within the organisation. The NLC advised BHP that it was withdrawing from the process until the Federal Government had arrived at a final decision concerning mining development in the area.[26] In other words, the NLC would not now discuss development of the Coronation Hill project unless the government decided that the project would proceed.

As had happened previously, there remained the possibility that the ASSPA might authorise further works. The NLC was therefore explicit in again identifying the Aboriginal constituency to whose interests the government should attend. In his letter to the Minister for the Environment, the NLC director argued that the NLC's presentation of a collective Jawoyn position should be preferred over any inconsistent statements made by the ASSPA on behalf of the site custodians.[27] The ASSPA director had long believed that the custodians' concerns over Coronation Hill did not amount to a total opposition to development, and that the project could be negotiated if carefully presented for approval in incremental stages. By December 1987, however, he perceived a shift in the views of the senior custodians against mining. In February 1988, the ASSPA deferred to the larger processes in train and agreed not to issue any further development approvals to BHP until the NLC–Jawoyn submission to Government was finalised.

[25] Copy telex Hand to Ah Kit, 8 October 1987, NLC file 87/391.
[26] Copy letter Ah Kit to Rush, 26 November 1987, NLC file 87/391.
[27] Copy letter Ah Kit to Richardson, 12 February 1988, NLC file 87/391.

Pursuant to its new expanded brief, the NLC set about the task of ascertaining the extent and nature of Jawoyn concerns in the area, and of formulating political submissions to advance those interests. Over the following months, it became convinced that most Jawoyn were absolutely opposed to exploration or mining at Coronation Hill or anywhere else in the Conservation Zone. A consultancy project for the NLC canvassed Jawoyn opinion widely, and not only concluded that most Jawoyn were opposed to mining, but argued that development activities in the Bula region were responsible for major social stresses within the Jawoyn community (Josif 1988). This was the formal Jawoyn position that the NLC passed to the Federal Government, and continued to insist upon as the dispute intensified. Development work at Coronation Hill was able to proceed for another dry season on the basis of existing approvals, but came to an end early in 1989.

1987 thus proved to be a deceptive year for BHP. On the surface of things it appeared to be a period of steady progress at every level. Development approvals had extended to the use of explosives, and by November the BHP team had embarked on the initial stages of negotiating a mining agreement with Aboriginal interests and the company was able to mount strong arguments for favoured treatment for the joint venture in the allocation of exploration rights in the Conservation Zone. At the same time, however, its fortunes were being undermined by the major transformation of that year, in the role of the NLC. From its early position as occasional advisor, the NLC had succeeded, through a combination of enabling legal change and evolving political strategy, in inserting itself as the mining company's counterpart in negotiations, and had been recognised by the Federal Government as its chief source of policy advice regarding Aboriginal interests in the area. From that position it supported and advanced a case both against mining and in favour of Aboriginal ownership of the Conservation Zone.

The Jawoyn and the Custodians

As the political dispute over Coronation Hill intensified during the next two years, public statements from the Jawoyn Association, the Jawoyn Working Group and the NLC repeatedly represented the Jawoyn collectively as the group responsible for the Conservation Zone area in Gimbat (for example, JWP 1989). The Josif Report of June 1988 established the terms of their argument against development: that it was the Jawoyn community that bore the stress and social detriment attendant upon any inappropriate interference in the vicinity of the Bula sites. The three senior custodians were accorded distinctive status for their special knowledge of Jawoyn traditions and sites in the area.

When in 1990 the Federal Government referred the issue to the Resource Assessment Commission for inquiry and advice, it created a space for a return to ethnography and analysis. A large, predominantly Jawoyn meeting at Gunlom in Kakadu Stage III told the commissioners that the three senior men had the primary right to speak about Bula sites and mining in the Conservation Zone (RAC 1991a: 176). The Commission accepted anthropological findings that this status was a function not only of age and knowledge, but of clan membership, and that both their Wurrkbarbar clan and another, Jawoyn Bolmo, maintained primary responsibility for sites in the Gimbat area (Keen and Merlan 1990: 12, 35, 41–3; Levitus 1990: 21–3; RAC 1991b: 285–6). These clan identifications marked a reversion to a more discrete level of structural affiliation between people and country within the Jawoyn language group. During the Katherine Area Land Claim hearings, with respect to the Gimbat sections of the claim, the clan level of social organisation had been argued as a modification of the unitary language group model of traditional ownership, but had disappeared from currency in the lobbying over Jawoyn interests in the intervening years.

In 1989 the Federal Government had radically reduced the Conservation Zone to a remnant 47 km^2 area around Coronation Hill and a neighbouring prospect as a pre-election appeal to the environmental vote. In June 1991, following the Resource Assessment Commission inquiry, the government ended the Coronation Hill dispute by prohibiting mining and incorporating the remnant Conservation Zone into Kakadu National Park. An endogenous discourse of traditional ownership with respect to Gimbat soon reasserted itself during the subsequent preparation of the Jawoyn (Gimbat Area) Land Claim. As anthropologist for the claim, Merlan initially advised the NLC that, consistent with the position recognised by the Resource Assessment Commission inquiry, the strongest model of traditional ownership would be clan-based. This occasioned some concern within the NLC over the task of satisfying the Aboriginal Land Commissioner that the single language group model presented during the Katherine Area Claim was not appropriate for this section of Jawoyn country, and over the political implications of abandoning that model at a time when feelings about Coronation Hill were still strong.

The question of which of these models of landownership should be used was put to a meeting of prospective claimants, including the three seniors, other Wurrkbarbar and Bolmo and other Jawoyn, in April 1992 at Barunga. The meeting told the advisors that the claim should be run primarily on a clan model, and that other Jawoyn would provide evidence as people interested in the land with separate representation. The meeting further instructed that the claim should be extended in two ways, firstly with respect to area, by applying for a repeat claim over the northeastern corner of Gimbat that had been lost in the Katherine Area claim, and secondly with respect to claimants, by including Matjpa as a third clan with localised attachments to Gimbat. The lawyers for the claim had misgivings about the first and were taken unawares by the second.

Merlan thus argued to the Aboriginal Land Commissioner that Aboriginal identification with Gimbat operates simultaneously at two structural levels. The

Jawoyn as a collective language group are affiliated with Gimbat because it is Jawoyn country and recognised to be so by other Aboriginal groups, while the members of three particular clans — Wurrkbarbar, Jawoyn Bolmo, Matjba — 'have historically special and continuous relationships to this area' (Merlan 1992: 7). She ascribed to Wurrkbarbar a general attachment across all of Gimbat, recorded a close attachment of Jawoyn Bolmo to north-eastern Gimbat as well as responsibility for the more dispersed Bula sites, and, on the basis of recent research findings (ibid: 65), reported a particular attachment of Matjba to the Katherine River around where it enters Gimbat from the east. These two levels of affiliation, of language group and clan, produced respectively larger and smaller claimant groups, the latter a subset of the former, and these two groups were argued in the alternative to satisfy the statutory definition of traditional ownership, with the clan group model given the primary running (ibid: 62–9). The claim was accepted by the Land Commissioner on that latter basis (ALC 1996: 16–21, 38–9). The three senior custodians played a leading role in both preparing and proving the claim during site visits on Gimbat, and by their success reasserted a local-level agency for discriminating relevant dimensions of attachment between subgroups within the Jawoyn.

Conclusion

Conflicts between indigenous and non-indigenous claimants to land, and between competing groups of indigenous claimants, are both common scenarios in Australia. The Coronation Hill issue demonstrated another dimension of conflict. There, the registration of indigenous land interests under Federal and Territorian laws recognised different dimensions of land interest exercised by differently conceived groups of interest holders, one a subset of the other within the same language group and group territory. By vesting representation of each interest in different bureaucratic agencies, the registration process created one of the conditions for contest over how indigenous interests were to be represented and advanced when land management became a political question.

My exegesis of that theme in the external history of the Coronation Hill dispute has demonstrated a level of complexity in its management that arose from competing strategic imperatives at the organisational level. I examined the way political agency took advantage, or wrestled with the limits, of law, in a context of persistent uncertainty often arising from the difficulty in interpreting Jawoyn wishes. There were disagreements over how to proceed within both the ASSPA and the NLC, overlapping personal commitments to Aboriginal and environmental values, and competing assessments of attainable political outcomes. Finally, from above, there were the contingencies of Federal policy making: arbitrating between competing land-use values, shifting the legal ground on which the players stood, widening or narrowing the terms of debate, and playing for electoral advantage. In other words, no actor in this story was a simple reflection of any other actor, and the rules they played by were not fixed. In discussions of sacred site protection issues the roles of organisations representing Aboriginal interests are usually left opaque, with the implication that their actions are to be understood simply as directly guided by the instructions of their local-level Aboriginal constituents, or as the discharge of administrative obligations prescribed by their governing statutes. The roles of such organisations need to be made transparent in order that we invest them in our analyses with the significance they are widely understood to have, as separate loci of active political agency.

Significantly, the NLC operated throughout from a position of weakness relative to that which it usually occupied in mining issues under the *ALRA*, as the representative of traditional owners of freehold Aboriginal land. As early as 1986, NLC legal officers had pointed out the strategic importance of finalising a land claim and thereby fixing an Aboriginal property right over the area before decisions about mining were made. Throughout the Coronation Hill dispute, Gimbat was not, in a legal sense, Aboriginal land, and the NLC intervened in the affairs of the area more as an act of political volition to assert an Aboriginal stake than as an act of administration of an existing legal right.

That intervention was predicated upon a conception of the indigenous interest that was broad both structurally, residing in the Jawoyn language group, and politically, encompassing future land-use regimes. As the dispute intensified during 1988 and 1989, the NLC also emphasised Aboriginal concerns from beyond the Jawoyn, among neighbouring Arnhem Land groups. The ASSPA had similarly tried when possible to promote the legitimacy of a general Aboriginal interest in the area, but its management responsibilities required it to have resort to a more particularised niche of Aboriginal authority, in the individual senior custodians. As politics gave way to ethnography, analysis and modelling, first during the Resource Assessment Commission inquiry and then in the Gimbat Land Claim, the more discrete structural level of the clan was elevated to attention, and the Aboriginal interest, conceived in terms of the formal entitlements of traditional attachment, became vested in those more narrowly defined entities. As part of that process, local claimants took charge of the elucidation of the clan-based model of attachments to sites, revealing again an endogenous discourse of land interests that had been submerged beneath the imperatives of political lobbying about local rights carried out at a supra-local level.

References

ALC (Aboriginal Land Commissioner), 1996. 'Jawoyn (Gimbat Area) Land Claim No. 111, Alligator Rivers Area III (Gimbat Resumption - Waterfall Creek) (No. 2) Repeat Land Claim No. 142.' Canberra: Australian Government Publishing Service.

CoA (Commonwealth of Australia), 1977. 'Ranger Uranium Environmental Inquiry: Second Report.' Canberra: Australian Government Publishing Service.

Cooper, D., 1985. 'Report for the Registration of the Upper South Aligator Bula Complex.' Unpublished report to the Aboriginal Sacred Sites Protection Authority.

Dodson, M., 1986. 'An Original View.' *Katherine Times*, 8 May.

Josif, P., 1988. 'A Report on the Social and Cultural Effects of the Proposed Coronation Hill Project and the Conservation Zone (Within the Alligator Rivers Stage III Land Claim) Upon the Jawoyn and Other Effected Aborigines.' Unpublished report to the Northern Land Council.

JWP (Jawoyn Working Party), 1989. '"We Want That Country Kept Safe".' *Habitat Australia* 17(1): 7.

Keen, I., 1984. 'A Question of Interpretation: The Definition of "Traditional Aboriginal Owners" in the Aboriginal Land Rights (N.T.) Act.' In L.R. Hiatt (ed.), *Aboriginal Landowners: Contemporary Issues in the Determination of Traditional Aboriginal Land Ownership*. Sydney: University of Sydney (Oceania Monograph 27).

———— and F. Merlan, 1990. 'The Significance of the Conservation Zone to Aboriginal People.' Canberra: Australian Government Publishing Service (Resource Assessment Commission Kakadu Conservation Zone Inquiry Consultancy Series).

Levitus, R., 1990. 'Historical Perspective.' In *Aboriginal Areas Protection Authority Submission to the Kakadu Inquiry*. Canberra: Resource Assessment Commission (Submission 77).

————, 1996. 'The Resource Assessment Commission and Coronation Hill 1990–91.' In J. Finlayson and A. Jackson-Nakano (eds), *Heritage and Native Title: Anthropological and Legal Perspectives*. Canberra: Australian Institute of Aboriginal and Torres Strait Islander Studies, Native Title Research Unit.

————, 2003. Sacredness and Consultation: An Interpretation of the Coronation Hill Dispute. Canberra: Australian National University (PhD thesis).

Merlan, F., 1992. 'Jawoyn (Gimbat Area) Land Claim: Anthropologists' Report on Behalf of Claimants.' Darwin: Northern Land Council.

————, 1998. *Caging the Rainbow: Places, Politics, and Aborigines in a North Australian Town.* Honolulu: University of Hawai'i Press.

————, 2004. 'Development, Rationalisation, and Sacred Sites: Comparative Perspectives on Papua New Guinea and Australia.' In A. Rumsey and J. Weiner (eds), *Mining and Indigenous Lifeworlds in Australia and Papua New Guinea.* Wantage: Sean Kingston Publishing.

———— and A. Rumsey, 1982. 'Jawoyn (Katherine Area) Land Claim.' Darwin: Northern Land Council.

RAC (Resource Assessment Commission), 1991a. 'Kakadu Conservation Zone Inquiry Final Report – Volume 1.' Canberra: Australian Government Publishing Service.

————, 1991b. 'Kakadu Conservation Zone Inquiry Final Report – Volume 2.' Canberra: Australian Government Publishing Service.

Ritchie, D., 1996. 'The Land Rights Act and the Official Recognition of Sacred Sites.' In *Land Rights Past, Present and Future: Conference Papers.* Northern and Central Land Councils.

Rumsey, A., 1989. 'Language Groups in Australian Aboriginal Land Claims.' *Anthropological Forum* 6: 69–79.

SSCERA (Senate Standing Committee on Environment, Recreation and the Arts), 1988. 'The Potential of the Kakadu National Park Region.' Canberra: Australian Government Publishing Service.

SSCNR (Senate Standing Committee on National Resources), 1986. 'The Potential of the Kakadu National Park Region.' Darwin: Official Hansard Report.

Chapter Thirteen

A Regional Approach to Managing Aboriginal Land Title on Cape York[1]

Paul Memmott, Peter Blackwood and Scott McDougall

In 1992 the High Court of Australia for the first time gave legal recognition to the common law native title land rights of the continent's indigenous people.[2] The following year the Commonwealth Government of Australia passed the *Native Title Act 1993 (NTA)*, which introduced a statutory scheme for the recognition of native title in those areas where Aboriginal groups have been able to maintain a traditional connection to land and where the actions of governments have not otherwise extinguished their prior title.

Native title as it is codified in the *NTA* differs from Western forms of title in three significant ways. Firstly, it is premised on the group or communal ownership of land, rather than on private property rights; secondly, it is a recognition and registration of rights and interests in relation to areas of land which pre-date British sovereignty, rather than a formal grant of title by government (QDNRM 2005: 3); thirdly, it may coexist with forms of granted statutory title, such as pastoral leases, over the same tracts of land.

While native title is a formal recognition of indigenous landownership and sets up a process of registration for such interests, it remains a codification within the Western legal framework, and as such is distinct from, though related to, Aboriginal systems of land tenure as perceived by Aboriginal groups themselves. This distinction is exemplified in the sentiment often expressed by Aboriginal people that their connection to country, and the rules and responsibilities attaching to this connection, continue to apply, irrespective of the legal title of the land under 'whitefellow law'. The very fact that Aboriginal systems of land tenure managed to survive without any form of legal recognition for two centuries in the face of legal and political denial, and the actual appropriation of their land — that is, that there are still systems capable of recognition under the *NTA* — alerts us to the fact that Native title is not the same as Aboriginal land tenure. As a codification which draws upon features thought to be characteristic of Aboriginal land tenure, it neither is, nor replaces, the indigenous

---

[1] This chapter is based upon research undertaken in 2001 for the report *Holding Title and Managing Land in Cape York* (Memmott and McDougall 2004).
[2] *Mabo & Ors v Queensland* (No 2) (1992) 175 CLR 1.

system itself. Indeed, there is considerable room for debate as to whether there may be a unitary system of Aboriginal land tenure over the continent or whether such systems reside at regional or even more local levels of Aboriginal polity (Sutton 2003).

Native title thus exists in a complex legal, administrative and cultural environment of intersecting and sometimes conflicting interests. While this complexity tends to be viewed by the wider Australian public in terms of indigenous versus non-indigenous rights, what is less well appreciated is that many Aboriginal groups find themselves caught within this same web, trying to integrate and reconcile their newly recognised native title rights with other forms of Aboriginal landownership. This is especially the case in remote northern Australia where, as a result of state and territory based statutory land rights schemes introduced over the past 30 years,[3] many Aboriginal groups have acquired land under a variety of titles which include pastoral leases, statutory Aboriginal freehold and trustee arrangements. Much of this land is also now subject to native title claim, often by groups comprised of, or including, those who at the same time already hold, or in the future may hold, the same land under one of these other forms of title. What these title forms all have in common is that, in their own ways, they are attempts at drawing systems of Aboriginal land tenure into the broader Australian system of landownership. But this transition has a high potential to distort and even rigidify the indigenous system, both in its description and in its practice, in order for it to 'fit' the legal requirements of the various statutory schemes and their requisite landowning corporations.

This complexity offers both opportunities and challenges. In Queensland, for example, native title claimants and the state government have taken the opportunity to resolve native title claims through a 'tenure resolution' process whereby the land needs and aspirations of Aboriginal people in a particular area may be settled through a combination of native title determination and the grant of Aboriginal freehold land under Queensland's statutory land rights legislation, the *Aboriginal Land Act 1991* (*ALA*) (QDNRM 2005: 16).[4] The challenge is to find ways of more effectively and efficiently integrating the ownership and management functions of the multiple Aboriginal landholding entities which result.

---

[3] These schemes are based on various state and commonwealth government acts and are specific to the particular states and territories to which they apply, and therefore quite variable in their legislative nature. During the same period there have also been a number of land acquisition programs, mostly funded by the Commonwealth Government, through which Aboriginal groups have been able to purchase land, especially pastoral leases.

[4] As of 2005, this tenure resolution approach was a matter of State policy (QDNRM 2005: 16). While the authors' experience is mainly in Queensland, we believe similar mechanisms for negotiated land settlements operate in other states.

This chapter argues that there is an important role for anthropologists to work with particular Aboriginal or Torres Strait Islander claimant groups, ethnographically document the system of Aboriginal land tenure and customary decision-making processes at the earliest possible opportunity in anthropological claim research, and advise claimants' legal advisers about the implications of this system for the design of Aboriginal landholding corporations. To ignore the opportunity to observe customary decision-making processes is likely to be counter-productive if the sort of corporate structures prescribed by the various land rights legislations are imposed without attention to how things actually happen in an emic political sense on the ground and in the community. The imposition of such legislative requirements are exacerbated further when multiple corporations must be established in a particular region due to multiple overlapping claims that fall under different legal and tenure regimes. Our view is that claimant representative bodies, such as land councils, should allow anthropologists to be proactive in this regard, and that such an approach should result in a closer 'fit' between the membership structures and decision-making processes of Aboriginal landowning corporations and the systems of Aboriginal land tenure as they are understood and practised by claimant groups themselves. While it may be unrealistic to expect that this 'fit' will ever be seamless, incorporating anthropological analysis at an early stage in the planning of corporate structures should minimise the distortion to the emic Aboriginal systems and result in greater consonance between people's experience of rights and responsibilities toward their land under their own system of Aboriginal land tenure and the practice of ownership within corporations set up under native title and other land rights regimes.

This chapter considers some practical aspects of applying such research in two case study areas of Cape York Peninsula in far north Queensland where there are multiple and overlapping Aboriginal entities for the ownership and management of lands and waters. It examines what will be required for the successful operation of the various registered title-holding bodies in these regions, namely native title Prescribed Bodies Corporate (PBCs)[5] and Aboriginal Land Trusts (ALTs) set up to hold title under the *NTA* and *ALA* respectively, as well as Aboriginal corporations holding pastoral leases and other forms of title. It proposes options for rationalising and possibly combining ALTs and PBCs, and models for cost effective coordination of Aboriginal land management at a regional level. Its premise is that this will be best achieved by giving primary consideration to using elements of the local Aboriginal system of land tenure and its associated decision-making processes as the building blocks in the construction of corporate landholding entities and land management structures,

---

[5] PBCs must be set up by claimants to hold their native title. Following a successful determination, the PBC is registered as a Registered Native Title Body Corporate. Throughout this chapter 'PBC' will refer to both entities.

rather than allowing these to be subordinated to legal and administrative convenience.

The case study areas are the Coen and Wik subregions of Cape York (CYLC 2001), selected on the basis of variation in the complexity of local land tenure and coexisting land and sea management regimes (see Figure 13-1). Between them, these offer a gradation of scenarios which we believe provide exemplary models for the operation of Aboriginal landholding corporations that are adaptable to other regions and other Aboriginal groups in Australia.[6]

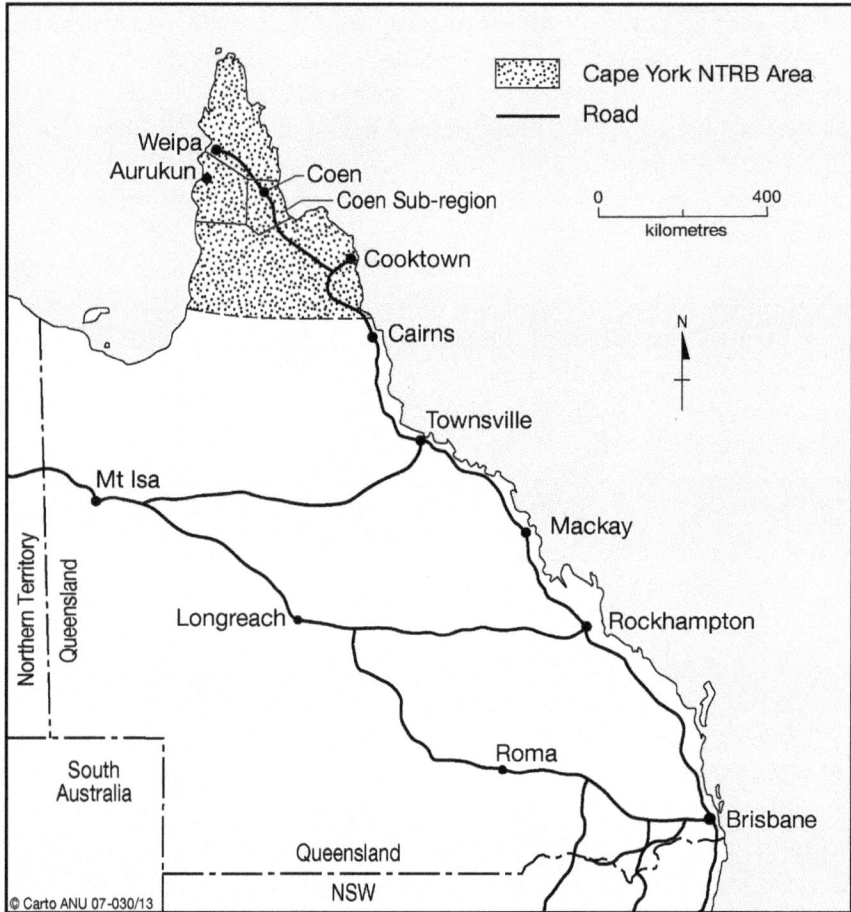

Figure 13-1: Cape York Native Title Representative Body's area of administration and the subregions of Wik and Coen.

[6] Unless otherwise indicated, the data presented in this chapter reflects the situation on Cape York up to 2001/02, the time of the original research.

Cape York Peninsula

The Cape York Peninsula Region covers approximately 150,000 km^2 of remote far north Queensland. The Aboriginal and Torres Strait Islander population comprises at least 60 per cent of the region's total population of 18 000. There are more than 50 named traditional landowning groups in the region. At the time of writing there had been native title determinations over lands of three of these groups — the Guugu Yimithir, the Wik and the Kaurareg — with more than 20 other active claims yet to be determined.

With the exception of parts of the Northern Territory, Cape York has the highest proportion of land in Australia which is, or which has the potential to become, Aboriginal owned and managed. Since much of this land will be held as either Aboriginal freehold or leasehold, and since most groups on Cape York have been able to maintain continuous traditional connection to the land,[7] the incidence of successful native title determinations over much of Cape York can be expected to be high.

Forms of Aboriginal Land Tenure on Cape York

Native title is but one of several categories of Aboriginal owned land on Cape York, each of which is associated with its own particular corporate landholding entity and each of which may also sustain coexisting native title rights over the same land.

In 1984 Queensland established Deed of Grant in Trust Lands (generally known as DOGITs) in respect of Aboriginal residential settlements and surrounding lands which had formerly been government- or church-run missions and reserves. DOGITs are inalienable and are held in trust by the local Aboriginal Council on behalf of its community.[8] Over 11 per cent of Cape York is comprised of DOGITS and there is a large DOGIT area in each of the case study subregions.

In 1991 a form of inalienable Aboriginal freehold title was introduced in Queensland under the *ALA*.[9] This provides for land to be granted usually on the basis of either 'traditional affiliation' or 'historical association', with the land title, once granted, held by an ALT which is usually comprised of a representative group of the beneficiaries of the grant. As of 2005, approximately 5 per cent of

---

[7] The *NTA* requires that claimants be able to demonstrate that they have maintained an unbroken connection to the land, which is interpreted by the High Court to mean that they have continued to observe traditional law and custom, and to have maintained a 'vital' society based upon this law and custom, in a substantially uninterrupted way since sovereignty.

[8] These councils were originally set up as exclusively Aboriginal local government organisations under specific legislation; they have since been replaced with conventional shire councils, similar to those operating in any town in Queensland. The local communities characteristically comprise a mixture of traditional owners for the area and other Aboriginal residents with historical ties going back several generations.

[9] Readers are referred to Memmott and McDougal (2004) for more detailed explication of the operation of the *ALA*.

Cape York Peninsula was *ALA* Aboriginal freehold held by 19 ALTs (QDNRM 2005, Appendix 2). This freehold may be granted as a result of either a claim process requiring claimants to prove their traditional or historical connection before a judicial tribunal, or by an administrative process referred to as 'transfer'. Both mechanisms rely upon the government to make the land available by gazettal, and this provision has enabled some creative tenure resolutions to be negotiated between the Queensland Government and native title claimants. The DOGITs already discussed are transferable, and the *ALA* requires that in time they must be converted to Aboriginal freehold.

A number of Aboriginal-owned pastoral leases also occur in each subregion. The favoured structure for pastoral lease landholding entities are corporations of traditional owner groups formed under the *Commonwealth Aboriginal Councils and Associations Act 1976 (ACAA)*, the same legislation under which native title PBCs must be incorporated.

Neither DOGIT nor Aboriginal freehold extinguishes native title rights and interests, and the *NTA* provides for any past extinguishment on Aboriginal-owned pastoral leases to be disregarded. Potentially, therefore, traditional owners' full native title may be recognised on all these tenure types, leading to the duplication of landholding entities in ALTs, PBCs, and Aboriginal corporations.

Native Title — Prescribed Bodies Corporate

Successful native title claimants are required to incorporate as a PBC under the *ACAA*.[10] Claimants may nominate to set up their PBCs to function in one of two ways, either as an agent or as a trust. The essential difference is that under an agency arrangement, decision making rests with the native title group as a whole and the PBC acts only as its agent or representative, while under a trust arrangement, decisions may be made by a small group of trustees without necessarily involving the wider native title group. The choice is of significant consequence as it determines the legal and operational relationships between the native title holders, the PBC as a corporate entity, and the actual native title rights and interests. Traditional owner groups on Cape York have generally expressed a preference for agency PBCs because this structure is perceived to give them greater control over decision making and avoids an additional level of legal complexity interposed by the operation of a trust structure.

---

[10] This Act has not proved to be altogether suitable for the purposes of PBCs because, in practice, it has not been able to successfully incorporate customary group recruitment mechanisms and decision-making processes (see Fingleton et al. 1996; Mantziaris and Martin 2000: 183–232; Memmott and McDougall 2004: 14–15). In 2005, the Commonwealth Government introduced a *Corporations (Aboriginal and Torres Strait Islander) Bill*, which it claimed would better serve the contemporary requirements of indigenous corporations, including PBCs (RAC 2005).

It is anticipated that eventually the majority of Aboriginal-owned land will have at least two coexisting types of titles and the consequent establishment of two landholding corporations for each area: either (a) Aboriginal freehold and native title, with an ALT and a PBC; or (b) a DOGIT and native title, with a Community or Shire Council and a PBC, or (c) leasehold and native title, with an Aboriginal corporation and a PBC. As it is possible to lease land from the trustees on both DOGITs and Aboriginal freehold, there is further potential for three levels of Aboriginal landholding entity on these tenures, all of which may have substantially the same membership of traditional owners — namely the DOGIT trustees or an ALT, a native title PBC and an Aboriginal corporation holding a lease (see Table 13-1).

Table 13-1: Tenures on Cape York Peninsula showing potential for overlapping Aboriginal ownership.

Tenure Type	Land area (ha)	Land area (%)	Potential for Ownership by Aboriginal Groups		
			Native title	Aboriginal freehold	Aboriginal-owned lease or freehold
Leases	8 063 000	59.2	Y		Y
National Park	1 647 709	12.1	Y	Y	
DOGIT (Deed of Grant in Trust)	1 551 500	11.4	Y	Y	Y (leasehold)
Aboriginal Freehold	736 600	5.4	Y	Y	Y (leasehold)
Unallocated State Land	475 800	3.5	Y	Y	
Statutory Mining Tenure	597 800	4.4			
Reserve	269 361	2	Y	Y	
Timber Reserve and State Forest	189 613	1.3	Y		
Freehold	90 600	0.7			Y
TOTAL	13 621 983	100			

Source: The figures for each category of tenure are taken from CYLC (2001).

Native title holders may make and register agreements about the use and management of land and waters with other land users, such as miners, governments, pastoralists and developers. These are known as Indigenous Land Use Agreements (ILUAs). ILUAs require the consent of all the native title holders for the area covered, and once made they bind all native title holders (including future generations), as well as the other parties to the agreement. ILUAs provide a mechanism by which governments, native title holders and other land users may come to agreement about the use of land and the recognition of indigenous rights and interests without necessarily requiring a formal determination of native title (Lane 2000). Importantly, where there is a PBC over an ILUA area, it must be a party to the agreement. This enables PBCs to use the ILUA provisions to assist in their function of protecting native title for traditional owners, as well as a range of other land management and economic benefits which might flow from such agreements.

Active and Passive PBC Structures

Models for PBC design fall along a continuum from 'passive' to 'active'.[11] The passive PBC is a minimalist structure. It is best suited to the agency PBC type since it will not itself hold the native title interests. These will remain with the native title holding group who may continue to exercise customary decision-making practices. The PBC's role is to consult with and implement the group's decisions, and its membership may be limited to that necessary to meet the minimal regulatory requirements; it may therefore have a 'representative' membership structure, rather than a 'participatory' model (which aims to include as many as possible of the native title holders as PBC members). The passive PBC will have limited demands for resources, but is likely to be reliant on the support of regional representative bodies, such as Land Councils or the Land and Sea Management Agencies proposed in the operational models described below.

In contrast to the passive model, the active PBC assumes greater responsibility for the making of decisions within the determination area. The trustee PBC type is better suited to an active role, because it 'holds' the native title and has greater authority to make decisions on behalf of the native title holders. Active PBCs could adopt either 'representative' or 'participatory' membership structures. There is a degree of expert design required here to ensure there is no conflict between the traditional processes and those of the 'active' agency, for which anthropological advice will be essential to minimise such conflict.

The distinction between passive and active relate not only to PBC functions (for example, whether it is an agency or trustee PBC) but also to its membership and its general mode of operation. The decision as to which model is best suited in any particular case will depend upon a variety of factors, including the PBC's responsibilities in relation to other landholding entities owned by the group and the levels and sources of funding.

Importantly, the choice reflects the spectrum of opportunities available in apportioning decision-making responsibilities between the PBC and the native title holders. At one end of the spectrum, a passive/agency/representative structured PBC would have no role other than to 'rubber stamp' decisions (including non-native title decisions) made by the native title holders. At the other end, an active/trustee PBC, even with a minimal representative structure, could make all decisions, including those involving native title rights and interests. A condition for the operation of such a PBC would be that it is possible to replicate traditional decision making within the PBC governance structure itself. The obvious dangers of creating such a representative/active PBC include the lack of accountability to other native title holders, who as non-PBC members

---

[11] See Memmott and McDougall (2004, Chapter 6) for an in-depth discussion of the design and function of PBCs.

would be forced to rely on their status as beneficiaries to redress any concerns about the management of the PBC.

These decisions may reflect the extent to which the wider membership of the native title group is prepared to cede the day-to-day running of the PBC to an operational and decision-making representative subgroup. As in the case of the Wik PBC described below (in general terms a passive/agent/participatory type of PBC), it is likely that many native title holders will prefer a hybrid of the models to meet their particular requirements.

Structural Options for PBCs in Relation to Land Trusts and Other Indigenous Landholding Entities

The prospect of ALTs and PBCs operating independently of each other with respect to the same land is a source of concern to traditional owners and is recognised by the Queensland State Government as one of a number of practical matters needing to be addressed in order to improve the articulation of the state and commonwealth legislation (QDNRM 2005).

There is a significant level of frustration about the respective operations of ALTs and PBCs in parts of Cape York, particularly where they have similar memberships and perform functions with respect to the same areas of land. From the perspective of traditional owners, the expectation (and hope) may have been that native title would result in a unitary system within which their customary system of land tenure might be recognised and exercised. In practice, however, it has failed to produce such a simplification of their position, but rather resulted in greater complexity, ambiguity and consequent confusion.

In the Coen subregion for example, there are approximately 10 existing or proposed ALTs, and as of 2004, five native title claims, the membership of whose PBCs will overlap those of the ALTs (see Memmott and McDougall 2004: 93). Given the importance of both the *NTA* and *ALA* regimes to the traditional owners of Cape York Peninsula, there is a need to reconcile the practical day-to-day operations of the landholding and managing entities to reduce not only the confusion and frustration of traditional owners, but also that of external parties trying to engage in negotiations, communications and contracts with the traditional owners. It is to be expected that similar situations occur in other Australian states and territories where there is a form of state land rights legislation.

The integration of PBCs and ALTs into single corporate entities for suitable large-scale socio-geographic units (for example language-based tribes in the case of the Coen subregion) would not only simplify arrangements and reduce confusion but also reduce the administration costs through a more effective (and larger) scale of economy. There are three options for coordinating the operations of ALTs and PBCs. On the face of it, the determination of an ALT as a PBC is the preferable option since it would limit the resultant structure to a singular corporate entity. However, it is unavailable without amendments to the PBC Regulations by the Commonwealth Government and possibly amendments to the *ALA* by the Queensland State Government.[12] Further, since the criteria for *ALA* land grants and for determination of native title are so very different, combining the two sets of responsibilities into a single entity may not always be the best option because of resultant conflicts of interest for the members.

Given that there are no legislative impediments to appointing a PBC as the sole trustee of an ALT, this constitutes a second option. However, Queensland government policy in the past has discouraged the use of corporate bodies as sole members of an ALT. This option would still entail the formation of two distinct corporate entities, but Table 13-2 sets out how the two entities may be harmonised within a single operational structure.

A third option is that of coordination between the PBC and ALT by agreement only. The PBC and ALT operate as independent entities with respect to the same land, with activities coordinated through formal agreements, such as Memoranda of Understanding, setting out their respective roles and responsibilities in relation to land use and consent. In practice, because the membership of the two entities is substantially the same, members of the ALT will have to make agreements with themselves as members of the PBC. This option is the least efficient and provides the greatest scope for fragmentation of indigenous interests. However without the regulatory or policy changes required to implement either of the preferred options, it remains the only practical (and legal) option currently available.

---

[12] Recognising similarities in the structure and intent of *ACAA* corporations and *ALA* land trusts, the Queensland Government has recently canvassed the option of doing away with ALTs altogether and granting land directly to *ACAA* corporations, which could include PBCs, thereby avoiding the duplication of organisations with almost identical functions. It has also acknowledged that the integration of land trusts and corporations may be facilitated by allowing land trusts to be formed prior to the granting of the land (QDNRM 2005: 33–4).

Table 13-2: Model of harmonised rules for a PBC as trustee of a Land Trust.

Issue	Land Trust Rules	PBC (as Grantee) Rules
Objects	Objects are for purposes set out in the Aboriginal Land Regulations 1991.	Objects to include acting as grantee of land trust and as a PBC.
Membership	Limited to one grantee — the PBC. Alternatively could include 'historically affiliated' persons as grantees. Historical members to be qualified with no voting powers.	Open to adult native title holders only. Note 'historically affiliated' persons are ineligible for membership.
Committee	Limited to PBC. PBC is Chairperson.	By election at AGM.
Meetings	Annual General Meeting (same day as for PBC). Committee meets quarterly.	AGM (same day as for land trust). Committee meets at least quarterly.
Decision- Making Processes	As set out in rules and in accordance with code of 'permitted dealings' provisions in ALA. Same as PBC.	Prescriptive decision-making processes set out in rules. Same as land trust.
Administration	Separate accounts/audit. Annual statement to Land Claims Registrar.	Separate accounts/audit. Reports to Registrar of Aboriginal Corporations.

The Wik Subregion

The Wik subregion is comprised of coastal flood plains and forested inland country drained by several major westward flowing rivers on the central western side of Cape York. It contains an Aboriginal land lease held by the Aurukun Shire Council, on which are located the township of Aurukun itself and a number of outstations that are seasonally occupied by Wik families. The region is occupied predominantly by the Wik-speaking peoples,[13] the majority of whom live in Aurukun and the Aboriginal DOGIT settlements of Pormpuraaw and Napranum, as well as the towns of Coen and Weipa which lie just outside the region. This region and its people are well known nationally and internationally through the Wik Native Title High Court Action which established that native title may coexist on pastoral leases.[14]

The Wik people comprise a broad linguistic grouping sharing a range of cultural similarities, within which there are a number of identifiable linguistic subgroups, namely Wik Way, Wik Mungkan, Wik Ompom, Wik Iyanh or Mungkanhu, Wik-Ngencherr and Ayapathu (Sutton 1997: 36, Chase et al. 1998: 59). The distribution of languages is often mosaic-like and language affiliation may be shared by clans with non-contiguous estates. Further, languages are not necessarily coterminous with political or social groups such as riverine groupings and regional ritual groups in a given region. Commonality in language use does not necessarily correspond to a unity of political or social identity (Sutton 1997: 33).

The building block of their land tenure system is the clan estate, in which membership is based on the principle of descent. Such estates can be aggregated

[13] See Thomson (1936: 374); McConnel (1939: 62); Sutton (1978); von Sturmer (1978) and Martin (1993, 1997) for an ethnographic history of these peoples.

[14] *The Wik Peoples v Queensland & Ors* (B8 of 1996). While there have since been determinations over areas of crown land, the Aurukun Shire lease and some pastoral leases, determinations over several pastoral leases and areas of the bauxite mining leases were yet to be achieved at the time of writing.

into various types and levels of configuration (Sutton 1978: 126–8, 140, 1997: 28), the most inclusive of which are 'large estate cluster' identity systems, including riverine groups, ceremonial groups and language groups. These are differentiated by particular principles of social and political organisation, totemic and religious geography, and language and land tenure (Sutton 1997: 29–32). Eight of these larger cluster groups comprising the Wik and Wik Way claim group are the social units on which the Wik PBC representative membership structure is based. These include five ceremonial groups and three based on either language or geographic affiliation (Memmott and McDougall 2004: 96, 125).

As of 2005, within the native title claim area, there were at least 33 parcels of land of coexisting (but non-extinguishing) tenure. These included parcels of DOGIT land at Pormpuraaw and Napranum, the Aurukun Aboriginal land lease, pastoral leases under both Aboriginal and non-Aboriginal ownership, and areas under mining leases. Outside the claim area, but still potentially subject to future native title claims, were two large national parks which had been successfully claimed under the *ALA*, and further pastoral leases. As well as the PBC for the determined areas of the Wik and Wik Way claims, there were two DOGITs held by the Pormpuraaw and Napranauum Shire Councils, the Aurukun Shire Council which held the Aurukun lease, and at least two proposed ALTs.

Planning authorities in this region included such regional agencies as Aurukun Shire Council, Pormpuraaw Community Aboriginal Council, Napranum Community Aboriginal Council, and the Cook Shire Council. In addition there were a wide range of government and indigenous agencies and departments that had jurisdiction over the wider Cape York region, including Queensland National Parks Service and other government agencies. Forms of planning agreements which were in place included Wik and Wik Way Native Title ILUAs covering pastoral leases under claim and the Western Cape Communities Co-Existence Agreement which brings together native title holders and Aboriginal communities with Comalco, owners of the extensive bauxite leases which have had a significant impact upon Aboriginal communities in the region since the late 1950s.

A mature outstation movement existed with some 24 or more outstations, most of which were serviced from Aurukun, with a smaller number being serviced by an Aboriginal resource agency based in the adjacent Coen subregion. Almost all of these were on the Aurukun Shire lease or on Aboriginal-owned pastoral leases.

Management problems perceived by the traditional owners included a mixture of both customary concerns relating to their traditional responsibilities for looking after their land, as well as seemingly more contemporary worries relating to access and security: over-fishing and fishing industry impact on dugongs and crocodiles; lack of coastal management and dune damage; poor road access to country; cultural heritage protection; and impacts of visitors to country, including theft and vandalism at outstations and littering. Their aspirations included: greater control over natural resources and the environment; access controls over non-indigenous land users and the prevention of vandalism of outstations and other property; cultural heritage protection and site mapping; improved infrastructure and access to traditional sites and living areas; and greater economic engagement within the region, including employment and commercial venture opportunities.

To develop and implement land and sea management programs across Wik traditional owners' lands, two resource centres known as Land and Sea Management Agencies had been proposed for the Wik region. These would provide a base for research into the environmental impacts of mining and post-mining rehabilitation, aimed primarily at generating real options for indigenous people to gain economic and employment opportunities from lands impacted by bauxite mining. They would also become a hub for the training of a skilled indigenous workforce that would build land management capacity across all Cape York communities (ASC 2001).

The Coen Subregion

The Coen subregion is located on the east of Cape York and contains the small service township of Coen as its regional centre, as well as a number of Aboriginal outstations. It straddles the Great Dividing Range, and includes the uppermost tributaries of the western-flowing Coen and Archer rivers and the streams flowing east from the Geikie and McIlwraith ranges. Aboriginal people of the Coen subregion reside in Coen and in some 10 outstations, the largest of which is Port Stewart on the eastern coast. Many of the traditional owners and native title holders live outside the actual Coen subregion at such large Aboriginal communities as Lockhart River, Hopevale and Aurukun, and also in Cooktown.

There are four language groups with native title interests in the Coen region: the Kaanju, Umpila, Lamalama and Ayapathu. While these groups maintain their distinct linguistic identities and are each associated with well-recognised linguistic and tribal territories, they share a system of traditional land tenure, laws and customs which is regional in character (Chase et al. 1998: 37).

Due to historical forces, the Aboriginal system of land tenure in this subregion has shifted from a patrilineal clan estate system toward that of cognatic descent groups and the 'language-named tribe' as the primary social structural units by which people identify with country and around which their ownership of land is organised and conceptualised (Chase et al. 1998: 35–9). However, the extent to which these transformations have occurred varies among different groups, so that patterns of land tenure, social organisation and identity are not uniform.

By the end of 2005, while there had been no native title determinations in the region (though there were several outstanding claims), there had been four grants of Aboriginal freehold land. Altogether there were eleven existing or future ALTs. There was one Aboriginal-owned pastoral lease, and several smaller blocks of conventional freehold held by Aboriginal corporations.

The regional planning environment included a central indigenous service agency, the Coen Regional Aboriginal Corporation, which delivered outstation, land and sea management services, as well as various administrative and welfare services. It serviced approximately a dozen residential outstations established on the various areas of Aboriginal land in the region, and assisted the operations of several ALTs in the region. As noted above, it also provides services to some outstations in the Wik subregion, and is likely to have a greater role in this subregion in the future. As well, the Lockhart River Shire Council had a land and sea management program with interests in the northeast corner of the Coen subregion. It oversaw the activities of a ranger service on the DOGIT which had responsibilities for natural and cultural resource management (LRC 2001).

Land and sea management issues of concern to the traditional owners of the Coen subregion included: cultural heritage protection; fire management; the problem of non-indigenous squatters encroaching into remote areas on Aboriginal land, often associated with illegal marijuana cropping; feral pigs; fisheries management; and under-developed infrastructure limiting access to country. Their aspirations included: the establishment of more outstations, bores, water tanks and other related infrastructure; the development of land management; the protection of sites; joint management of the national parks in the region and greater access to and use of national park lands; and small-scale enterprise operations at their outstations and on Aboriginal land, including for cattle herding, tourism, prawn fishing and pig farming or harvesting.

Operational Models for Land Use and Management in the Case Study Subregions

The models to emerge for each subregion both have, as a core structural element, a centralised Land and Sea Management Agency, providing administrative and other functions to the various Aboriginal landholding entities in its subregion. In other respects, however, the models differ, reflecting the different cultural, demographic and socio-geographic landscape of each subregion.

Whereas the Wik have opted for a single PBC and have not chosen to formally incorporate each of their eight subgroups for local land management purposes, but rather to work through existing organisations (such as the Aurukun Shire Council), the traditional owners in the Coen subregion wish to formalise their four language-named tribal groupings into four corporations to carry out land and sea management contracts, outstation development, and enterprises. In the interests of rationalising the multiplicity of 18 or more titles in this latter region, a method is proposed to amalgamate these entities for each language group or tribe. This will result in all of a tribe's land and sea areas having a single PBC, which also acts as a trustee of their freehold ALTs.

Administrative and consultative complexities are identified that are likely to be encountered at and near subregional boundaries where groups may choose to seek land and sea management services from centres in adjoining subregions, and where land tenures on ILUAs straddle subregional boundaries.

The Wik Subregion Model

Wik and Wik Way claimants expressed a strong preference for having all Wik people represented on a single PBC ('all Wik people have spoken as one').[15] Their preference was for an agency type PBC with minimal membership based upon representation by regional and ceremonial subgroups from across all Wik and Wik Way country. There was an additional need to ensure that some of the representatives resided in each of the Coen, Napranum and Pormpuraaw communities, and to ensure adequate representation of native title holders in these communities for the purpose of communication and feedback. Thus the translation of customary membership into contemporary landholding corporations has to take into account those post-contact demographic factors that have taken people away from their country.

The Wik PBC model, as detailed in Figure 13-2, lies somewhere between the passive and active PBC types.[16] It has at its centre a 'passive', agency-type PBC based upon representative subgroups and with limited objects and limited executive powers. But it also has 'active' features, such as participatory representation providing for widespread PBC membership and a representative Governing Committee based upon the eight ceremonial and language groups discussed above. The latter characteristics may support the growth of corporate governance culture within the native title group, possibly causing the PBC to take on a more 'active' role in decision making in the future.

---

[15] This PBC, named Ngan Aak Kunch, was incorporated in 2002.

[16] This Wik PBC model is very similar to the 'tripartite' statutory model of the *Aboriginal Land Rights (Northern Territory) Act 1976* (Memmott and McDougall, 2004: 89).

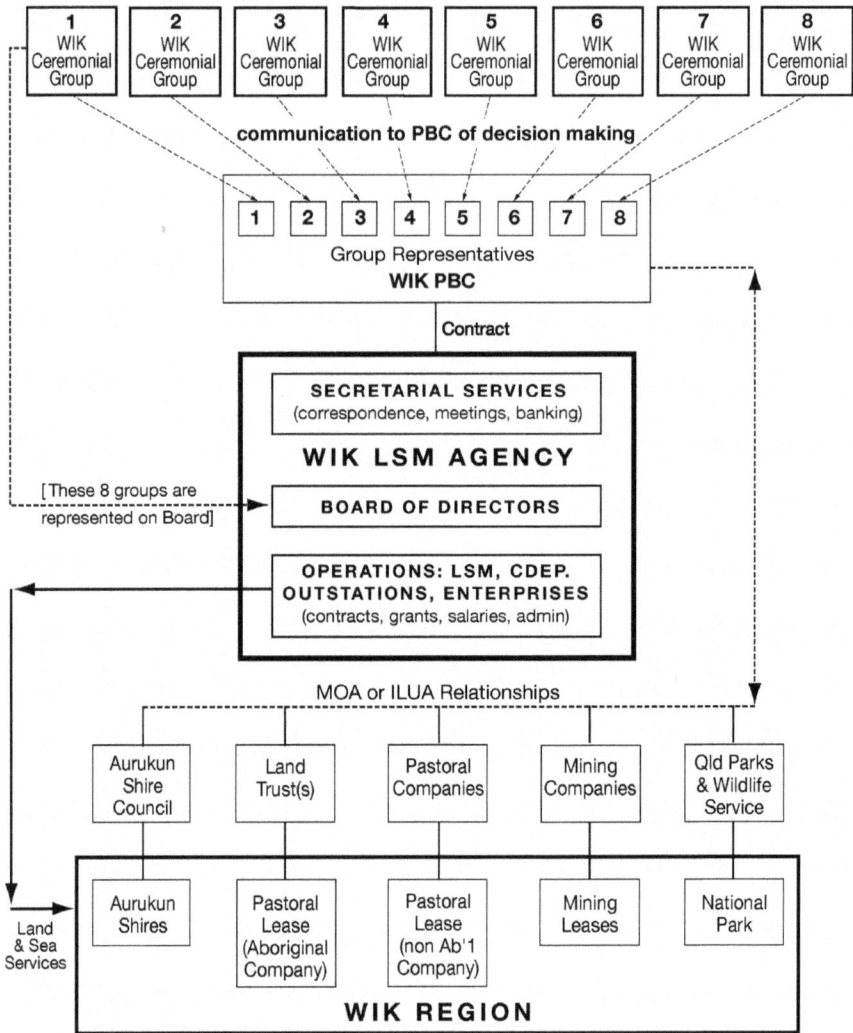

Figure 13-2: Wik subregion model.

Note: This model shows the proposed structural relationship between the Wik PBC and the Wik Land and Sea Management Agency.

A core feature of this model is that each of the representational groups will need to have a capacity to meet by themselves on occasions in accordance with their customary methods of decision making, to make decisions about critical events affecting native title in their respective regions. This is a most critical aspect of the model, necessary to ensure that Wik and Wik Way law and custom are incorporated into decision making on land and sea issues.

However, this is also a vulnerable aspect of the model, with potential problems including the difficulty of individual groups having a viable meeting when key personnel may be residing in dispersed centres (for example, Aurukun, Coen, and Pormpuraaw), the need to raise funds to facilitate transport for adequate consultation, and the possibility of apathy amongst members of the representative groups to attend meetings.

It should also be noted that decision making within each of these groups may still have to devolve to the clan or extended family level, before being brought back to the group level, because the ceremonial and regional groups are not landholding units, nor are they units of political, social, or economic action. They do not correspond to corporate units within Wik society which are particularly relevant to the operations of native title. The basic appropriate groupings in which such discussions would be held are 'families' within regional associations.[17]

It is not proposed that any of the representational groups be separately incorporated for business activities (as was the case for the four language-named tribes of the Coen subregion). On the contrary, there is some concern about the likelihood of 'fissioning' or the subdivision of such corporations if they were formed, as it is a commonplace feature of the political dynamics in the Wik universe, both socially and corporately.

The most plausible and efficient method of providing the PBC with an administration facility would be for the PBC to contract the Aurukun Shire Council as a service provider through the council's Land and Sea Management Unit (which in turn could draw on wider council resources by internal arrangements). The minimal administration services required of such a secretariat would include: dealing with correspondence; holding bank accounts, minutes, legal documents and the like; calling meetings for decision making, elections among the representative groups and information dissemination; providing feedback to native title holders; representing the PBC at meetings with development companies, government departments and authorities, and so on; and raising funds to provide such services. While there are advantages of centrality of location and economies of scale and resources in the council taking on the administration role, there is also potential for conflict of interest in that the civic interests and responsibilities of a Shire Council may not always coincide with those of native title holders. There would therefore need to be protocols in place to deal with such eventualities by separating off the council's local government functions from its PBC-resourcing functions.

In addition to the PBC having a service agreement with the council's Land and Sea Management Unit for administration services, there is traditional owner support for this unit to eventually contract out a range of land and sea management services on behalf of the native title holders, including: land and sea management planning; provision of outstation services; provision of rangers

---

[17] Personal communication, David Martin, February 2002.

to monitor country and carry out management projects in country; negotiation with developers of various sorts, including mining companies and tourism operators; cultural heritage assessments and socio-economic impact studies prior to land developments; and employment of native title holders to participate in the range of land and sea management activities.

The Coen Subregion Model

Traditional owner groups expressed a preference for a structure which retains independent corporate vehicles for each of the four language-named tribes while at the same time recognising the need for a central agency for the subregion that will provide the necessary administration functions common to all four groups. Preference was for agency-type PBCs for each group.

This model is structurally analogous to the relationship which has been established between the Coen Regional Aboriginal Corporation and the outlying outstation communities which it has serviced for the past 20 years. The model, as outlined in Figure 13-3, has two key structural dimensions. The first of these is an overarching corporate structure which brings traditional owner and native title groups from the subregion together to form a decision-making committee for common purposes, such as financial administration, subregional land and sea management, resourcing outstations, and liaising with National Park Boards of Management.

Within this wider structure, separate traditional owner decision-making committees for each of the four tribal native title groups will act as trustees for their respective local areas of land. These committees will have responsibility for making decisions about budget allocations for their own groups, use of local assets, businesses and so on, as well as PBC- and ALT-relevant matters, and overseeing land and sea management contracts on the group's traditional land. Eventually, this model should lead to the structural amalgamation of PBCs and ALTs for each tribal group, though this may still be some way off since it will depend upon the resolution of the political and legal impediments discussed above.

There are persuasive arguments for having one central agency for the Coen subregion as a point of contact with outside agencies, government departments, industry groups and so forth. One is to achieve economies of scale; another is that it is already a requirement of most state and federal government funding agencies that funding goes through a regional organisation rather than to individuals, family or outstation groups.

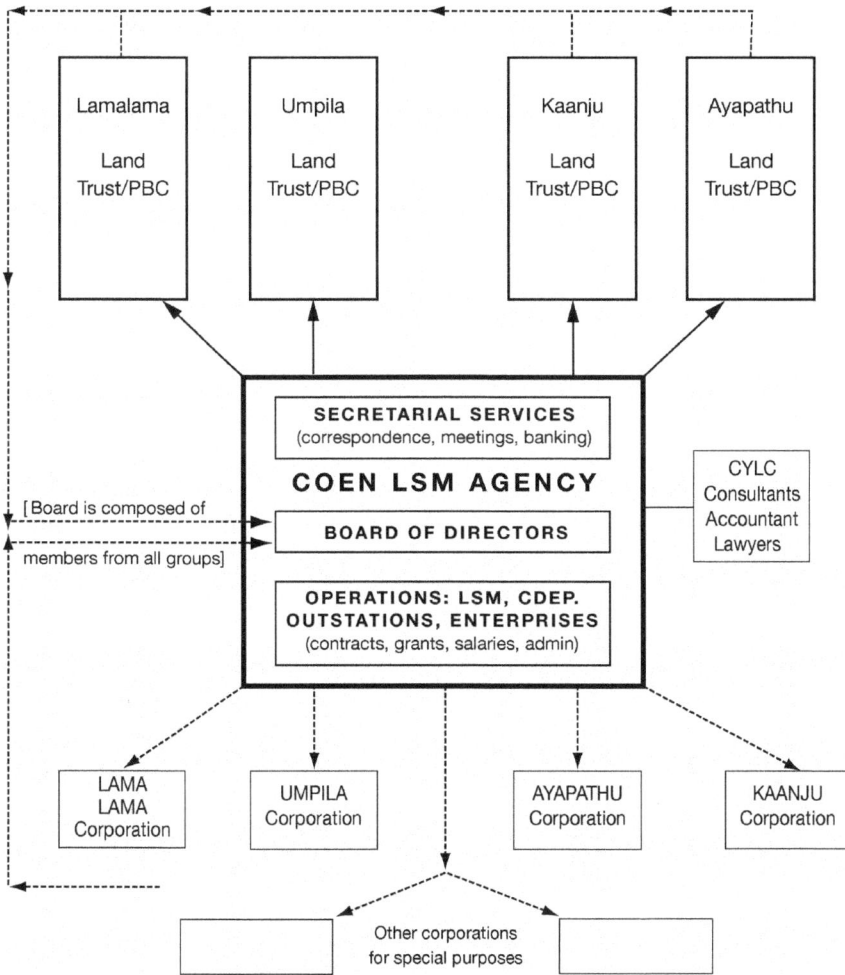

Figure 13-3: Coen subregion model.

Note: The model illustrates the proposed Coen Land and Sea Management Agency, a set of tribal PBCs which also serve as ALTs, and a set of four tribal corporations for day-to-day business in the Coen subregion. This would result from an amalgamation and rationalisation of all existing PBCs and ALTs.

The most plausible and efficient method of providing an administrative service to the various PBCs and ALTs is for them to contract to one service provider. Using one agency will reduce the complexity of transactions, given that for the foreseeable future there is likely to be a number of PBCs and ALTs for any one language group, as well as PBCs and/or ALTs for multiple language groups. To some extent this role is already being played by Coen Regional Aboriginal Corporation, but this role will need to be mandated separately from the four constituent language groups as they establish their PBCs or ALTs. The administration services required from a central agency are likely to be similar to those described above for the Wik Agency.

The Coen subregion is economically 'poor' from the indigenous perspective. As of 2002 there were no viable Aboriginal commercial enterprises in active operation, nor were there any prospective mining projects from which cash flows were imminent. Nevertheless, viable prospects for tourism, cattle herding and prawn farming have been identified and form part of traditional owner aspirations.

The Right to Negotiate and the ILUA provisions of the *NTA* also provide a valuable basis for negotiating benefits in return for access to native title lands, and in compensation for any extinguished or impaired native title resulting from land and sea developments (for example loss of resource collection area, damage to a sacred site, and so on). Mining and other development companies may also be legislatively obliged to carry out a social and environmental impact assessment in relation to their projects. Through such studies a range of economic activities can often be designed in which local Aboriginal groups can engage and which can 'piggy-back' on the main project. The proposed gas pipeline from Papua New Guinea constitutes a project of this type which could provide such opportunities in the Coen subregion.

Managing Aboriginal Title Holding Entities at the Subregional Level

Three key components common to the land management models for both subregions are centralised Land and Sea Management Agencies providing support to landholding entities; predominantly passive, agency-type PBCs; and a strong desire for the amalgamation of PBCs and ALTs, at least to the extent possible under state and commonwealth regulations. This arrangement is predicated upon an understanding of the traditional social organisation, land tenure and decision-making systems among groups in each subregion, but constrained by the necessity of incorporating traditional decision-making practices into organisations which will be economically sustainable and will comply with the legal and regulatory environment imposed by state and commonwealth legislation for the registration of Aboriginal interests into various forms of title.

The role of the regional agencies is to provide sufficient economies of scale for their affiliated title-holding bodies to be able to accommodate a more traditional mode of operation. They would provide contracted secretarial services to PBCs, ALTs and leaseholding corporations. PBCs and ALTs might also outsource some of their functions, for example the management of certain areas of native title land, issuing of entry permits onto Aboriginal freehold land, and so on. The agencies' activities will intermesh with a range of the native title rights and interests being claimed in the region with respect to: the general use of country; occupation and erection of residences; hunting, fishing and collecting resources; management, conservation and care for the land; the right to prohibit unauthorised use of the land; and cultural, heritage and social functions.

Therefore the most critical external design factor in the regional models is the development of satisfactory consultation and communication among landholding entities (PBCs, ALTs, corporations holding leases and so forth), the native title holders and the regional agencies. In order to respond to consent requests for planning and development activities from other parties under the *NTA*, properly resourced consultation of native title holders needs to be ensured.

In the case of PBCs, the extent of outsourcing to a regional agency will depend on whether an active or passive PBC model is adopted. However such an arrangement would ideally require that the native title holders agree to consent to the regional agency performing certain acts or classes of activity. This would enable day-to-day transactions to take place within such an agency without its staff having to continually consult with the native title holders — for instance a policy where the agency staff can approve permits for certain scales of tourist activity, camping, fishing and so forth, without having to worry the PBC membership.

The proposed regional agency model also allows income derived from compensation or other benefits, such as those negotiated under ILUAs, to be channelled through the PBC to the agency, which can then engage practically in a range of land-based operations, drawing upon any available infrastructure, Community Development Employment Program workers, community rangers, or consultants, on behalf of the native title holders. In all cases there needs to be a close coincidence between the membership, and to some extent the structure, of the landholding entities in the subregion and that of the agency to prevent conflicts of interest, although it would be possible to incorporate spouses, and those with historical interests in land, in the membership of the agency where that is not possible for a PBC.

A key problem for indigenous landholding groups is to develop a capacity to independently fund their operational as well as infrastructure costs. At the very least, a minimum income is required for a base secretarial and administration service to fulfil the legislative duties of ALTs, PBCs and leaseholding corporations (including meeting organisation and travel costs). Therefore the ability to use ILUA agreements to finance not only title-holding bodies but also their regional service agencies will be vital because ongoing grant funding is likely to become increasingly limited. Neither the commonwealth nor state governments were allocating money for the recurrent administration of PBCs or ALTs. Yet these corporations will be unable to perform their prescribed functions without some base funding, and this is a critical limitation on the ability of Aboriginal landholders to derive real benefits from either native title or statutory land rights legislation in Queensland (QDNRM 2004: 20).

Poor funding already results in low levels of minimal corporate compliance (such as failing to hold annual general meetings, lodge financial reports and hold elections and so forth) (ibid: 21). But it also results in poor levels of consultation and places limitations on traditional owners' abilities to engage in the interactive social practices that often characterise traditional decision making. This in turn increases the likelihood for dispute amongst native title holders and poorly negotiated outcomes marked by corruption, lack of accountability and legal uncertainty.

There is a substantial dollar investment required to maintain Aboriginal traditional connection to country through customary land tenure systems incorporated into contemporary corporate entities. Traditional land management does not equate necessarily to a cheaper alternative; indeed, because of its communal nature and a general tendency toward consensus decision making through intra-community consultation, resources are required to run what might be termed the 'software' (such as the recurrent administration) of traditional land management, as well as the 'hardware' (such as the management operations). Funding bodies all too often fail to get this balance right, so that while there may be resources available for 'doing' things (often termed project, implementation or program funding), there is little provision for maintaining the capacities of the organisation to function effectively over the longer term.

Clear rules of agreement will have to be established amongst traditional owners (including native title holders) as to how monies coming into the regional agency will be distributed, to complement those set down for PBC and ALT income (if any). This is particularly the case where a subgroup of native title holders has an established income stream from an ILUA or other agreement, but the other subgroups in the PBC do not. There is thus a need for an economic plan that allows, on the one hand, Aboriginal income into the region to be equitably spread to groups across the region for basic regional agency functions, but which at the same time recognises local native title rights in compensation outcomes or acknowledges local enterprise initiatives by individual groups.

Conclusions

In this chapter we have discussed the possibilities within the existing Australian planning and legislative framework for rationalising and integrating the operations of PBCs, ALTs, and Aboriginal landowning corporations so as to improve the outcomes possible from land acquired by Aboriginal groups on Cape York and elsewhere under a variety of tenures. A key to the models proposed has been to take a regional approach and, to the extent possible, to pool resources and to service landholding bodies on this basis. However all such attempts are severely constrained by limitations on funding within the public sector, and by legislative and legal constraints which apply to PBCs, ALTs and the operations of Aboriginal corporations.

These constraints may only be readily overcome with policy and legislative reform of the commonwealth native title and state land rights legislations (and their associated regulations) to harmonise the amalgamation of tenures and landholding entities, to provide adequate levels of base funding for landholding and management entities and to amend them to enable greater flexibility in the types of corporate landholding structures available for native title holders and traditional owners under statutory land rights regimes.

In both the *ALA* land claim and the *NTA* title claim process the structure of the title-holding corporation is often the last aspect to be considered. In our view the preferred approach is to work with claimants from the outset on designing and establishing their PBCs and ALTs. This would shift the initial focus from the frustratingly lengthy and legalistic processes leading to a determination, to consideration of the long-term outcomes people wish to achieve from their native title. It would assist in achieving desired outcomes because, as the claimants pursue their claim, important dynamic aspects of their political processes and social structuring are likely to be revealed, and these may hold valuable clues as to how their title-holding corporations might operate in reality.

Anthropologists can further assist by promoting landholding corporation design and operation as a component of effective community government. A basic design assumption should be that the customary system of Aboriginal land tenure cannot be divorced from the social relations of its 'owners', nor from their systems of internal group authority and governance. At the same time, it is important that PBCs and ALTs are structured to ensure congruency and compatibility with the planning frameworks of state and local government bodies. This may best be done through the sort of regional land and sea management agencies suggested in the case study models. Other specific governance aims would be to minimise unreasonable and unnecessary friction and obstruction with respect to community settlement planning and development processes, through ILUAs between native title holders and DOGIT-owning councils.

In the introduction we drew attention to the distinction between native title as a recent construct of the Australian legal system and Aboriginal land tenure as the emic system of indigenous landownership. A key principle is to inform the PBC design process, and that of ALTs and other landholding corporations, with an understanding of the social structure and decision-making dynamics of the autochthonous Aboriginal land tenure system. This presents a classic opportunity in applied anthropology for the practitioner, based upon his or her research on the emic system, to mediate the transition from the Aboriginal system of land tenure to the holding of title under a corporate, statutory entity, whose objectives include the replication of 'traditional' membership and decision-making processes, into a structure capable of articulating with a variety of non-indigenous planning and land management entities. Major design challenges include: maintaining the integrity of traditional decision-making processes whilst responding to the legal and administrative requirements of the various statutory regimes for Aboriginal land rights; structuring the membership to reflect traditional social organisational arrangements; and having a capacity to subsume any politicisation and power politics within the native title group.

References

ASC (Aurukun Shire Council), 2001. 'Wik Waya Land and Sea Management Centre.' Application for a Project Grant from the National Heritage Trust 2001–2001, Aurukun, 29 January 2001.

Chase, A., B. Rigsby, D. Martin, B. Smith, M. Winter and P. Blackwood, 1998. 'Mungkan, Ayapathu and Kaanju Peoples' Land Claims to Mungkan Kaanju National Park and Lochinvar Mineral Field.' Cairns: Cape York Land Council (unpublished claim book).

CYLC (Cape York Land Council), 2001. 'Three Year Strategic Plan 2001–2004.' Cairns: Cape York Land Council.

Fingleton, J., G. Crough and T. Libesman, 1996. 'Final Report — Review of the *Aboriginal Councils and Associations Act 1976* (Cwlth).' Canberra: Australian Institute of Aboriginal and Torres Strait Islander Studies.

Lane, P., 2000. 'A Quick Guide to ILUAs for Governments.' Paper presented to National Native Title Tribunal Agreements Workshop, 13 September 2000.

LRC (Lockhart River Council), 2001. 'Position Description for the Lockhart River Homelands Land and Sea Management Coordinator.' Lockhart River: LRC.

McConnel, U., 1939. 'Social Organization of the Tribes of Cape York Peninsula, North Queensland (Part 1): Distribution of Tribes.' *Oceania* 10: 54–72.

Mantziaris, C. and D. Martin, 2000. *Native Title Corporations: A Legal and Anthropological Analysis*. Sydney: The Federation Press.

Martin, D., 1993. Autonomy and Relatedness: An Ethnography of Wik People of Aurukun, Western Cape York Peninsula. Canberra: Australian National University (PhD thesis).

———, 1997. 'The "Wik" Peoples of Western Cape York.' *Indigenous Law Bulletin* 4(1): 8–11.

Memmott, P. and S. McDougall, 2004. *Holding Title and Managing Land in Cape York. Indigenous Land Management and Native Title*. Perth: National Native Title Tribunal.

QDNRM (Queensland Department of Natural Resources and Mines), 2004. 'Review of the *Aboriginal Land Act 1991* (Qld) and the *Torres Strait Islander Land Act 1991* (Qld).' Brisbane: QDNRM Issues Paper.

————, 2005. 'Review of the *Aboriginal Land Act 1991* (Qld).' Brisbane: QDNRM Discussion Paper.

RAC (Registrar of Aboriginal Corporations), 2005. 'Meet the Bill: A Guide to the Introduction of the Corporations (Aboriginal and Torres Strait Islander) Bill 2005.' Canberra: Office of the Registrar of Aboriginal Corporations.

Sutton, P., 1978. Wik: Aboriginal Society, Territory and Language at Cape Keerweer, Cape York Peninsula, Australia. Brisbane: University of Queensland (PhD thesis).

————, 1997 'Wik Native Title: Anthropological Overview, The Wik Peoples Native Title Determination Application QC 94/3.' Aldgate, South Australia (manuscript for Wik Native Title Claim).

————, 2003. *Native Title in Australia: An Ethnographic Perspective*. Cambridge: Cambridge University Press.

Thomson, D., 1936. 'Fatherhood in the Wik Monkan Tribe.' *American Anthropologist* 38: 374–393.

Von Sturmer, J., 1978. The Wik Region: Economy, Territoriality and Totemism in Western Cape York Peninsula, North Queensland. Brisbane: University of Queensland (PhD thesis).

Index

www.ingramcontent.com/pod-product-compliance
Lightning Source LLC
Chambersburg PA
CBHW061242270326
41928CB00041B/3373